June
A Life Study

Published by APML
Book production by The Bluecoat Press
Designed by March Design, Liverpool
Front cover, *June Furlong* by James Lloyd Kitchen
Printed and bound by Biddles Ltd

ISBN 0 9534461 1 5

The contribution and support of Professor Cecelia Crighton and Colin Fallows along with many other members of staff, past and present at Liverpool John Moores University is gratefully acknowledged. I would like to express my thanks especially to Reg Phillips for his tireless efforts in reproducing my photographic records – of which only a glimpse is included. Additional thanks to The Bluecoat Press, the University of Liverpool, the Williamson Art Gallery, Birkenhead and National Museums and Galleries on Merseyside for their continuing support. Many past students and artists have kindly written their thoughts and comments and have encouraged me to make a record of my experience as a life model. The limited space available has not permitted the inclusion of all contributions, nevertheless my thanks and appreciation is extended to you all.

June
A Life Study

June Furlong
Jill Block

APML

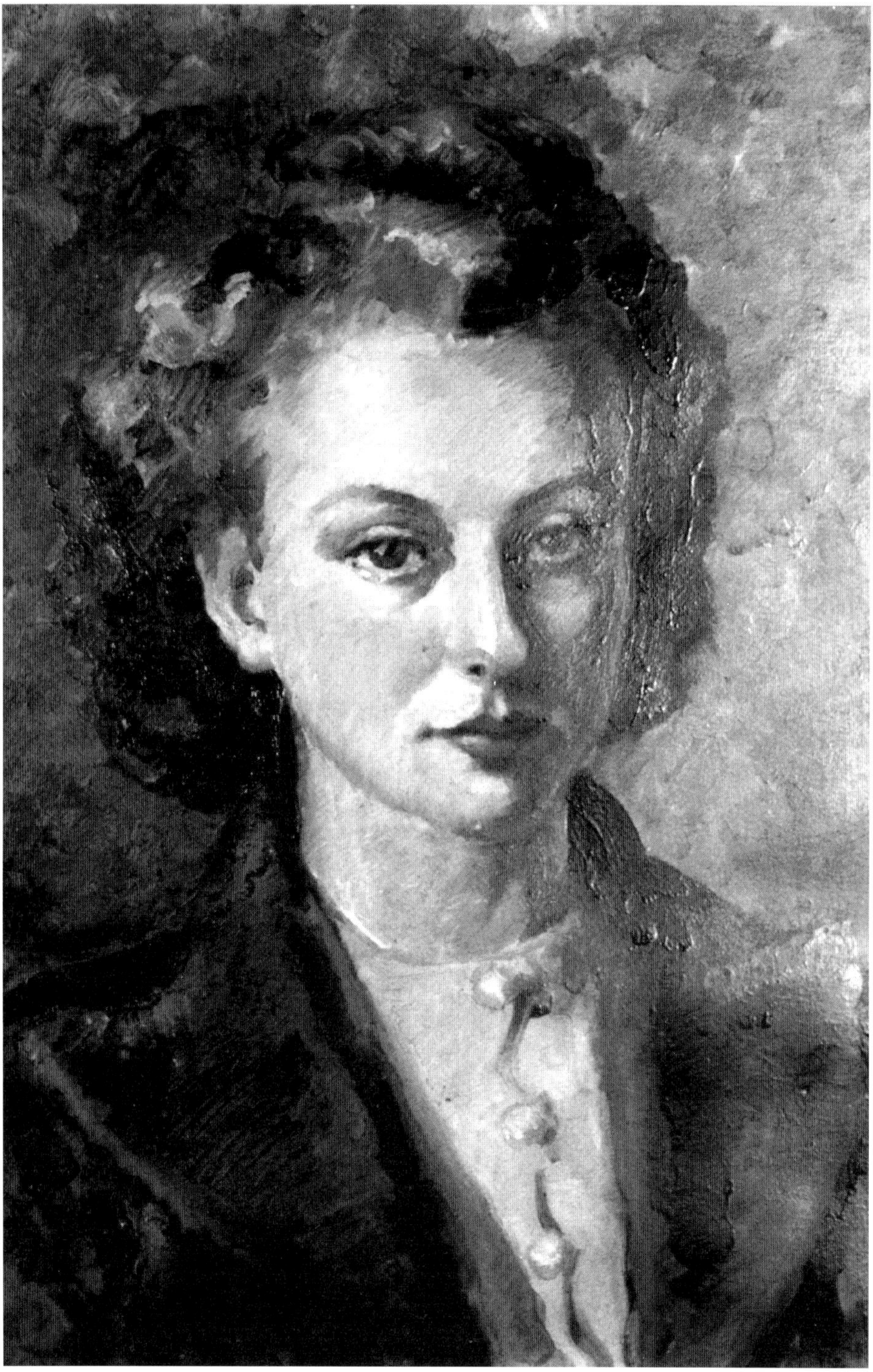

June Furlong, 1946, oil on canvas. Witold Witoski.

Foreword

by Peter Davies

The life model has played a significant, rather than silent and passive role throughout the history of art. The social standing of the life or portrait model has also made its presence felt in every academy or artistic bohemia, whether the situation be the roaring inter-war Parisian art scene of Kiki or the more recent, self conscious, transatlantic art scenes frequented by the legendary Quentin Crisp. She, and occasionally he, has played friend, lover, confidante, counsel or muse to artists, and those that made a career from this oldest of professions inevitably formed an intimate knowledge of the various artistic movements to which he or she was privy.

The nude or draped figure has also provided the most valuable single exercise for the training of eye and hand. Draw the nude well and an artist can draw anything. It is a blueprint for all natural form – the most perfect and complete object in nature. The human figure functions as landscape, portrait and still life all rolled in to one. It elicits a whole range of graphic responses – for some a descriptive or pedantic line expresses the infinite variety of postures, from standing to reclining, on offer in the life room. For others the fall of light on the undulating subtleties of figurative form calls for a more circumspect and sculptural approach in the successful depiction of lit convexities or shadowed concavities.

As far as British art is concerned, June Furlong has been a remarkably long-standing model, with wide experience of the many different artists who have made art in this supposed artistic backwater such an unexpectedly rich and rewarding an experience. Her career has been mainly based in Liverpool and London. I first heard about her through June's friend, the Wirral-based surrealist painter George Jardine, whom I befriended as a result of writing *A Northern School* (1989) and *Liverpool Seen* (1992), a book about post-war Merseyside artists, published by Redcliffe Press. My first encounter with June was, perhaps appropriately, in the life room at the Liverpool College of Art, where she stood, holding court in more ways than one, and ready to put a mouthpiece on her unrivalled enthusiasm. She would talk endlessly, in a kind of anecdotal, yet not uncritical, stream of consciousness, about those painters and sculptors I was including in my survey of northern artists. Her extraordinary powers of recall were immediately in evidence as it became quite clear to me at the outset that she had known about pretty well every artist, teacher, student or hanger-on who had ever set foot in the Liverpool art scene.

With the exception of the renowned artist's colony of St Ives, Liverpool has possessed perhaps the most distinctive and lively art scene outside London – if indeed we can call the 'capital of Wales and Ireland' English – and June is justly proud of her Liverpudlian background. Yet interesting though her native city is, her knowledge and experience of art so entertainingly encapsulated in this anecdotal volume would not have amounted to the valuable document it is were it not for the several years spent in London. In the capital she became life model at both the Slade School of Fine Art and the Royal College of Art, the two foremost bastions of fine art education in this country. The artists and tutors for whom she posed – Carel Weight, Ruskin Spear, Robert Buhler and Roger de Grey at the RCA, Adrian Heath, Frank Auerbach and William Coldstream at the Slade, have been amongst the most important artists of the period. The academies of Exhibition Road and Gower Street have also reflected different tendencies in art – the latter responsible for a disciplined and analytical approach to form construction, the former perhaps undertaking a romantic approach to picture-making using narrative, anecdote and fantasy. But the importance of life drawing remained undiminished in both and has, thankfully, survived the onslaught gratuitous iconoclasm, the encroachment of basic design concepts on traditional drawing and the inexorable growth of the new 'Brit Art' charlatanism.

June moved freely around the social scene in London. Augustus John, in the late 1950s, the grand old man of English figurative painting, wrote to suggest she pose for him. That it never happened was down to his old age. She also knew Jacob Epstein, perhaps the most brilliant practitioner of the modelled portrait head in Britain this century. But age was no factor when it came to her dealings with Frank Auerbach and Lucien Freud, today the two most successful living English painters, both of whom she came to know intimately. The gossip, the intrigues, the colourful life and times of such an exciting world are all recalled here without rancour, but with overflowing tides of enthusiasm and gratitude.

But it is ultimately to Liverpool that June's loyalties return and where her essential identity resides. She was 'discovered' by Don McKinlay, a talented if unambitious Liverpool artist who as a student in 1947 met her outside a telephone booth. McKinlay recommended her to the charismatic Arthur Ballard, Liverpool's most significant postwar artistic personality who, a few years later, would teach the talented Stuart Sutcliffe and the irascible John Lennon at the art school. Both founding members of the greatest ever rock 'n' roll band, Sutcliffe and Lennon knew June, the former making several excellent studies of her. But more significantly, June observed them with the fresh and unsuspecting eyes of someone involved in the same dramatic and historical moment, a moment that saw many individual, though less celebrated, talents spring forth.

I have often considered June Furlong as a 'conscience' of the art scenes to which she has been privy. Her enthusiasm for the art world as a whole, which she has humanised through an inherent sense of humour concerning the perversities and idiosyncrasies that attend the artistic life, has provided the gloss of a community spirit that it has often lacked. Yet there is a common endeavour – indeed mission-like passion – shared by all serious, ambitious or talented artists and her role in the present context is not only that of an important chronicler but also a binding influence. The lady with the lamp illuminates and makes sense of the diverse personalities and conflicting interests that have gone to make up the creative soul of a modern renaissance.

Peter Davies

Introduction

When I was young, aged about six or seven and at St Margaret's Junior School in Princes Road, Liverpool, my clearest memory is of my teacher saying: 'Now June will tell us a story'. My stories would go on long after the bell signalled the end of class, but there was never any rush to get away. Teacher would have to say, 'Well, yes, we can certainly continue with this story soon', just to satisfy my classmates. Now I am telling you my story, the story of my life and times remembered from fifty years spent in the rarefied world of professional art, beginning in 1947. I hope that you will not want to rush away!

June Furlong 1999

The Early Years and Family Life

I was given the name June to mark the month of my birth. The long-awaited arrival of a healthy daughter on 3 June, 1930, brought me into a Liverpool teeming with activity. Our family house was in Falkner Street. This area of town houses was built to meet the demands of a wealthy middle class. My grandparents moved into the house nearly one hundred years ago. My grandfather used to say that the area from Croxteth Road to Rodney Street was a top-class area with lots of hansom cabs taking gentlemen from and to town. At the turn of the century, women ruled the household and the city was dominated by professional gentlemen. The area saw a lot of coming and going well into the night. Business families would entertain, servants would walk in and out and the well-to-do would always have visitors.

Our house has large windows which help to give the house a light and airy feel. I was born in the fourth-floor back bedroom. It was a large, square room with a high ceiling. Like the other rooms, it had an imposing square-paned window, which threw sunlight into the room. The fire was set every morning and there was a comfortable and homely feel to the place. My grandfather used to tell me a story about the day that I was born. He said he came home from work and said, 'Where's Flo? I haven't seen her since yesterday.' He was told that my mother was in bed with a sore foot, but it might be a good idea if he took her a cup of tea. He took it, and when he went into the bedroom saw me in the cot – he always maintained that nobody told him anything around here!

I remember that in my nursery room the decoration seemed typically expressive, loose and boldly patterned in gold, pink and green. The colours remind me of Christmas time. I remember what seems to have been a tradition in Liverpool – a big pillowcase filled with toys. So many marvellous toys, bright colours and lots of them. All the children from the neighbourhood would play with me because they said I always had the best toys. I tried hard to remember my favourites: the Artmaster crafts, my doll that would spin around like a ballet dancer in a trim tutu with arms outstretched, effortlessly graceful and elegant. I could imagine myself as a star, balancing delicately with every inch of my stature held in theatrical pose. I loved mosaic sets. The diamonds, squares and rectangles in jewel-bright colours of painted tin gave me a lot of satisfaction as no sooner had I made a design it would be tipped up and a new structure would begin to take shape. All this may well have developed my eye for pattern or formal order at an early age. I loved creative toys, it was a magical power to be able to create and make patterns.

I would look forward so much to the joys that Christmas would bring in the years before the war. I would go to bed fresh and clean and full of excitement. The ceremony of hanging up my bolster pillowcase still tantalisingly haunts my memory. It was all I could do to sleep, and when I woke in the night it was barely visible, hanging at the end of the bed. I would scarcely dare to look. Was it full? Did it have anything at all in it? Had I been good enough to deserve a Christmas present? All these questions wrenched the emotions in a split second in the dead of night. I found it impossible to contain myself. The minute that my eyes grew accustomed to the light I could see the changed shape of the pillowcase. When its outline suggested there was weightiness and bulkiness to the crisp cotton, I was off! Racing down to the end of the bed to haul aboard the Christmas treasure. It was full of oranges, sweets, beads, and small toys. Everything was out, tossed adrift over the bed as I felt down deep into the pillowcase. The smell of starched cotton fanned through the air as the toys and gifts poured into the light. I did not know what to touch first. My eyes would dart across the goodies to search out that special gift. At the same time I would be passing personal judgement on the success of the occasion. I was never disappointed.

I recall at the same time an early gramophone. When Christmas Day was underway, the family would congregate downstairs and my parents would say to me,

'Go and get a record and put it on'. It must have been one of the earliest things I learned – how to pick out the right record. I used to love the colours of the records. The lettering was always gold and shiny, making the record sleeves look special. Records were heavy things. Their speed was much faster – 78 revolutions a minute – in those days, and they became scratchy when they were played over and over again.

It was probably His Master's Voice records, the label showing the attentive black and white dog, that I found such fun. It had its head tilted over to one side and the hint of tongue lolling out of its mouth. I always thought the dog was smiling, as it seemed drawn towards the depths of the horn where the sound jerked upwards and out of the gramophone. Simply looking at him was as much fun as putting on the records. The dog looked so clever, but always seemed to be waiting for something to happen. It was a great game. The gramophone was a trumpet type that had to be hand wound. It would go for so long, then start to sound all funny, making everyone laugh. I had to do the winding bit, loving every minute.

Our Christmas was always special. Everyone has their own special memories, one of mine being images of gingerbread men hot from the oven. I also remember being given a spoonful of olive oil to take every day of the year except Christmas Day. My grandmother used to give me olive oil by the bottle to drink; she said that it was good for me. I have no idea why I should remember this unless it was quite unusual at that time. Most other children were given cod liver oil, which must have tasted like poison. There is no doubt that it was the connection with Merseyside trade that provided exotic additions to our Christmas fare.

The mid-1930s were prosperous years for our household. The city had a modern glamour that I can recognise now as an adult, but at the time, even as a child, there was always the sense of something that was good. I would listen to our visitors, or notice how they dressed, or go down into town to shop. Liverpool was (and is) a great place. It has a personality of its very own. Around Dale Street there were hundreds of bikes and telegraph boys, wearing small pill box-shaped hats as part of their uniform. They were easy to spot in their red colours. I would say that all the offices in the city employed junior boys as runners, especially those companies connected with shipping. Boys would take messages from their employers about cargo and bills of lading, or do their master's bidding in competition between ships' brokers. It used to cost about a penny a word to send a telegraph. The sharper boys would shorten their telegraph messages and earn a penny or two to spend on a bun. A lot of wheeling and dealing went on. The city centre always seemed to be very full and noisy. The arrival of the motor car was significant as it made Liverpool an even busier place.

My father never owned a motor car. Instead he preferred the freedom of a motorcycle with a sidecar. We travelled everywhere in the sidecar with me on my mother's knee. At every opportunity we were off, particularly to Wales to go camping. Trips to north Wales were the thing to do. It was commonplace for young people to cycle all the way to Rhyl and Colwyn Bay from Liverpool, not something teenagers today would consider lightly. Later on, we bought a cottage in Moelfre Bay in Anglesey as part owners with the Hobbs family to share as a holiday home.

Father's motorbike was kept in the shed. He loved to tinker with it. I travelled in the sidecar until I was just too big to fit in any more. The first motor car that I remember belonged to Uncle Philip, my father's elder brother. Uncle Phil lived in Blackpool with his wife Annie. He worked for Colonel Washbone as a despatch rider and confidante in the war and was left the Bentley car and a house in Westbourne Avenue in the colonel's will. Westbourne Avenue was one of the best residential areas in Blackpool. We would all go there to visit and ride in his car. It used to hold us all, Grandpa and Grandma too, rattling along at a fair old speed, and it was a real treat to be driven around Blackpool in it.

The experience of growing up in Liverpool has given me my character, a character that has been nurtured and developed, a body that has been well travelled and a mind that has met a multitude of others. It is strange to hear people describe you as a local hero, someone the city recognises as one of its own, and for people to mark your existence as worthy of recognition. My commitment to Liverpool and its artists is very dear to me. A Liverpudlian upbringing has made me acutely aware of a good opportunity when I see one, a bit like the telegraph boys.

Until I started to collect my thoughts together to write this story, my childhood years were way in the past. As I started to think about the path that my life followed, it was the little insignificant pleasures that were surprisingly still in the corners of my mind. There are grand academic arguments that suggest that all art is nothing but memory and recollection of experience, but no one can say for sure. My own aesthetic sensibility may well have developed as a result of my comparatively privileged background. However, I was to experience two great cities, radically different and yet joined together in art: a symbiotic relationship between Liverpool and London, with art as the fertile catalyst. Art in Liverpool encompasses a rich cultural heritage closely tied to the city. In time it drew attention from a much wider audience, as a hotbed for talent so revered in London in the 1960s.

Thinking again of my formative years, life had a good rhythm to it. In winter, when we had snow, Grandma would make a huge snowman at the back of the house. Grandpa was always at the office, which meant that my childhood memories are filled with images of my grandmother. We would always use pieces of sharp black coal to look like real eyes. Our snowman never seemed to get his personality until he had his eyes. The old felt hat and coal pieces for buttons made him look quite dapper. I thought it was great. The children from St Bride Street would come around to see what he looked like. I would play outside for ages, making snowballs and trying to make snow figures. I always wanted to make things. When it was eventually time to go inside Grandma would say: 'There's the man in the sun. Look at the great big orange sun,' and I would run in as fast as I could. I don't remember what I thought was there. Perhaps it was the fear of the power of the sun melting the snowman. The colours and changing hues of light on snow are quite peculiar and somehow eerie. The gentle gold that falls into the strong orange glow. The small blue chinks of ice that reflect the colour of the rainbow if you look closely.

These early visual experiences have stayed with me. There are elements of those winter evenings and the still curiosity of the winter palette that remain lively visual engagements with the colours of nature. It was much later in life before my romantic childhood pleasures would resurface in my love of art. Sometimes, I look at a painting where the artist has captured a feeling or mood of nature and I am instantly transported back to the snow and ice. Their watery existence, fragile and unstable nature skilfully captured by marks on a canvas. The sense of underlying solidity that waits for the return of spring once again to make the landscape active and alive. There is a strange settling down as night falls in winter. Children sense it when they return indoors to the warmth of firelight, piping hot drinks, cheeks glowing with a mixture of pink and russet. Outside, winter steels the cold air. Nature holds a fascination for the artist, a childlike desire to explore their youthful memories or an adult desire to be master of all they survey. The harsh realities of daily life soon impose on the idyllic, imaginative world of childhood.

Much of my time was spent skating. From the age of about ten until I was eighteen my mother had wanted me to skate professionally because it was terrifically well paid in those days. I was certainly very strong on my feet and legs. I think back to the strength that you need when skating for very long periods and now I realise that it must have developed a really good muscle tone. It must certainly have helped me as an artist's model to retain a particular pose. I developed a knack of supporting my weight on my right leg with my hands clasped behind my back. This pose proved to be my most distinctive feature as a model. Now I realise it must have been all those years skating and perfecting my balance that later enabled me to be adept and keep my weight distributed evenly on my frame. This made it easier for my outline to be drawn because the central axis of my posture was well supported, meaning that I could hold still with perfect poise for as long as an artist demanded. Other models would frequently tire, which meant that the artist would be forced to stop. This must have been a problem in moments of inspired creativity.

Skating was a popular pastime in the Liverpool of the 1940s. It was both a way of keeping fit and healthy and a way of socialising. I learned to dance and carried on skating until I was about eighteen years old. My father used to take me. We went to the local rink about three times a week. After each practice session my legs would ache, usually when it was time to play hockey at school the next day. It was, all the same, a family activity that we could enjoy together.

The heart of my family is firmly embedded in our peculiar city. As a busy international port, Liverpool has played host to untold thousands. Traditionally, the Port of Liverpool swelled with the in-migration of travellers: people who were outsiders, expectant emigrants to the Americas in the last century, soldiers or sailors in this century. As a westerly point of seaward departure, Liverpool attracted the traffic for most of Europe. This resulted in a multi-cultural society of all tastes and attitudes ranging from gay abandon to serious business. It could be argued that the fierce torrent of the River Mersey, coupled with its renowned dangerous waters, and the excitement of 'making the tide' concentrated the minds of its inhabitants, encouraging the enthusiasm of a culture of hope, of exploration and experimentation. Liverpool people have a peculiar insularity from the rest of England and a culture that has suffered ebbs and flows over the decades. Liverpool in the 1990s is a calmer but nonetheless active city, bustling with a successful port.

The Furlong family has long been connected with the port and the image of a prosperous, middle-class, white-collar family is ever present in the exterior of my family home. Situated at the far end of Falkner Street, the four-storey family terrace house is redolent of the eighteenth-century grandeur of old Liverpool. Coach and horses, cobbled streets and the sharp, chill river wind blowing up the hill towards Upper Parliament Street. The academics and the well-heeled took residence here. There is always the sense of history present. Even today the streets are frequently used as period settings for film makers as well as for modern television drama. A popular misconception is that Liverpool is a place to be feared, as desperate, poor and hopeless. The reality is different. There is indeed hardship and poverty in such a large city, but it should be said that Liverpool has a wealth of success and positive aspects to its credit. The Port of Liverpool and the Mersey Docks and

Harbour Company (MDHC) have been a major success. Even in the recession of the late 1980s the company made substantial profits and is today financially strong.

There has been a long tradition of association between river and city. The shipping companies drew travellers from all over the world. The Great Western Hotel adjacent to Lime Street Railway Station was the height of luxury for visitors. It was built for the Atlantic Sea traffic and has only recently been acquired and converted by Liverpool John Moores University for student accommodation. In the 1930s wealthy travellers would arrive at Lime Street station and then take a passenger train to the quayside. At the quayside, the boy-runners of the shipping companies would be bustling between the dockside and the hotels in the city to carry the bags and shepherd the travellers safely between hotel and ship and vice versa. The shipping families of Merseyside have been patrons of the arts for two hundred years. More recently, the MDHC have carried on that tradition in their sponsorship of the art of the city, too. Numerous images of the Port of Liverpool have been produced and sold worldwide.

The Irish Sea can be particularly inhospitable at times and the Mersey Estuary is one of the most treacherous in the world. Well-seasoned sailors always say that the Liver Birds on the Liver Building as they turn into the estuary are a welcome sight. Even if they did not come from Liverpool, the birds symbolise a warm, safe haven for the seafarers. During the war, after sailing home from dangerous missions across the Atlantic, sailors could celebrate in the city at night.

It is possible to smell the river: the salty, musty scents still haunt the long time-worn streets. Romantic images of tightly packed bales of cotton, tobacco and paper flood the mind with the fleeting breeze and then disappear as if carried to some far away place in an instant. Old timber and brickwork towering above the hessian-bound, decaying cargo stand in the mind's eye alongside the murky, cold water that sends the salty air over the dockside. Only a short distance away, in the 1930s, the scrubbed steel liners with their luxury fittings would swell the portside beckoning aboard travellers off to America and the excitement of New York. Liverpool and America were brought so much closer in the 1930s. Liverpool was a gateway, a threshold of hope and a place of transition and growth. The people grew ever hopeful of a more prosperous future, as they looked westward. The charm and elegance of the wealthy travellers, who sailed with the likes of White Star or Cunard, was a sharp contrast to those immigrants travelling less grandly and to those left behind in the city.

Many were too poor to move on and faced poverty in overcrowded tenement buildings or court slum dwellings. Liverpool City Council carried out a massive slum clearance programme in the 1930s as much of the city's Victorian past was swept away. Buildings were levelled and a sense of optimism was slowly generated. Our family was indeed fortunate; many families saw extreme hardship and poverty. Dockworkers in particular struggled with the dock labour system, although as an infant I was obviously not aware of this at the time. By the time I reached nine years of age, war had broken out and the 1930s were soon sucked into an idealistic bubble of memory. The sheer size of the huge liners loomed awesomely over the dockside during that golden age. Passenger terminals vying with warehouses and the competitive juxtapositioning of vessels queuing to go like horses at the Grand National as soon as the river demands. The benefit of the western Port of Liverpool took on a new mantle with wartime. The once fair, beautiful people were soon a thing of the past and army and navy uniforms took their place.

My grandfather was Chief Clerk at the Port of Liverpool, after being educated at St Xavier's Catholic School for Boys. He worked as head of the checking department at the MDHC. His sisters went into teaching, and his son, my father, became a manager at the Cotton Exchange after the war. In the 1920s and 1930s it was only the well-educated who could move into the large corporations, insurance companies or Port Authority. A grammar school education was essential, not only for employment but for entry into the officer corps in the forces, too. Without a grammar school education it was unlikely that in later years you would be able to get a pension. In the 1984, my cousin Trevor Furlong was appointed Managing Director and Chief Executive for the Mersey Docks and Harbour Company after having worked for the Port since the age of sixteen, following his father. Trevor has thus continued the family presence. The Cotton Exchange, where my father worked, was a prime employer of considerable standing in Liverpool. Work in the Exchange was regarded as a good job and it was a reasonable measure of success and social status to be employed there, even though the level of trade had peaked in the nineteenth century. Liverpool provided all the raw cotton for its hinterland and the Lancashire cotton mills. I always tell visitors to the Liverpool Museum to look out for the bales of cotton on display. They belonged to my father and were presented to the Museum by Eldon Worrall. Eldon is a long-established antique dealer and close family friend. We first met in the Sandon Studios at the Bluecoat Chambers when I was having a meal with the artist George Jardine, who had a studio at the Sandon, number 10 at the top.

Growing up in Liverpool and living through the experience of wartime made friendship very important. I remember that the children around and about seemed poor. My friends used to like to play with my toys and call around for tea and cakes as a treat. One was Paul Thomas, whose father had a dairy in St Bride Street. He would walk the cows around the vicinity and deliver the milk directly into the pails brought out by the servants of the great houses along the road. We had eight bells above the basement kitchen door which would be used by Grandfather to summon the staff. The house bells were very large and had quite a loud ring. Paul would never want to go home, and my parents were always concerned that his parents would be worried about him. The only way to get him to leave was for Grandma to go upstairs and ring one of the servants' bells. Paul would then fly off back to the dairy. Friends like Paul, Edna, Rosie and Jennie called regularly, liking the opulence and the food. Grandfather's connections meant that our house had quite unusual foodstuffs with a sense of mystery about them. Not the run-of-the mill pantry, but one that would lead the senses on a curious and inquisitive journey around the dinner table.

My best friend Dorothy (Dot) Lawrence, with whom I spent a lot of time as a child, has now retired and lives in West Kirby. We tend not to see a great deal of each other nowadays, although we keep in touch. Her married name is Buchanan, she had four children, one of whom, Nick, is a fine teacher. Dot lived in Egerton Street near the Rialto Cinema. The Rialto was razed to the ground in the Toxteth rioting in 1981 in symbolic defiance of the modern decay of the traditional, authoritarian static nature of Liverpool society, stuck in the doldrums of hopeless despair. Before the riot and in more affable days Dorothy and I would call for each other and go to St Margaret's School in Princes Road together. We spent our girlhood together as much as possible. We went our separate ways when I left St Margaret's to enrol at the very-well-to-do St Edmunds College in Devonshire Road. The school colours were black and purple, colours that oddly are still favourites of mine. It was a prestigious college that encouraged girls to have a good education. The games mistress, Miss Formby, coaxed me into the hockey team. I couldn't wait to get out of it, especially as my elaborate, curly hairstyle ended up as flat as a pancake after hockey, which meant I looked a disaster when I got to the skating rink. As a games captain I was, however, responsible for collecting the subs from everyone. I had a big tin for the money and all my friends were well aware of this. Whenever the latest Metro-Goldwyn-Mayer film was showing at the Rialto Cinema they came to me to borrow from the tin. Harriet Naylor took over the hockey team in due course and I was let off the hook, but not before gaining the Red Girdle for my Spooner House for sports and deportment. Miss Celia Hennings was our headmistress, a stickler for discipline, very kind at the same time, though. I was given a good report when I left along the lines of 'June Furlong will no doubt succeed in anything she decides to pursue. a natural born leader. I have always found her a pleasure to deal with'. Armed with that glowing reference I thought I could take on the world.

Between Falkner Street and Sefton Park was the most affluent area of Liverpool, certainly one of the wealthiest cities in Britain. It was quite a fashionable area, with stockbrokers, shipping magnates, surgeons, professionals of all kinds living in the grand terraced houses up to the park. Falkner Street was the best place for grandfather to live. He bought the house in 1903. The best areas were all within walking distance from the centre of commerce and the city's dock heartland. As soon as he came home he would recline on the big black horsehair chaise longue. His supper was always ready and he would then have a snooze until six o'clock. Even when Grandpa retired, he was used to walking down to the river. He would take a walk each day to the landing stage at the Pier Head and feed the pigeons. He had a good routine to his life. He would call at the market, then to Credens for a Guinness and then on to the library. He would pick up his book, bring it all the way home and then say: 'Oh blow, I have already read this!' He smoked an exquisite rosewood pipe, from which the ash would tumble down the front of his waistcoat when he sat in the large armchair in front of the fire. Dad would arrive home about six – he would generally walk from his office in Old Hall Street, and say: 'Dad! Your waistcoat is on fire!' It was a family joke really. I remember Grandpa spoke magnificent French and said that Paris was his favourite city. He had a love of art and used to take me to the Walker Art Gallery when I was only four years of age. It was a real treat. He died at home aged 87 after one of his morning walks to the landing stage, dearly missed by everyone.

My maternal grandmother, Florence Ureka Garrett, married Tommy Garrett. She had inherited three businesses from her father who worked as a tea blender at premises near the Liverpool Institute.

Mother was born above the business in Mount Street, near Rodney Street. The business of tea merchant and blender was a good one to be in, but it was hard work. It must have provided a good income for the family. I was always amazed at how different blends of tea could be identified and named. Early in the 1960s they had moved out of Falkner Street after buying a business in Windsor Street. It was a grocer's shop, newsagents and a snuff/tobacconist shop. There was accommodation over the shop which is why they had left Falkner Street in the first place. After father had died, aged 65 in 1965, mother retired in 1970 from their business in Windsor Street and she came to live with me and Uncle Fred in Falkner Street. She would have been officially retired when they bought the business in the first place. When most people are starting to slow down we seem to pick up speed and motivation to try new things! It was a sad time when she died soon after.

The family name, Garrett, was Irish. Grandmother Garrett was born in Duke Street, the house later became the Knightsbridge Club and a regular haunt of mine in my forties when I used to visit with Steve Hardstaff. Steve is the wonderful teacher who produces such high quality silkscreen prints in the Art School at Liverpool John Moores University. Steve came to Liverpool from London in 1969. I am not sure when my grandparents originally came to Liverpool but the city has a strong Irish tradition of immigration. I do know that my great-great-grandfather Furlong was a rear-admiral in the British navy and my great-grandfather's connections were all in education, with all the family working in teaching at some time or another.

My mother's family had three businesses in all. This makes me think that they must have had a good start in Liverpool as it would have been difficult in the nineteenth century to begin in business. The businesses were in Slater Street, Scotland Road and Mount Street. They lived over the premises in Mount Street as they worked very hard. I remember there were huge tea chests all around. The smell of a tea chest is quite distinctive and I was always reminded of it when I went into the Kardomah and other coffee-houses in the city. My grandparents on my mother's side also sold high-class provisions which would account for the wide variety of different kinds of foodstuffs and exotic tastes in our household. The shops were in very long rooms; it wasn't a bit like going shopping for Tetley teabags! All their teas were blended on the spot to the whim of the customer.

They went to Ireland, and when they came back to Scotland Road and Slater Street their businesses had been burned to the ground around 1928-9 in the riots that accompanied the Depression. Life was hard for most people in Liverpool and riotous behaviour was not unusual, and still isn't if we think of the Toxteth riots not all that long ago. Grandmother had been living in Pilgrim Street but went to live over the business in Mount Street for about 37 years after that. I remember when she was in Mount Street she used to have a selection of the advertising posters for Pears Soap, together with other Victorian posters pasted on the ceiling in Mount Street. When she retired she gave them to some of the students from the college who asked for them, along with the old fashioned black and gold lacquered tea chests. She had carried on the business for many years.

On my father's side, my grandmother Amy Furlong was a florist who used to make the most magnificent bouquets and create the grand decoration for society weddings and banquets in Liverpool. She had amazing panache. Her brother-in-law was Fred Fishlock, the Fishlock florist with premises still in Castle Street. They were the number one florists in Liverpool, selling only grade one flowers. My grandmother always had the house full of flowers. Nevertheless, grandmother would never refuse to buy from the 'Mary Ellens' who called at the door. They were the old flower sellers of Liverpool, poor Irish who lived around Scotland Road. They would walk about with baskets balanced on their heads and wore heavy black woollen shawls, draped about their shoulders. They were always dressed in black. If the flowers were not good or even if grandmother had plenty already she would still pay them to take their flowers to the cemetery. They would knock on the door and say: 'Is the Mrs in?' She never turned them away.

When I was young, Grandma didn't go out to work and neither did my mother. Both were at the house all the time. We had quite a strict timetable. There was a variety of food every day and plenty of it, always served at a set time, and I was not allowed to miss a meal. If I were outside playing in the backstreets with the local children, my mother would always come and call me home. My father encouraged me to mix with people of all classes and types, from all walks of life, saying, 'On this bumpy road called life, you will come into contact with all sorts of people from all sorts of places and it is just as well that you should be able to cope with it'. It was good advice, which has stood me in good stead.

All my uncles were born in Falkner Street. My grandfather had seven sons and a daughter. My father was third from eldest. The first uncle was Phil, the driver for Colonel Washbone I mentioned earlier. The colonel left him his

Bentley and his house in Westbourne Avenue in Blackpool. The family sold this house and bought something smaller, but I did manage to visit regularly every summer.

Then there was Uncle Fred. He was shipping master for P & O and remained a bachelor for life. He lived at home in Falkner Street with the family and eventually took over the running of the house, paying the bills and keeping everything organised. I was not under any pressure to manage the household affairs. Generally, young women would be expected to take on these responsibilities, especially if they married. It was because Uncle Fred was living at home that I was able to take up evening posing and work so hard. Uncle Fred retired from work when he was about 54 and lived for only another four years. When he became ill I gladly took the responsibility to nurse him, as we had been so very close. The last couple of years of his life were especially difficult for me. As well as being emotionally drained watching my dear uncle suffer, I was trying to keep working full-time at the Art College in Hope Street. The years between 1975-80 were very testing. Uncle George, a refrigeration consultant, would take Uncle Fred around and about until he eventually needed the ambulance service.

Next came Uncle Leonard followed by Auntie Marjorie. Uncle Leonard was a good dancer, good looking too. He ran two of the most popular places in the city, the Bear's Paw, an elegant and prestigious restaurant and dance hall at the corner of North John Street, and the State, in Dale Street. He was called manager/host. There was no television then and dancing filled the time and provided a way to meet other people. He lived at Falkner Street before getting married. He would go out of the house at five in the afternoon for the tea dances and not arrive home until about two or three in the morning. The Salvation Army would play by the hospital and I remember Uncle Leonard saying to my mother, 'Pay the Sally Army two pounds and tell them to move on, as I need my sleep!'

Leonard was best described as a professional dancer. He was lively and a tango expert. He had immaculate and beautifully cut evening clothes. I remember his white bow tie; he always took a second white collar with him to change as the evening wore on. It is such a shame to think of more recent times when the State lost its licence because of a drug problem. There were no such difficulties in Uncle Leonard's day. People did not need to get drugged up before they went out. Uncle Leonard's was the time of great style and panache, the elegance and beauty of everyone giving a good feeling to a night's dancing.

There was always – and I think still is – a generosity amongst the people of Liverpool. Uncle used to receive wonderful gifts from his clientele when he ran both the Bears Paw and the State. I particularly remember him being given a big white parrot and a silky-haired Pomeranian dog called Teddy. This was a real event – what a gift! All the ladies adored him.

As a professional dancer his hours were erratic, so he never ate at the house with the family, but exclusively at his clubs, and then he would be tea dancing at five o'clock, anyway. He was in with all the tip-top ladies of society in Liverpool at the time. He would introduce people as host, looking every bit like a film star. I suspect that he was really quite a sharp gentleman, although he was a romantic hero to me, living in an adult world. 1930s Liverpool was avant-garde, wealthy, with charm. Grand-dad always used to wonder what Leonard was up to, and could never understand the type of world that he mixed in.

With regard to the wealth of the family, it was grand-dad who had the money, but he always spent it on his own tastes, including my grandmother. He loved partying and good food. Although he earned it, he certainly spent it, and made sure that he had a good time doing so. Perhaps that is where Uncle Leonard got his love of life.

My next uncle, Percy, was harbour master of Herculaneum Dock at Liverpool and lived in North Sudley Road in Aigburth. He was the father of Trevor Furlong who is chief executive of Mersey Docks and Harbour Company.

Then we have Uncle Bruce. He was originally in the navy but he hated it, as he was always seasick. His brothers had to get him thoroughly drunk before each sailing, pushing him on the boat as near sailing time as possible. After one particularly rough sea he decided that his days as a Jolly Jack Tar must come to an end. He found a place as head waiter at the five-star Grand Hotel at Llandudno. As an elegant Victorian and Edwardian seaside retreat, the bay is beautifully rugged. There were regular sailings from the Pier Head in Liverpool to the pier at Llandudno and the town thrived on the day-trippers from across the region. The tramlines and quaintness of the fishing port of Conway made the area especially attractive to visitors.

The Grand Hotel was very plush and would attract the rich and famous stars. The singer and actor Paul Robeson once stayed there. Robeson, appearing in Showboat in London, paid for food for the miners at the end of their historic walk to London, suffering from a lockout and literally starving. Robeson helped their trade union and became very popular in Wales. He, like many visitors, would holiday in Llandudno before sailing on to Liverpool and over to America. The sweeping bay nestles between the steep Orme headlands that both protect and disguise the bay. Artists have been drawn to the region for inspiration and the challenge of capturing its many moods and seasons. Whenever I visit the Royal Cambrian Academy gallery at Conway I think of Uncle Bruce and Aunt Kitty. She was quite an eccentric, even at 85 years of age swimming in the sea for charity, or playing golf. Kitty was an admirable character, surviving until 1997, loved by everyone.

My mother's sister moved to Cheshire. There were eighteen years between my mum and sister. Peter, Michael and Jeffrey are my cousins, but didn't keep in close contact over the years. They have all done quite well, probably because they were all educated at Liverpool College. Peter lives in Halewood and has a quarry business.

Grand-dad Furlong was a Catholic and a Conservative, although I was raised in the Protestant faith. Both grand-dad and grandmother (and mother Florence) were all good whist players. They would play twice a week, especially with the Bon Marché (now George Henry Lee) crowd. Dad hated cards. Nevertheless, the family would hold high tea in the back room and play a hand or two.

In our house at meal times, the trolley would rattle through the playroom from the butler's pantry, the distant kitchen sounds and smells drifting through the open shaft. Our meals were always served in the front living kitchen room without fail. The upstairs dining room was reserved for special occasions such as Sunday, birthday teas or wedding celebrations etc. the grand back room was just right with its imposing architecture and substantial furnishings.

My childhood was happy. The houses around Falkner Street were not flats or apartments as they are now. They were all full of life and there was plenty of activity. My parents never excluded anyone from our home even if their circumstances were different from ours.

There were no black people living in the area when I was a child before the big immigration campaign of the late 1940s. Many people from Jamaica were recruited to come to Britain to help rebuild our industry after the war and they were encouraged to settle here. Liverpool has a good mix of multi-racial families and a wide variety of ethnic groups. I think that this has opened up Liverpool culture, which nowadays shows in different uses of colour and pattern in the city's art that brings it alive. The cultural heritage of Liverpool should provide great inspiration to the artists who live and work here. Certainly, compared with the art produced from Leeds, where the formal elements promoted by the influential critic Herbert Read are clearly visible, the art of our own pasture is more daring and colourful. The formal structure of our art appears to be far more elemental, although the Post-Impressionist influence has remained. Many examples are dotted about in private collections, distinguished examples of the Liverpool talent.

My education began at St Margaret's Primary School about fifteen minutes' walk from home. Happy at school and successfully accepted by St Edmunds High School for Girls, I couldn't wait to move onto my secondary education. Articulate and intelligent, I was top of the class in some subjects, especially art which was my favourite. I was hopeless at mathematics, algebra and geometry. It is just as well that I wasn't around in the days of the Renaissance, when mathematical structure and calculation was everything. Trying to calculate the perspective in a painting would not have been my forté at all. I began to try my hand at painting through part-time study at Saturday morning classes in Princes Avenue when I was about ten years of age. I learned a few practical skills which have helped me appreciate the work that artists put into a piece.

Initially employed in an advertising studio at an agency called Lee and Nightingale in North John Street, my future seemed secure – but also predictable. It was expected that I would work in an office for a few years, do the social scene, and find a young man who would make a good husband and get married. There wasn't any specific pressure to marry, but it was regarded as a natural path to a good life. After all, any such certainty was luxurious after the uncertainty of the war years.

I was 15 at the end of the war and most of my childhood memories were of wartime. School was disrupted and lessons were always unusual. Nevertheless, as a child I accepted wartime as just part of life. Wartime Liverpool has been well described by others. My own experience was of the excitement of uncertainty. For adults, a return to calm stability and the routine of family life and ritual must have been justification in themselves for self-limitation, both through geography and in personal relations. I felt like something different, though. I thrived on self-belief and independence. Never being suburban by inclination, and although it suited others, I didn't fancy the predictable role of secretary, wife and mother.

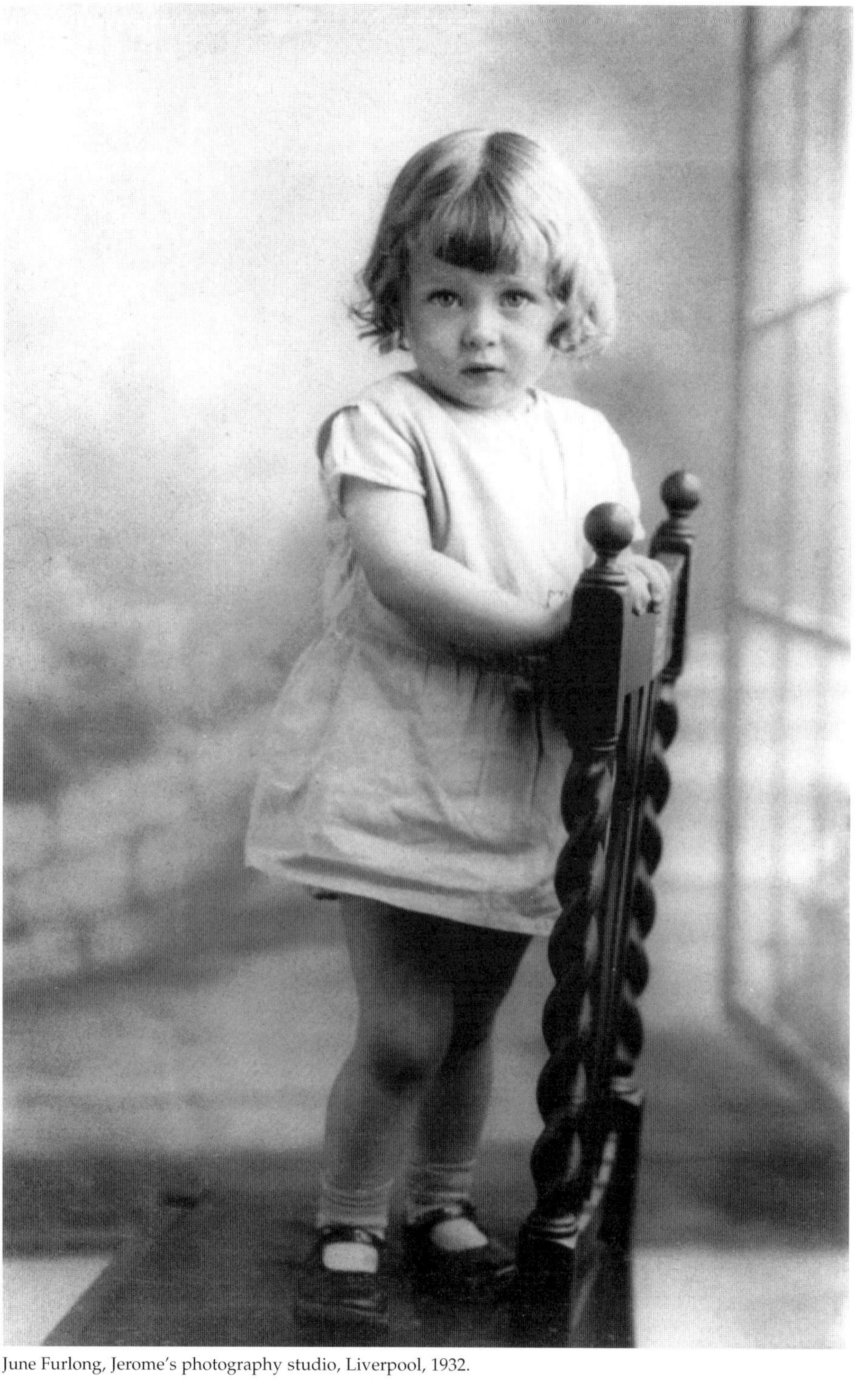

June Furlong, Jerome's photography studio, Liverpool, 1932.

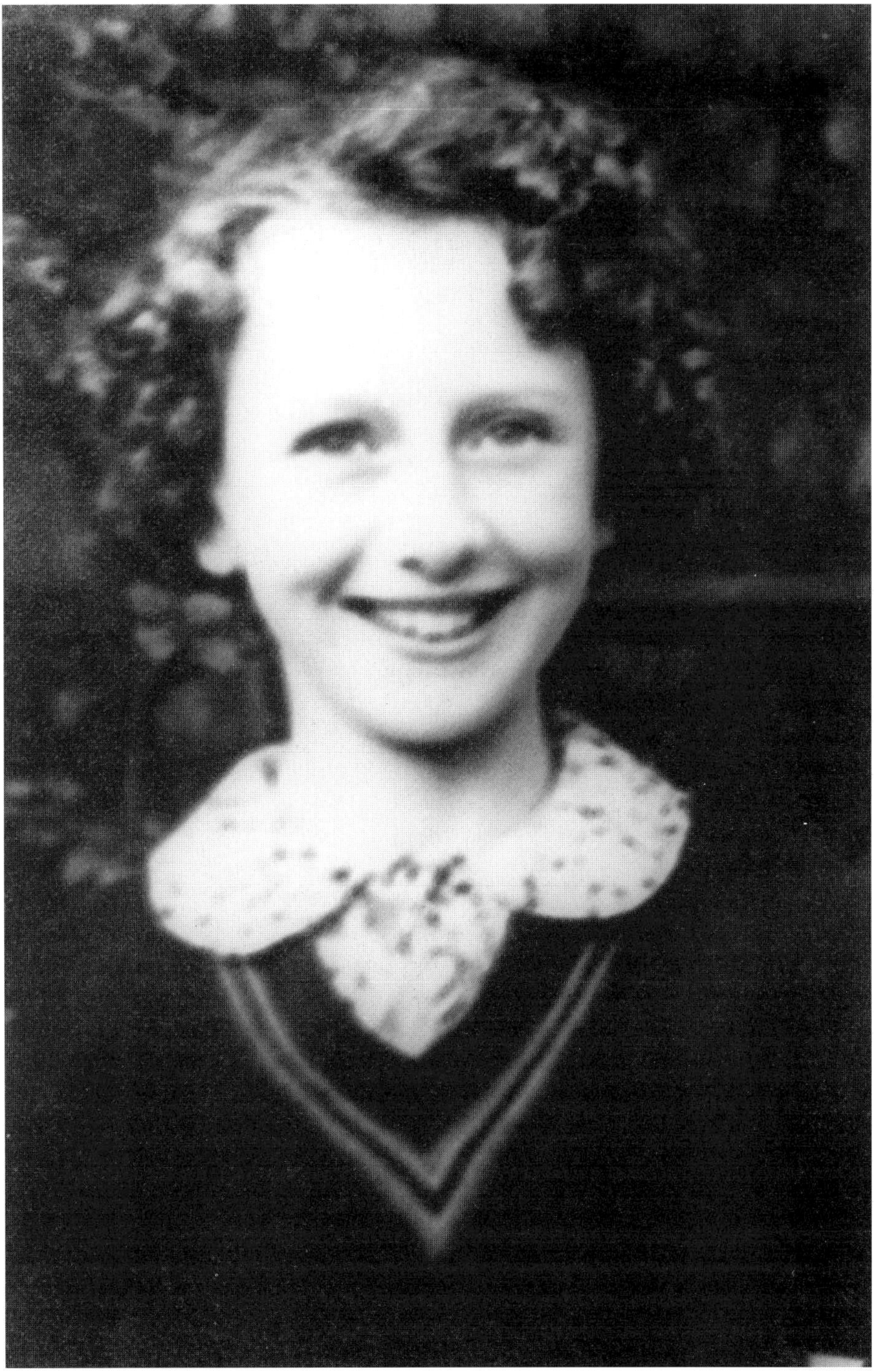

June, wearing St Edmunds School pullover, 1944.

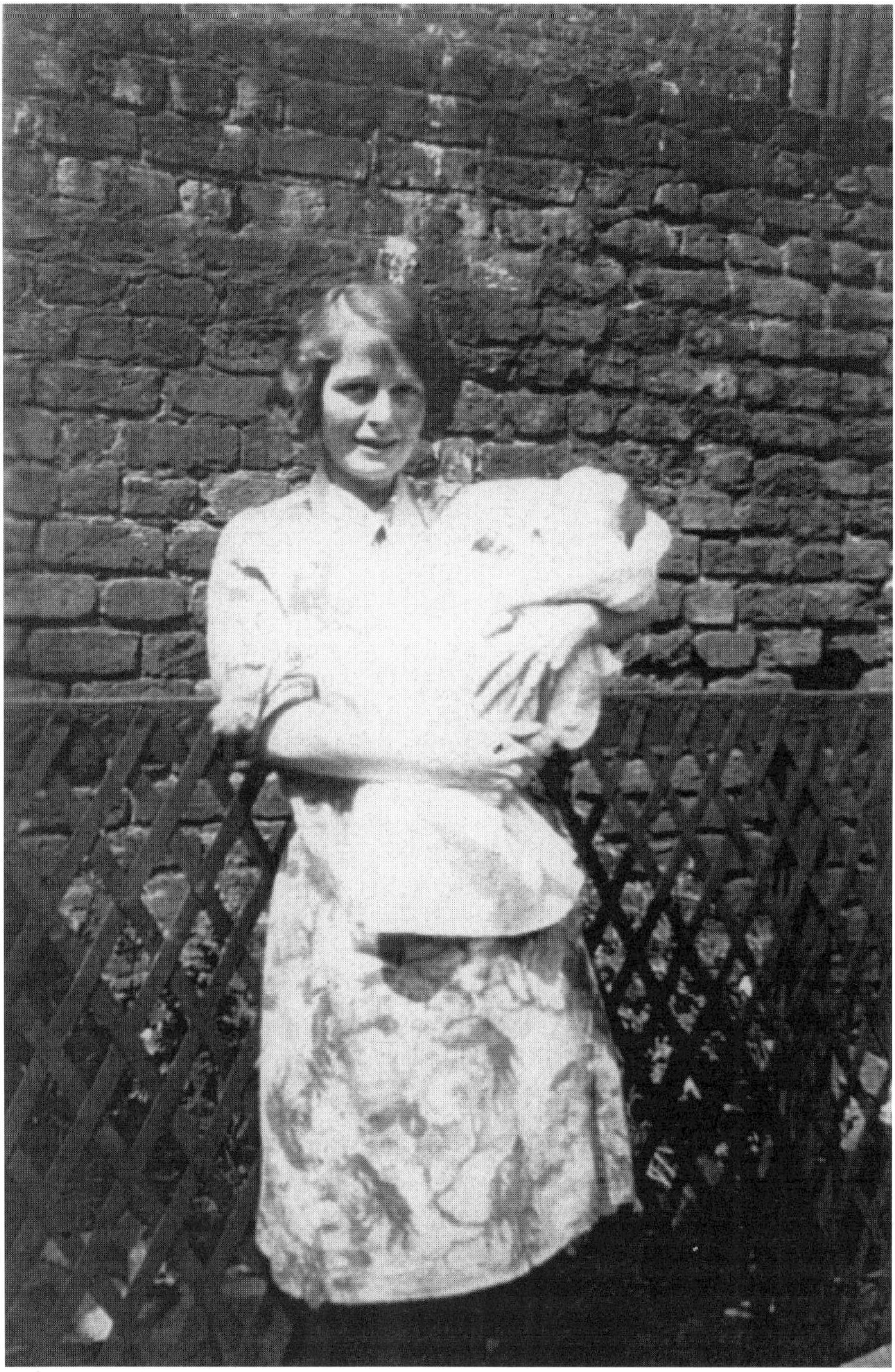

Mother – Florence Furlong holding June, Liverpool, 1930.

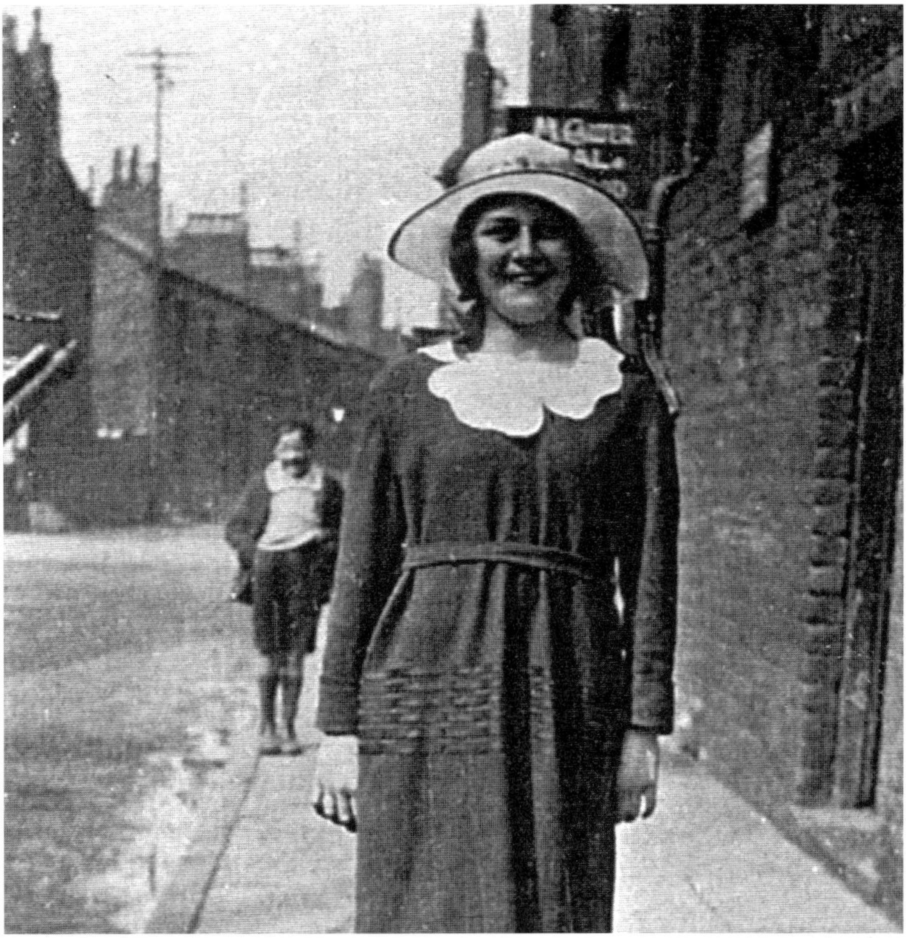

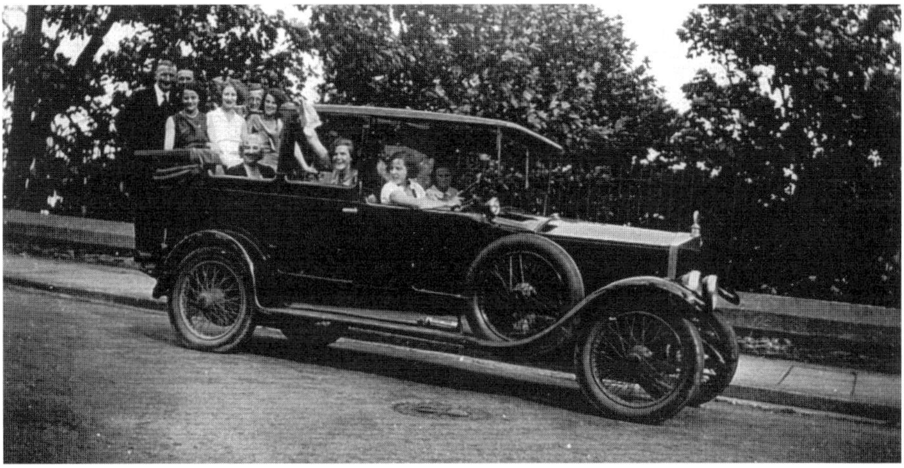

Florence Furlong.
Uncle Phil's car and the Furlong family.

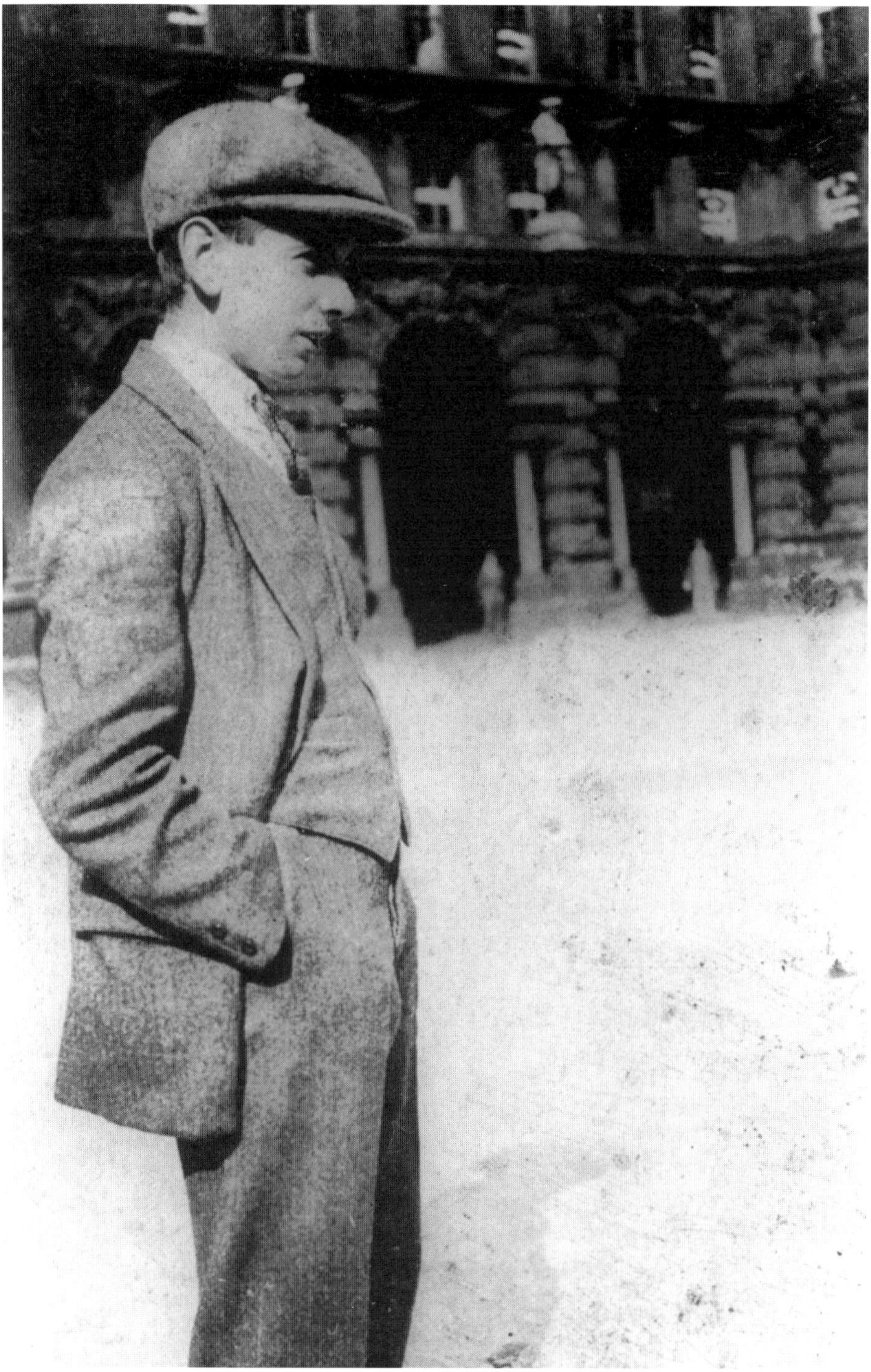

Father, Cyril Furlong at Exchange Flags, Liverpool, 1926.

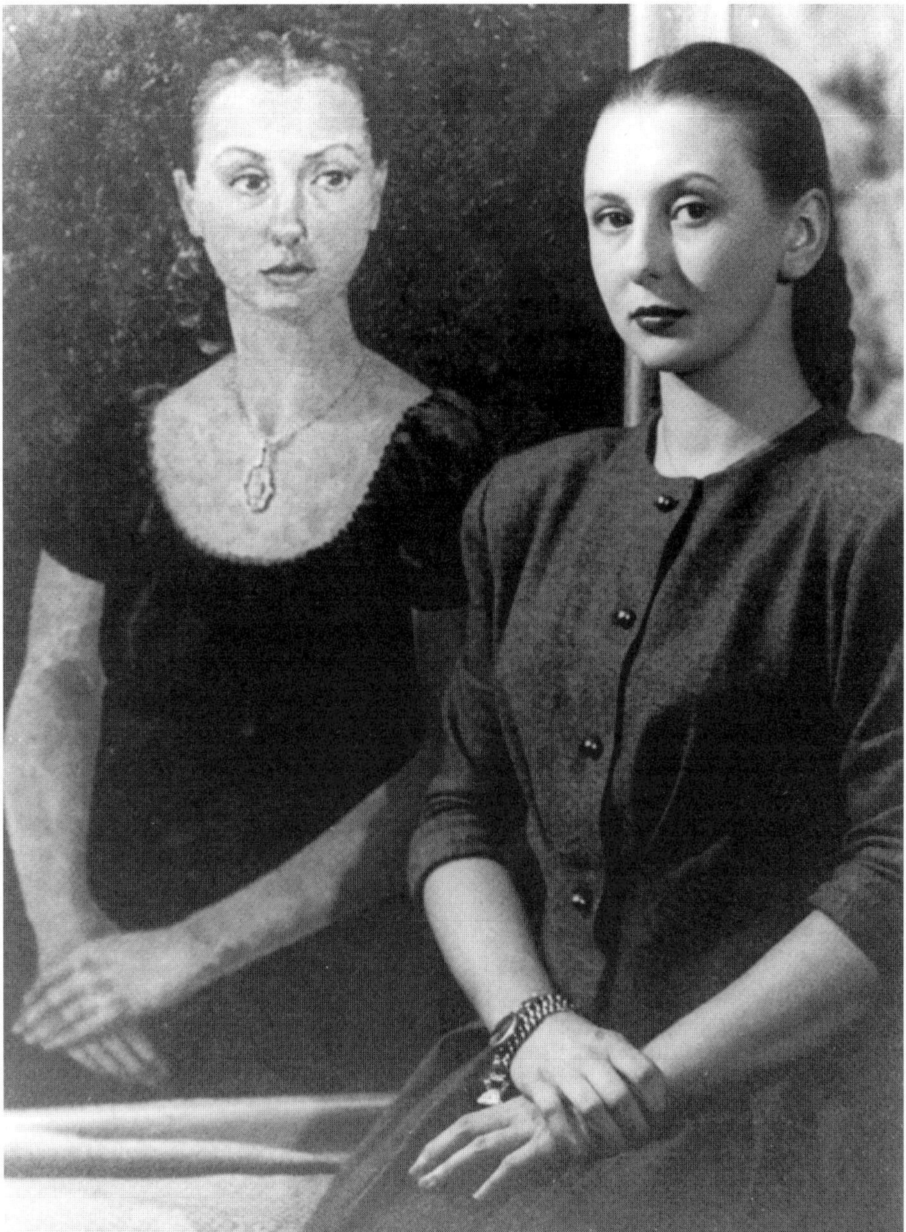

June Furlong, oil on canvas. Austin Davies, 1948.

In My Liverpool Home 1947-1951

Far from predictable was my encounter with a young man called Don McKinlay while I was 17 and still at school. I was using the public telephone in Catharine Street when a cheeky young man said, 'You would make a wonderful model – a natural' and asked if I would model for the students at the Art College. Startled and flattered, I learned that he was himself a student there and seemed genuinely keen to persuade me to sit for him. I didn't agree, as he had no money to pay for models. I wasn't even sure about the idea of working at the College but finally decided that nothing ventured meant nothing gained. So I agreed to give it a go. Don's father was the chief crime reporter on the Liverpool Daily Post & Echo. I think he would be surprised to learn that our contact has continued all these years. As recently as 1997 I was sending Don a cheque for the sale of a series of etchings entitled Anna that were very much in demand. He was continuing to exhibit in Liverpool in 1999.

Don McKinlay is one of the most prolific northern artists of today. His teaching was expert and without doubt the students in Manchester have benefited greatly from his input and influence. All speak well of him. His antics, however, persuaded the genteel Furlongs that Art College might not be the best place for their daughter. He would arrive at Falkner Street at all hours, frequently after midnight. Many a time he called with a group of other young artists. He was a bit of a joker. He sent word around to his friends that my father always did his gardening at night as there was this lovely smell – it was night-scented stock!

I loved the cheerful and fun-filled atmosphere that Don brought. I felt part of life, tasting freedom and revelling in undivided attention as I learned my craft. There is something magical about the age of seventeen, as the stepping stone between youth and young adulthood. Life is the promise of excitement, of an immense future that stretches into the distance, too far to be seen or fully understood at such a young age, when responsibility looms large. This cannot be truer than for those of us who had experience of war. In the post-war years we were told that our future was going to be fresh and bright, austerity a way to ensure a greater happiness and success in the future.

Don had a lot of energy, captured in his work, and which he expressed through his originality and terrific output. Even as an art student, his verve and commitment were obvious. He thinks through his work and prepares well, he possesses a natural ability to draw well and has a creativity charged with feeling. He could look at a figure in space, measure it up and produce a free-hand drawing directly onto the canvas, a drawing of such exquisite quality and freshness that the figure has a life of its own. Such direct interaction between eye and hand was uncommon and against the grain of meticulous, methodical tradition, so that meant that his work was always inspiring when compared with that of other students.

Attention to detail and expert copying were the main elements of traditional pre-war art education, but a new freedom of expression through line was emerging. Traditional line drawing often looked static and heavy. Students always had difficulty in making their representation look as if it had a life. Only a handful mastered the skill of making their drawing vital and lively, Don being one of them. He should have moved to London to one of the national colleges, but his father was against the idea. Don became a close personal friend. I developed a trust in him that was reflected in his work. At the time, I simply enjoyed the life, but as time went by I began to look and to get a better understanding of what art was all about. I found myself being drawn in, quite literally.

When I began to model, I was in the full bloom of youth, but never thought I would still be as enthralled 50 years later. I was told that I looked like an English rose. Bob Mossman, art historian and painter, once said that I 'looked like a Fragonard' and that my face was 'quintessentially eighteenth century'. My hair fell about my shoulders light brown and blonde in colour and starting to darken with an auburn glow that seemed to appear in a particular light.

I remember at the Regional College of Art, Alfred Wiffen would be teaching anatomy and he wanted my hair swept back off my face. He said that as it was long the students would spend all day simply drawing my hair. My features such as my well-defined cheekbones looked more pronounced, although when I first started my career my cheeks were fuller. My skin tone was good. I have been told that my eyes were a crisp, penetrating blue/grey that would contrast sharply with the auburn red gloss in my hair, that my hip line was linear and graceful, and that my face is well balanced, symmetrical and of good proportion. I have since these early days and Mr Wiffen's advice, worn my hair up off my face and pinned into a sort of oval, the oval line reflecting my oval-shaped face. Much of my appearance has been discussed over the years, but it is continually rewarding to see how different artists have captured different aspects of my body.

The earliest painting of me was by a Polish artist named Witold Wotiski, who went over to America and became quite successful. Commissioned by my mother, it was painted in 1946 when I was just 16. The work is very much in the academic style. It reminds me of the techniques used in the painting by Albrecht Lipzinski (nicknamed Lippie) entitled The New Testament, 1915, which is held in the collection of The University of Liverpool. The colour palette is very similar, with expressive brush strokes. Lippie was known by reputation only as he returned to Poland after the Great War and died there in 1974. This academic style of English painting changed considerably between 1946 and 1956, colours becoming brighter.

My likeness was to be reproduced in line more times that I could have imagined at that early sitting. I had not before now really thought about the difference between the model sitting for commissioned work and posing for an artist to practise his craft. There is a distinct difference. When someone is sitting for a portrait, the aim of the artist is to capture personality, that something unique to a person, enabling the essence of his or her spirit to be momentarily caught on a canvas. When one is sitting as a model, however, the artist's task is infinitely more difficult. The artist does not necessarily know my personality, or have an opportunity to familiarise him or herself with my character traits or eccentricities. Thus, the seeking out of the formal elements of the structure of the body, the parts of the human skeleton that support weight, for example, or the parts that reflect light require a more objective approach. The most demanding task for the artist is to make the drawing have a life, not necessarily a character. This objective view, in my opinion, ensures a much more disciplined technical proficiency. This is the very basic demand of the life room. On the other hand, where I have had an opportunity to get to know the student artists and their tutors, there seems to be a blurring of the line between sitter and model. It is always the area around the eye that produces a likeness, especially if an artist is commissioned to portraiture. If the eyes are not right the whole painting becomes unstable and unsatisfactory. Even in some of the line drawings and sketches of me, I can feel a warmth of knowing between their creator and myself. People can identify my silhouette as: 'Oh, that's June!', but most of the artists for whom I have particular regard could capture part of my spirit, too.

Few other people can have had their physical appearance recorded in as many different styles. The 50 years of my modelling career have seen significant developments and changes in artistic style. All the artists who have worked my image into their work have recorded not only their own talent, but also my growth. More importantly, my changing image has mirrored the stylistic changes in art over almost half a century. I have endeavoured to include in my story that story too. That is, a short recollection of the experience of the model, the experiences of the artists in the making and, at the same time, the changing process of art itself. The early images of me from Anthony Butler, Jim Kitchen, Arthur Ballard, Stanley Reed and Ronald Scarland through the London years to the swinging sixties scene in Liverpool all show subtle changes.

I have often been asked what has helped to make me a successful and long-standing artist's model. Having a classical look has obviously helped, as has the ability to hold a pose. Equally important is to have the stamina to sustain the pose, not just for the hour or day, but every day for weeks at a time. It is difficult for me to judge, so I just record how pleased and encouraged I am by the thought that my image has been recorded and produced by so many talented artists throughout such a long period and in so many well-respected institutions, accumulating into a visual record of the skills and creativity of the artists who worked in Britain from 1946 to1996. The changes in artistic style, technique and interpretation during this time have arguably been the most wide-ranging in the history of art to date. I am pleased to have played my part in that. Such an experience of the magnitude of stylistic change may not recur for decades. Our current art appears to move at a slower pace; but then again maybe it will be possible to judge only with the benefit of hindsight

Nervously, but encouraged by the dashing young student Don, I began my first modelling session, as opposed to my first 'sitting', on the top floor of the Art School in 1947. The session was for two hours from 7.00 to 9.00pm in Room 78. As I remember, I managed quite well, I kept my pose and found the experience interesting and enjoyable. Undressing required a lot of courage but was certainly helped by the very professional atmosphere of the School. Contrary to popular belief, it was and is not a den of iniquity, even if there is a certain freedom from prudishness. I have to admit that for a teenage model there were always opportunities for sexual liaison. However, at the Art School business is business and any intimate attractions are strictly out of bounds until after hours. I was fortunate to have a number of admirers and could be as flirtatious as I wanted, but my very private relationships remained just that.

I wanted to succeed as a model. I also wanted to have a good reputation as the girl who could put art first and help to produce fine work by being disciplined when working. As well as seeing my likeness reproduced I knew that I was part of a greater whole. These young artists were learning a craft, I was a part of the tutoring of that craft and over the years have enjoyed the pleasure of their successes as well as my own. Perseverance and dedication were the attributes that I was to learn. They paid off. I could hold my pose, and I was encouraged by the staff to undertake further sittings and at their suggestion speak to the Art School about working permanently as a model.

At that time the School was modelled on the average provincial art teaching system with its students receiving tuition in anatomy (from Alfred Wiffen) under the headship of Will C Penn with strictly structured disciplines. Anatomy classes were always exercises in drawing. The teacher would often sketch the muscles, but the students would have to work in repetition. When the light failed and prevented painting, the students would concentrate on their life drawings. Using only line and shading meant that they could work as long as they wanted. However, there was a regular timetable and students were encouraged to be good all-rounders. Post-Impressionist expression was evident in the style of the paintings with loose brush strokes but with limited palette, reminiscent of the Camden Town Group. Liverpool's Sandon Studios was the first group to put on a Post Impressionist exhibition in the British provinces in 1911, which gives some indication of the region's outward-looking attitude. Attention to detail was drummed into the students and laborious practice, practice, practice was everything. Drawing everything, repeating pencil sketches, tackling different parts of the body individually and as a whole. Balancing proportion, bringing life into the human physique in the two-dimensional manner was not taken lightly and required devotion and hard work. When students made it into the Art College on a full-time basis their time was spent in anatomy lessons working from the skeleton. After a day in the life class drawing, students worked from the traditional plaster casts. Many artists have since told me that they learned far more as a student from those classes than from anyone with the latest set of trendy gimmicks.

It was at this time that I first met Arthur Ballard at the night class. I was working full-time in North John Street, combining my day job at the advertising agency and part-time modelling. Arthur was the son of a cabinet maker and boxing promoter. He was head of the Junior Art College in Gambier Terrace and later became head of foundation studies at the Regional College of Art. As an artist he was influenced by Jean Dubuffet. Arthur was responsible for the formation of the foundation studies, improving the way the study of art was organised. As more students were encouraged into training, the administration of the college needed to move with the times too. Don McKinlay was one of Arthur's students. It was Don who suggested that I had a trial run at posing on a Monday night in the end room, the life room, at the Regional College of Art under Arthur's tuition. I did the class and was a great success. Afterwards Arthur Ballard asked if I would like to join them in Ye Cracke, the local pub. I went along, but all evening Arthur tried to put me off modelling. He said I would be better off staying in advertising.

Later he tried to put me off going to London, and insisted that I should give it all up and not be lured by the promise of life there. I think he was really worried that I would come to some great harm, being vulnerable on my own, and so young. We were young for our years, too, not even allowed to vote until 21. The social standards in England were not yet challenged to the extent that they would be in the 1960s. The war years had left a contradictory legacy. On the one hand life was precious and to be lived to the full, with people voicing their intolerance of things that did not seem right. On the other hand the safe traditional values of the home and family were cherished and the immediate task at hand was to rebuild the nation on good foundations. Young people still held their elders in a great deal of respect. For a young 17-year old, this was real fatherly advice from Arthur, yet he was only about 36 and just out of the army. Arthur became a great personal friend who some years later coined the phrase: 'June is the Gertrude Stein of Liverpool'. He was a real gentleman: quite paternalistic to the women who worked for him, and always protective both of his staff and his students. I am convinced it was as a result of his excellent teaching that a good number of students went on to become successful artists in their own right.

As a painter, Arthur was not particularly prolific, although he kept a studio in Back Bedford Street near the Children's Hospital. I was fortunate to visit him there to see his paintings and to pose for him at the Art College. He would sometimes work long and intensely on paintings only to discard them later. He had, however, achieved a certain measure of national success, exhibiting in Cork Street at the Roland, Browse and Delbanco gallery. His friendship with the architect Quentin Hughes meant that his circle of friends extended to both artists and architects. Although Arthur stayed in

Merseyside and latterly moved to Wales, he did travel and went to Malta on one occasion with Quentin to give a lecture series. Our association was to continue for about 45 years. Neither he nor I thought further than the current art session and the immediate tasks at hand when we first met in 1947. It was exciting to see Arthur's retrospective exhibition at the Williamson Art Gallery in Birkenhead, in 1996, along with the launch of Peter Davies' book about him.

Another long association also began in these early years, my contact with Ron Scarland. I worked for Ron at his studio in Percy Street. He was a very good professional artist who taught amateurs to paint at evening classes as well as teaching the full-time art students at his evening class, working for Arthur Ballard. Professional artists would attend his classes, as he was a very proficient technician as well as an excellent and committed teacher.

Ron and I first met when he was just out of the army. He was then teaching at the Bluecoat School. I saw him at the Philharmonic pub where I said to him, 'I gather you need an artist's model?' 'Can you come on Sunday?' he asked. So, on Sunday I went around to his studio class where we had lunch and it turned out to be my first freelance posing job. After that I started to get hooked and went to the night classes at the Regional College of Art where Ron and Arthur were teachers of the night classes. I think Ron held two classes a week when he was art master at the Bluecoat School. Ron was appointed head of art at the Ethel Wormald School and had a studio built in Rodney Street to his own specification with a huge window. It was great to see out of and let good light in. I was posing at his studio for life classes. This studio is now part of Liverpool John Moores University housing the Central Administration Department at 2 Rodney Street. Ron also took night classes in the main Art College buildings in Hope Street. His Friday evening night class at the foundation studies department at the Polytechnic (before it became John Moores University) was very popular. I worked for him for about four years before I went to London and then again when I came back to foundation studies in the early 1960s.

Also in 1947, whilst working for Ron Scarland, I first met Richard (Dick) Young. He came onto the art scene as a student in Ron's evening class. Dick is an outstandingly good draughtsman and today could be regarded as Liverpool's best local artist. His wonderful retrospective show at the Williamson Art Gallery in 1995 included some superb drawings of me. He had began as a qualified electrician in the navy and carried on that trade after the war. He started his full time art education only in the 1970s, graduating with a first-class honours degree. Dick is a very nocturnal character and I often see him going out as I am coming home. He has been a good neighbour for many years. His sketching and line drawing style is unique, often filling the entire canvas with subtle shading and blending his figurative work into the backgrounds to capture the whole scene. This differs strongly from other portraits that set themselves against a background. With Dick, the background and the sitter become interchangeable and one enhances the other. This is especially noticeable in his self-portrait of 1975, in his small 1987 sketch of me as well as the larger drawing done in 1980.

Through my involvement at the college and with the small but select group of artists in Liverpool I met Roderick Bisson who worked as the national head of interior design for Lewis's Department Stores. A practising artist he also became art correspondent at the Liverpool Daily Post & Echo and used to attend private views in his slippers! Roderick Bisson was a member of the Sandon Studios Society and he invited me along to pose for the evening art society based at the Bluecoat Chambers. Bisson had an exciting retrospective at the Walker Art Gallery in 1987, but died unexpectedly before the show. His work is not yet in the public forum. A very private painter, he had a modernist style that brought an original flatness to his canvas with carefully crafted but simplistic form. He did, however, have complete mastery of the three-dimensional representational skill. I would like to see more of his work on view for all to enjoy.

Recalling another of the predominant artists of this particular period brings back memories of the smell of the oils that permeated everything. That studio smell of turps and paint, created a sultry and heavy atmosphere. As I think about the final compositions made from the life sketches, I have the image of a painting on display at the Royal Cambrian Academy art gallery, Conway, at my retrospective show in 1979. It was an early nude in oil entitled June and was painted by GA (Tony) Butler in 1949. He is a good academic painter. Tony was born in West Kirby and against the advice of his tutor, Martin Bell, decided to stay in the north. He decided not to apply for the Slade and has instead spent his career in teaching, firstly at the Laird and then at Birkenhead Grammar. The Slade was not geared towards job-seeking, unlike the Royal College of Art. It was small and very selective and prestigious. Pure painting and sculpture as well as drawing attracted students from all nationalities. The Royal College on the other hand, was practical, where designing for industry, textiles and graphics flourished and students found work as designers reasonably quickly.

In those days, students had to draw from the skeleton and plaster casts before they were even allowed to do any life drawing. I feel great affection for them and their talent. I like that oil painting that Butler did of me. It is a reclining nude but is foreshortened, as I am seen from the upper right-hand side of the image, as if the spectator is looking slightly down, rather than directly at me. There is an obvious distance between the artist and model and the essence of the pose expresses this distance. My character is not captured in this particular canvas, but the experience of my work is held as a snapshot of the moment. It is an objectification which reflects the whole sense of detachment between the artist and the model. The canvas is thoroughly worked and illustrates Butler's almost Impressionist handling of the paint. There is a strong sense of the materiality of the oil supported by a drawn framework to give a hidden skeleton of the formal outline of the reclining nude. Although there are substantial line drawings of me of the time, I find this little academic oil painting very satisfying to look at, the sort of work of which Tony Butler is master.

Stanley Reed was art master at Liverpool Institute for Boys in Mount Street at the time and he would attend the art classes at the Bluecoat Chambers Sandon Studios in School Lane on Friday nights. I sat for him both before I went to London and also on my return in the 1960s. His drawings reproduced in this book are again of very high quality, successful representations of me. Stanley Reed would sketch away, time and again, continually repeating his lines in order to capture the image. He wanted the lifelike character, the personal reflection of the sitter as well as the proficiency of technical ability. As I said before, we had the absolute regime of practice, practice, practice and there are certainly a number of images of me that have survived as testimony to his output. Of all the local painters, Reed's images are the strongest and most classically proficient. He has a gracefulness of line that exudes warmth and the roundness of his work is always very easy on the eye. His drawings of me continue to give me pleasure whenever I see them. They are held in the collections of the Williamson Art Gallery, Birkenhead and in the University of Liverpool.

Reed was part of the group at the Sandon Society in the Bluecoat Chambers. The fee for a Friday night art class was 10 shillings (50p) for two hours, seven o'clock until nine o'clock. The rain poured in through a leaking roof, summoning stoical persistence on the part of the members. Eventually the fee was put up to 15 shillings. As soon as our work was finished we would all hotfoot it to the bar for a relaxing drink, often with Edgar Grosvenor. Grosvenor was art master from the Liverpool Collegiate School and was an excellent cartoonist often lampooning in sketch the activities of the group. The bar at the Sandon was unique, not quite on the lines of a gentlemen's club, perhaps more an up-market local pub. The conversation was good and the mix of characters ensured that the place buzzed. Some years later, after the demise of the Sandon, Gerry Grindley was found dead in his studio. Gerry, who was famed for his discovery of an original Caro painting, had taken over the Sandon life room for his personal studio. He improved the room and encouraged an apprentice to work with him. It was his apprentice who discovered the body.

A sense of mystique about the Sandon persists amongst those who lived through those days. It is difficult for newcomers to appreciate the foibles and eccentricities of the crowd who stuck it out. I loved it; the collection of artists who congregated together was amazing. The supporters of the Sandon such as George Tyson Smith or Jack Coburn Witherop would come into the classes during breaks to talk with their friends, making it a lively place to work. Today, the rooms are used for craft fairs and arts events, and the visitor can only try to imagine the ghostly doings of the Club members whose presence permeates the very fabric of the building.

My regular work at the Sandon put me into contact with professional and amateur artists. I was paid in cash at the end of each session, which was a good thing as the Sandon Society always had periods when it was financially stretched. Coburn Witherop, who lived near my grandmother in Mount Street and was the picture restorer at the Walker Art Gallery, would volunteer to throw a party whenever funds dropped a bit. Not only did this lift the spirits, but it also boosted the cash flow as a fundraising bash. The Sandon sadly lost direction when it abandoned its artistic base. There was an influx of architects and musicians, with the artists marginalised from the core activity. Although it was very much a social activity, membership of the Sandon began to fall and it drifted towards exclusivity. This was its downfall, as the membership became a bit too high-faluting. The original core of artists carried on in contact with each other, but with growing competition with the Liverpool Academy, the Sandon did not quite hang on to its traditions. This cannot have been helped by the poor condition of the buildings. For a time in its history, the Bluecoat Chambers, housing the Sandon Studios, needed a considerable amount of money spent on it to maintain the fabric of the building. The studio rentals could not cover the cost of maintenance and the parties could not provide enough money as the artists spread themselves about a bit more in other directions, leaving the musicians and architects to take over the running of the Society. The Sandon was a good place for me in the post-war years, but by the time I returned from London it had all changed. In 1977 it faced bankruptcy and after closure was absorbed by the Bluecoat.

Roderick Bisson has catalogued its demise in his excellent history of the Sandon Studios Society. In the course of a chronological history of the society he gives some idea of the business connections of its members and, of course, the patronage of the artists who were members. Taffy Jones, a great friend of Bisson's, has added that Roderick Bisson, although very much part of the establishment background, was also a prolific and talented artist.

Some years later a painting of Bisson's was attributed to the French Post-Impressionist school as the work of artist Albert Gleizes. Bisson was passing the London gallery and saw his painting on sale. He had sold the picture in 1935 and some 30 years later there it was with his signature over-painted. He entered the gallery and pointed this out to the owner who seemed disinclined to believe him, modest as Bisson was. Nevertheless, some months later the painting was published in the Daily Telegraph with an accompanying article declaring that our Liverpool artist may be well be hiding his light under a bushel. He was now hailed as a significant modernist, ahead of his time and one to be watched. Unfortunately for the general public, much of Bisson's breathtaking work is in private collections. He shied away from publicity and did not court fame.

Although his work is of an intimately personal nature it contains a hint of political comment. For some strange reason he appears left wing, but I have no reasoned argument to support this theory. Bisson's work would fit neatly into the formalist camp of Herbert Read with regard to style and technique; the artist was also adept at detailed representation. The University of

Liverpool held a retrospective of his work in December 1997 giving an opportunity to the general public to see some of his smaller pieces on loan from private collections, along with the large scale pieces owned by the University.

The other local business-meets-arts club was the Artists' Club in Ebele Street, just off Dale Street, in the city centre. This centre was really a gentlemen's dining club where they would meet for luncheon and dinner in Edwardian surroundings of oak-panelled walls and tables laid with silver. The Artists' Club houses a large painting by Will C Penn of Joseph Green at the piano which takes pride of place in the members' dining room. There are also many examples of paintings of seascapes, landscapes, shipping and various domestic genres hanging about the walls. A tradition is to have the portrait of its president painted by a local artist, not necessarily a member of the club. In some cases, a member of the club who is a competent amateur painter paints the portrait. The Club is still open, membership in the 1990s being mostly made up of local businessmen. It has an excellent exhibition space and I was lucky to extend my contact with the club in the 1970s to enable Major Merseyside Artists to exhibit there today. Successful in business, many collectors realise that investment in our cultural heritage is both worthwhile and profitable

While the city of Liverpool was busy trading, for me a new world of activity opened up through the College. A tempting and attractive easy-going world of artists and sculptors, these were people who were thinkers as well as creators. They thought about what they wanted to achieve and could escape from the shackles of city life. The business world was courted for commissions but not bowed down to for support. I liked what I saw. After my introduction to working as an artist's model on a part-time basis at the College my interest grew. I was asked if I would consider taking on even more work. While I was working in the advertising studio of Lee & Nightingale, in North John Street, friends would call to see me at my coffee break at about four o'clock in the afternoon, before I finished and started the dash home ready to take on my life classes.

Peter Graham was one of these friends. I had met him when he was a medical student at the University of Liverpool along with his friend Frank Plumb. Frank was funny. As bald as a billiard ball after being bitten by a tsetse fly in South Africa, he was sensitive about it and wore very good wigs. He would always say that he could get anything he wanted at public school by exchanging one of his wigs for profit! I remember he used to wear an orange one. Hair technology not being what it is today, the colours were still in the developmental stage. Still, he at last gave in to his fate leaving himself with a smart bald pate, very fashionable nowadays.

Frank would regularly stay with Peter, who lived in Caldy, on the Wirral. Frank was not used to Peter's grand style of life and was one night found wandering around in Peter's father's bathroom, wearing borrowed pyjama bottoms. 'Heavens! Use your own bathroom old man!' said Mr Graham,

Senior. Frank, not realising that every room had its own facilities was extremely embarrassed and subsequently was banished to the outhouse to sleep.

Peter owned a smart red MG sports car and was a very talented photographer, producing the first glamorous photographs of me. He was well educated and worked in public relations as a speechwriter for George Kennerley, chairman of Littlewoods, amongst others. Peter married and had four children, Jonathan, now runs a boutique in the King's Road that has the rock singer Mick Jagger as a client. After Peter had returned to Liverpool we again struck up our friendship, meeting with George Jardine regularly in West Kirby. Our last visit was followed by a great shock. George, Peter and I were planning to go to Essex to visit Roy Cross when Peter called it off because of illness. Within a couple of days he had died, at only 58, from mumps of all things. We didn't believe it, as it was such a shock. I have been left with fond memories and a video made by Peter that will forever remind me of a gentleman and good friend.

My first photographic work was done with Peter. He said I was photogenic, but just as important I learned to differentiate between photographic modelling and posing in the life room. The end result is considerably different and it was far more important to have good looks for the camera than for the easel. I found photographic posing the fun side of my work, as the poses were held only for a short time. There was always time for a little conversation and relaxation, which would have been unheard of in the life classes. I found that posing for the camera was more like striking a pose, very Vogue-ish.

One day we went over to Hilbre Island, at West Kirby, Peter announcing that his father owned half of it. He was Dr Graham, managing director of Vernons Pools. We had tremendous picnics in the early days, dried bananas (it was just after the war), good patés and the best champagne. We would picnic with another friend, Ronald French. Ronald, also a photographer, persuaded me to pose au naturelle for them on the Hilbre rocks. These photographs were sold to the naturist magazine Health and Efficiency and I earned my first photographic fee as a result. Ronald also photographed me in my striped sweater, again very Vogue-like and glamorous. Life was good, even luxurious for such an austere time. There was a stark contrast between the haves and the have-nots in those days. Definitely part of the haves, Ronald had a cabin cruiser in the Conway bay and at weekends we would sail over to Puffin Island or Anglesey to the family house in Malfra Bay. Life was wonderful and every day brought a new experience or challenge.

There has always been a close link between the north Wales coastal towns and Merseyside. It goes back as far as the early nineteenth century when the Welsh builders travelled to Liverpool as stonemasons and later in the century came in their droves to build the terraces so familiar in the city. The shipping industry has ties with Anglesey, too. Going to Conway or Anglesey was very popular with those who were comfortably off and some of the family shipping companies had their dry docks on the north Wales coast, using Liverpool for access to wider markets. Certainly, the Royal Cambrian Academy in Conway reflected some of these traditions, many of our local artists showing successfully there for years.

Back in the busy city, the coffee houses – in particular the Kardomah next to my office – sent wafts of freshly ground roasted coffee beans into the street. The delicious aroma permeated the whole area. Passers-by could not resist being drawn into their cosy halls. Coopers across the way offered temptation beyond endurance as sanctuary against the cold river draughts. Even in the unbearable heat of summer they were welcoming, offering suggestions of lands beyond the sea to the timid traveller who ventured no further than the city streets.

Much of Liverpool's activity is part-time. Piecemeal activities or, rather, the keenness to engage short-term projects, is an integral part of the region's history. Where else would such enthusiasm be engaged for a young model to accept the post of sitter 'across the water'? This local expression is used for travelling between the Pier Head and Birkenhead, by ferry across the River Mersey, by train in the old tunnel or bus through the relatively new Mersey Tunnel, which opened in 1934. Every Wednesday, after working at the advertising agency in town until 5.00pm, I would dash home for a quick tea and then off on the ferry to Birkenhead. I then caught the bus to the Lady Lever Art Gallery to sit in the basement modelling class under the stewardship of Will C Penn who was in charge of the art class at the time. In the spring and summer months, my reputation grew.

The artists here were part-time students or hobbyists, many from the bourgeoisie such as bank managers or civil servants. For me the Lady Lever was an attractive contract, warmer than the School of Art. The students attended the classes regularly and worked very hard. The modelling class was decorated luxuriously with heavy drapes of the richest colour in the deepest reds and blues. These provided a sensational backdrop to the high-quality watercolour and oil representations they produced. I can quite understand that watercolour is regarded as the British tradition, by professional and Sunday afternoon amateur alike.

In the art schools just after the war, as everywhere else, there was a great sense of relief. The freedom to go where one pleased, when one pleased was overwhelming. With this new experience and an insight into the world of fine art, I felt destined for bigger things in modelling, and London beckoned.

My parents were not very keen. Their past was encapsulated in Liverpool, London seemed a long way off with goodness knows what evils waiting. Perhaps all students were like young Don McKinlay, adventurous and bohemian? What made it worse was the fact that I was also off to France for my first holiday abroad. Travelling, of course, was much more basic in those days. There were no package tours or coach trips. Life was still returning to the pace of the pre-war years. Nevertheless, I had saved enough money to provide a holiday. I had a wonderful time in France and I didn't have any money left to get me to London. There was a big panic at home as the rumour was that I had hitchhiked all the way.

I at least knew that I had a job to go to in London, if I could get there. I had managed to organise myself before I left for France, securing a contract with the Slade. I had written as soon as I had turned 21, sent in my photographs (taken by Peter Graham) and was thrilled to be accepted for a three-week contract starting on 26 September, 1951. I was forced to wait until I had turned 21 before I could go abroad or even to London. My parents had until then called my bluff. They said that if I was so determined that I could succeed in the world of art, I would have to prove it by making a living from it. Financially unsupported and with something to prove to my parents I gritted my teeth and stubbornly launched myself headlong up (not down) the path to success.

In the late 1940s when I first started as a professional artist's model, the art scene in Liverpool was nothing like it is today. There were hardly any art galleries, apart from one or two rather élite dealers. The Bluecoat was the only really stylish place with public access for viewing, along with the established Liverpool Academy and the Walker Art Gallery. There were few outstanding artists of the day. Most of those of note were members of staff at the College such as Will C Penn, Martin Bell, AP Tankard, and Alfred Wiffen, Stanley Reed and George Jardine.

Of the students of the newly arrived Arthur Ballard, a handful holds special interest to me. Josh Kirby, of science fiction illustration fame, was a student of Arthur's who had come from the Junior Art School (1943-5) in Gambier Terrace and has since achieved great success. He was classically trained when life drawing was compulsory and the training had basically remained unchanged since the days of the Renaissance. He left the School of Art in 1949 and now lives away from Liverpool and provides the world of illustration for Terry Pratchett's successful novels in the extensive series Discworld and The Colour of Magic. Josh has an interest in intense use of colour; his vivid and gigantic canvases were on display at the Williamson Art Gallery, Birkenhead in 1996. One particular favourite of mine is his Alfred Hitchcock painting. The portrait is expertly produced as a likeness, well crafted and tonally accurate. However, Josh's interest in the unusual and imaginative is also evident. The whole of the left-hand side of Hitchcock's face is drawn in with maggots and crawlies in pencil line. The detail is minuscule and precise. This unusual depiction of the suggestion of the eerie, of the unnerving thriller is typical of the artist. Josh can create a whole world within a world in his paintings. His science fiction pieces are very stylised and immediately recognisable as his.

Ted Atkinson was a friend and contemporary of Josh Kirby's. Born in Liverpool 8, he went to the Art School in 1944, was conscripted to National Service between 1947-9 and finally graduated in 1950. He was accepted by the Slade School of Art and spent four years in London. Ted achieved success quickly when he was appointed head of sculpture at Exeter in 1954, moving to Leeds in 1960 and then settled in Colchester in 1966.

From my point of view, working in the sculpture department was hard. Plaster dust covers everything. In the early days, students would tidy their workspace every day and leave the studio in good order. This standard gradually slipped over the years and the dust began to affect my breathing. Nevertheless, it is exciting to be able to see the work in progress. This was in complete contrast to posing for a painting, where the model never really sees the work in progress, only feels the gaze of the artist scouring every nook and cranny to translate the idea into the two-dimensional on the board. Three-dimensional sculpture offers a different challenge. Here the likeness is important; the character of the model needs to be captured to make the piece breathe. Seeing clone-like images of oneself is disconcerting at first and one becomes quite critical. Is that my leg? My hair isn't like that. I didn't think I looked like that, and so on. One never said these things to the artist though. Artists are always their own severest critics in the search for perfection.

The third member of this particular trio of friends was Roy Cross. I met Roy in 1948 when I was only 18 and he had just finished at Art College after gaining his degree. He had a studio in Hope Street, opposite the College. He was tall and dark. I was attracted to this very handsome young man and fell deeply in love with him from an early age. We went out together for quite a long time and I have some special memories. An early photograph of Roy next to one of his paintings, based on studies of me, was taken by Adolph Morath in 1949 and offers a glimpse of the significant style and expressive quality of Roy's painting. Although Roy and I were very close, it was too early to make a commitment as we were both relatively young. Instead we remained friends and went our separate ways, me to London and Roy to Essex and eventual marriage, until his untimely death after a dreadful illness in his fifties.

All three felt there was not much future for their particular talents in Liverpool and looked to fresh horizons. By this time I was 21, going to London, and Roy, Ted and Josh had moved down to Wivenhoe, in Essex, where Roy's relatives had a pub and gallery. Both Cross and Atkinson eventually settled in Wivenhoe which became the artistic enclave of Essex University in the Kingsley Amis territory of later years. Fortunately for them, property values soared and they could comfortably retire from teaching when the time was right. Ted Atkinson is still there living in the house he designed himself, concentrating on his sculpture. I was fortunate to receive a book featuring Ted's etchings and Josh regularly sends me a copy of his work as each new book is published. Recently I received the latest copy of his etchings that accompanied the exhibition at the Williamson Art Gallery. I get great pleasure from watching the progress of artists who have become personal friends. Part of this enjoyment lies in being able to follow the subtle changes in their work.

Another sculptor, Edward Carter Preston, was father of Julia Carter Preston, the wonderful local ceramic artist. Carter Preston was a noted medallist in Liverpool in the years of the Great War as well as a sculptor and painter. His most popular pieces, exquisite statues, can be seen in Liverpool's Anglican Cathedral. I do not have many memories of Edward Carter Preston, as he was a contemporary of my parents and grandparents, living nearby in Bedford Street. He was well established by the time I was born and working on commissions, many of which are now in private collections. However, his influence in the sculpture department was evident. Students could see plenty of his work locally, he was represented in the Walker Art Gallery collection and he had made his presence felt through the Sandon Studios Society as a founder member in 1905. I first saw examples of his work in the Walker Art Gallery collection.

When I was eighteen, the best photographer in Liverpool was Adolph Morath who took very dramatic portraits of the stars who were performing at the Empire Theatre and the Old Vic. Repertory Company at the Playhouse Theatre. He displayed his work outside his studio in Church Street and also took photographs of the general public, but they were expensive to buy. Everyone was very impressed with his photographs. They were, of course, in black-and-white in those days. One day I arrived home from the studio in North John Street to hear from my mother that I had had a caller who was wearing a cowboy's hat and who wanted to meet me. When I saw the card I realised it was Adolph Morath, so I went down to the studio the next day thinking that I would indeed like some photographs of myself taken by him. He was very pleased to see me but I soon realised that it was not me he wanted but my dog! – a large bull mastiff called Carlo who came up and down Bold Street with me and all over town.

I had an eye for business even then so I agreed that he could photograph Carlo if we could settle on a price. Adolph did not want to pay to photograph a dog, though, so instead he took some photographs of me and my boyfriend Roy Cross. I must say they are superb. I left Carlo at the studio for a while, and when I went to collect him, Morath was in a foul mood. 'Carlo bit me,' he said. 'Why, what were you doing?' 'Well, I wanted a photograph of the dog in a baby's high chair. Carlo bit me when I tried to lift him up.' Morath later published the photographs in a book with the title Man barks at dog. He took all the marvellous photographs with a German Leica camera but the age of colour was looming and although he knew it he always resisted as he never liked colour photography.

It was to be quite a few more years before I would be involved again in the Liverpool scene and part of the 1960s avant-garde with the arrival of Dick Young, Maurice Cockrill, Mike Knowles, Ray Fields, Adrian Henri, Sam Walsh and the new work of the younger generation. Before crossing their paths, I was to cut my teeth on life in London and the international art scene.

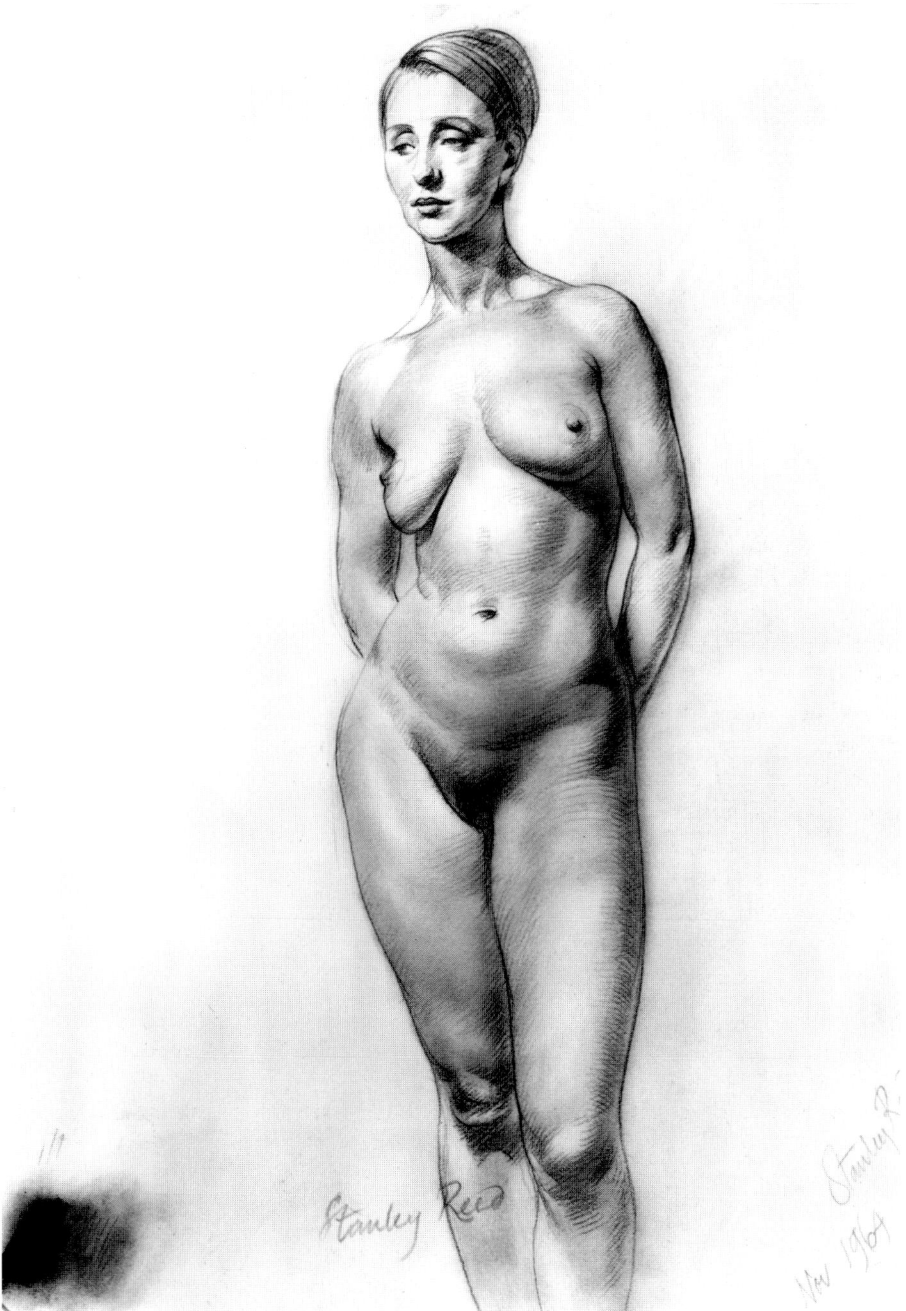

June Furlong Study, by Stanley Reed. By kind permission of Williamson Art Gallery, Birkenhead.

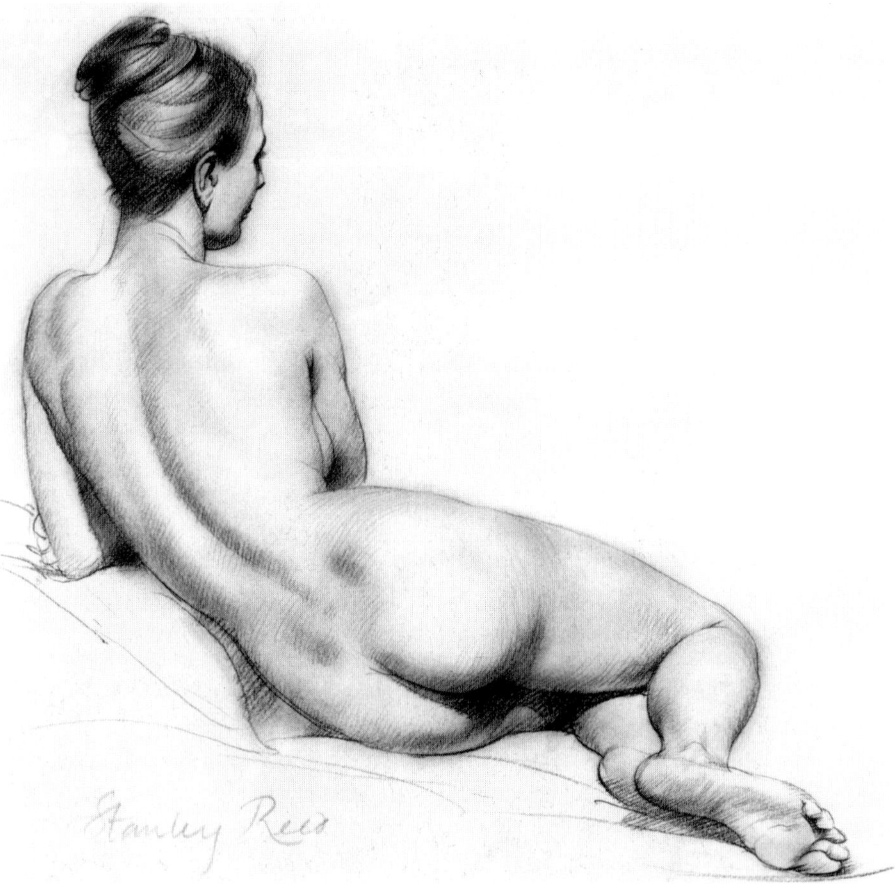

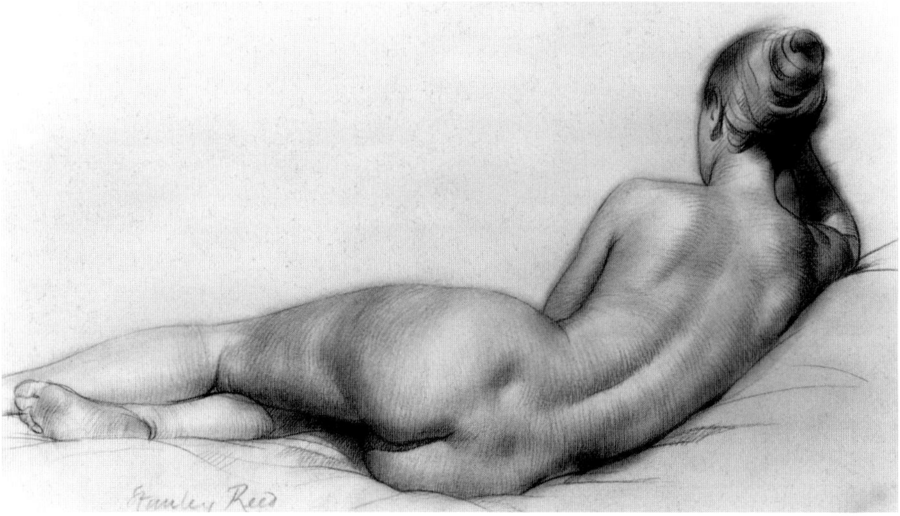

June Furlong Study, by Stanley Reed. University Collection.
June Furlong Study, by Stanley Reed. By kind permission of Williamson Art Gallery, Birkenhead.

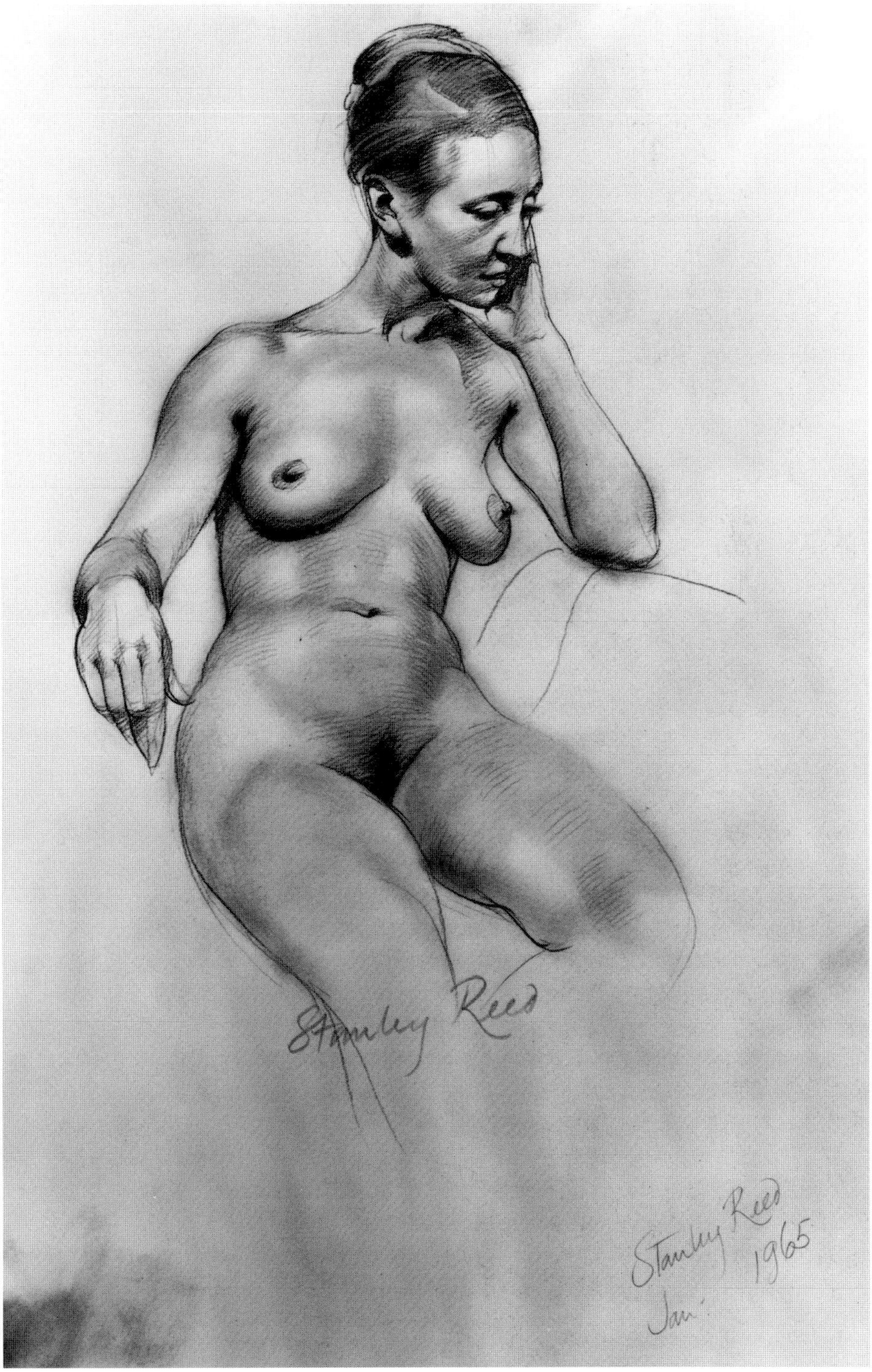

June Furlong Study, by Stanley Reed. By kind permission of University of Liverpool.

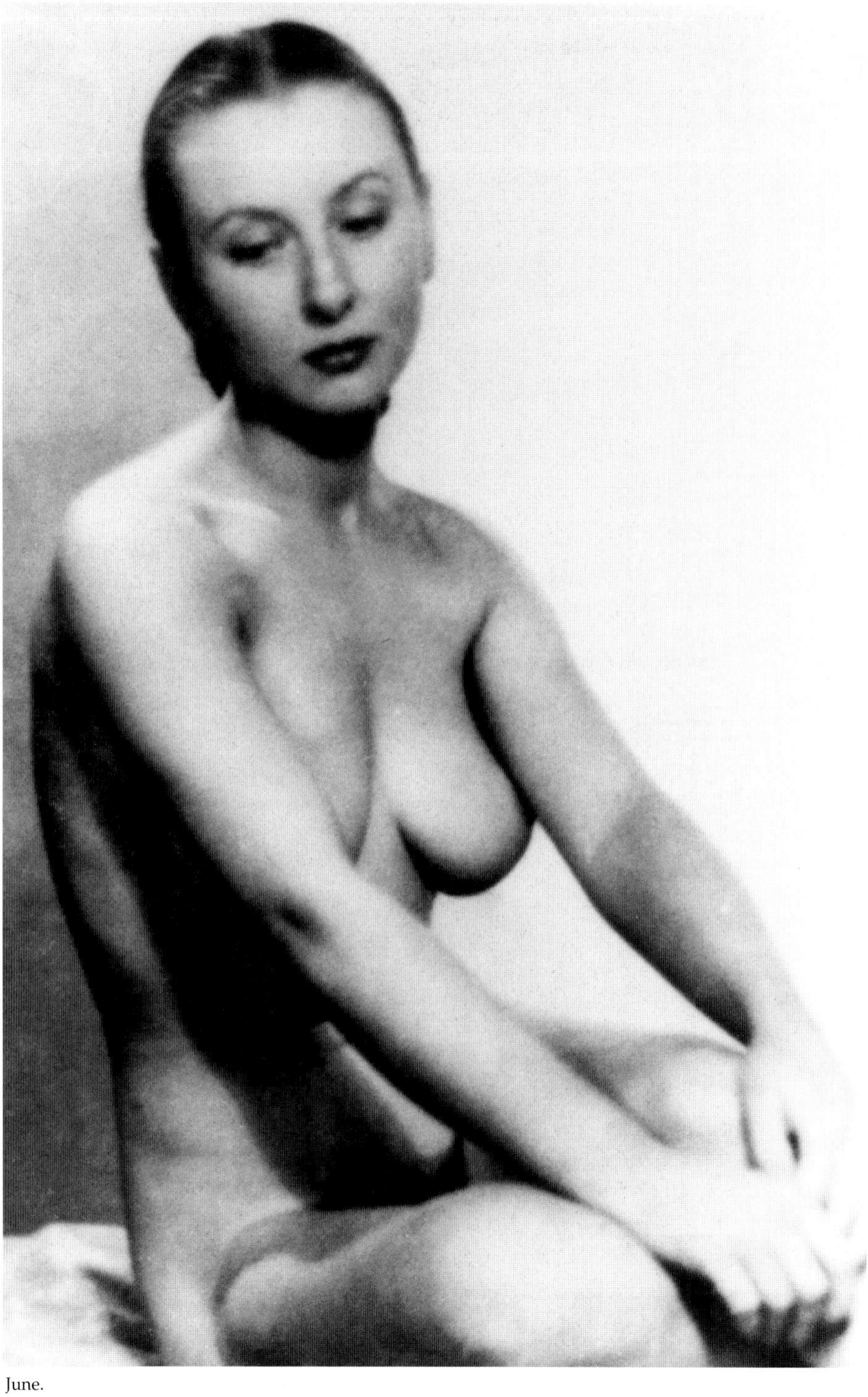
June.

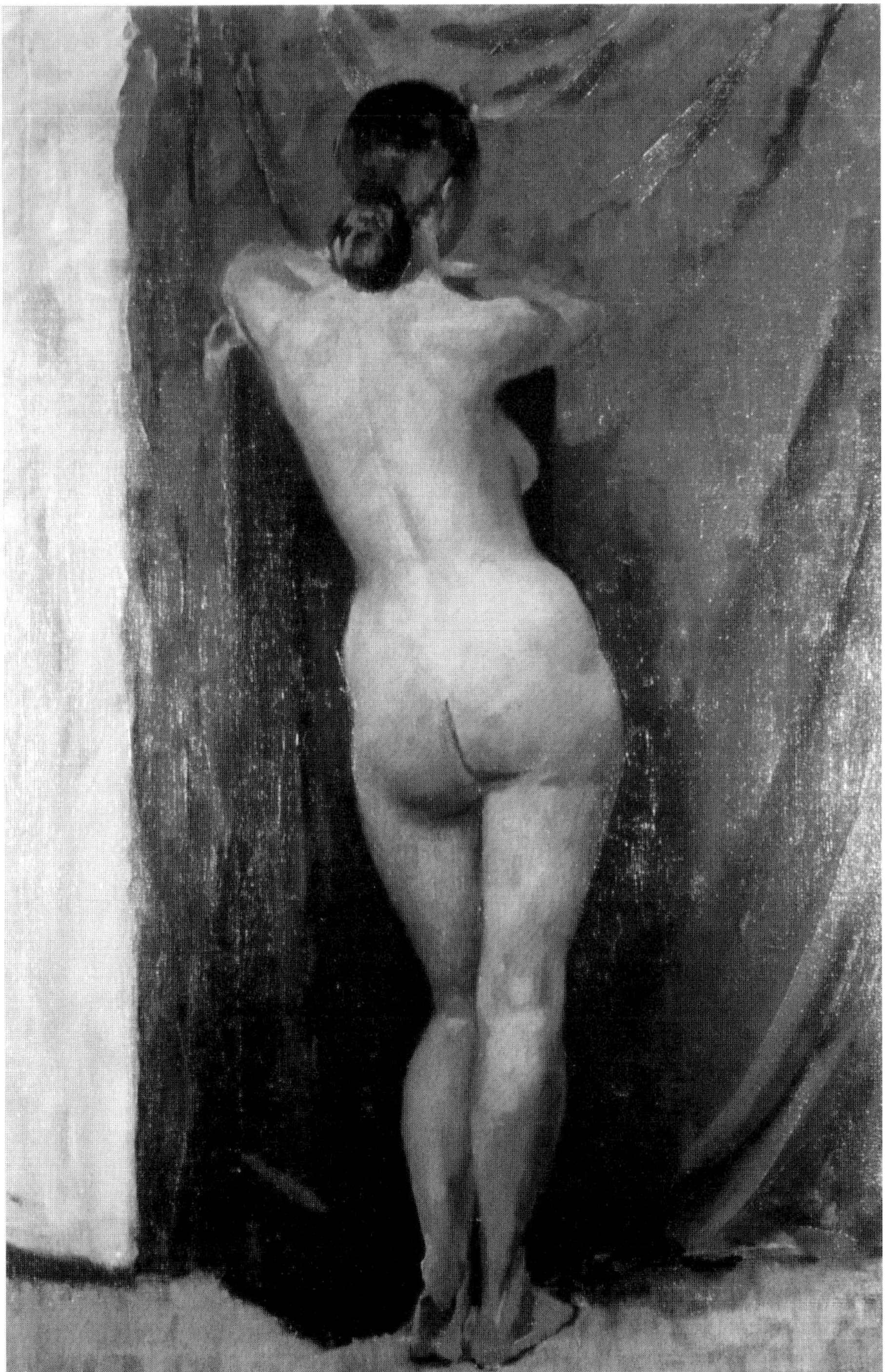

June Furlong, oil on canvas. James Lloyd Kitchen. Life Room, Liverpool Art College.

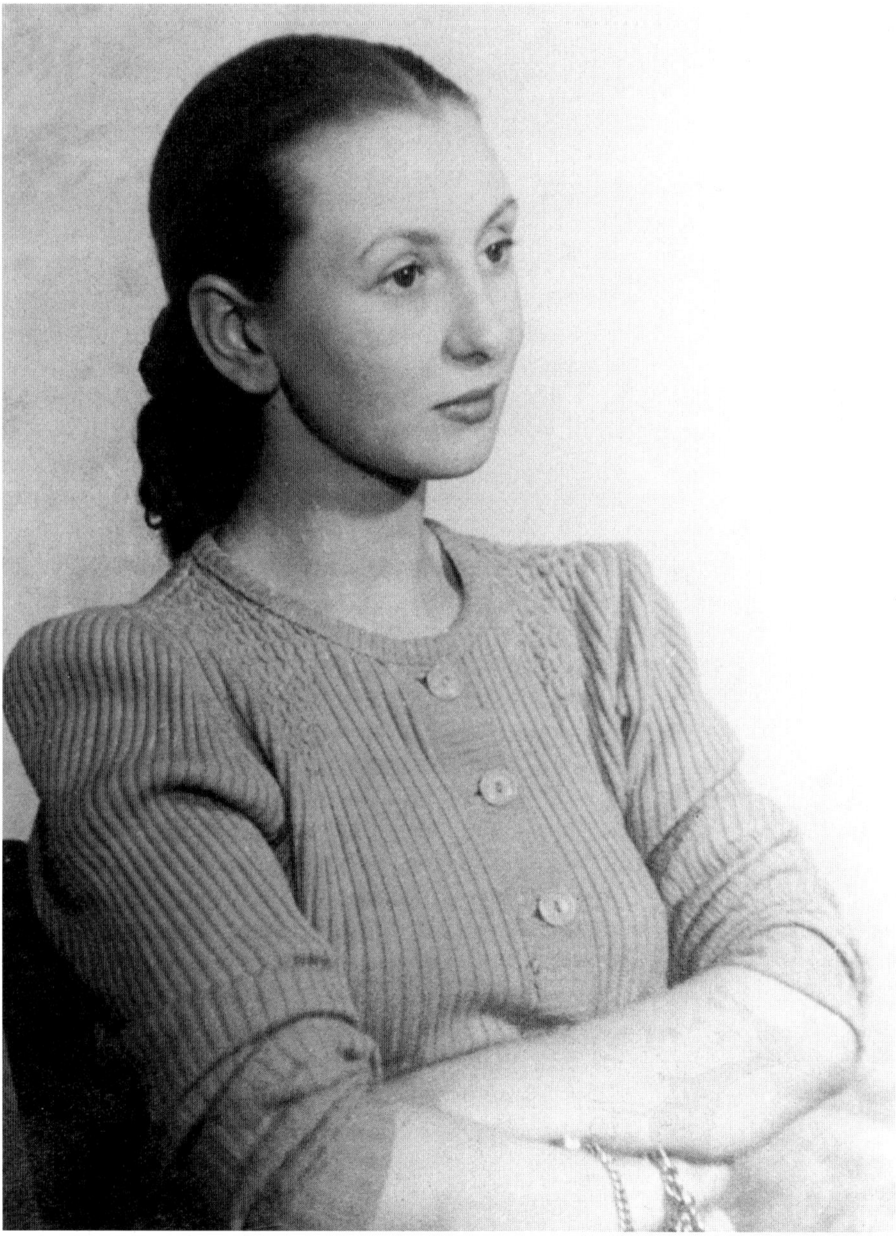
June.

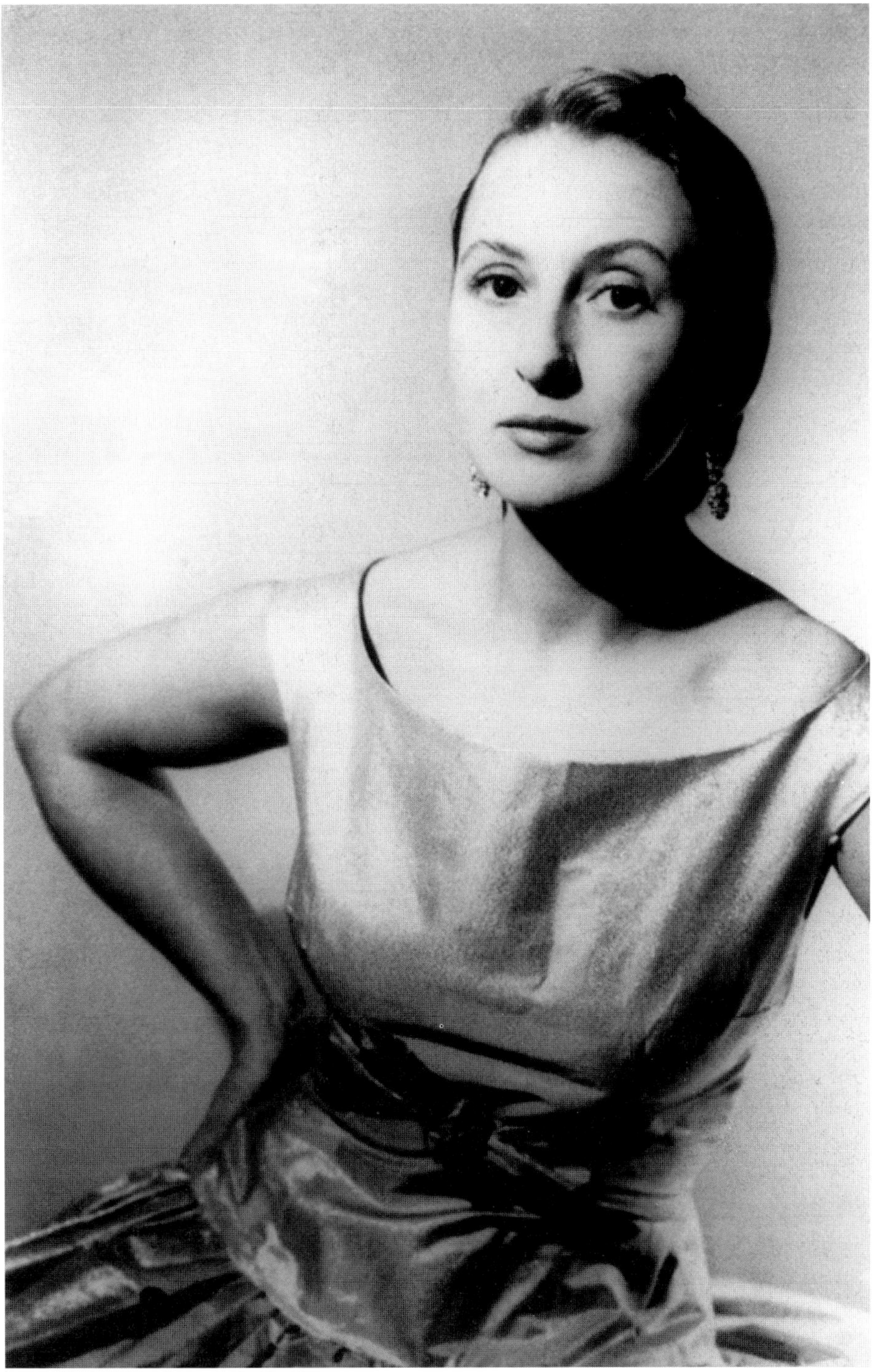

June.

Auerbach, Freud and Friends From the Fifties

My initial three-week contract at the Slade was the standard arrangement for an artist's model. Having started on 26 September, 1951, however, it continued until Christmas that year. There were no Christmas or summer retainers, so hard work during term time was essential. I managed to keep working at the Slade until March, 1952, by which time I had built up more contacts. It suited me fine. The Slade paid on Thursdays, and by Monday or Tuesday of the following week the money had gone, but I did not worry as I realised that I could work harder and I was so pleased to be in London. I was just about supporting myself and growing up in the art schools without any financial support from my parents.

Through the staff and students, I began to make enquires about additional work and discovered the rate of pay for models was a little higher at the Royal College of Art. I called in at the College and was interviewed by Colin Hayes. He is a very popular English Fauvist painter, now a Royal Academician, whose work appears in the Summer Exhibition. I did not, of course, know that at the time. He sent me into the office at first, saying that he wanted to see if I could do the job. From there I began to creep from the lowest rung as a penniless model to top of the ladder through sheer hard work. It helped, of course, to have lots of requests from artists for my sittings. The ability to pose was everything. Models were certainly not appointed on their looks alone. Their character was all important and their technical skill in projecting an image in space and in holding the pose.

The first character to stay in my mind from those days is Stanley Spencer, who I first saw when I went to Cookham in 1947 with Roy Cross, Josh Kirby and Ted Atkinson. We went to the wedding of Ken Woodward and Margaret Bickel who worked for Walt Disney's film studios. Stanley Spencer was outside doing some drawing. An inconspicuous figure, he sat at the end of the platform sketching what he called 'the Liverpool contingent' on our arrival at the railway station. I stayed for about one week after the wedding and thought Cookham to be a wonderful place.

It was some time before I saw Stanley Spencer again, when I was working in the men's life room at the Slade. He was an unusual man and his paintings reflected a neurotic religiosity. As I entered the Slade, often with Claude Rogers and William Coldstream, we walked on up the stairs and there was the Spencer mural, between the first floor and the life room. He had painted men on the one side and women on the other, defining the role of each. Spencer shuffled around in a huge ill-fitting coat and shoes, wearing those little intense silver wire glasses which have since become fashionable. Stanley Spencer was trouble in that he made people feel a certain unease.

Some time later I met his daughter Unity at the Slade. Unity's work is different from her father's.

However, in the early days, to go to Spencer's beloved Cookham was to enter completely into his world: all his marvellous pictures sprang to life. He must have packed a fantastic number of painting hours into each day. He was a very eccentric character – hair always full of hay – because, although he owned two houses, neither his wife nor his mistress would let him into either of them. Anthony Tooth's son, a friend of mine, said that the gallery owner who handled his exhibitions dealt only with the works of dead artists after finishing with Stanley Spencer as 'it was less trouble'. Although his character was so unpredictable, to me his art is timeless.

When I was posing around this time I called on all the old Royal Academy artists in Chelsea, asking them if they wanted any models. They would come to the studio door and say no, then change their minds, asking if I would like a cup of tea or something. I would then be there for hours which usually resulted in fixing up a couple more dates for a pose. I visited them regularly and always got a great welcome. There was an atmosphere of adventure and a feeling of being at the centre of the nation's creative heartland. The concentration of talent in a small area gave a buzz to the most mundane aspects of daily living. One thing I always remember with affection is that all the other professional models, well established in London when I arrived, accepted me immediately. 'Young June' they called me, all those great characters – all ages, all shapes, all nationalities, I liked them all.

I got to know the gallery owners, too, who also extended a warm welcome, full of joie de vivre. I felt as if I was one of their best customers. I realise now that I was lucky to be born with a sense of style and a good eye, which I always took for granted. I had never thought twice about it until recently, when it has added a new dimension to my present life: organising and promoting exhibitions in Liverpool. It helps me to keep a mental note of every work on view and its essential positioning for greatest effect. No one pays me anything for this. I have never received huge grants or salaries, but just cover my expenses.

When I first arrived in London and had my job at the Slade I lived in Earls Court, but did not think very much of the district or the accommodation. It would be all right to start with, but I did not envisage staying long. It was a boarding house with dinner included in the price of the board. Not one of the boarders thought much of the food, and I decided that instead I would organise it. A Persian gentleman called Jasper P Jasper occupied the best room in the place. After a chat with the other guests, it was decided that we would all move into his room to co-ordinate our eating.

The boarders were an interesting lot. I remember there was a Miss Crossley, who had come to London to find a rich husband. This admission was delivered in an Irish accent so broad one could hardly decipher what she was saying. Looking at her, it did cross my mind that she did not stand much of a chance of achieving her objectives!

Jasper seemed to have plenty of money and was fond of dancing, even to the point of sporting black patent leather shoes in the morning. His hair was slicked back and shone like his shoes. He thought he was so impressive with the ladies who partnered him. He could afford to frequent Casa Pepe's expensive Spanish restaurant, inviting a lot of other Persians. What with the food we all bought (which he preferred) and eating together in his room, life took a turn for the better until one day the landlady said to me: 'I am running this establishment, Miss Furlong, not you', which I translated as meaning that it was time I moved on.

Nevertheless, my domestic arrangements did not upset my working day. At the Slade I found all the models were real characters. There was an elegant male model, and a gypsy amongst others, as well as Iris Martin and myself. I found that tales of models being grabbed and harassed were untrue. The professional models were very serious, knowing that they wanted to be engaged on a regular basis. It is possible that the more casual models may well have had loose liaisons, but they could not be regarded as professional artist's models.

Our day was quite strict. During working hours there was quite a clinical atmosphere, which was also quite competitive. Art was not like mathematical problem solving where you either got it right or wrong. There were so many variations on a theme. Other considerations did not come into the life class as work always came first. It was here that I met Euan Uglow. I had made friends with Iris Martin and we became flatmates. Uglow was a student when Iris posed for him at the Slade. She would come home at night after working a standing pose with her feet badly swollen from trying to hold the pose far too long in a standing position. I had to get surgical spirit to rub on to help relieve the pain. She was not as used to the standing poses as I was, especially after my skating years. I went in to tell Euan that Iris was suffering and needed rest. He said that he had to get the painting finished. We had a brief chat, I saw from the canvas that his method of working was measuring tone in a mathematical way down through the form in typical Slade fashion. Knowing what the artist is working towards gives me an idea of what I would be required to do and how long it might take to complete. It was not even half completed, but when I was walking away Euan called me back and asked if I was interested in work outside Slade hours as he needed to complete the piece. Years later he won first prize at the John Moores Exhibition at the Walker Art Gallery, Liverpool, for a similar painting. It became a Slade technique of painting from life taken to its ultimate conclusion.

So, did I undertake private modelling work? he asked. I said that I would if the fee was suitable. 'No problem,' he said. He had a friend called Gary who had a beautiful studio in Barons Court and who wanted to run additional sessions. He asked if I would be interested in Sunday work for about three weeks taking the full-day sessions. We agreed on a good rate, refund of my fares and my Sunday lunch for posing. And guess who was in the front row but Euan Uglow! The arrangement lasted for about six months and Euan did some wonderful drawings of me.

Frank Auerbach says that Euan is one of England's best painters. I believe that Frank is right about this and only recently I saw a marvellous exhibition in Cork Street of Euan's work. His work is typical of the Euston Road School and Slade approach. Slade teaching emphasised the division of the golden section, a proportional system of painting but with an abstract approach. It focused on the Renaissance plumb-line and the relationship of people to the room using meticulous sizing up as part of the creative process. Renaissance painters, of course, allowed the measurements to remain in the pictures to show their skill and enable the spectator, or patron, to see how the piece was done. With this thoroughness paintings took a long time to finish. Coldstream, in particular, painted slowly, a portrait taking maybe dozens of sittings to complete. His work can include dingy, dark interiors: he brought to the Slade a view of drab London life inherited from Sickert and the Camden Town School. Rodrigo Moynihan and Graham Bell had a following for this style of work. The colours were black and ochre in the post-war years; it was as if no light colours were allowed near the canvas. Perhaps it was just post-war pessimism compounded by a shortage of new materials.

Euan was a contemporary of Paula Rego. I remember Paula joining the Slade as a student in 1952. She arrived as a part-time student and her drawings were not of the same standard as the full-time students. She would spend much of her time in the cinema instead of the life room. Paula developed her own unique imaginary style, which has since become inseparable from her work. The over-sized figures and the brutality of her art have made her work immediately recognisable. At the Slade she met and eventually married fellow student Victor Willing. Vic Willing was a much more intellectual artist, and I would suggest that their partnership helped Paula gain the artistic confidence she needed to succeed. His early loss was tragic, she loved him from the moment they met.

London must certainly have seemed an exciting place for Paula. She had spent some months at school in Kent, after arriving from Portugal. Perhaps the atmosphere of the Slade and the unusual characters who worked there were a liberating experience for her art.

As luck would have it, after having newly discovered exciting London and Soho myself (which was wonderful in those days, not full of strip clubs), I bumped into James Stirling who later became one of England's most notable architects. I had originally met him when he was a student of architecture at the School of Architecture at the University of Liverpool, a friend of Arthur Ballard. After the usual pleasantries, I told James that I had moved to London and was working as an artist's model at the Slade. He invited me to tea on the following Saturday. When I arrived in Hampstead I was absolutely delighted with the area. This was the place for me, I thought, forget Earls Court.

Jim was living in a flat with some other architects, all with good jobs, mostly as it happened graduates from Liverpool University School of Architecture. At the top of the road was the Magdala Pub, where Ruth Ellis, the last woman to be hanged in Britain, had murdered her lover David

Blakely. I was installed in Hampstead at the time of the murder and recall the episode and the publicity vividly. Ellis was executed on 13th July, 1955, in Holloway Prison, an event which caused a public outcry to get hanging abolished. More of this, later.

After meeting James Stirling I started to look around for somewhere permanent to live. The rents were high in Hampstead and Belsize Park and all I had was my salary from the Slade which was not particularly substantial. I had, as mentioned, formed a friendship with another model called Iris Martin from Falmouth in Cornwall. I asked her where she lived in London. 'Balham,' she said, and she invited me to visit her as she was staying with her aunt and uncle. Well, Balham was not for me so I talked Iris into a tour of Hampstead, and naturally she liked it very much. I suggested that we share a flat and the rent, to which she was agreeable. Eventually we found just what we were looking for, a marvellous attic near Hampstead Station in Haverstock Hill. Three houses were owned by the same Polish family and were set back from the road, and only five minutes from the High Street.

Whilst in Hampstead, I became friendly with Pat Gardener who lived in Fitzjohns Avenue. She was not in the art world but was simply looking at the outdoor art exhibition that was held regularly on Hampstead Heath. She was a beautiful girl who later married the boss of Decca Records, Dick Rowe. Dick turned down the Beatles for a recording contract, but on George Harrison's recommendation, picked up the Rolling Stones – would you believe it! I was a witness at Pat and Dick's wedding and often stayed with them for long periods in their flat in St John's Wood. But Hampstead drew me back, it fascinated me. Iris and I had become quite settled in Hampstead and were now great friends.

Not long after this Lucien Freud came to visit us regularly. It was quite amusing the way we struck up our friendship. Both Iris and I were working at the Slade, where Iris became besotted with this handsome, dark-haired man. Lucien came to the Slade to teach one day a week, on a Friday. I did not know who he was at that time.

In the Slade they had a really big men's life room for the male students to draw. It had three models in it. Professor Coldstream had a balcony above the room and when he came out of his studio he could stand at the edge of the balcony and peer over the top to survey the industrious activity below. It was indeed industrious, everyone worked consistently in a good atmosphere. I remember the students at the time included the Cohen brothers (Harold and Bernard, who later taught at the Slade). There was Craigie Aitchison, an awful student but an artist who would mature into success, and Alfa, an Ethiopian prince. Coldstream was very interested in Alfa. I worked for him doing private work. His guardian, always at his side, was called Bobo. Bobo would read poetry to us while Alfa made his drawings and worked on his painting. Professor Coldstream would get Alfa to organise the parties and cabarets in the men's life room. At Christmas time they would have a huge table with all the party food cooked by the students in the Slade's student halls of residence in Bentham Hall on Gower Street. The wine flowed like water. Iris and I turned up and loved every minute. In summers we went on the boat trip outing on the Serpentine and had strawberry teas at the other end.

Well, Iris had set her cap at Lucien Freud but she was not making much progress at all. She had not even said hello to him. She would go weak at the knees when he came to teach at the Slade. I thought this would go on forever and decided that action was needed to get things moving. Lucien never walked into the life room, he would walk around the outside edge and then deposit himself on a chaise longue. On other occasions he would sit half way up the stairs where everyone had to pass on their way to the canteen. Later, he told me that the Friday teaching session was the only opportunity he had to have a rest as he was busy painting the rest of the time.

Lucien never seemed to be a natural painter. That is, although expert at his craft, he had to continually work at the canvas from his original brilliant drawings. His skill in paint gradually developed, as can be seen from a comparison of his early portraiture with his later work. There is so much more character and depth to his late work. He was probably undergoing this change in stylistic interpretation in the early 1950s as there is a noticeable increase in the amount of paint on the canvas as his subjects become less hard edged. This would certainly marry with the popular trends in the art schools of the time. In those days, my interest in art was growing alongside my interest in life.

I remember Iris and I made an enormous Valentine card for Lucien as a combined effort. It was about two feet high. One of the students composed a verse and when Valentine's Day came we left it upstairs next to the signing-in book. The models, students and staff had to sign in in those days. The staff had their own porters and beadles to look after them; it was all rather refined. As it happened, Valentine's Day was a Friday so he collected the card himself. The next moment he was glaring at everyone in the studios wondering who had sent him the card. Iris was terrified, she thought if we were discovered she would get the sack. When our tea break arrived at about a quarter to four we all went over to the canteen. I dashed upstairs and asked Lucien if he had got his Valentine card to which he replied: 'My dear girl, it is the biggest envelope that I have ever received in my life!' He thought that I had sent it to him. I thought I had better get Iris into the picture quickly. She was pushed forward as we all went for a cup of tea. After we had been talking for a while, I realised that it was Lucien and me who were talking. Iris was still shaking, so I managed to turn the conversation around to get Iris to ask him over to dinner. Lucien accepted and over the next few months we struck up a good friendship. He confided in me that he was constantly aware of opportunists who would want to talk to him for some sort of social gain. He said he liked me simply because I was vague about who he was.

We had a great time as a group of Bohemians in the big city. Lucien, Iris and I went to the West End quite often. I remember he used to look very dashing in his green Blackwatch tartan trousers with a green jacket. His piercing green eyes were emphasised by the dark tones of his outfit. He had dark sideburns that framed the exquisite features of the extremely handsome and elegant man he still is to this day. Iris remained besotted.

Lucien came to dinner, but we realised our flat was nothing like the surroundings that he would be suited to. On one occasion he had a heated argument with the gentleman who answered our door for us. Lucien would want to come in but if the door were not opened immediately he would stamp his foot and shout 'Imbecile!' at the poor chap. Although our flat would pale into insignificance compared with his abode, we thought 'so what!'

It is thanks to Lucien that I got to know London so very well. I think he was probably married to Epstein's daughter at the time. He used to take us everywhere and live a grand old style of life. He would change his money into ten-shilling notes and stuff every pocket with them. He said he had a Bentley motor car but always used the Underground so that he could look at the adverts as he travelled around! We were wined and dined in the very best of places. Iris was to be disappointed, though, as their friendship dwindled away.

When I was working at the Slade, Lucien came over one day and asked, 'Are you going home to Liverpool for the Christmas holidays?' 'Yes,' I said. 'Oh well, will you do me a favour and go into the Walker Art Gallery and see where they have hung my painting, Interior near Paddington? This is the image of Harry Diamond in a raincoat standing by a large plant. 'See if it is in a good light and see what is hanging next to it would you?' he said. I replied that I would do just that. Again, he reminded me before I left to make sure that I would not forget.

I duly visited the Walker, looked all over the place for this painting but saw nothing. Up came Hugh Scrutton, the director of the Gallery in those days, and greeted me. After the usual pleasantries, I asked: 'Where have you hung Lucien Freud's painting?' He looked straight at me, 'What did you say?' So I repeated it. 'Well, what an extraordinary thing,' he said. 'We have been waiting for this picture to arrive for weeks, the transaction has gone through with the payment, but we have not yet received the painting'.

As soon as I got back to the Slade, Lucien said: 'Did you go into the Walker Art Gallery?' 'Yes,' I replied. 'What did they say?' I told him exactly what Scrutton had said, that they had not received the painting. To my amazement, Lucien said: 'Do they really want my painting, are you sure?' 'Yes, definitely!' I confirmed. 'OK,' he said, 'I will get my agent to send it to them tomorrow, I thought they had some spare cash and thought that they might as well spend it'!

Lucien was not nearly as confident as he appeared in those days. Externally he appeared self-assured, and was in so far as his social standing was concerned, but he was modest about his art. At that time Lucien put fewer hours into it. He would keep a pad in his top pocket and make pencil sketches of the people he was with, but he kept it private and would rarely show the sketches. Lucien looked deep within a character and produced contemporary images of a fresh nature in the 1950s. As his personal style matured and his tonal palette broadened, his portraits offered a glimpse of the whole person. This differed from other artists who could capture a pose and public persona. Lucien's pieces cut back the very public images of the well-known to reveal their more human side, not always flatteringly, but certainly more likely to suggest characters who were affected by the everyday, by the real living of a life.

A salutary lesson was learned from Lucien. He once said to me: 'There is no permanent value on anything or anybody.' This was a sobering thought, keeping things in perspective for the twists and turns of fate. I have found it an observation that made more sense as one journeyed through life.

His eccentricities were common knowledge. 'Well, that's Mr Freud' was a turn of phrase bandied about regularly. 'You are a strange exotic creature with a deep penetrating mind,' he would say to me. 'Blimey, not half as strange and as exotic as you!' I would think.

I consider myself fortunate to have known him in his early career. Over the years his comments have proved absolutely right. I often thought 'Yes, Lucien said that.'

He was a great friend as well as a great artist. He worried about his surname, as he had a lot to live up to. I used to say to him: 'If you were called Joe Smith and lived in an ordinary house and could paint like that everyone would still appreciate it'. We would often laugh about this. I was reminded of this recently, with the announcement that Lucien may paint a portrait of Her Majesty the Queen, which many would consider the final accolade. Freud was well respected by the students. Although he never refused to look at the work of any of them, they would have to pin him down and ask him directly for a critique. He seemed ill-at-ease and looked as though he was being forced into saying something.

As things continued my friend Iris and I found our way around London and got to know some of the other good places to live and work. Our next stop was 4 Belsize Park. This flat was a wonderful place with a black marble sunken bath, very art deco. The only problem was that you could not get people out of the bathroom!

When we were still living in the flat in Haverstock Hill, one Saturday morning I was having a sleep in, about 10am, when a black hand came around the door. After being woken with a start, I sat bolt upright. 'Iris Martin is it?' 'No,' I replied. A man was in my room. He stood quite still for a moment looking at me, and I felt quite uneasy. He was Indian and looked rather majestic, like a mystic of some sort. Eventually he told me that he had come to ask her to model for him as he was a student at the Central School of Art, Holborn. 'You would be fine,' he said.

What happened next escapes me, but we arranged that I should go to his studio, not far away, for private work. He was paying at three times the rate of art college fees. This man proved to be a genuine artist and later became a good friend. At the time I was keen to earn extra money, as I have said. He had me wearing a sort of silk sheet draped like a sari, and a flower behind my ear. 'A very odd painting,' I thought at the time. Then it dawned on me, Indians do not think three dimensionally in art, and the cultural heritage to which he belonged used flat pattern to a much greater degree than we did in England. After this, he was so delighted with the painting, he was always calling to see me.

He kept the most peculiar hours I have ever known. Once he called at 4 am. 'You will please get up, wash your face, comb your hair, I have a gift for you.' He presented me with a beautiful necklace of white beads. As it was summer I took to wearing it frequently. We would go to the most expensive restaurants. He would consult a magnificent huge menu and then announce: 'Egg and chips, is it?' This happened three times, and I was beginning to think I was being taken for a ride. I told my friends, who said that as he was either Muslim or Hindu he would not necessarily be able to eat the same things as me since he didn't eat meat. This made sense, plus the fact that he always had a cow in the centre of his pictures. 'What is it with all these cows?' I would ask.

He would smile, and only later did I realise it was a sacred animal in India.

It is strange to imagine nowadays the naïvety of the English at that time. We have a better understanding of other cultures nowadays. He was Shiva Mukerjee, a name that apparently translates to Smith. Mr Percy Brown, principal of the Central School of Art, used to say: 'What can we do for you Mr Mukerjee?', realising that he had a very mystic mature student on his hands. Iris was not impressed, but I was fascinated by all of this, as I could learn so much. I felt like the artist's muse.

I now began to make a lot of money by sheer hard work. I never stopped working, all the big names in the Chelsea art set employed me at their wonderful studios.

That superb artist John Ward, now private tutor to Prince Charles, drew me in his studio in Glebe Place, where I was to model shoes for Vogue magazine, for which he then illustrated. He would work in line and wash drawings. If I had to choose an artist to paint my portrait, it would probably be John Ward. He recently resigned from the Royal Academy in response to the 1997 Sensation exhibition. John is an upholder of academic standards, of which he is a true master. He taught at Wimbledon and enthusiasts for his work could see his portraits in the Academy Summer Exhibition. Picking up the tricks of the trade in commercial work was extremely advantageous, and certainly paid off with his marvellous illustrations.

While I worked for John amongst others, I worked all the time – at weekends, and evenings. Iris only worked at the Slade. Iris decided she preferred Cornwall, and returned to settle there. I have since learned that she has been successful in St Ives.

So I was on my own again, but was earning enough money to manage. I stayed on until the owners decided to sell the house. My next place was 15

Gayton Crescent, Hampstead. Not very far away and on the corner of Willow Road lived an artist called Don Fisher. He now works as a television set designer and is doing very well. Don and his French wife, Lillian, became great friends and every weekend I worked at their beautiful studio/house, then modelled the art class where Don was a teacher. I left Gayton Crescent from time to time and for a while I went to live in Swiss Cottage with Dick and Pat Rowe who I knew from Hampstead. I remember there was always a lovely atmosphere of friendship in London at the time. Everyone was very cosmopolitan and sociable, it suited me and my lifestyle extremely well. I loved Hampstead Heath, especially from spring to autumn. It was such a special and unique village atmosphere yet so close to the hub of the city.

I first met Frank Auerbach when I lived at Gayton Crescent and was working at the Royal College. He drew me in the life class, as did Leon Kossoff. David Bomberg trained both Kossof and Auerbach. Bomberg was somewhat like Van Gogh, for he had little commercial success during his lifetime, unlike Auerbach and Kossoff who are both successful. Perhaps this is a symptom of changing times. It is possible to be successful at an earlier age today, thanks to the growth in the media interest in the visual arts in general. Kossoff was quite easy-going, although his wife was a little aloof. He was a complete opposite to Auerbach, who was more highly strung, very intense.

One night in 1954 I was in the Studio Club in Swallow Street, off Piccadilly, and Frank was there. Later I said goodbye to my friends and took the train back to Hampstead. Frank got on the same train, introduced himself and started talking. When Mornington Crescent loomed he said to me: 'If you don't get off at this stop, I'll never see you again.' 'Well, your loss would be greater than mine,' I thought. Instead, I said he could come for a cup of coffee at my place. 'Where do you live in Hampstead?' he asked. When I told him he just said 'Oh yes, I can do that.' So we left the train together. He obviously liked my place and became a frequent visitor and invited me to his studio in Mornington Crescent.

When I got there I thought it was a dump. Nowadays, it is a very smart place to live and not a bit like the garret it appeared then. His studio squelched in paint, it was all over the floor. Whatever you touched, taps, chairs, cups – everything, paint oozed out of it all. It must have been inspirational, at least. The studio had one great advantage: it had northern light. It felt like a real studio, good light and the smell of oils. Even though the space was limited it enabled him to produce his large masterpieces in rich earth colours. I wonder these days how he ever got far enough back to look objectively at his work. I am amazed how superb it looks when hung in international galleries, given that Frank had such a small space in which to work. His work needs a good setting in our major art galleries, and although there have been good reproductions in books, they cannot illustrate his paintings to perfection. The spectator needs to experience his work, be there to see it in three dimensions, not just have an idea of it. I remember sensing that he would be a big star in the art world one day.

Frank said he had been offered a place at the Slade, but had opted for the Royal College of Art. Only later did he go back to the Slade to teach, where he became the godfather of the students and budding artists. This is something he never felt particularly flattered by. He always said that any influence and similarities in the work of others should merely be a jumping off point from which to strive for even greater artistic ambitions. The last time I saw him he was thankful to be out of teaching, as it exhausted him. He would put himself into his art to a full one hundred per cent. Teaching was a distraction that meant that he could not sustain his desperate commitment to his own work, which always had to come first.

Frank was never easy company, a bit like the fabled difficult or tortured artist. When we were together we quarrelled endlessly. I can smile about it now. I was young and interested in putting myself where the money was. London was an expensive place to live and I worked every hour God sent to ensure I would stay away from the less desirable places and people. It was important to me to live in Hampstead, to enjoy the company of good people and to have a certain quality of life in keeping with my upbringing.

Frank never had any money. I always kept an eye on him and we were good friends. He used to say that I was his most severe critic. I would never hesitate to offer my opinion. He said that I was also very good to him when he had nothing, not even food to eat. He was always short of money because he used so much paint. Everything went on his art, in buying paint, mixing and blending it, only to dismiss it and start again with more paint. I used to say things like: 'Well, how thick is it going to be?' 'Well, I don't know. I have got to get this picture working,' he would remark. About sixteen hours later he would stagger out of his studio to cross London and join the human race again, visiting friends.

I knew a lot of artists in Hampstead, but they would never reach the international heights of fame that Frank did with his work, even though they were nice people, kind and friendly to me. They were very sociable. Frank would look at their work and say: 'What else do these people do?' He meant of course that they must have had day jobs, as they were not destined to make a living from their art. Frank could not quite take in that people would settle for something in their art that he would consider inadequate or trivial, while he strove towards perfection. He rarely admitted that a picture was complete, often discussing it with Leon Kossoff in the process.

At the Royal College of Art, the staff would say: 'June, please remind your friend Mr Auerbach that the term started two weeks ago!' To which Frank would absolutely explode in fury saying: 'What the hell do they think I am doing? Going on a slow boat to China, or something!' Meanwhile, he was dedicated to the canvas on which he was engaged, working away in the studio regardless of time or dates. His commitment has certainly paid off. He would not be the major British painter he is today if he had compromised his endeavours. The sensual and emotionally expressive quality of his work is truly outstanding.

His main model was called Stella. He used to cross London to paint her. She was his landlady at one point, as well as a lifelong model. I didn't really like posing for him as I needed to be where the money was. I wanted to mix in high society, and feel at the forefront of the action. Nevertheless, Frank and I continued our friendship over many years. Once I received an invitation to London, with his sending the fare to make sure that I went. We visited beautiful restaurants as his success increased, and he began to receive acclaim for his work.

Settling into his work and eventual family life has been good for Frank, even though he is now a bit reclusive, avoiding a demanding public. Frank and I were very close for quite some time. On our last meeting, twenty years ago, I was hoping that he would paint a portrait of me in the manner of his paintings of his cousin, Gerda Bowan. They were superb paintings. However, the pressure of the sitting and the short time available to us both proved a disaster. We parted company after an exchange of strong words and the painting was abandoned. On the train back to Liverpool I thought over the work and decided to let it be. Frank was now in a different world and our paths would be unlikely to cross again for some time to come.

He had a lot of professional Jewish relatives living in Belsize Park. While Earls Court was full of Persians, Hampstead and Belsize Park had Jewish German and Polish residents, culturally influencing the area. Frank never saw much of his relatives when he was a young man as he said that they thought he was some sort of dilettante messing about in art. Now he has made his name and earned international recognition they would doubtless be falling over themselves to entertain him!

Frank was struggling and unknown in those days. Years ago he was trying to get into the Young Contemporaries Exhibition at the Beaux Arts Gallery run by Mrs Lessore. He used to go over to this particular gallery all the time when he was a student at the Royal College. He barely had the fare and it was his dogged perseverance that eventually persuaded her to take him on. My last words to Frank were that 'it must be wonderful for you, now you are a famous artist.' 'Famous artist!' he said, laughing. 'It is harder now for me to do anything that I think is any good with the spotlight on me. I was painting better as a young man when no one wanted to know.'

There is no doubt that his work is marvellous and his portraits are especially exquisite. He learned to paint in earth colours, making them work for him, as he could not afford expensive pigments.

It was through Frank Auerbach that I was invited to pose for Augustus John, around 1954. Frank knew his grand-daughter, Anna John, who knew that John was looking for a model. Frank recommended me, gave me the address in Fordingbridge in Hampshire and said that I was to send photographs of myself and let John know when I would be available. Augustus John kindly replied, returning my photographs as they were of very good quality, saying that he would contact me when next in London and would be happy to draw me anywhere I suggested.

My time in Hampstead was the best ever for a young woman. When I lived in Albert Terrace, the Rowes visited me and through them I became friendly with film star John Gregson. At the time, 1954, I was the Beauty Queen in Hampstead. After working at the Royal College of Art I went to visit my friends Lillian and Donald Fisher at their studio in Willow Road. Lillian, as I have said, is French and was obviously keen on all the French films. I was not very keen myself, but enjoyed watching Brigitte Bardot. Unlike many young girls, I did not change my image to that of Bardot, I looked the same as I always did, only older. I used to be at their studio nearly every Sunday, and I would pose for them all day.

Those weekends in Hampstead were heavenly. The day of the pageant was a lively affair. I was dressed as elegantly as possible and on the Saturday afternoon I arrived at about three o'clock with the Pearly King and Queen and we drove back to Hampstead Village. It was a celebrity party day with their friends from the Temperance Seven group (who later recorded their successful hit Home in Pasadena) along with all the students congregating in the pubs.

The area had its criminal side. Gladys Yule lived in the same road as The Magdala pub near to James Stirling and also near the spot where Ruth Ellis shot Derek Blakely. The murder took place outside the Magdala and Gladys got shrapnel in her finger from the shooting as Ellis pumped bullets into her lover, Blakely. I remember Gladys calling to show us her wound! She was a student and was summoned as a witness in the Ellis case. 1954-55 was certainly the time and Hampstead the place where it all happened.

Hampstead in those days did not have any traffic problems. It was a lively and creative place to live where you would meet trend-setters and the soon-to-be trend-setters just walking along the street. I gather Hampstead was the model for Greenwich Village in New York, another enclave for creative artists and writers. Even though times were financially hard, there was this sort of electric verve echoing around the art world on the threshold of change. The film industry in Britain was reasonably strong at that time, too. But the American influence was growing in the arts as elsewhere. England was looking west and film theatre was promoting the concept of stardom. I met the film director David Poltangis who always liked me because I was about the only person he knew who did not ask him to put them in a film! The draw of the silver screen must have been immense. I did, however, appear in one film about the life of Toulouse Lautrec. Students from St Martin's School of Art at Charing Cross acted as extras, and I am among them somewhere.

The only occasion on which I found life difficult also happened to be when I lived in Hampstead. I had a very bad dose of the 'flu; there was a raging epidemic at the time. I could not model and spent days in bed. I remember I had neither the money for food nor the strength to get out of bed. My friends helped me, bringing meals and vitamins and nursing me back to health. I thought I was going to die. This was probably my all time low, but it taught me to make the best of things when they are going well.

One particularly theatrical character at the Slade was Quentin Crisp. He would talk to us in the model room where there would be up to fifteen models at any one time. He was so melodramatic. He would demonstrate how to pose and would suggest standing 'as if waiting for a bus.' He would then add 'a number 35!' and fling his arm out as if hailing the oncoming bus. He would hold the image in a wanton stance of self-determination. Quentin was posing at the Royal Academy, as I remember. Although I never worked with him our conversations were often quite philosophical in a down-to-earth sort of way. He would say it is important to remember that people live as part of their place in time, given the particular set of circumstances that they have been dealt. His way of life, and the places that he visited, combined to put other people with whom he came into contact into his life at the same time. This way he could track the ebbs and flows of his life without great bitterness or regret, as if it was meant to be. It did not stop us being wistful or wishful, but it did help one to keep things in perspective and get on with life in a positive frame of mind.

By now I had extended my work to the Royal Academy. I had also changed over to the Royal College of Art from about March 1952 as the pay was better. I was still working by the term for the life-size sculptures which meant that I had very long hours. I used to see the notorious Lord Lucan returning from the previous night's gambling in full evening dress at about 9.30 in the morning when I was entering the Royal Academy via the back entrance near the Burlington Arcade. We never entered the Academy from Piccadilly but went in near Cork Street. The Royal Academy Schools were poor payers. For my one room in Hampstead I paid about £4 per week (say, £125 today), which was then a great deal of money to be earned before travel, food and (more importantly) clothes. Still, as Quentin Crisp said: 'I put a lot of trust in my friends and can say that as a member of the professional art world it is to me more like having a wonderfully big family with all the success and none of the problems'.

After my days at the Royal College of Art, I had to spend weekends and nights on private work. I needed to earn as much as possible during term time to be able to pay my rent over the holidays. One of my favourite places was Glebe Place, near Chelsea Town Hall. It was here that a lot of the well-known artists had their studios. I would find out where these where and knock on their doors to ask if they needed a model. Our Liverpudlian confidence stands us in good stead in difficult times. If I had not had the confidence or determination to succeed then I would have starved or returned home to a sympathetic 'I told you so!' I knew I was good at my job and also knew that if I could get the opportunities to prove it then I would always have work. I was very willing to do the work that was required of me, even though it was exhausting to pose almost seven days a week.

My perseverance paid off. Through it I got to know David McFall, the sculptor. David was a very funny chap who would cartwheel out of a room whilst wearing a kilt. McFall, who used to do a lot of casting for Sir Jacob

Epstein, had a studio in Glebe Place and had been a student at the Royal College at the same time as George Jardine. I remember McFall leasing his studio when he went to Madeira. When he came home he couldn't get in. Eventually he got the door open and walked into the room only to be bouncing and squelching about in rubber. The studio had been sub-let to a rubber doll factory by Jacob Epstein's illegitimate son, the artist Theodore Garman.

One day while walking along the Kings Road I saw some of the students from the Royal College. There were lots of studios around this area, especially in Manresa Road, and I could usually find work quite easily. The students walked over to say hello and said that they knew of an artist who needed a model urgently. I went over to this big house on Kings Parade, now demolished, rang the bell, but no one answered. I pushed the door lightly and it opened. I wandered in to a house full of Epstein sculptures and collected pieces. There were lots of objets d'art around the place and a massive grand piano in the big room to the left. I heard someone shout: 'Up here', so I walked upstairs and tentatively pushed open the door to one of the rooms. There was Theodore Garman, the son of Kathleen Garman, Epstein's mistress and second wife. He had painted everything in the room white and had flung whitewash at the cupboard. He was propped up, half sitting, half lying on the bed. The door closed behind me and I was stuck in this unknown room with a huge, strange man.

He was very friendly as he introduced himself. Even so, I sensed danger, there was something a little odd about him and there were, after all, only the two of us in the room. It did not feel right or comfortable, and I thought that I had better get out.

He asked what I did. I had to think quickly and said that I was a model and that I thought I might have been the butt of a practical joke by some students outside. I realised that I knew of the family as I was a friend of Lucien Freud. Lucien had married Theodore's sister Kitty Epstein, and I told Theodore that I was a friend of Lucien. Theodore sulked and said the name of Freud was never to be mentioned in the Epstein household. Suddenly, his mother came in and announced that tea was ready. We looked at each other and I promptly said that I thought I had better be going. He asked if I would come back again. I made my excuses and bid a hasty retreat from that chilly atmosphere, back into the safety of the Chelsea streets. After I had become friendly with David McFall I remember telling him about the encounter and he said that Theodore had some social difficulties and was not a well person, because of his epilepsy.

In 1954 I was again in the area, when there was a lot of commotion and police and an ambulance were called. Apparently, Theodore had had an epileptic fit and was being bundled into a straightjacket, tragically suffocating on his way to hospital. I do not think his family ever really got over it. Certainly, when I met his father, Jacob Epstein he had a sort of subdued air about him. We often sat chatting on the bench at the Royal

College of Art. We vaguely discussed the possibility of my posing for him for his sculpture. At the time he was working with the male model in the sculpture department at the Royal College of Art at Queen's Gate but we never made any progress. Perhaps this was just as well after the incident with Theodore.

Anyway, I eventually posed for his contemporary, Frank Dobson, in his Chelsea studio, where he generously paid three times the college rates. Mr Dobson produced very bulbous results – his drawings were just the same – and as I was slim at the time this primitive enormity was not very flattering. I was, of course, exceedingly vain in those days when I wore a size eight dress.

The professor of sculpture at the Royal College was John Skeaping. He had a vivid yellow Rolls-Royce motor car, and was the first husband of the sculptor Barbara Hepworth. They had met at the Royal College of Art in the 1920s and had one son who was tragically killed in a plane crash. Barbara Hepworth was by then working and living in St Ives. On one occasion John, who became a good friend, encouraged his second family to produce a caterpillar sculpture. They planted grass seed on it and it grew a hairy green coat. I did his life classes at night in Queen's Gate. There were usually about six or so students and his friend Rita Ling. We quite often ended the evening all drinking wine and chatting late into the night. John Skeaping could speak many languages and could also play the guitar as well as sing. He would entertain everyone, telling all about his life spent in Mexico, his favourite place. John was a very good friend to me always.

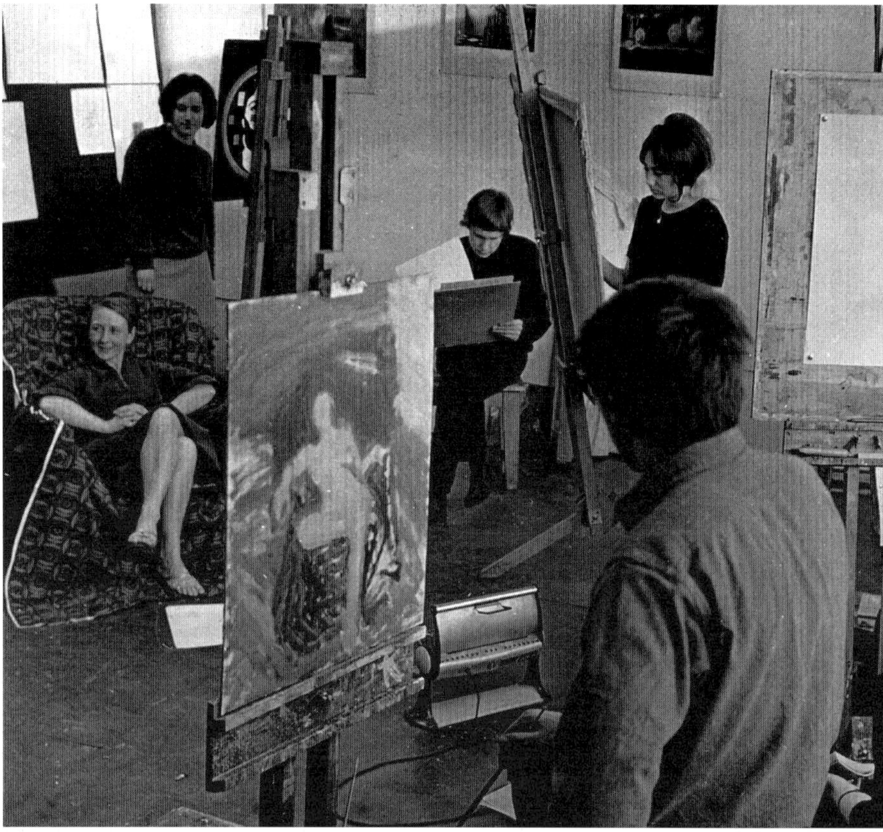

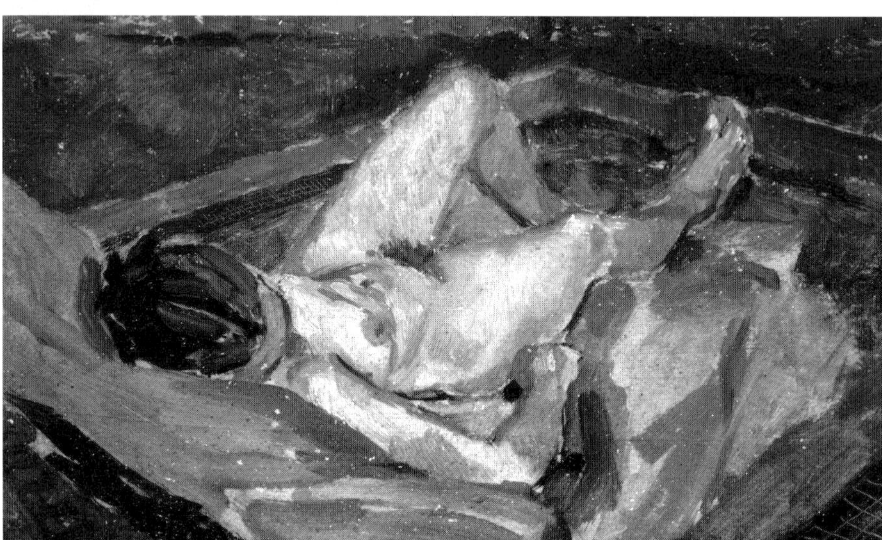

Life class.
June Furlong, oil on canvas. Anthony Butler, 1949.

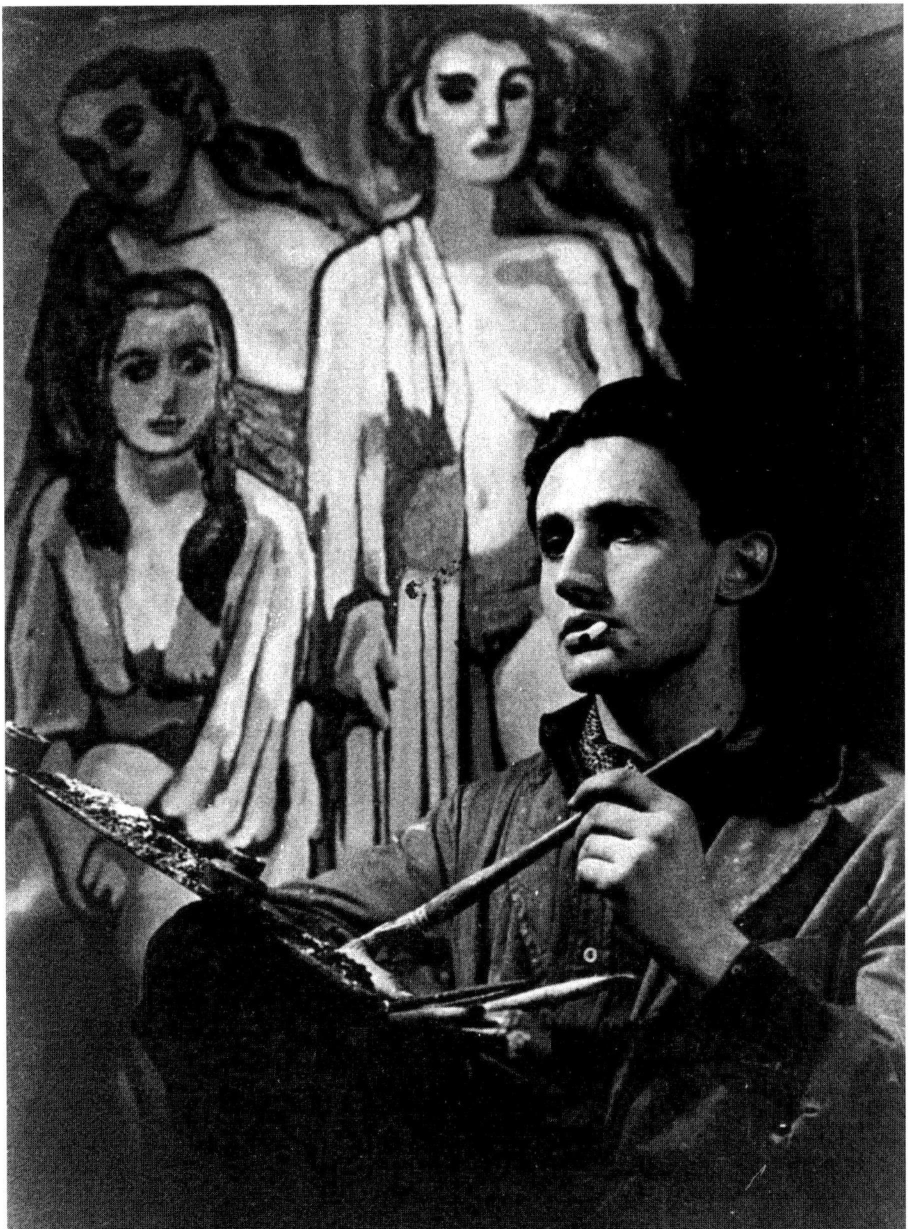

Roy Cross painting *June Furlong*. Oil on canvas, 1947.

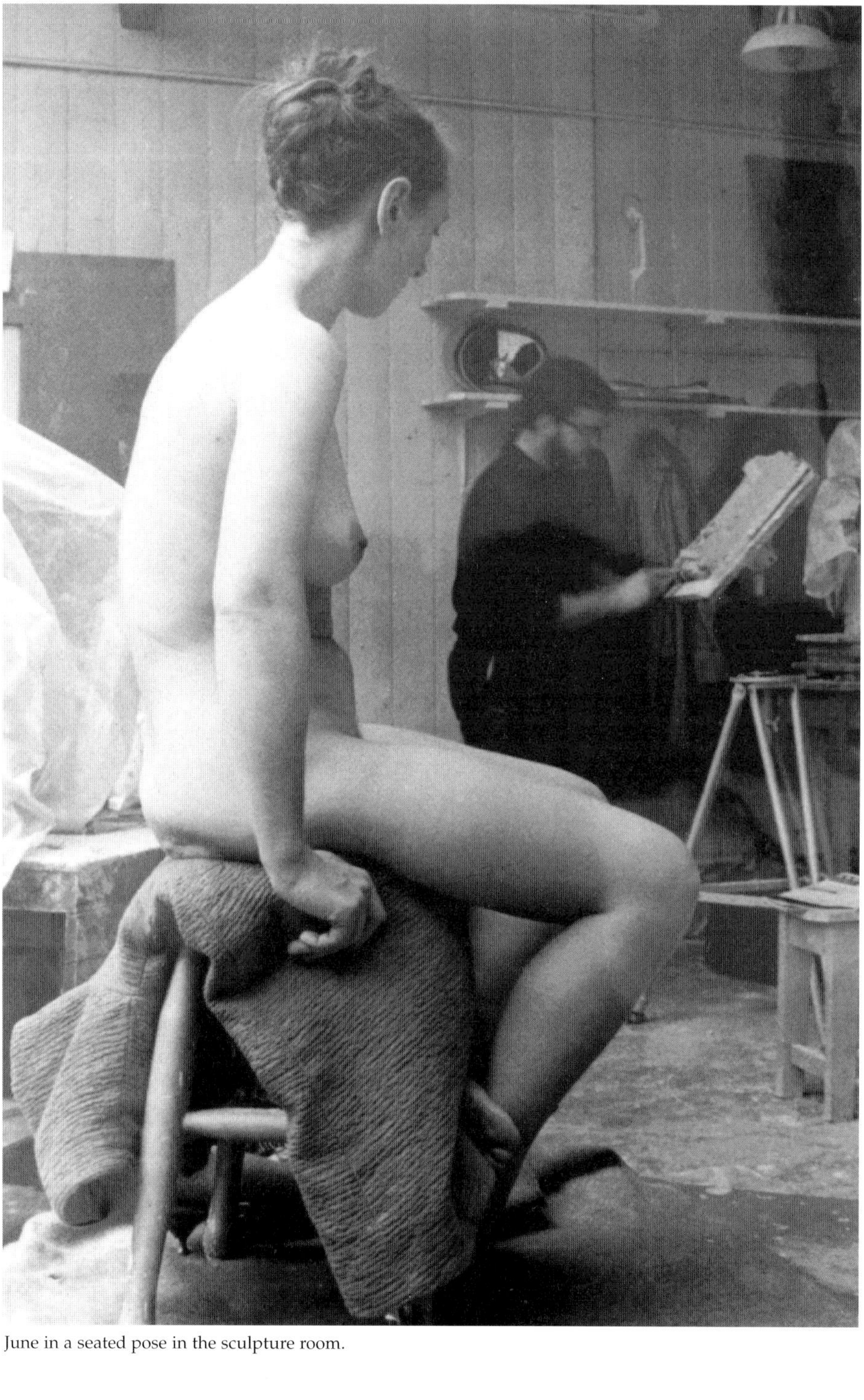

June in a seated pose in the sculpture room.

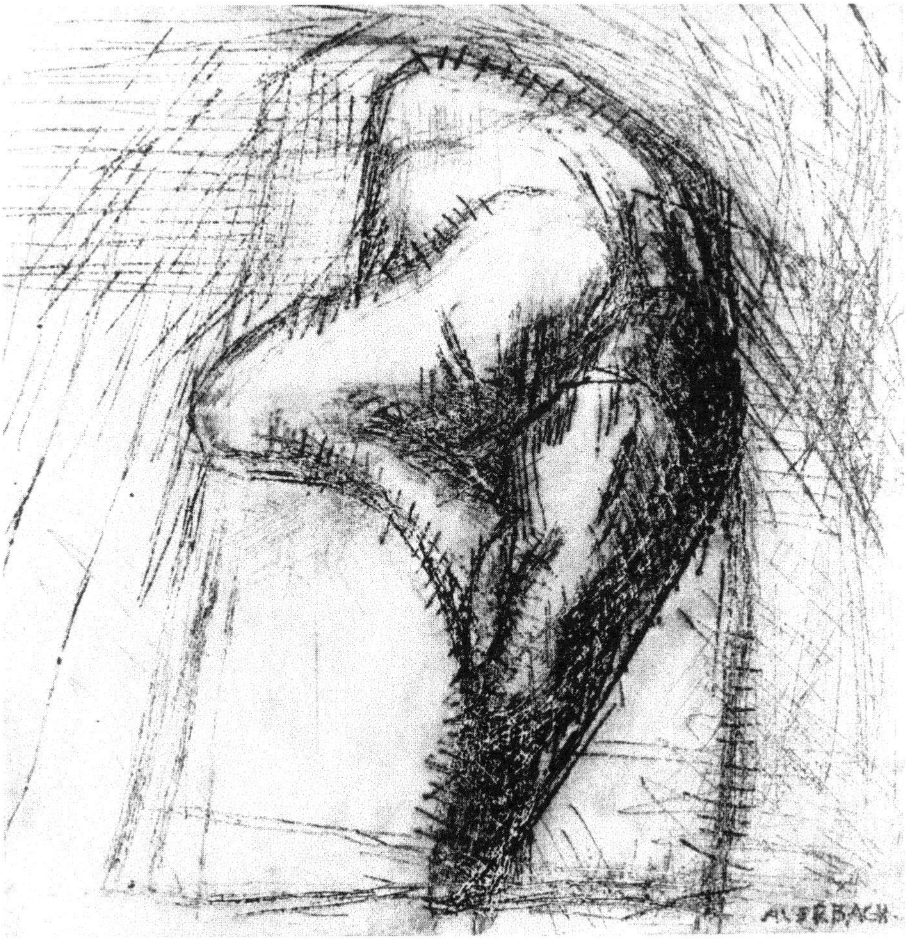

June Furlong, Etching. Frank Auerbach.

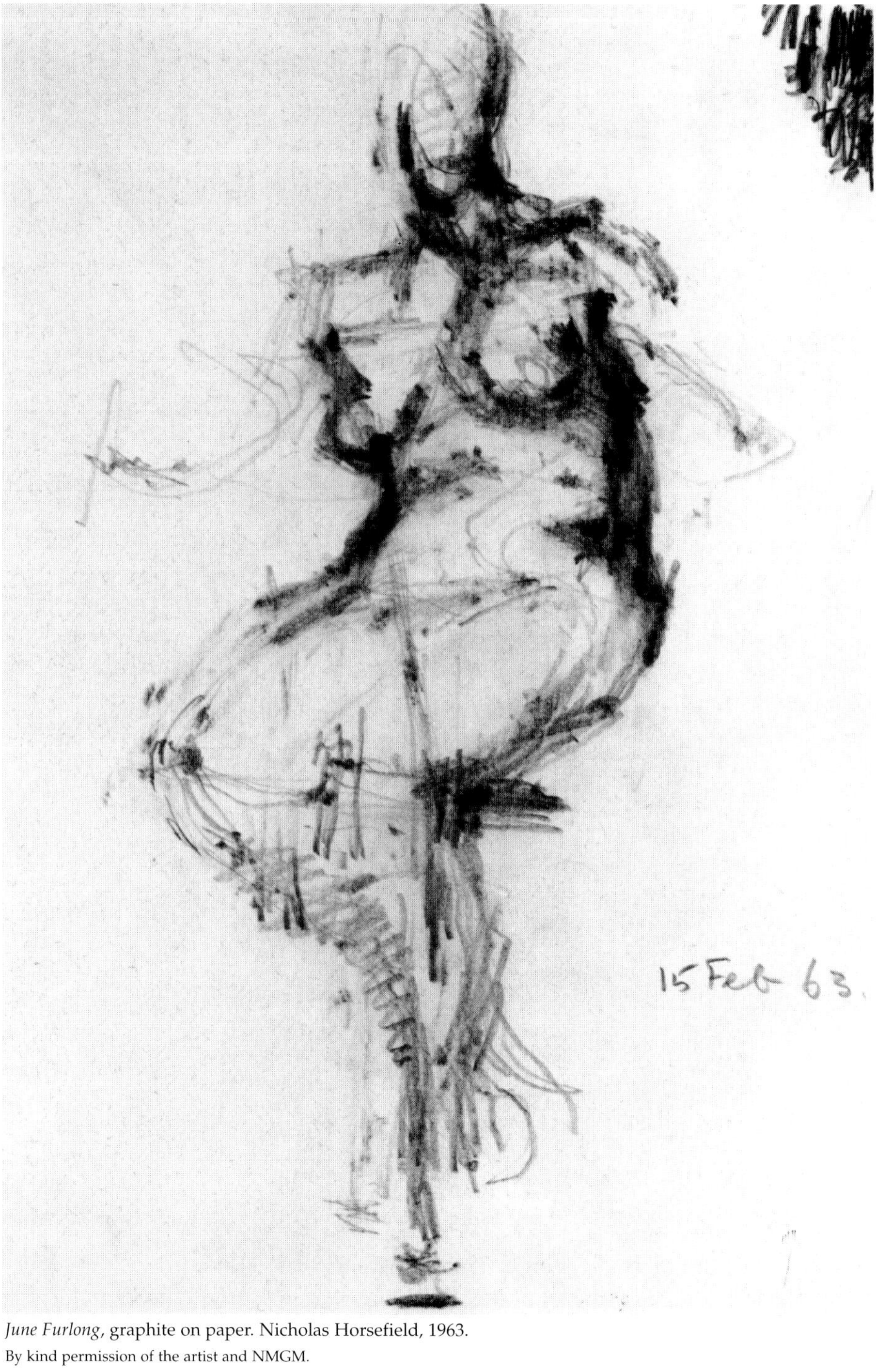

June Furlong, graphite on paper. Nicholas Horsefield, 1963.
By kind permission of the artist and NMGM.

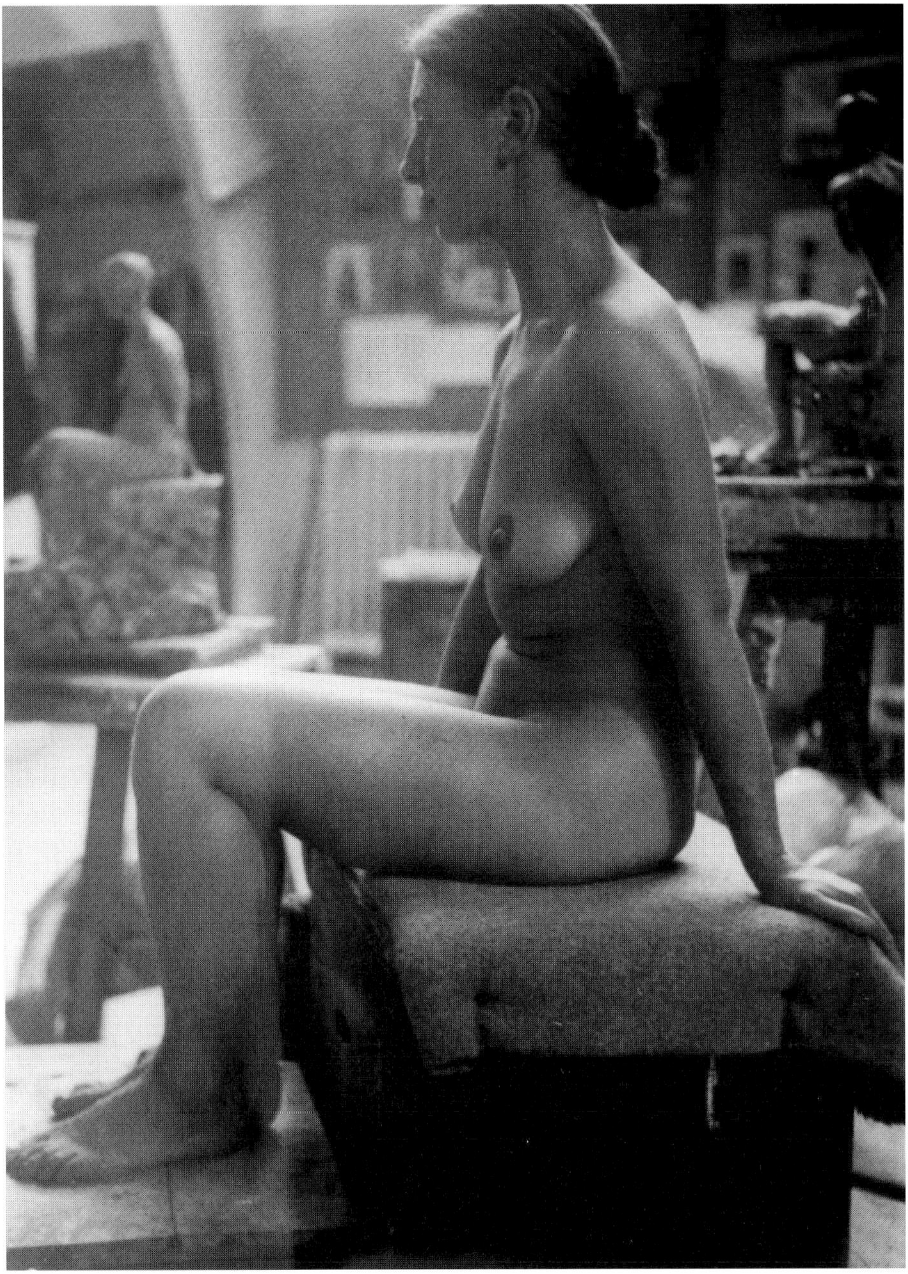

June in a seated pose in the sculpture room.

London and the Royal College of Art

After moving from Liverpool to London, my friend Adolph Morath had set up a studio off Cromwell Road. When I went to investigate, it turned out that he had come to terms with colour photography after all and had landed a contract for Shell, the oil company. Colour photography was in its infancy in the 1950s. When I called on Morath I was quite impressed to see the whole of his wall displaying huge commercial blow-ups, technically brilliant as always.

I find it a little ironic that Shell International has played such an important part over the years in the art world. In the inter-war years Shell used artists like Paul Nash for their advertisements. Their art department was one of – if not the, leading patrons of young artists from the world of fine art. It was a good way for artists to earn a living and become established working on graphics-based advertising promotions. Their success opened the door for the rapid growth in the graphics market and in the employment of young artists. I was so pleased that Morath was recognised as able to produce top-quality photographs for the commercial world, given that his interest had strictly been in studio portraiture in the first place.

I was fortunate to be able to pose for the leading photographers of the time, Bill Brandt, Zolton and Stephen Glass as well as Joan Craven. Joan took the photograph that promoted my retrospective at the Royal Cambrian Academy gallery. Always very photogenic, I was in great demand, and was widely photographed in the 1950s. Many of the pictures look like Hollywood stills, very poised. Striking a pose became second nature. I could increase my earnings by posing for advertisements, sweaters for example, or shoe advertisements for Vogue and the other glossies. I used to spend hours on my appearance to make sure that I looked my best for this work

Public attention focused on London in the 1950s. Not only because it was the capital and Britain was regarded as a leading nation in post-war Europe, but because of the Festival of Britain. The Festival had taken place by the time I arrived in September 1951. However, its impact remained and was to spill over into all the art schools for a number of years. The new elements of design that the Festival publicised captured the public imagination. London had welcomed many thousands of Festival visitors. The buzz and atmosphere that the show created was my first impression of London, a whirlwind of enthusiasm for contemporary art and architecture.

Pure form was to creep into everything. I can remember students discussing the possibilities of commercial contracts and commissions at the Royal College of Art. The trendy organic art forms were taking off and this era heralded the demise of the life room as we knew it. I feel that the period 1951-1955 was a halcyon age in the art schools. It was an age increasingly influenced by European modernism, then gradually American modernism.

Although a great deal of fuss was made about the modern image and the new architectural styles that were on show, as part of the Festival exhibition, I cannot remember being really bowled over by the aftermath of the event. With hindsight this has really surprised me, especially as the event has in later years been heralded as a significant watershed in post-war modernism. I suppose I was engrossed in the figurative and traditional aspects of the art world. The radical young artists such as Victor Pasmore used function and form in representational art. This shift was outside the normal experience of the life class and like-minded artists tended to associate in their own small cliques. I remember Pasmore had a close friend in Alan Reynolds. They came from different artistic backgrounds, both figurative but with different perspectives. Alan doted on Victor, but had a bit of a schizophrenic nature towards his artwork. He was divided between organic form and the reproduction of thistles, crocuses and spiky neo-romantic imagery from the tradition of Paul Nash and John Minton. He shows evidence of attentive geometric construction in relief between his early and later work.

Reynolds has said that he has burned all his early work. He almost turned away from art to return to work on the railway but, as the story goes, was so attracted by the rocks and natural forms of the kerbside that he collected samples together. Back in the studio he started to paint natural organic images based on his kerbside collection. Reynolds paid to have his work expertly framed to show it at its very best. The framer knew the owner of the Redfern Gallery and the link was made. Reynolds went on to show through the Redfern.

The link between Reynolds and Pasmore can be seen in their sudden interest in a geographical, abstract type of work. Spiral motifs in Pasmore's 1940s work and a hard-edged geometry was likened to the 'road to Damascus'. As an established English painter of the Euston Road style, Pasmore's sudden conversion was widely reported in the press, and there was a tension of loyalties within the art schools. Abstract art had arrived. The Royal College of Art, I remember, was split into two camps. I was not involved in the debate or discussion between groups myself, but certainly one could not help but be aware of the changing attitudes between staff and also notice the emergence of little groupings of like-minded fellows.

Carel Weight was head of painting at the Royal College of Art when I was there. He was approachable and kind to me, and I have great admiration for him. We were friends and he was loved and respected by artists, a fatherly figure always willing to put himself out to help.

He has since said, in an interview in 1996 with the author Peter Davies, that 'June Furlong has made a valuable contribution to British culture', of which I am very proud. I like to think he meant that my image has been at the root of the training of many of today's great artists. I would also like to think that I have made a contribution through the exhibition organising that I have since undertaken.

Discipline, resilience and persistence, with a continuing striving for success and truth in art, are all qualities that I would associate with Carel Weight.

I have a painting entitled The Road to Charlestown (circa 1956), one of my personal favourites. It is in Professor Weight's realist style, showing a man and a girl on bike, painted in a dark palette of green, mustard and brown tones. I like it because it is set in a semi-industrial landscape, showing the merging of town and country. It is not a romantic picture, but there is a sense of old England. The picture captures a sort of post-war time of change that excludes fear of the future. War has finished, life has been hard, there has been rationing but factories are again working. There is no directional light on the canvas and the artist has worked in expressive short handling of the medium. There is a discreet central light source from the distant town, which looks quite comfortable with red chimneys suggesting secure warmth. The whole painting evokes feelings of safety and security. It could be late summer or autumn, and there is a hint of yellow and blue with grey and cream to the horizon. To the sides are scratched branches that offer a hint of a shady lane leading into a deep, woody backdrop. Professor Weight gave the painting to me when I worked at the Royal College of Art.

It is a typical example of his work. He was antipathetic to abstraction and never tried it but favoured symbolic, narrative art. I recall a visit to his studio in Putney, where he lived until his death. He put me inside a cupboard to pose for him, with the door open. He produced a good painting and we always had a nice tea at the end of our work.

A particular favourite of Carel Weight's was John Bratby, of the Kitchen Sink School with Middleditch and Greaves, a Social Realist painter of great strength. Bratby was a student of the Royal College of Art when I worked there in 1954. He was quite anti-social for most the time. He married a painter called Jean Cooke, but she left him. His second wife, called Patty, was an actress and John was very happy. He would travel around Europe, staying in expensive hotels and painting her in exotic attire. Even in their rambling mansion in Hastings he had an eye for unusual quirky subjects – his wife in kinky underwear and so on. I remember he won the Prix de Rome scholarship for his work. He painted the pictures for the Alec Guinness film The Horse's Mouth and went on to win a prize in the Walker Art Gallery's John Moores Exhibition.

Bratby was a big, gangling fellow and was often seen with his student friend Martin Chapman from Ipswich, parking Chapman's car in the principal's spot. It caused a row when Professor Darwin could not get his Rolls-Royce in. When the Queen Mother was expected in Exhibition Road there was uproar. Martin Chapman's old Singer car had broken down exactly where the Rolls was meant to be! We all thought it extremely amusing. The staff, however, thought differently. Darwin came storming into the studios looking for Chapman, who calmly said: 'Well you move it! I certainly cannot, it's broken down'. I have no doubt it wasn't there for long.

I remember that Chapman would rush into the studio shouting: 'Where is Reason? I must see Reason!,' This was highly amusing, of course, as he meant fellow-student Cyril Reason who would eventually appear wondering what was so urgent. Carel Weight produced a series of paintings about Cyril. Martin Chapman was a fan of stately home sales and would buy up whole lots to get just one piece he found of interest. He was constantly short of money. Martin would invite Cyril over, with Cyril saying that there was not really anything that he particularly needed or wanted. Nevertheless, Cyril would say: 'Well, if you insist, I will have this piece.' As a result, Cyril ended up with a house full of treasures and Martin a house full of bric-a-brac after needing to sell the good stuff to make ends meet.

I was encouraged by the students to write a piece for the Royal College of Art journal called Ark, issue number 14, 1955. I offered a piece called 'Self Portrait', which gave a brief outline of my involvement in the art world and included a couple of sketches and a photograph. I was furious when it went into print. It bore scant resemblance to the piece that I had written and the editorial team had added bits and pieces and stretched the details to suit themselves. Looking at the journal today I notice that in the list of contents mine is the only name not included. All the other contributors are there. Maybe I was so well known that I needed no introduction, or perhaps it indicates the élitist nature of the college. As a model, and therefore an employee of the college, my position was obviously different to the teaching staff. I can smile at my closing statement, which reads: 'I am quite vague about the future. One thing I am determined to avoid is becoming one of those old familiar faces (and figures) which keep returning to art schools year after year.' What a thing to say! I was only 24 at the time and had been in London for just over three years. I cannot imagine what I thought I would be doing in future. Here I am, fifty years later, still working.

It was not all work, of course. Most of our spare time was spent on the London night-club scene. The post-war years saw a steady growth of entertainment of all sorts. Theatre, cinema, casino and club all had their individual charms. I loved the cinema, but the night life buzzed in the night-clubs and I had a great time.

Even part of my life at the Slade and the Royal College of Art involved the many dances and parties that were held. We had a fantastic and colourful time with Humphrey Lyttelton playing in the common room at the College. I recall that Lucien Freud had a regular haunt called the Gargoyle Club, in Soho. Lucien introduced me to Francis Bacon on a visit there. Bacon was a non-conformist and he used to offer talks on set pieces, for example, the play Under Milk Wood by Dylan Thomas. He would give a critique on the whole thing. Bacon was not a member of staff and was self-taught, but often Bacon and Freud would team up at the Slade afternoon tea. In the 'huts' they would talk about the set pieces that had been worked up over the last month. The paintings were as different as the artists were. When Bacon hit a stumbling block in a critique Freud would prompt him. However, it was quite a rare experience to witness Bacon stuck for words. He always seemed to be so spontaneous and the students liked his visits.

His contemporary at the Slade was Robert Buhler. His mother owned the

Café Journal where everyone went to pass the time. Robert's son, Michael, has a gallery and has been promoting his father's work since his death. Robert was a portrait painter of some talent but he had a problem with drink and was a chain smoker. Both habits were commonplace in the art schools. Robert was a member of the Chelsea Arts Club and produced a big painting of Carel Weight in the 1950s. He taught at the Royal College of Art and mixed in the right social circles, but could cause some consternation amongst his associates. One evening Buhler was drinking heavily and Lucien, always red-hot on scrupulous behaviour in public, was trying to get Robert home. Robert lived around the corner in Cromwell Gardens, off Exhibition Road, and had a studio in South Kensington. Before he could make his exit, Lucien had disappeared from sight for fear of a scene.

The Gargoyle Club itself was a fascinating place to me. I used to visit it on other occasions with the painters Robert Colquhoun, Robert MacBryde and John Minton. They drank a lot between them and mixed with the gay crowd. The two Roberts were the darlings of Cork Street. They hit London from Glasgow and lived life to the full. John Minton, however, was from a well-connected family and totally disliked social climbing. I was fortunate to feel comfortable at all levels and to be invited to some of the grand parties. With John's Royal College colleagues and our usual crowd we found ourselves made very welcome.

I remember coming out of the Gargoyle Club one night in 1952 to be greeted by a slim young man with a mop of black hair. He asked the way to Peterborough from London as he had to be on stage in about two hours. It turned out to be George Melly, the jazz singer, who was appearing with Mick Mulligan's band and thought he had seen me around Soho on a few occasions. He decided that as time was tight they had better get a taxi. George has never changed. At the launch of Peter Davies' book on Arthur Ballard, at the Williamson Art Gallery in Birkenhead, George was supposed to be opening the associated exhibition and was about an hour and half late for the lunch, giving the same excuses. Still looking for Peterborough, I expect.

Of the other night-spots there was also the Beaux Arts Club and all the college dances that were swinging with life. Lucien was really keen on the West End. My own favourite London clubs were the exceptionally plush Milroy and Les Ambassadors, where you had to be suitably dressed, of course. In those days I spent a fortune on my clothes, shopping at Harrods or Galerie Lafayette or the well-known fashion houses. I enjoyed the glittering social scene and thought I had really arrived when Princess Margaret was seen at the next table in the Milroy night-club! I was wearing a superb dress, gold in colour, that I had bought from Galerie Lafayette in Regent Street, which was just as well, given the royal company. The food and the music were marvellous.

The staff of the Slade frequented the Soho restaurants, and I was always made welcome. In those days I learned how to live life stylishly, after those early lessons acquired on my grandmother's knee. There is a superficial emphasis on the culture of 'life-style' nowadays but it is all rather artificial. An inner style is what kept me right up there where I wanted to be. I can still detect the good stuff in others, although it is only occasionally noted nowadays. There is a distinct difference between the brash style gurus of the nineties and those who cultivated and displayed style in the 1950s. I would put it down to the change in culture. The old stuffy style of besuited gentlemen was being rapidly overthrown by the international style. Food, music and art were becoming more international.

This was at the time right before the blossoming of the pop art scene. There was a shift in emphasis on the way people lived. Visits to night-clubs, restaurants and socialising were part of this dramatic change. However, it was not a change that was open to everyone. The dawn of pop culture, which was the natural progression, brought that into focus. The period in time that I am trying to recall was still gracious and selective and you either had it or you didn't. There was a fine mix of the American influence and the European influence. With so many people from overseas using London as their post-war focus it was bound to be a haven of the extraordinary and I wanted to be part of it. It was as if we all sensed we were on the threshold of momentous change. What sort of change we couldn't define – yet it permeated everything. The art world began to capture the change and record it through new approaches to art, to teaching art and to the reflection of society through art.

Louis Le Brocquy was another artist who stands out in my memory. He had a lovely studio in Battersea. I used to work for him after meeting him at the Central School of Art where he taught. He would paint in an immaculate white coat and never make any mess. Louis exhibited exquisite tapestries at Gimpel Fils gallery. I think he was of French/Irish descent, educated in Dublin. He was strikingly avant-garde. When we first met he was wearing a pink suit, something that would be perfectly acceptable in the 1990s but forty years ago could have been risqué. It was an outrageously expensive pink suit in hand-woven tweed. I would wear my black velvet coat with the red satin lining, which he admired greatly, as did others. It seemed to be my distinctive trade mark for a while.

I would visit studio after studio. Frank Dobson's was off the King's Road, opposite the Chelsea School of Art. He made quite a few drawings of me as part of my Saturday morning work. Dobson was a major sculptor during the 1920s and 1930s who was unfairly eclipsed by Henry Moore and Barbara Hepworth. He was not as adept as the 'Yorkshire Mafia' – Read, Moore and Hepworth – as a self-publicist. He was seen then as retrograde, unclassical and although modern, not abstract enough. As I have mentioned previously, he produced huge sculptural figures, full-bodied and voluptuous along neo-classical lines.

Adrian Heath held his classes in his large establishment, near the Slade. Heath was ex-Royal Air Force and was an acquaintance of St Ives artist Terry Frost during the war. His studio was in the Fitzrovia area, north of Oxford

Street, and he was part of a Fitzrovia artists' group. As well as Adrian, the group included Pasmore, Robert Adams, Anthony Hill, Terry Frost and Kenneth and Mary Martin. The wife of Gustav Delbanco attended Adrian's life class. His studio classes were expensive and Heath had a wealthy background, living near Bath, with good connections. Nevertheless, as an employer he paid well and always offered refreshments, which were most welcome, when I was working hard throughout the holidays to be able to pay my rent.

Other memories of my days at the Royal College are rich in delight too. Robert Buhler once asked me: 'June, do you like strawberries?' 'Yes,' I said. 'Wait one moment,' he replied, and came back with at least twelve pounds of fresh strawberries. 'Here, take these,' he said 'Some madman sent them from the country and I am allergic to them.' I went staggering back with them to Hampstead, and all the artists sat on the Heath eating strawberries. I laughed to myself and thought: 'Slade strawberry teas have nothing on this!'

Robert Buhler drank so much I wondered how he could see the canvas, never mind the sitter! Nevertheless, a marvellous artist he certainly was.

Thinking back to the Royal Academy days, I don't think I ever sat for an artist whose work I did not like. The standard of work from the students is always very good. I try to look critically at all the work I see, but I never think whether or not a piece appeals to me on the basis of whether I simply like it or not.

There was always the odd unusual event to smile over. I remember a chap called Matthews, a good friend of mine at the time. He was a car dealer and while I was waiting to prepare for a sitting he gave me a tatty box tied up loosely with string. It was stashed full of £5 notes. That was a considerable amount of money at that time. He said I could withdraw any amount of money from the bank up to £100. It certainly paid my rent and I could shop at Harrods, of course. Always one for good taste and the best in life, shopping was my personal reward for hard work.

Frank Auerbach saw all this money constantly carried around by me in a brown paper bag, for emergencies. I offered him £5 to help him out, a lot of money then. He said he could not possibly take it, so I quickly offered to buy some of his etchings as a fair exchange. Frank agreed that he could accept the £5 in return for his work, so I got the etchings and he got the £5. He went straight out to buy bread, tea and more paint! I went off with the etchings and had them all identically framed at the Royal Academy where I was working and have cherished them ever since.

After working at the Royal College of Art, we would finish about 4.00pm, I would go with some of the artists to a Polish café next to South Kensington tube station, the Daquise. It is still there. This was a quick break for a lemon tea before moving on to Soho and St Martin's School of Art for the 6.30pm class. Ruskin Spear would arrive. He sported a big red beard and would select his model from the row, all of us seated outside the studio. I was always fortunate to get the work at that class, which finished about 8.30pm.

Frank Auerbach would often arrive after the class and we would go either to the French pub or to the cinema in Soho.

During the 1950s I used to work at Adrian Heath's art class in his beautiful house and studio in Fitzroy Street. He was a very distinguished non figurative painter and always charming to me. I went regularly to his class for a number of months and met all sorts of good people there including Lilian Browse, of the Roland Browse and Delbanco gallery in Cork Street. No stranger to the art galleries of Mayfair myself, I was encouraged to call into her gallery to see the shows. I was always fascinated by the personalities of the gallery owners and their ability to survive with the fantastically high rents and rates of Mayfair. I spent all my spare time there whenever I was in the West End.

Around 1954 Alan Reynolds was at the Royal College of Art and was making a name for himself even though still a student. He was exhibiting at the Redfern Gallery, under the direction of Rex Nan Kivell. I often went in with Alan when he lived in Blackheath,Victor Pasmore's territory. Lionel Levy, director of the Portal Gallery in Grafton Street, I knew vaguely as a student at the Liverpool College of Art. I now love his gallery as the character and atmosphere never changes. These days Lionel is a personal friend whom I see regularly in the Mediterranean as he has his boat and apartment there. Lionel is a true gentleman, one of a dying breed who often shows a kindness and always extends a warm welcome to George Jardine and myself when we visit. George was a regular exhibitor at the Portal Gallery some years ago. When we visit Lionel in the Mediterranean we are offered champagne on the terrace with his delightful wife and son and we discuss the crippling costs of maintaining a gallery in such a wonderful and exclusive area. The commitment to keeping a gallery open and accessible is not just one of money, although that obviously plays a big part. There is an ambience and feeling of great satisfaction when you are involved in the art world, and a visit to the Portal Gallery is always a rewarding experience.

At the Piccadilly Gallery in Cork Street I would meet Mr Godfrey Pilkington. Anne Redpath would show there. She was from Edinburgh and is regarded as a premier Scottish woman painter, producing rugged still lifes in that country's painterly tradition. They were very marketable and always collectable. We would often meet when she was exhibiting in the June show at the Pilkington's gallery. She would ask about the art world in London, as Scotland made her somewhat distant from it all and she had three children which prevented her painting to any degree for about ten years. Anne Redpath and Elizabeth Blackadder are two of my favourite female artists.

Each time I visited a gallery I was careful to study the hanging and literature as well as the work itself. Having spent so many hours in the art galleries of Britain and Europe I have learned much about the organisation of exhibition hanging. Eventually I was going to take a more active role in promoting our home-grown talent.

Before that, though, my work in London was to end. I had been in the city for some eight years but home was always Liverpool and Liverpool was warming up to become the bright city of the 1960s. Youth culture was born and I was young enough to see and experience its embryonic beginnings. The scene shifted as London and Liverpool battled for stardom.

It was 1959 and the world of pop was upon us, quietly and musically at first, but there was a new breed of student who looked to popular culture for inspiration. We were on the threshold of a dream. The twenty-somethings were about to drag the teenybop age into the 1960s kicking and screaming. Peter Blake and Pop Art were the rising stars. Blake was an illustrator taught by Edward Ardizzone and Edwin La Dell. As a forerunner to Hockney, he was to benefit at the Royal College of Art from the emphasis on design and graphic illustration encouraged by John Trevelyan. The College spawned, from as early as 1954, a talent for print-making in the pop art field. Blake is properly renowned for his famous Beatles cover for their Sergeant Pepper album. The early 1960s saw huge changes in the academic style. Pop Art made a media-conscious commercial world aware of it. It is a world that I feel has promoted a descent into triviality and decadence, with a decreasing emphasis and appreciation of craft.

In 1997 a visit to a Hockney exhibition at the Manchester City Gallery demonstrated his popularity in reaching such a broad audience. Schoolchildren recognise his work and he has fame. Blake, on the other hand, who later exhibited at the Whitworth Gallery in Manchester, proved a little less familiar but his work was shown in good light in a good show.

The message is the thing, and generally the American artists are better at it. Blake and the other British artists made a more subdued attempt at Pop Art. It was not as big and as brash as the American style, but had a distinctive European flavour. The influence on the student body was screeching west. Fascination with American culture and style was everywhere. For my part, the local College in Liverpool was as far west as I would be heading. They were desperate for a model for the National Diploma in Design exams. Teddy Griffiths visited my home and asked my mother to help entice me back to help out at Liverpool over the busy examination period. The work piled up, and what should have been a temporary visit turned another page in my life as family ties tugged and I stayed.

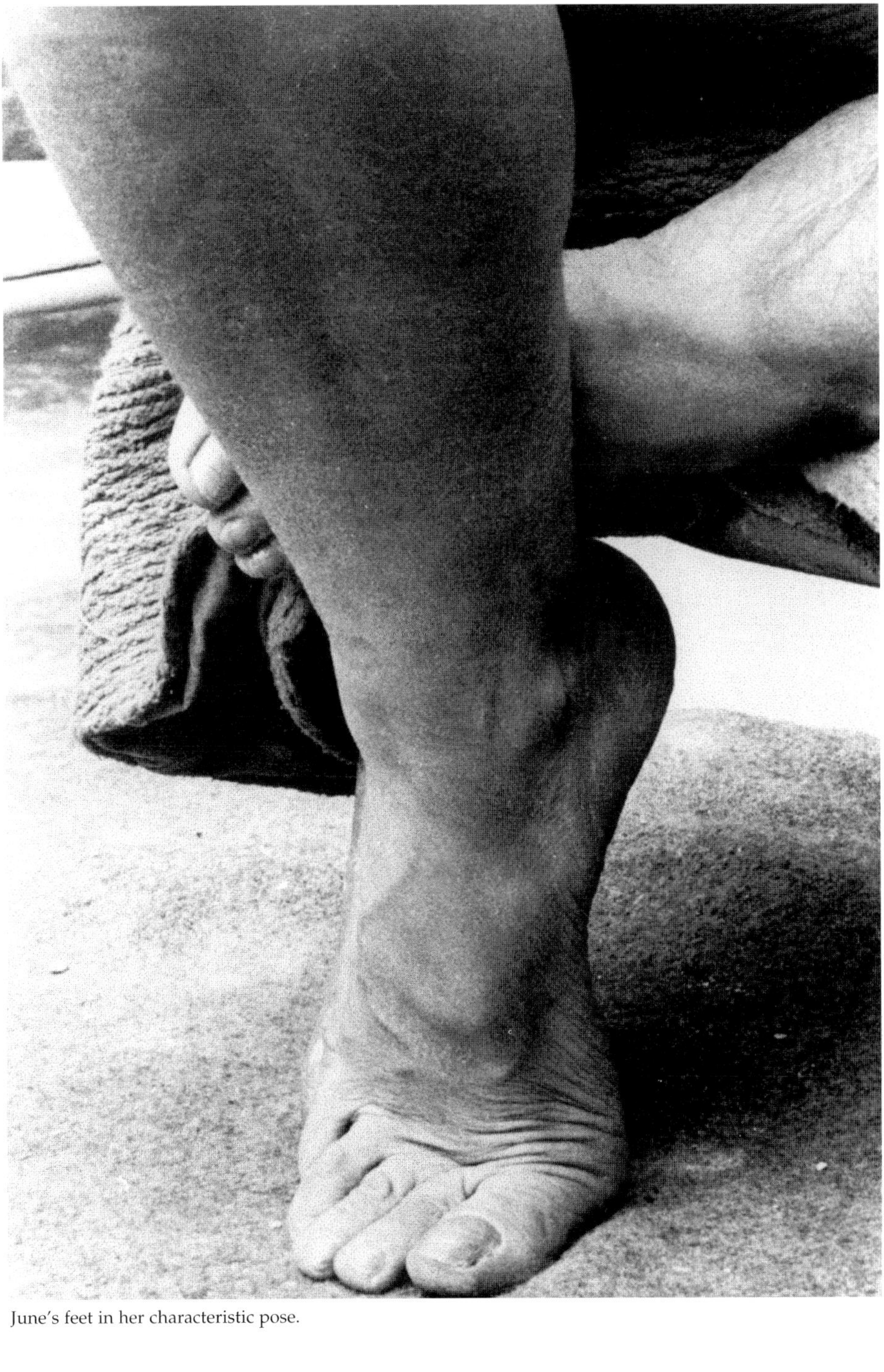

June's feet in her characteristic pose.

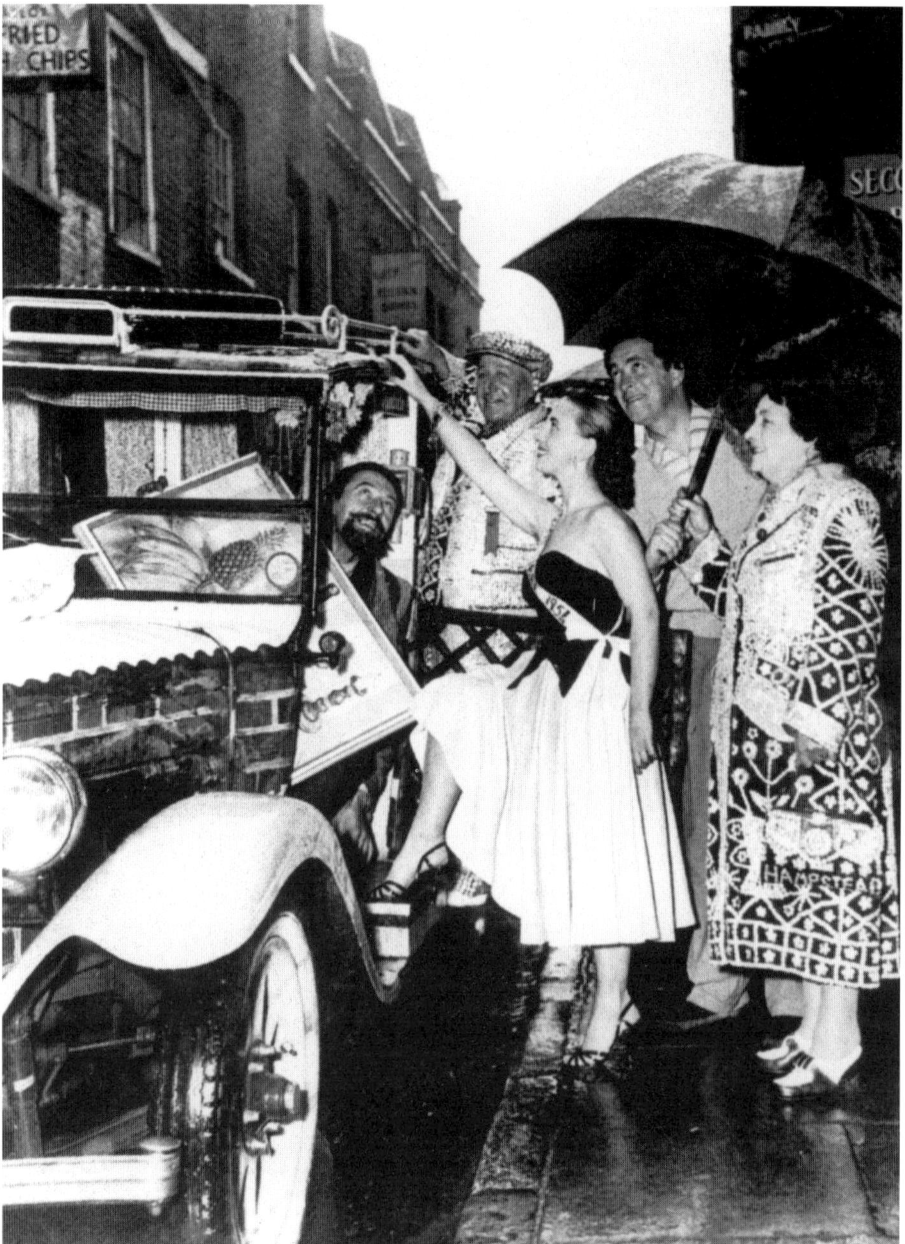

Beauty Queen June Furlong with film star, John Gregson and the Pearly Queen, Hampstead,1954.

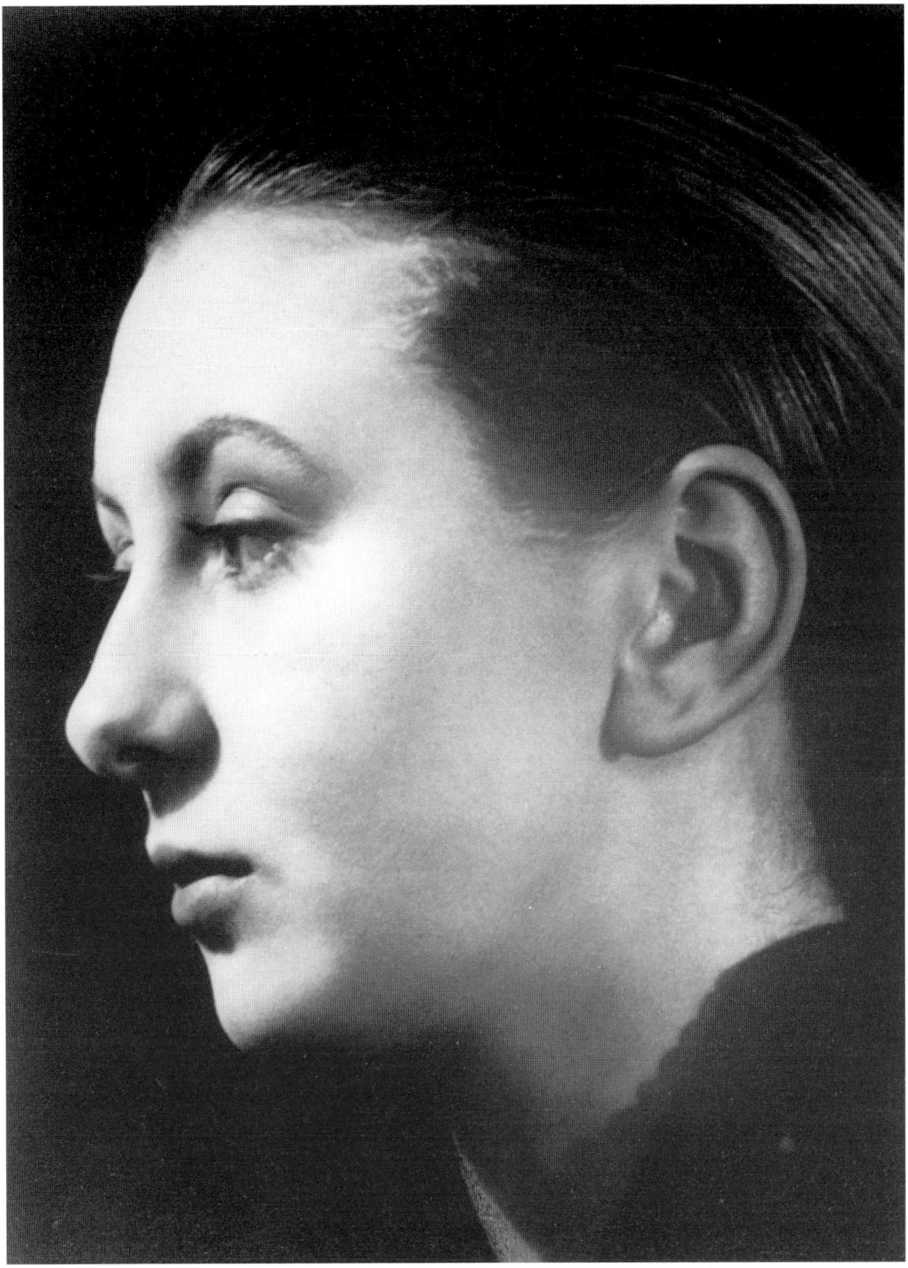

June profile photograph, Norath Studio, Liverpool.

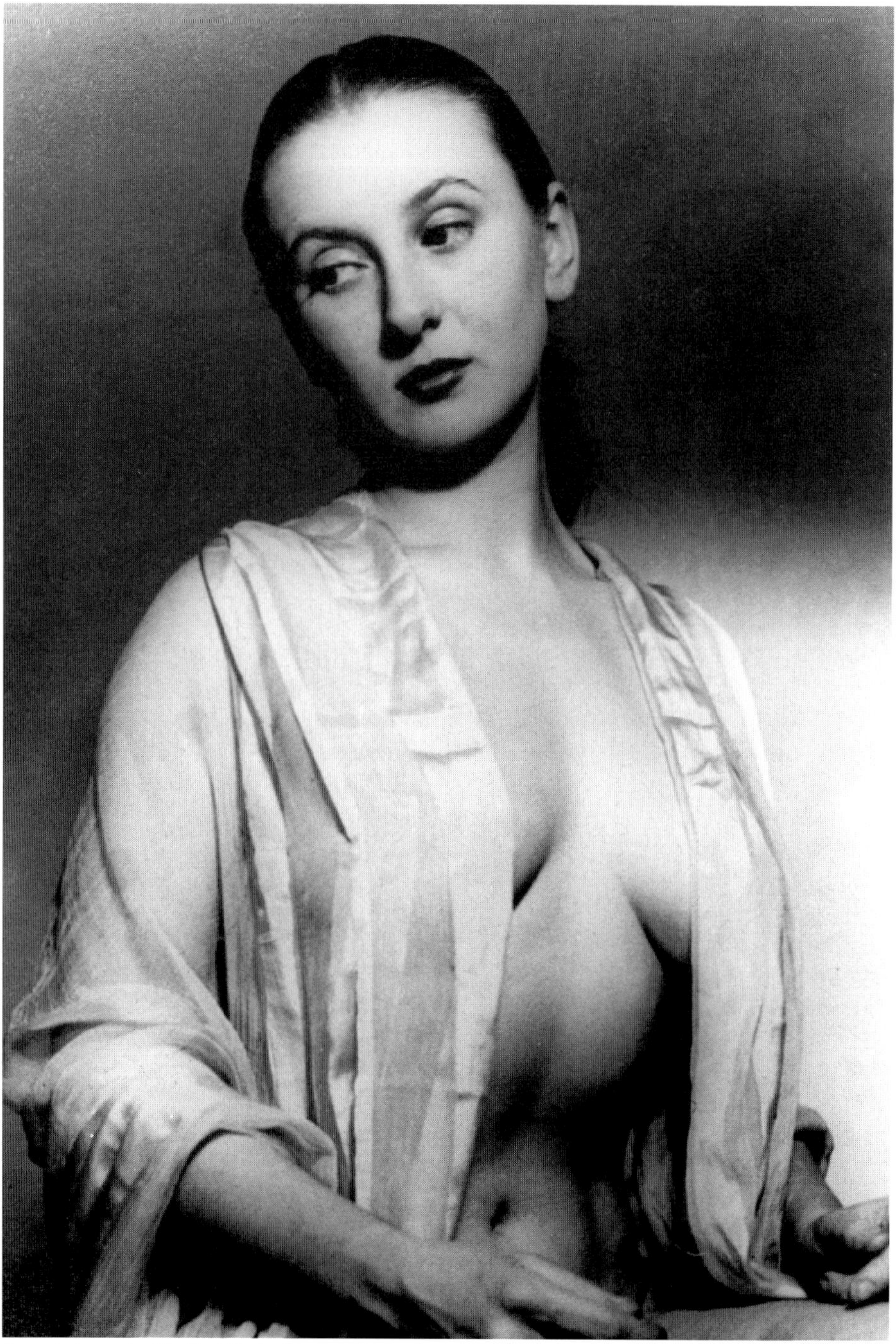

June photographed by Bert Drake, Liverpool.

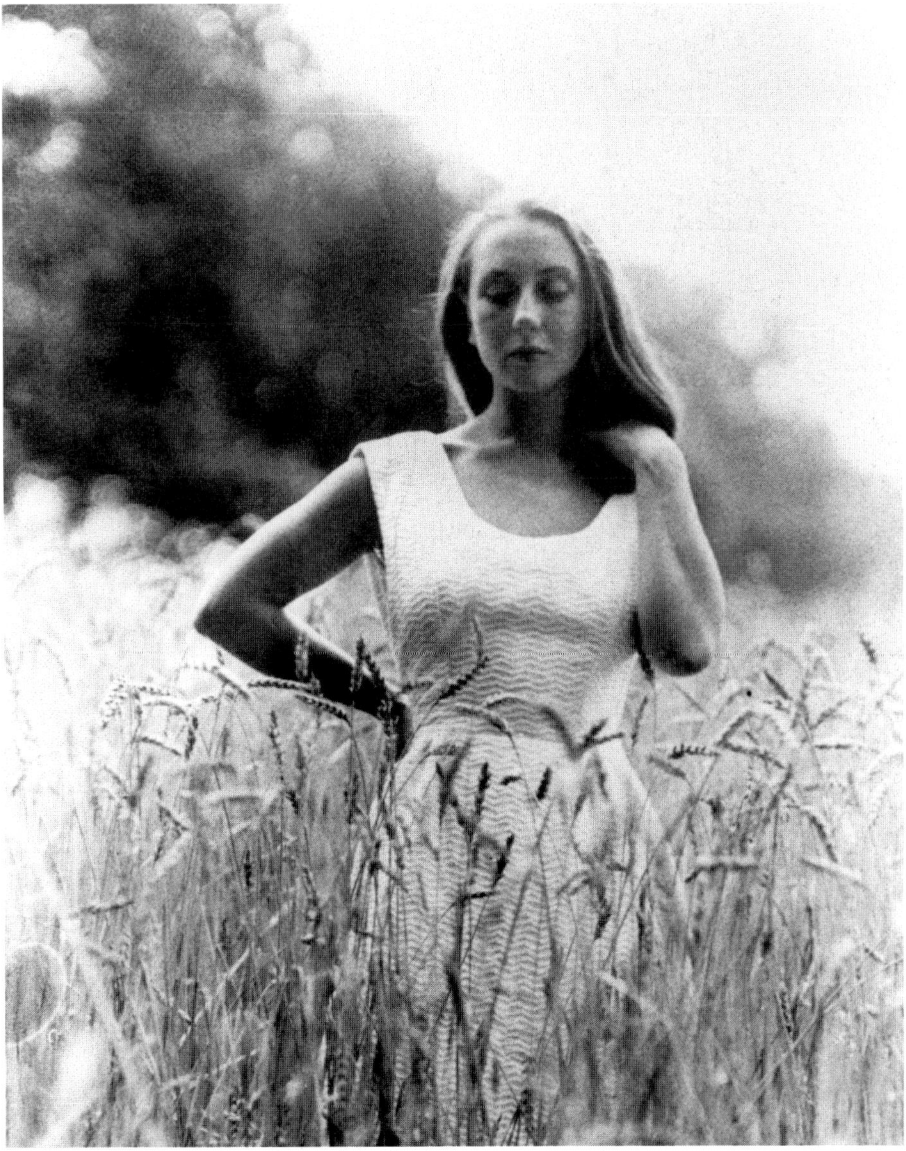
June, photographed by John Underwood, London.

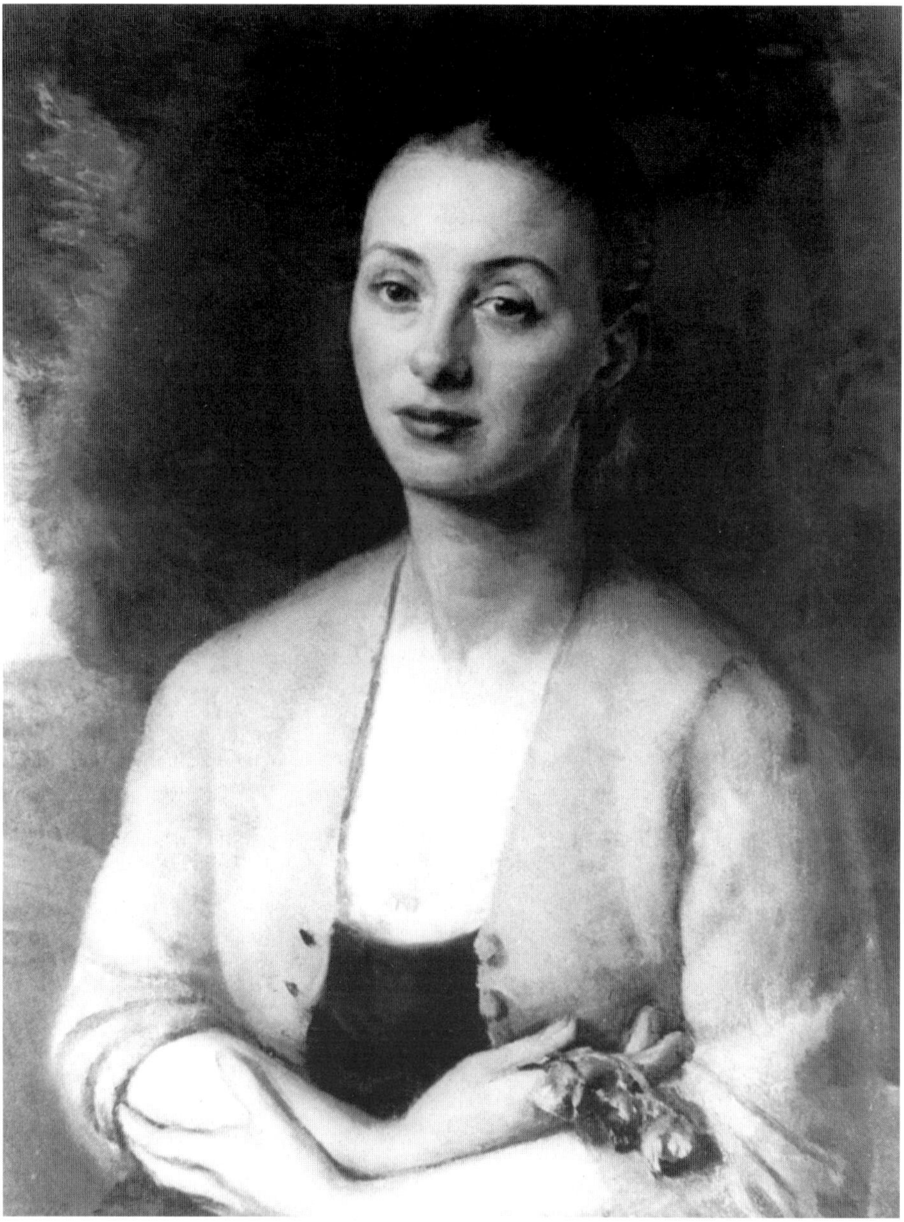

June Furlong, oil on canvas. Arnold Machin RA.

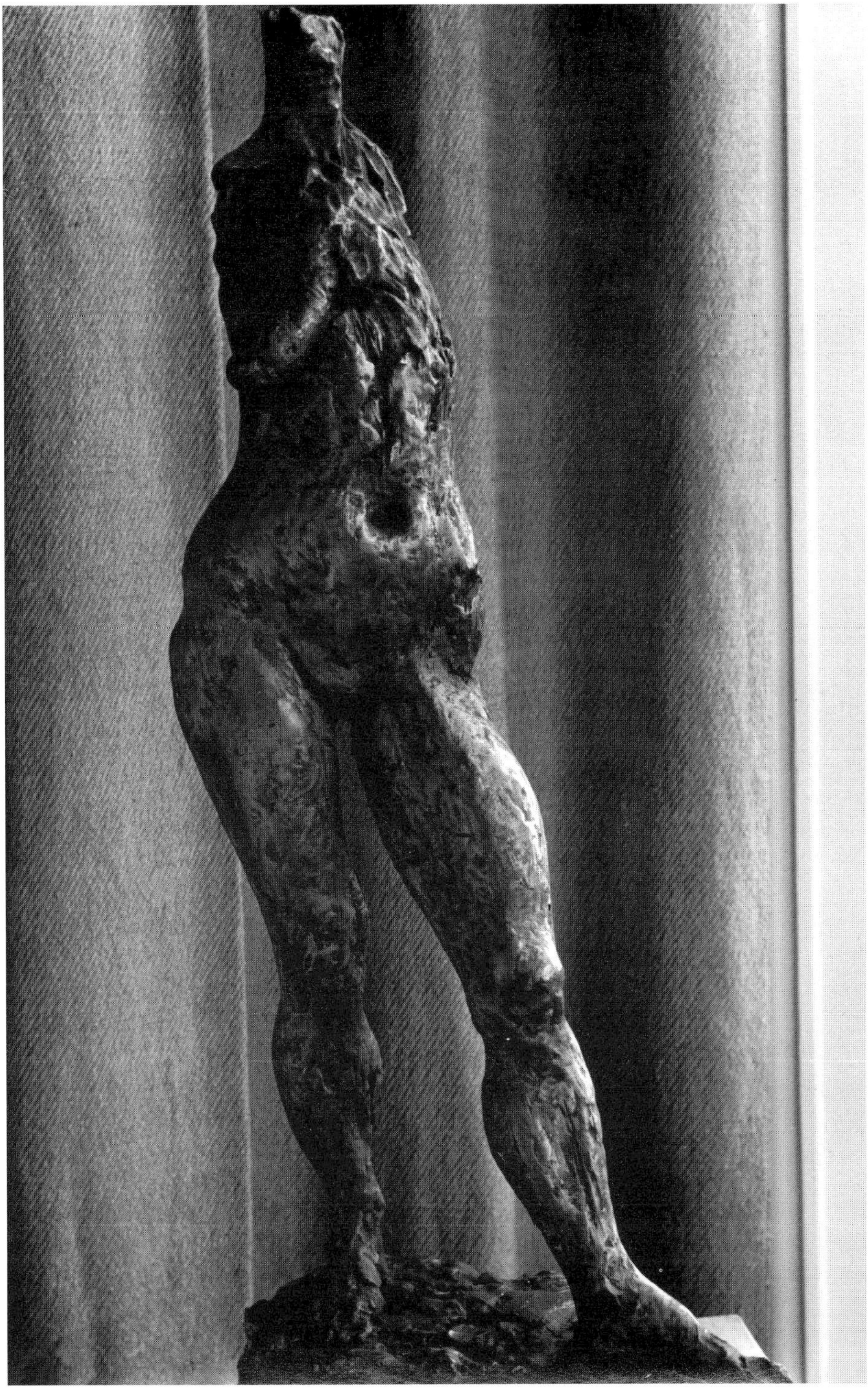

June Furlong, Sculpture Study, work in progress, Roger Dean, Sculpture Studio, Myrtle Street.

Mediterranean Visits

Before going to London in 1951, I travelled overland to Perpignan in the south of France. I started off hitching a lift, not something I would recommend today. I could not wait to get there. Life was an adventure and the underdeveloped post-war landscape held an enigmatic allure all its own. The grass on mainland Europe is different, the colours have an umber-like dryness to them, scorched and tinted in a golden hue by the strength of noonday sunlight. My journey was pleasant. I am reminded of the French visits of the Bloomsbury set, so familiarly described.

Life took on an altogether different pace. I was heading outward, bound away from the city of my birth, launched into the wider world. France was my first stop, and little did I realise that my annual sojourn in the Mediterranean would be such a refreshing and revitalising event. The hotel was in the Rue de la Cloche d'Or. The French were very warm and welcoming, and I became quite friendly with a local family.

I had saved hard to get to France, and spent all my money on the trip. I did not have any to pay for a fare back to London when it was time to return. I knew I had secured a place of work at the Slade for a three-week contract starting in September. I also knew that friends who worked at the Walt Disney studio in Wardour Street could put me up when I arrived in London.

My French friends Madame and Monsieur Mayneu turned out to be very kind, and invited me back for later visits. I managed to get there again with Gerry Worsley, the painter, who was to be another lost talent as he died quite young. We both went back the next year, and I knew that I was hooked.

After my French visits, I thought I would try Spanish life and hospitality. My first companion was Tom Landry and we went to Ibiza together. He was a London friend, who was a Maths student from Oxford, whom I met as part of a group of German acquaintances living in Hampstead. Tom and I hitchhiked through the Pyrenees in the days when a trip in a truck or lorry would not be seen as risky. We had coffee and cognac to keep awake. We would take the boat to Barcelona and then on to Ibiza. Travel was primitive and basic. Paying our way was difficult. We would sleep rough, eat when we could and save our cash to splash out without really thinking whenever we thought we deserved it. It was a carefree and happy time.

One year, I was visiting a café in Dean Street, London, called Casa Pepe. It was a Spanish restaurant where I got to know Pepe Solsana and his wife Maria. They had a restaurant in South Kensington that became one of my favourite eating houses. They were good friends from the London scene. I told them I was going to Spain and they suggested I visit their friend Santiago Soteras, who had nine restaurants in Barcelona and who, they felt sure, would give me a good welcome. Pepe gave me Santiago's address after contacting him and arranging for him to look after me. I made my way overland travel from London, then caught the Barcelona express.

Santiago's place was in the 'West End' of Barcelona, in calle Diagonale, which is the best part of the city, and here I was arriving in jeans carrying two casual zipper bags. I was sorted out by Rosita, the manageress, and shown to my room. She gave me a wonderful suite to use. I had intended to go to Ibiza quite quickly, but it was so luxurious and wonderful that I decided to stay for a bit, not thinking how I was going to pay for such a good room. It felt like the Dorchester of Barcelona. So I got out my grey silk dress, which I luckily had with me, and which looked very good, and thought that I might as well go out looking grand. I bought hand-made chocolates in the best areas of Barcelona as if I was made of money. I spent my days discovering the art galleries and learning to appreciate the different culture. I went everywhere, getting exactly what I wanted. I was still aiming to get to Ibiza, my original destination, especially as I knew my money would go further. Barcelona was expensive when compared with Ibiza, as the tourist area there was still relatively undeveloped. Nevertheless, I still bought more than I should, as there was so much that I liked.

Santiago Soteras had the most wonderful houses and land. He was infatuated with me, and took me all around Barcelona. It was marvellous. I left thinking I would get a big bill from the hotel. I said, 'Cheerio!' thinking, 'This has been fun,' but he wouldn't take any money at all. It was a great relief, as I was beginning to think I would be taking Shanks' pony back to Liverpool.

I eventually got to Ibiza, which was breathtakingly beautiful. I found I could get by and chat quite comfortably really for a novice. I used to get telegrams from Santiago saying that he had a place for me in Majorca, asking would I like to go for a weekend. He had been so kind in Barcelona that I decided to take the boat back to the mainland. I said my temporary goodbyes, leaving my Swiss coat and bag, intending to return in a day or two.

When I arrived by boat, he was waiting for me and we whizzed off to his place. He was a very wealthy man, owning farmland and property over a wide area. He had three houses as I recall, his, the staff house with maid, cook and gardener and a little guest house for me to use. He had only short holiday breaks himself but I stayed and stayed. His staff, Marguerite and Juan, were great and we had a private beach and pool. I thought it was all marvellous, but very lonely, and I was quite scared at night. There were the strange sounds of the country which were new to me. Spain was not commercial as it is today, with lots of comings and goings. I missed his company and although he wanted me to stay, I thought I would be too lonely without him as he was so busy in Barcelona. Although I did agree to spend my holiday there, a long-term commitment was too much to consider. I managed to see him when he could get away, and when we were together I enjoyed the lifestyle tremendously. He even came to Liverpool when I came home and met my parents.

I went to Madrid, Paris and London with him. He wanted to marry me but he was not really for me. I was not in love with him, and I enjoyed my freedom too much. I went everywhere in taxis, and was living very independently. Spain became a second retreat for me during the College holidays and I went back the following year, too. Santiago was a very jealous man and kept tabs on me all the time. He insisted on knowing what I did, where I went and to whom I spoke. It was all too much, I knew that I would not be able to stand it long, so one day I just left.

I called a taxi and, as I was way out in the country, I could only ask the driver to take me to somewhere good, cheap and clean where I could eat the food. He took me to a place called Hostal Gina where I was one of the first clients. It was a laugh from beginning to end. I went every year after that for about twenty-seven years until they closed up. I was their first client and their last. It was a small pension, full of fun people, German, French and English, with excellent food. It was before the age of package holidays, so there were never any 'tourists' in sight; only dancers and singers from the clubs who slept all day and appeared about six o'clock in the evening. They were all very theatrical or artistic in some way or another, which is probably why we all got along like a large and friendly family.

I went on to stay at the Hostal Borne, not far away, where I stayed regularly for some years. These days I stay five minutes from King Juan Carlos' palace Marivent, in Cala Mayor, and I see him depart each morning at 10 o'clock for the King's Cup, one of the most important events in the yachting calendar in the first week of August each year. All countries have a boat in the race, the locals usually win each of the night events, and celebrations carry on until dawn. I am made to feel very welcome every time I visit. I am always invited to the prestigious gallery owned by Senor Jose Pinya. Whenever there is a private view I am fortunate to be included. No expense is spared and champagne flows like water. As well as touring the exhibitions while I can, I spend my days taking a swim at about 4 o'clock.

I quite often recall when Santiago followed me hotfoot across Europe. He could not understand why I should just want independence, nevertheless, I did. I am pleased that we kept our friendship, though, that was important to me. I have stayed in touch with some of the people I met at that time. In particular, I remember Hotel Mediterreno and Senor Terrago, who looked like a big Spanish Winston Churchill. He invited me to have drinks with him and to use his hotel as a base. He was patron of the Ritz Hotel Barcelona, and I saw him each year I visited until he died some fifteen years ago. I was always made very welcome there. Sadly, the hotel has been converted into apartments. Lola Flores, the famous Spanish singer, lived there. The restaurant is still superb.

As I have mentioned, one of my regular pastimes is to visit the galleries. It is so enlivening to see the Spanish painters using their bold colours, sensuously and expressively. There is a certain vigour and vitality in their art. Senor Jose Pinya owns the best gallery in Palma, and I have become quite interested in a number of respected Spanish artists. On one occasion one of the great international artists was on exhibition, Joan Miro. He was born on the island of Majorca and fascinates me. I remember seeing him some twenty or so years ago, about eighteen months before he died. He had a retrospective exhibition in La Lonja, which was visited by the King of Spain. When I went into the exhibition, the first thing I saw were the outstanding paintings of Majorcan almond tree blossom. You could trace the development of Miro's art across time.

Another favourite is Anthoni Tapies, also held in extremely high esteem. I have seen Tapies' work in the Mediterranean area. His work is dramatic, the symbolism striking.

In Spain, the Bank of Spain often sponsors famous art exhibitions which means that money is available to enable high quality pieces to be shown. I look forward each year to the new treasures that await me on my visit and regret a similar lack of committed funding for art projects in Britain. I am invited to my old friend, Senor Pinya's private champagne receptions each summer. On the opening of his new gallery in Calle Can Veri, in Palma, which he had bought from the nuns, he had a Marlborough Fine Art gallery exhibition of international artists, including Freud and Auerbach, from London. Their paintings looked superb in the Mediterranean light. He as continued to stage a popular contemporary art show every August.

Every year I enjoy renewing acquaintances, seeing old friends and breathing fresh air in a lovely climate. The Mediterranean is my second home, leisurely drinks with George Jardine, John McFarland or Lionel Levey as the sun sets over the harbour is an ideal way to spend one's retirement. These are halcyon days indeed, which have a distant connection with my real home in Liverpool. There is an old tale which suggests that people who are born by the sea never really leave.

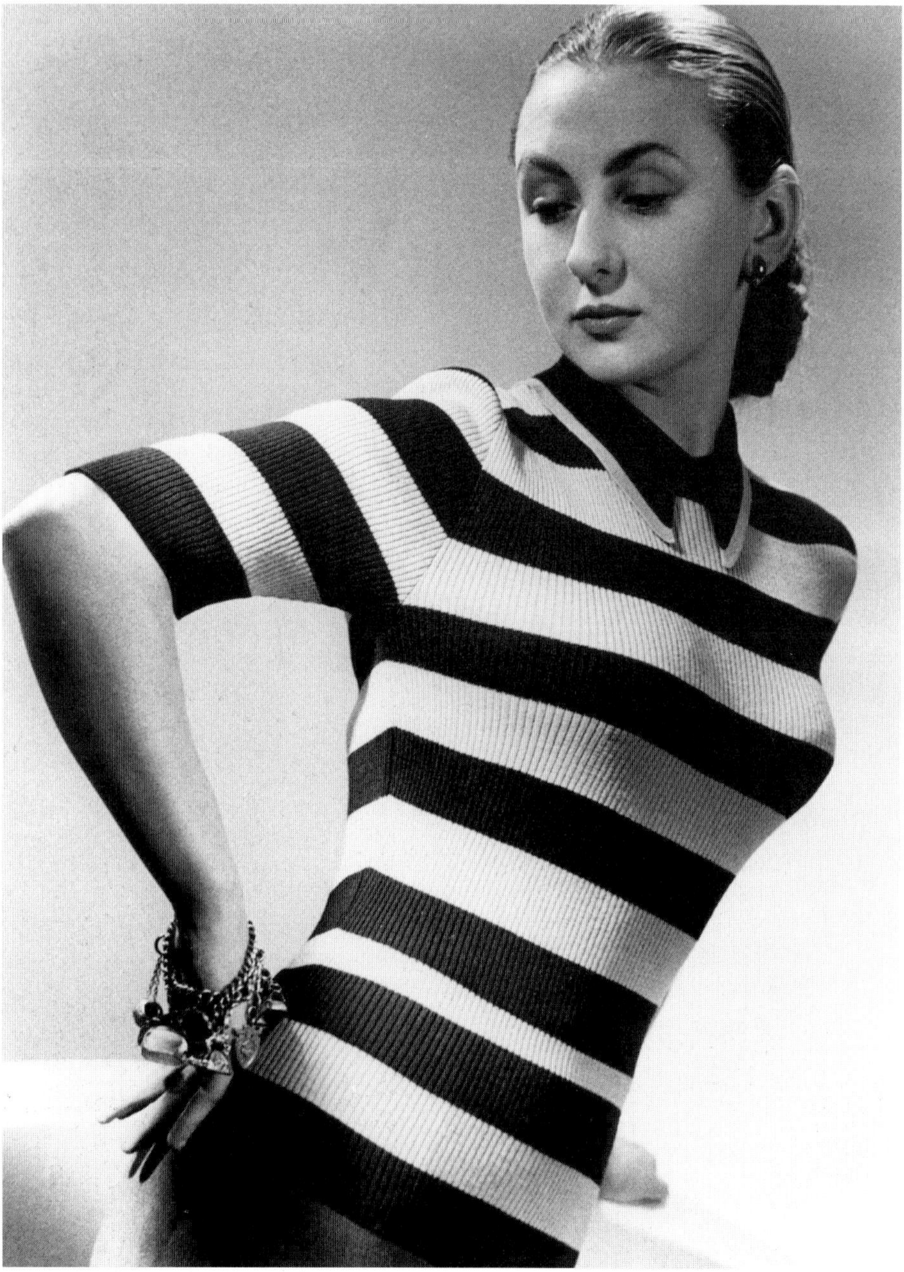

June Furlong, photographed by Ronald French.

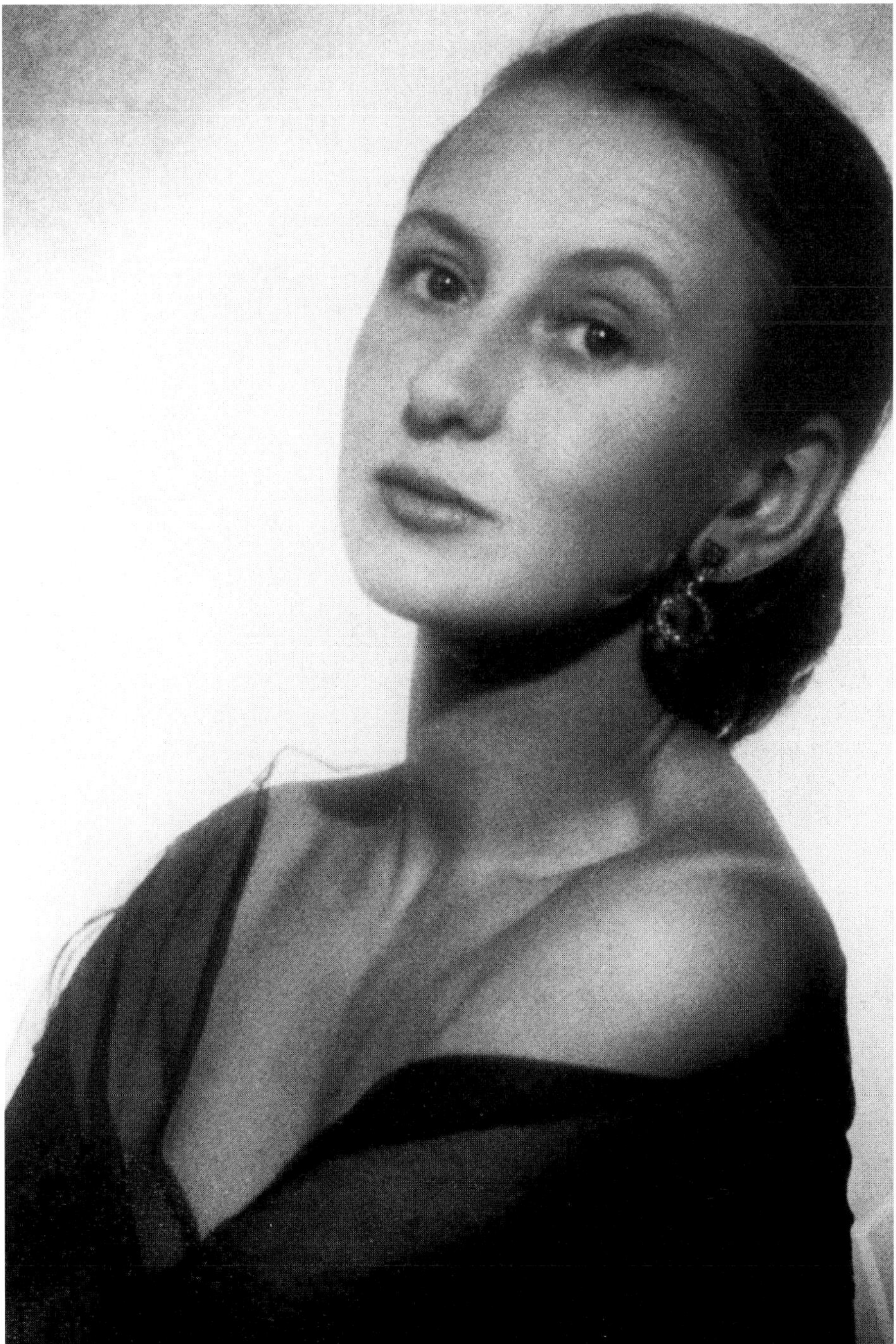
June, photographed by Bert Drake, Liverpool.

Full Circle – Back to Liverpool 1959-99

When I returned to Liverpool, things had moved on. Arthur Ballard was still in charge of foundation studies, but the students had changed in style and talent. There was freshness in the work that showed a mix of European academic discipline and the influence of popular culture and Americanisation of youth. Within a couple of years the content and interpretation of artistic form changed very quickly. The life class began to lose some of its formality as life drawing became an elective rather than a compulsory study option.

However, in Liverpool we were fortunate that we could keep a foot in both camps. The late 1950s and early 1960s kept in step with traditional academic discipline – I learned my craft with such discipline – and also became open-minded enough to take on new ideas. In the post-war years Martin Bell would teach painting in the studio on Tuesdays and Thursdays and the other days were drawing days. Bell was only an average painter, but had known Walter Sickert who was a friend of Degas. There was a solid structure and foundation to the School, but gradually the teaching relaxed as the culture of youth grew and students developed a more expressive and loose structure in their work. The graphics students were brought into the life room, then in the charge of Teddy Griffiths. Students were exposed to different concepts as design increasingly influenced art. Tutors who had received their own training in the national schools did try to emphasise the need for proficiency in drawing and copying skills in addition to innovatory and experimental work. Students showed their youthfulness by rebelling against the academic strictures that had been so prevalent the last time I was here.

The Art Schools were changing from the top down and from the bottom up. At the top, the framework was regrouping into a regional structure. From the bottom, the students were breaking new ground. By the time we reached the 1970s, the Regional College of Art had gone and the institution had become Liverpool Polytechnic, still with a substantially high-quality art department that I have since been told has proved far superior to other regional colleges. The foundation studies department was one of the first to use its models in a broader way. Initially I worked in the life room for about eight years non-stop. Then the models were allocated to work in all of the departments on a rota system which gave greater opportunities for students to work from life in disciplines that may not have previously been thought necessary. In 1969, Sue Lee, another good model, joined me but who had a different approach to her work. Three female models, me, Sue Lee and Marie Slott worked consistently, although I found my private work continued. There was an influx of talent into Liverpool, not just artistic but literary and musical as well as visual.

Liverpool was a great place to be from the 1950s and especially all through the 1960s. Much, of course, has already been written about the atmosphere and the beat scene. The many night-clubs were excellent and could compete easily with those of London. I had my own particular favourites and of course the background in music and dancing derived from Uncle Leonard gave me a passion for this type of socialising. We had great fun and the days seemed packed with activity. Even after a very hard day's work, we always had enough energy left to start again and carry on with the night life. Arthur Ballard thought I had an exotic social life and liked to congregate with the beautiful people. He was convinced that I knew everyone worth knowing in Liverpool. There was a great variety of music: R & B, jazz, tempo, slow blues and many live bands. Discos were unheard of then. The Blue Angel in Seel Street was a hugely popular place as was the Cabin Club, run by Mrs Winters. If I remember rightly, Jim Ireland's partner had won the football pools and opened the Pink Parrott club. Jim would regularly frequent the Adelphi Hotel, in those days the chic place to congregate. From there we would go to the Babalou Club.

Arthur Ballard believed that I was always where the action was. After the end of work at the College he could often be seen hurriedly dragging his coat over his arm, bustling to get the other arm in as he said 'Where are you off to now June? Don't mind if I come along do you?', as a group of us set off into town. One of the best commissions for a Liverpool artist to find was working on the artwork in the clubs, as the money was always good. The history of decoration of club and café society stemmed from the late nineteenth and early twentieth centuries, but has in the last fifteen years moved into the lap of design rather than fine art students. The students from the Royal College of Art in London and from the Liverpool College of Art in later years could earn money from painting the walls of various establishments, some of which are still visible in London and Liverpool clubland. There is a recently restored mural by John Lennon, Stuart Sutcliffe and Rod Murray in the Jacaranda Club.

Bob Percival ran the art department in Lewis's department store in Liverpool in the days when that firm had lots of money to run displays. Bob was dapper, he had a red beard and looked quite distinguished. I am not sure how he managed to get the contracts for the club artwork, but I do know that he painted club murals.

Early in the century in London artists such as Wyndham Lewis had decorated the interiors of London clubs. It would be interesting to make a comparison between their work and what was done in Liverpool. The Spencer mural in London could also be included. A good decoration creates the right atmosphere and so is important to a club's success. Nowadays, it would all be seen as a major part of the image-making exercise as a marketing tool and the designer would carry a huge budget. This is all far more formal than it was in the 1950s and 1960s.

I was particularly fond of Friday night in the clubs. Certain people in our group could drink most hardened drinkers under the table. We never had to pay to get in anywhere. I did not believe that membership nonsense, just turning up was enough for entry. Jim Ireland had the Pink Parrot club, also in Seel Street and a good club. We would finish the art class at about nine o'clock and then go to the Adelphi and on to clubland. At nine-thirty the next morning, regardless of what time I had got home, I would be back to work in the life class, fresh and ready to work. I was committed to my work as it was my career and I would never let anyone down – one hundred per cent reliability was expected from the models.

The Adelphi Hotel would serve a pot of coffee to you even at three o'clock in the morning. All the Jewish town boys would meet there. We were always made welcome. It was the place to be and had superb patrons.

The style in those days was to do the rounds of the clubs. People did not stay in one place, but would have a drink or two and then move on to the next place, until time ran out in the early hours. Such gatherings were important for making valuable contacts, as well as cementing a community of revellers. The clubs were much smaller than they are today and were always packed. An evening started with cocktails (an Orange Blossom if possible), when everyone would meet, then decide where to go. The local pub for the art students and staff was Ye Cracke, still going strong and the haunt of many a 'starving' artist.

One of the more avant garde clubs in Liverpool was the Masquerade, in Clayton Square. I used to go there with Eldon Worrall, the Liverpool antique auctioneer (now Dr Worrall). It was at that time an unusual club with a select clientele. My acquaintance with Quentin Crisp in London ensured that I could feel comfortable with all sorts of people of differing persuasions, such as gay men. The first time that Eldon and I went to the Masquerade we did not realise that it was a gay haunt.

Eldon and I were often looked at but not approached, which was just as well as some of the people looked like 'Bullring' types, the Bullring being a circle of flats that were behind Lime Street Station. This was a really rough area where, if you did not belong, you would stand out a mile and be at considerable risk. It was by its nature poor, with sharp reminders of the old tenement houses in Liverpool that had housed immigrants, usually from Ireland, before they established themselves in the city and found something better. Life in the Bullring was hard and cut-throat. However, not everyone there was bad, but could best be described as sharp.

The manager of the Masquerade club fascinated both Eldon and me, as he tottered around in his double-breasted suit with a phoney European accent, sporting Cuban-heeled shoes, and his hair dyed a cheap jet black. One of the barmen, recently beaten up in a bottle fight, wanted to be friendly with Eldon. The chap insisted on sitting at the table with us much to the annoyance of Eldon, who asked: 'It's OK visiting this exotic place but must I have to sit next to these people?' It could be described as hair-raising fun, that feeling of being in the crowd but at the same time breaking ground by pushing on the regular social boundaries.

Our other wily activity was a poker school. If I play poker I play to win, and if I am alert and awake I am capable of doing just that. I had a friend called Arthur Rose, who was a mild-mannered gentleman. He was an art student, a very smart fellow and reasonably well heeled. He was a pal of Matthew Calderwood from Liverpool University and who had connections with the Playhouse. They used to set up card schools with some tough Liverpudlians. Arthur at one point wanted to move new-found yobbo friends into his flat in Rodney Street. Unfortunately, he was naïve and liked people a lot, so would be taken for every penny he had.

Arthur's flat was next to Olivers the jewellers, and he shared with a 'county' chap, from the racing world, landed gentry or such-like. He would visit Liverpool on business. Arthur actually moved the awful 'friends' in, then went to pieces when he realised what he had done. A nervous person and anxious in public, he could not even get on a bus, so had to use taxi-cabs all of the time. When the friends appropriated the flat, Matthew Calderwood went to see Arthur but he could not get in. Matthew realised that action needed to be taken as Arthur would not be able to carry on living there. He arranged for Arthur to be taken into Winwick Hospital for help. Matthew then went to evict the friends, but this proved impossible.

I must have been tough and fearless in those days. I decided that the only way to deal with such people was to act as tough as they thought they were. I went in single-handed and said, 'Listen, I know the law with regard to mental conditions, and that you have no right to be here at all. I will have you arrested if you are still here when I come back.' I suggested that they all leave straight away. They had all flown by one o'clock the next day. After that episode Arthur's father took control, settled his son's debts and took him back to Wales, never to be seen again. Arthur looked like a broken-down theatrical in the end, really tragic.

By 1960, I had begun to suffer ill health. I had three attacks of viral flu in one year and became gradually worse over the year. I had originally felt ill on my return from Majorca, it started in the September. Ulrich West and I were going out at the time and we had been to Exchange Flags station after a visit to Hightown on the train. I was dizzy and sick. When I got home I left my taxi and took straight to my bed and stayed there for about two weeks.

My uncle was at home then. I was hot one minute, cold the next and could not eat anything at all. Dr Lipkin came to visit when I was apparently hallucinating. I was sweating and delirious, so within two hours the specialist Mr Gowe was called from Rodney Street. He said that I was to be moved to Mossley Hill Hospital immediately. I was diagnosed as having a kidney stone which had to be removed as a matter of urgency. My temperature had settled at 103 F.

I had some logical thought left. I thought my career would be over as I would have a large scar, and during the operation the surgeon had some difficulty in removing the stone. In recovery I did not make a very good patient. I was used to a jet-set lifestyle, and although I was forced to rest it was not the same as being still when posing. I was bored, missing out on the fun and atmosphere of the life class. The illness did have a great effect on me, though. One quiet day, after a party, while I was drinking gin and Dubonnet and my usual brandies, I decided to change my lifestyle. I was out every night, working all day, out at six o'clock, doing night classes, going on to meet friends for cocktails. I needed to take stock and protect my health, it was important to me. At thirty years of age I had spent the last thirteen living life in the fast lane. It was sensible to shift down a gear and maybe try the middle lane for the time being.

Liverpool in the 1950s still had most of the consulate offices. As it was a successful trading port and had continued its links particularly with America, the American consul's office was quite active. In the nineteenth century it had been housed in Abercromby Square (now the University of Liverpool). It was at No.19, where visitors are able to view the beautiful decoration still in place. Paintings on the ceiling show the slave trade connections with Liverpool: scenes of plantations and considerable wealth, painted in rich colours. A visit helps one to understand how important Liverpool was on the world stage.

Another consulate that became familiar to my friend Kay McEvoy and myself was the Peruvian. One of the diplomats had his own suite at the Adelphi Hotel. Kay looked exotic, with long black hair. I introduced them and they hit it off instantly. It worked out so well that we could eat on the house at the Adelphi, at his invitation and on his account. We had a great time and used every opportunity to live the good life. Kay and I used to laugh, not too unkindly, as our friend was quite old; we used to say that he was probably embalmed.

He used to have to fast one day each week. We did not have to fast, though, so we would all go into the French restaurant; he would not eat anything, but would still pick up the tab.

Kay and I remained friends for a long time.

After I had been back in Liverpool for about two years, one of the striking students I first met was John Lennon. He used to come for a day's life drawing into the very large art studio, Room 78 at the end of the top corridor in the main building. He would be with the rest of his group: John Haigh, Tony Carrricker, Jeff Mohamed, Ann Mason and June Harry as well as other students. John seemed to take to me immediately. He always included me in the conversation and usually asked my opinion on what he was attempting to persuade his group to do. I always responded positively, as it was not much use offering vague ideas that had no substance. Most of the time he was asking me about life in London or what it was like to mix with the rich and famous. He was determined to make a mark. In the early years, his mark was expected to be art. He had a basic talent for representational line drawing, but he was more attracted to performance.

John was always trying to get his friends to visit the theatre with him. This was still the age of twice-nightly variety shows at the Empire Theatre and The Pavilion (now a bingo hall) especially if Liverpool's own comedian Rob

Wilton was on the bill. The group usually pleaded lack of cash, but John, with his teasing and tormenting or pushy self, found they usually went along with him. He generally got his own way. Everyone knew they'd have a good time in the end. The next day (I could not normally go to the shows with them as I had to work three evenings a week and Friday at the Bluecoat Studios), he would be full of the show telling all Rob Wilton's jokes and doing a perfect impersonation of him.

I like all the good Liverpudlian humour; it mirrors and mocks life. Rob Wilton's records could always cheer everyone up. The most famous Liverpudlian comedian, Ken Dodd, was still a door-to-door salesman in the early 1960s, still to make the big time. Doddy played the working-men's clubs, which much later caused his much-publicised trouble with the tax man, as he was paid in cash on the night – usually very well, I might add. I also remember John talking about the comedian Stan Boardman, who was starting to get his act together. He is another Liverpool natural well-known today from his many television appearances and charity work.

Stan is a friend of Mike McGeer, Paul McCartney's brother, who went on to be part of The Scaffold pop group. Morecame and Wise were often at the Empire and were also much appreciated by John. John Lennon enjoyed all the theatrical and performing arts. He watched others develop their style, 'show' personalities or star qualities. He always wanted to know exactly what I had been doing in London, who I knew and which contemporary artists' work I preferred. He asked about their interests, their work, lifestyles and associations, having a craving for star quality in everything.

John knew that he could achieve his goals, and was prepared to work hard to achieve them. His writing of poetry displayed another side.

Paul McCartney was next door at the Liverpool Institute for Boys. The school is now the Liverpool Institute for Performing Arts. Paul was a serious sixth former, who had a very musical father but who himself only played for fun. Coffee breaks at 11.00am saw John going round to see Paul to persuade him to do something or other. I am absolutely certain that if John had not been asked to leave the Regional College of Art for disrupting the organisation there would not have been the world-famous Beatles. At the college he used to be quite rebellious and loud. His family was middle-class and John had this overwhelming desire to do something himself, to be somebody. He really did not seem to want what his family circle could provide. His mother had died when he was still quite young and his aunt brought him up.

John used to visit Nems in Whitechapel. This was a record shop, the boss of which was Brian Epstein, and as a student, John also went to the Cavern Club; I used to go but was not impressed with its cobble stone floor and the boiling hot sweat that drenched the place. It had a very peculiar fire exit and a narrow stairway to the basement. It was eventually improved to regulation standards but in the early sixties it was the most popular beat place in the city and in a very raw state indeed. It was quite some time before John and the

Silver Beatles (as they were originally called) could get a slot at the Cavern, and there were lots of smaller gigs that the band would have to do first.

John would have achieved great success in any performing capacity. He was very theatrical and had a feminine side to him that contrasted sharply with his outgoing rebel youth persona. John decided one day to put on a pantomime version of Cinderella in the College's basement canteen. June Harry was to be in it. He wrote, or re-wrote, the whole thing. Jeff Mohamed was one of the ugly sisters, John was the other. He asked for my assistance with the clothes. So I dug deep into my grandmother's ottoman and came up with a pair of large pink laced corsets, a navy flowered silk dress, a couple of lovely hats, a long pair of earrings and super Victorian bathing suit, the top half black, the bottom half bright orange. I have a photograph of my grandmother coming out of a bathing machine wearing it.

John was delighted with all this. He told me John Chase from the graphics design department would play Prince Charming; the only straight part in the whole play. Chase was a graphics student whose mother had been one of the original Bluebell girls at the Paris Lido. The only snag was that Chase, as I recall, did not want to do the play.

Well, John Lennon's power of persuasion succeeded. He went to a dress hire company in Liverpool's Bold Street to hire a theatre costume, coming back with the most beautiful stuff, including long pale green silk tights and brocade tunic all of it very rich looking and impressive. When John Chase saw it he agreed to join in. June Harry had a very long, pink satin night-dress affair for Cinderella. Jeff Mohamed wore the orange and black bathing suit belonging to my grandmother. The first night of this unique Liverpool theatrical event gave a glimpse of John's usual standard of musical performances. He had written poems about all of the teaching staff and set them to music which he then sang, with the help of a large microphone. They were always very funny and accurate. Our Cinderella, June Harry, was a mixed-race Liverpudlian, sister of Bill Harry, producer of his own Mersey Beat Music Echo newspaper. She had a huge mop of frizzy hair (later in the 1970s to become high fashion), and in the enormous pink nightdress she was quite a vision.

Everything was going well. John Chase looked superb and had really got in the mood, word-perfect and serious. All of the others forgot their lines and June Harry had got terribly drunk before the show started, much to John's dismay, but she kept staggering on stage saying what she was supposed to say. Someone mentioned that a Canadian boyfriend of June's had suddenly arrived. He said: 'Hello June, great to see you.' 'Oh, is that right?' she retorted, in a complete alcoholic stupor. Then, she punched him on the nose, declared the pantomime no good and went off to get the bus home like a ship in full sail. She was last seen queuing for a Number 86 bus in Catharine Street in the huge pink satin nightdress and attracting quite a stare from the general public. John Lennon was astounded, but everyone thought it was a storming finale.

John returned the costume materials to me at my house, all except the Victorian bathing suit. Later, all the clothes were sold at auction at Sotheby's and at Eldon E Worrall & Co.'s auction rooms. Included was some sheet music, Red Sails in the Sunset, a favourite piece of my grandmother's who liked to play the piano. John liked it, too, as it was the signature tune of Suzette Tarri; a famous professional comedienne of the day.

Some months later John said to me on a visit to the life class, after an encounter with Brian Epstein: 'This fellow wants to manage us, what do you think?' I said: 'Well, what have you got to lose?' John liked that and burst out laughing, and said: 'Yes, right, what have we got to lose, not a lot'. In those days the big time was not even on the horizon. He brainwashed Paul McCartney into turning professional by convincing him it was going to the best thing they ever did.

In April 1995 I was contacted to play a part in a film about John Lennon. The programme makers were German and the project was intended for German television. Their researchers had established that Helen Anderson, fashion designer, along with Pam Bancroft and myself could all recount memories of working at the college when John was a student there. The three of us and twelve of the best students available spent a fascinating time re-enacting our past lives. We reckoned the directors of the German television show must be the only people who had worked with the original players. All the other films and television reports have used actors to play the main characters. We, of course, thoroughly enjoyed ourselves, being transported back over thirty years. Mind you, this time around we had full wardrobe, drapery, make-up and hairdressing facilities.

The recreation of the life room, room 78, was very well done, although reconstructed in appearance. It was far cleaner than it would have been in reality. We could not help thinking that it was a bit of a laugh when you recalled those times. That is not to say that the life class was not taken seriously, just the opposite. In my experience the life class was more like a clinic with all the students and proficient artists trying to get their drawings and paintings looking good as well as technically proficient.

My own part in the film was simply playing myself, posing for the required study. I gathered that some of John's drawings of the time were going to be superimposed on to the screen. It would be more fast-moving, the way television approaches everything nowadays. The television programme could not capture the camaraderie, because John himself was no longer with us. Nevertheless, the important thing was that memories of John's time in Liverpool were being recorded. The essence of what he was, and of what Liverpool meant, was captured for posterity. He must have been greatly influenced by his experiences during that most impressionable time.

I had assigned the memories of John's friend, Stuart Sutcliffe, to the corners of my mind. Memories were brought back only when an early acquaintance would reminisce, usually about John, and then about Stuart because of the tragedy that surrounded him. It was as if the memories of both

John and Stuart were the strings of a kite, snapped off in the excitement of a heady wind to leave everyone sad or disappointed. Stuart's originality as an artist was very dear to him. His studies of the nude are characterful yet faceless, with many strokes of the pencil capturing the image. His non-representational work is unique and the colours have a suppressed vibrancy as if waiting to burst forth. The recently published biography from Genesis has done a splendid job in presenting Stuart as a talented artist.

My own memories of Stuart begin around 1958-59 soon after my return to Liverpool. His absolute commitment to his work immediately springs to mind. Stuart was one of the first students to recognise that my role was important. He always requested a standing pose, my hands clasped behind my back which he coined the June pose. This is the pose with which I have since become synonymous. The works of Stuart's that appear in his biography illustrate this pose along with others.

He would come in quite often by himself, with his large drawing board whenever I was in the studio, even on Saturday mornings, and would concentrate on his artwork. Stu (as John Lennon called him) would join a group of architects sent over from the University of Liverpool for art appreciation with our teacher Charles Burton. Charlie encouraged Stu to come in and join the class, if he could find a space and could be quiet. I think this was said looking over his shoulder, as Stuart was a friend of John Lennon. As I have mentioned earlier, John was well known for disorganising everything that was organised. Charlie would want to make sure that Stuart was there to work. As a result, the lovely inheritance that Stuart Sutcliffe has left are the super drawings, mostly of me. He said that I was his favourite model, as I could match his determination and concentration for as long as he felt necessary to produce a piece of work. Stuart could work tirelessly until he was satisfied. It helped that I was experienced and could appreciate the difference between those students who simply plodded along to their National Diploma and those who strove for success and who wanted to make a difference to art.

One of the ways to ensure the physical fitness needed for successful modelling is to have regular massage. I had a friend called Barry Nathan, a Jewish businessman in Liverpool and an avid collector of Sam Walsh paintings. Barry knew Bill Williams, a masseur with a consulting room in Rodney Street. I met them both when I was 17 when I would rush along during my lunch break or sometimes at four o'clock. I found that massage helped to combat the muscle fatigue that accompanies standing for long periods of time. I managed to have a massage at least every two weeks throughout my career, but whenever possible I would fit it in weekly. I would try to stand in front of a sun ray lamp to help to keep an even body colour and light tan, which always gives a sense of well-being. Bill moved premises to Mount Pleasant before emigrating to Australia in 1971 and I had to find an alternative.

Eventually, Bill came back to Liverpool and carried on keeping me in tip-top condition. He also became masseur to the city's football teams and would often say that the players wouldn't listen to him. They would not rest when they should, and would eventually come a cropper. I am grateful to Bill, for he got to know the particular pressure spots that were overworked when posing. His skill, I am sure, prevented me from suffering from varicose veins, the most common ailment in jobs that require sustained standing.

In 1995 I met Steve Goff and his wife Sandra. They have premises in Bold Street and have continued to be my masseurs since Bill died. It used to cost about £2 a visit with Bill, now it is around £10-15. Massage is to be highly recommended as it keeps a good skin tone for one's age and is, therefore, a good investment.

Back at work in the life room it would be all eyes concentrating on the task in hand. New students nervously starting their drawings, not knowing what they were to do, slightly apprehensive about asking. The early days of term were always exciting. Opinions and judgements often made in the first few days were accurate. Those students who were going to make the grade seemed to be that little bit more interested and committed – keen to carry on with their work beyond the normal classes. I remember Doug Harker arriving as a schoolboy; his local claim to fame is having designed the famous Yorkie chocolate bar wrapper with John Baum. Arthur Ballard would set up drawing tests in the main building in Hope Street. I would come in, take up a standing pose, dressed, and the youngsters would be required to draw me. Doug drew me and was accepted into the college. Eventually he became a successful teacher in foundation studies and had very high success rates from his own students, working under John Baum who had taken over from Arthur Ballard after Arthur retired.

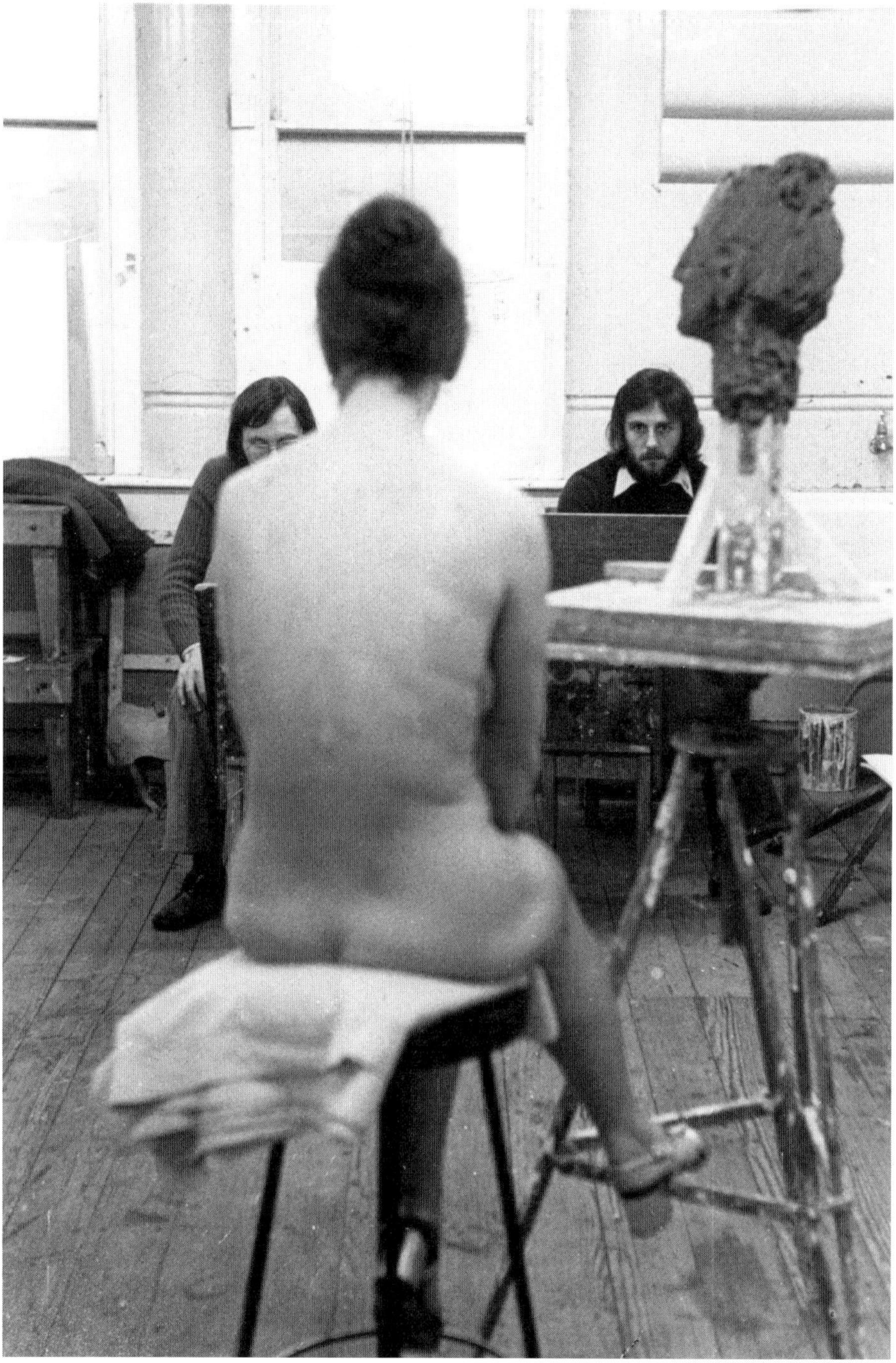

June, being drawn by Dave Shiers.

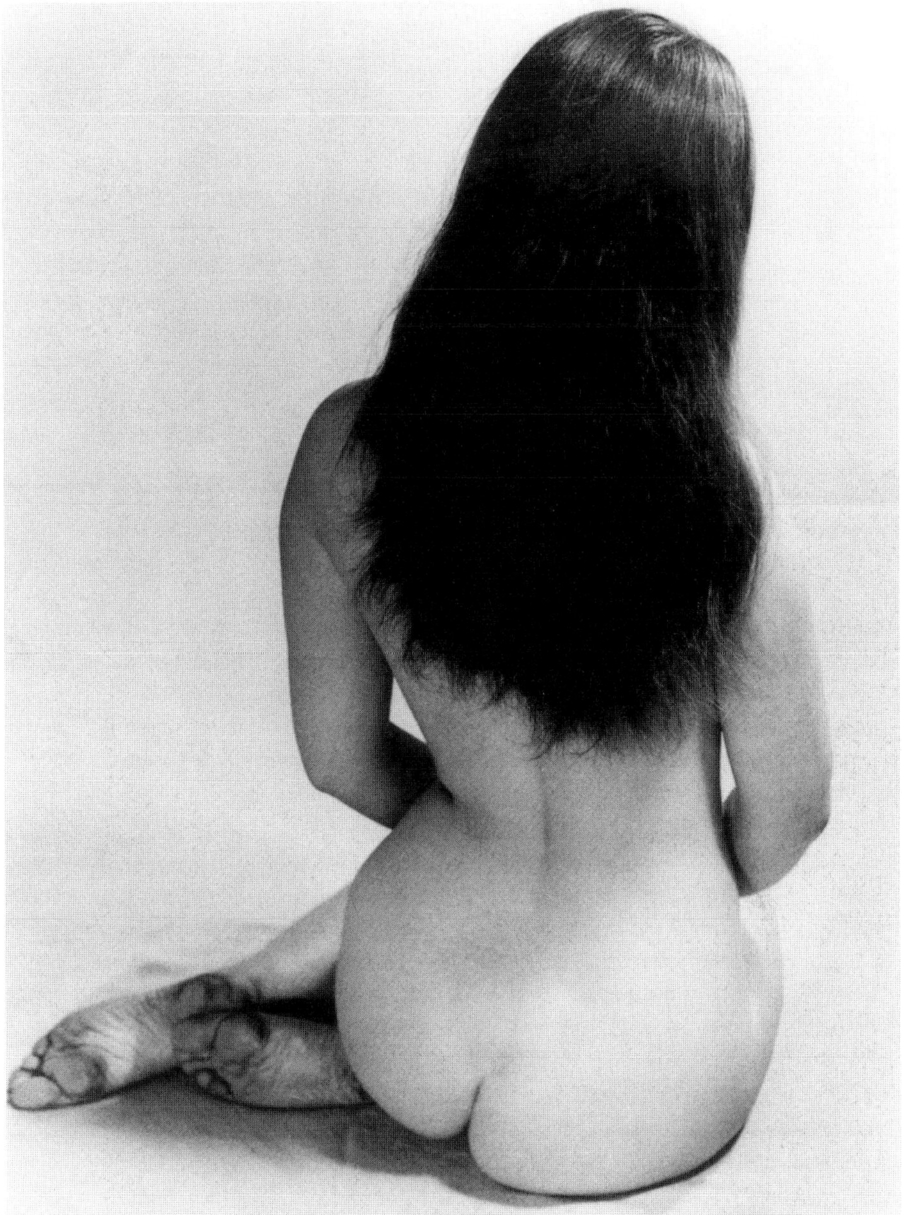

June Furlong, life size photograph by Bert Drake for Andrew Collinge hair dressers.

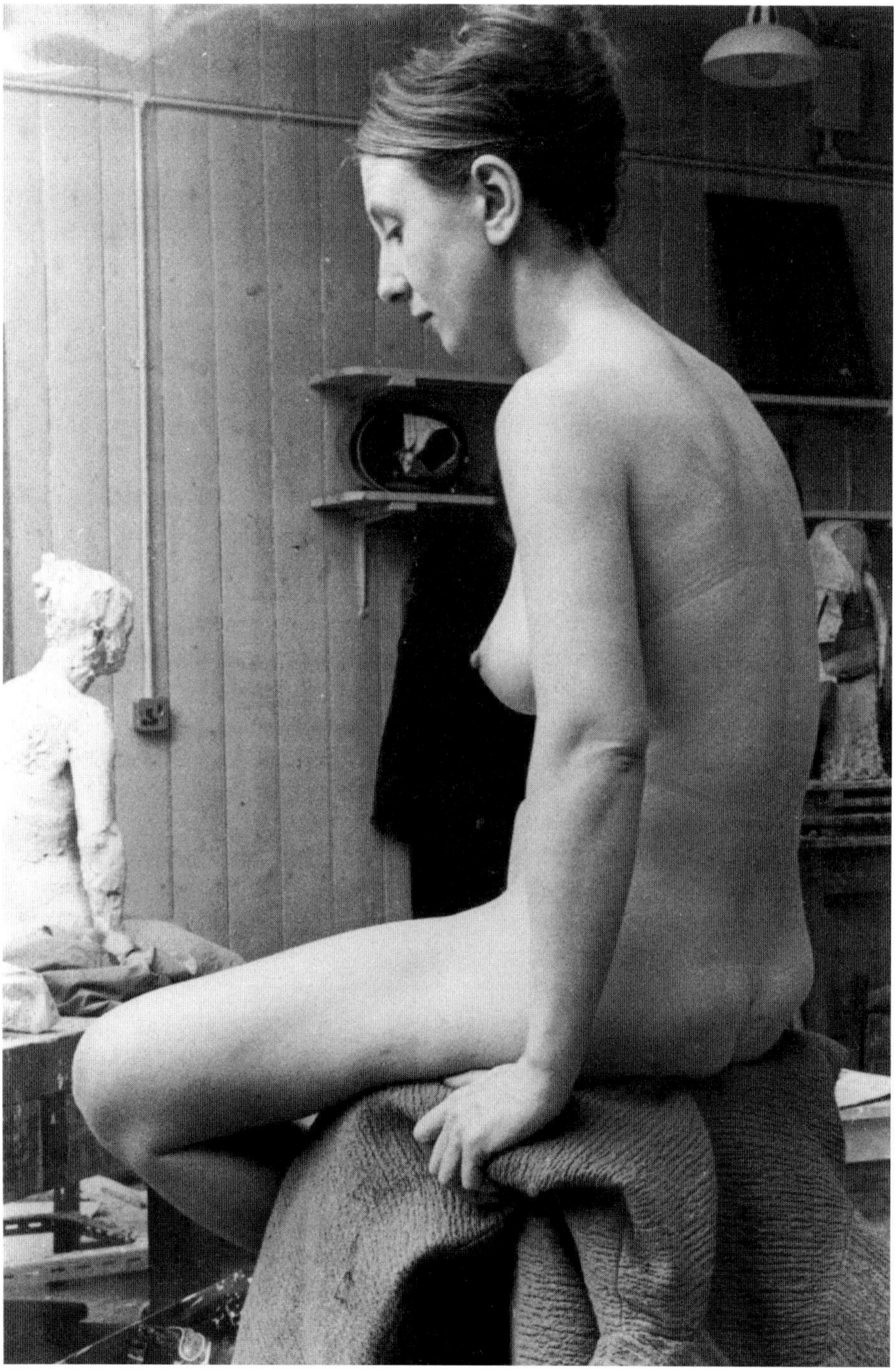

June posing in the sculpture Studio.

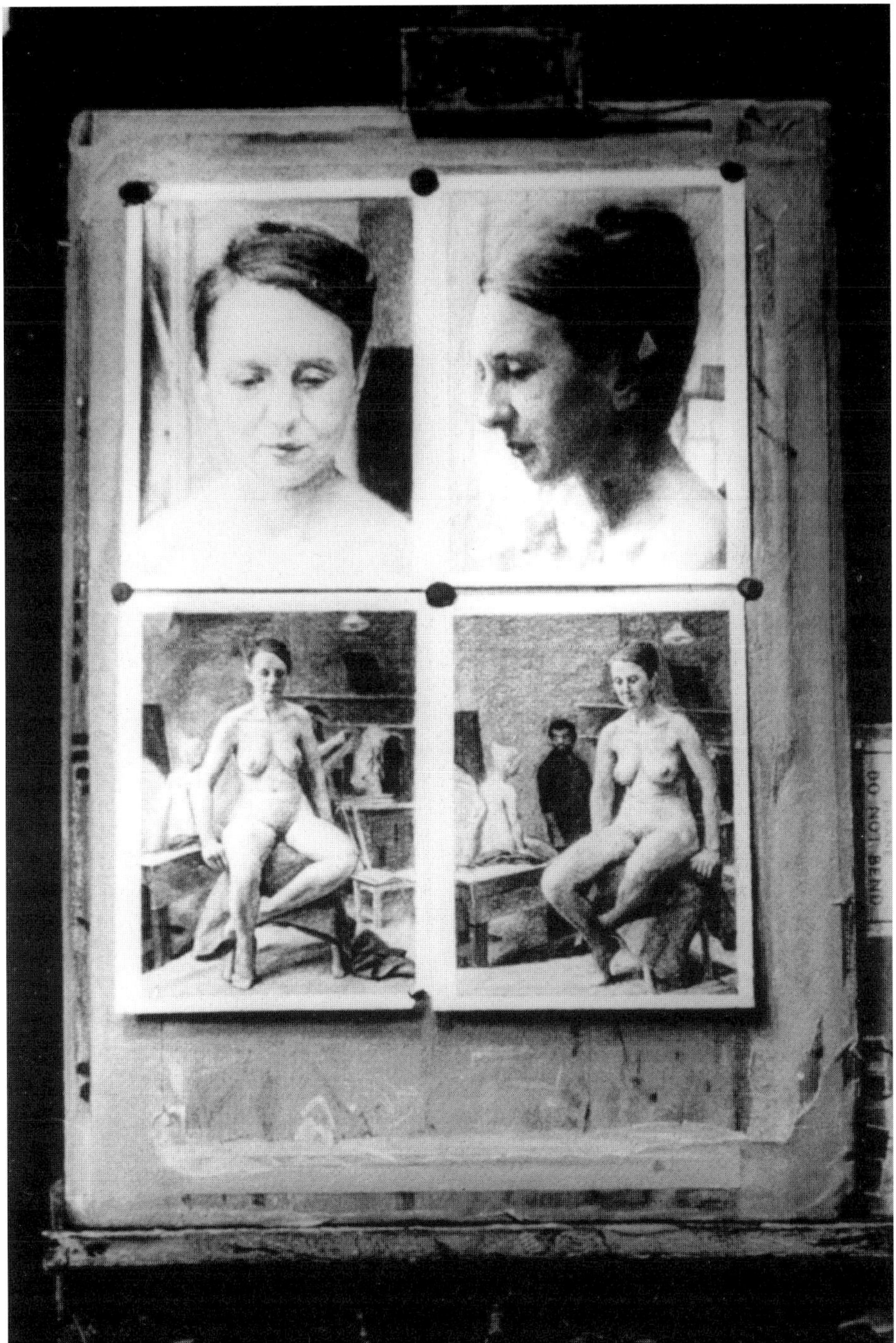

Painting the Photographed Pose, Geoff Yeomans.

The Artists

This has been the most difficult chapter to write. There are so many people who have special places in my memory. I have estimated that at least 25,000 pairs of eyes have studied me over the course of my career to date. In foundation studies at Liverpool, the intake was usually 98. Not many students fell by the wayside and dropped out. Over the years, this alone must have amounted to very nearly 5,000 students, without including all the other classes. In my London years, I was working at all the colleges and private classes, which considerably increased my exposure.

I have great respect for the artists who came to Liverpool and stayed: Sam Walsh, John Baum, Adrian Henri, Peter Mousdale, Jim Weston, all did a marvellous job at the foundation studies department of the Polytechnic. Maurice Cockrill is an artist I greatly admire, not just for his considerable ability but as a person. Mike Knowles, another wonderful artist, has an excellent drawing of me by Peter Prendergast. Maurice has several line drawings of me by Arthur Ballard. I have found that artists regularly collect each other's work.

After much deliberation, I have decided to record the major Merseyside artists in the form of biographical notes. Many of their pieces have been sold through my exhibitions and are now in the public domain or have private provenance.

I will begin with the students whom Arthur Ballard favoured. Peter Mousdale was a student who trained at Canterbury, achieved honours in his Art Teacher's Diploma in Liverpool and went on to a successful career in teaching, eventually as head of foundation studies. At that time he used to enthuse about the natural rhythm and grace of my poses. I expect my skating days helped considerably as I was able to shift my weight and move around at the same time, but with a certain style. He was enthusiastic and helped his students to see art as something that is not a static activity. Peter realised, along with Ray Fields, that movement should appear in graphics. To his credit, about 95% of his students won success in their first choice of further study. He was relentless in his commitment to Liverpool Polytechnic. He would regularly travel to other colleges to look at the work of their students, and on his return he would ensure that Liverpool students were kept up to date with national standards and often improved on them. This aspect of art education is often overlooked in research into artistic tradition and development. The sheer hard work and dedication of the organisational structure and funding are essential to create an environment in which students can work and develop.

Peter's dedication is one of the reasons why Liverpool's artistic development has been so successful when compared with other regions. As the city's history shows, we have always been outward-looking and our art is no exception. After Arthur Ballard had retired, Peter took over until the political wrangling over education funding meant that he spent more of his time fighting to keep the college open than in developing good artists. He once said to me that he seemed to spend most of his life on the train between London and Liverpool. He left to work in New Zealand, but we hope to see him in the city again some day.

Another of the teachers, Maurice Cockrill, had great personal success while his students also achieved their targets. Eventually Maurice forfeited his teaching career to concentrate on developing his own art. Seizing the opportunity, he moved to London in 1982. Maurice was much more prominent as an artist in Liverpool than many of his contemporaries. He was instrumental in forming the artist enclave of young radicals at the police station, The Bridewell. The project provided an opening-cum-studio/gallery space for new artists who wanted to strike out, away from the traditional academic strictures that bound their progress. For people outside Liverpool, knowledge of the Bridewell stemmed from the later television programme Boys from the Blackstuff, when 'Giz a job' Yozzer Hughes strides across the screen with the Bridie in full view as the backdrop. Not only was it appropriate to the plot but it was also symbolic of the quandary that contemporary artists faced, artists of all disciplines whether painters, sculptors, writers or whatever. A coming together of such talent made the place electric. I was on the outside of this particular project, as I was committed to the Polytechnic training. Nevertheless, the artists who collaborated in running the Bridie had come through our development process and it was tremendous to see them achieving so much.

Cockrill has now been in London over twenty years. He often says that I encouraged him to 'go for it' in the early years. He has a tremendous graphic facility and painted in Liverpool in a fashionable style, parallel to photo-realism. He produced realistic views of buildings, landmarks and landscapes in his early years. The University of Liverpool owns a great number of Cockrill's paintings, including Entrance, in acrylic on canvas. It is, as far as I know, his last photo-realist piece and is the ultimate example of that particular style, produced at that particular time, around 1973. By 1982 he had changed his style completely after moving south to London. He adapted the influence of Paul Nash and Ivon Hitchens and became expressionistic, mixing the two inspirationally in his output, and achieved considerable success as a result. His work contained an aggressive disquiet. The force of his use of colour squelches from the canvas, violent reds and powerful blues. From about 1988-89 Cockrill matured in style and his work appeared to be more thoughtful. Still expressive and loosely worked, his palette has softened and blended to a greater degree and became set, often, against a plain ground into more works of abstraction as he moved through the 1990s.

His contemporary, Mike Kenny, is another Liverpool-born who has moved his career on to the international circuit. He has lectured in America and latterly based himself in London, lecturing at the Slade and Goldsmith's as well as being Treasurer of the Royal Academy. He was a student at the

Liverpool College of Art in the 1960s and was part of the blossoming talent that the city has produced. Kenny is a widely acclaimed sculptor who has defied the tendency towards bulbous abstraction and instead concentrated on developing a linear style using hard materials. Multi-media artistic influences are few; perhaps Giacometti and Zen rock gardens. His wider influences are many: he has drawn on mathematics, religion, symbolism, alchemy to broaden his work. Kenny is not a derivative of any other style or artist; 'doing his own thing', he developed his drawing skills while at Liverpool, was accepted by the Slade earlier than most and began to fashion his individual style while in London. His sculpture is pictorial and he draws and paints as well. He mixes his images and his figures have no features. His painting has an existential feel and a sense of the loneliness of the figure. I would very much like to see a sculpture of Mike's purchased for the city. During the 1998 travelling exhibition of his work, I was fortunate to visit the West of England Academy in Bristol where it was shown to good effect.

Although Liverpool has a rich collection of sculpture there has been a cessation of public monumental sculpture in recent years. The Epstein piece graces the corner of Lewis's building, Phillip King's work is outside the Sydney Jones Library and the Barbara Hepworth in Abercromby Square. Tyson Smith has the Liverpool War Memorial and the local gentry fortify the city green areas. Now, who better to mark our entry into the next millennium than Mike Kenny, re-forging links between Liverpool and London that have for some many years run concurrently and simultaneously through the art world? Mike will be almost 60 in the year 2000 and could offer the city a suitable tribute and statement for the next decade.

One of the most prolific artists of his generation is Clement McAleer. McAleer was born in Dungannon in County Tyrone and went to Ulster College of Art and Design in the early 1970s. He came to England in 1972 with a place at Canterbury College of Art, moving on to the Royal College of Art from 1975 until 1978. I remember some of his very impressive shows at the Bluecoat Gallery in Liverpool between 1979 and 1985. He seems to have successfully exhibited between Britain and Ireland almost consistently since that time and is represented in many well-known collections, including the University of Liverpool, Ulster Museum, the Royal College of Art, the European Parliament and Granada Television as well as the Arts Council. One of his series of pieces from the early 1990s captures the beauty of nature and sets man against the backdrop of his presence in nature. The colours are earthy but ethereal and hint at something known instinctively, but he depicts changes of mood and almost sculpts his paint thickly on the canvas to chisel glimpses of the landscape he is portraying. Journey to the Sea (1995) is a large piece that pulls images of the deep with suggestions of sails, sea, shore, storm and the built environment. The mood is wholesome and although imprecise in line, is still recognisable as if gazing through a window, slightly removed from the place where the soul would like to be.

Back in Liverpool I could compare the studios of our artists with those in

London. The life room at the Sandon Studios in the Bluecoat Chambers was very draughty, heat came from one tiny electric fire and rain leaked through the roof. All the older members would pussyfoot about, too mean to put one shilling in the meter for the heater. So, while they held a summit meeting to discuss who would put the money in, the poor model would be freezing to death. Even so, I never let the group down, every Friday turning up without fail. The Stanley Reed drawings of me were produced at the Sandon. He drew me at a ten shillings a night class for two hours every Friday, seven till nine, eventually putting the cost up to fifteen shillings. At nine o'clock it was off to the bar with Edgar Grosvenor, the art master from the Collegiate. We would often go the Oyster Bar in Basnett Street as an alternative. The night's work would be set aside, but the memory always held the images of Reed's work at the close of the session. It is very linear in style and his drawings of me are exquisite.

What really fascinates me now is when young students who apply for a diploma course and produce life drawings at their interviews tell me afterwards that this fellow interviewing me said: 'Oh look, that's June.' That is fame indeed!

Nicholas Horsfield came to Liverpool's Regional College of Art from the Arts Council, in the late 1950s, and taught art history. At first he was in the painting studios, always a very good artist, his style exceptionally expressive, with paint thickly applied. When he taught foundation studies at the then Liverpool Polytechnic he was extremely popular with the students and they all treated him with great respect. In any year there are only about five or six students who are outstandingly good and outshine the others in their figurative work. Nicholas had one particularly good group with Ian Scarfe, David Ledell, and David Harrison in it. It was Nicholas who told me the terrible news about John Lennon's murder in 1980, at the start of the morning, just as I arrived for life class. John Lennon had been a student when Nicholas first arrived in Liverpool and he remembered his talent as an artist as well as a performer.

A contemporary of Horsfield was William Stevenson, principal of the Liverpool College of Art, and an interior designer by profession. One day John Moores senior came to the College as an amateur artist who wanted lessons. He spoke to William Stevenson who said that he would teach him personally. Stevenson went on to resign his position at the College and moved to work for the John Moores company. He vanished from the art scene in Liverpool and Mr Norman took over as principal. Some time later I was visiting friends and met William Stevenson at an exhibition. We had a brief conversation and I asked how he was getting on. He replied that the boss had him clocking on and off starting at 8.00am like everyone else.

Stevenson did not lose his interest in art and in making it accessible. He had the idea of having a big exhibition and convinced John Moores that the John Moores Exhibition would be a worthwhile event. This has been a two-yearly event ever since, successful for over 25 years. In the early years the exhibition had a French section that attracted a very high standard of European art. Since that time it has developed as an open competition and has gained in international status, recognised as one of the leading opportunities for artistic talent in the United Kingdom. It was never merely a local show, although many local artists have taken part. The judging is still by a panel and the exhibition continues to excite the art world.

Many of the artists in Liverpool seemed to stay regional because there was no organisation on a national scale to enable them to move around and become known outside their region. On the other hand, artists in Liverpool have a good regional organisation that has developed gradually over the last thirty years. John Willett in his book about art on Merseyside (Art in a City, 1967) described the scene very well. His questionnaire, asking the general public about their understanding of art, was revealing and quite sad. I do not feel that his findings would have been peculiar to Liverpool, though. Any regional city would have found the general public only vaguely aware of changes in the world of art.

The most fascinating bit of his report was about activity in the education system. Compared with the traditional art classes in schools, which usually involved the development of copying and drawing skills, it revealed a shift to the now familiar concept of modern art. Whether the swing towards collage or three-dimensional artistic expression was due to the particular personalities and interests of the teachers at the time I cannot say. However, the attention given to artistic development certainly created the right atmosphere to enable young people to become interested in art of all sorts. It might be coincidental that John Lennon attended Quarry Bank, which is the school that John Willett was to highlight in his book. The fact that members of his peer group are still active artists should be testimony to the special creative energy that Liverpool was generating in the heady sixties. Many of the artists I feature in my exhibitions of Major Merseyside Artists had their roots in that creative period.

After twenty odd years of organising exhibitions I suspect that what I do today the art world does tomorrow. I am very selective in the two special categories that I support and see myself now as one of the most active supporters and promoters of regional art on Merseyside. I must admit to feeling some disquiet today when artists make direct contact with the venues that I have traditionally supported. I suppose I feel a little cheated. Perhaps I should have been less trusting and insisted that the titles of exhibitions were associated solely with my name. Major Merseyside Artists now has a recognisable standard and can capitalise on the hard work (and it is very hard work) that I have done over so many years. Some artists though, genuinely appreciate and acknowledge the advantageous start that they had. It is very satisfying to know that you have in some way helped to promote a young artist and to see his or her work develop and become easily saleable.

It is as if your were dealing in diamonds. Each piece of work is a jewel in its own right, regardless of the type of painting that evolves. Like a diamond, each piece has its own identity, and in the same way that a raw diamond has to be cut, in some way the hanging and display of each painting is like selecting the best facet of a diamond to enhance its beauty. I take each piece of art on its own merit.

Take Ulrich West, for example. Ulrich was my boy friend for about three years after we met around 1963. Eventually he was unable to complete his course at the Regional College of Art because of ill health and our relationship came to an end. However, Ulrich has a vital and imaginative style that ensures his pieces sell well and are widely collected. We have since worked together on many exhibitions of his work. Ulrich is a regular exhibitor in the Major Merseyside Artists Exhibition collection. I included him, together with another local artist, Paul Cousins, in a number of shows, and I am pleased to see them successfully carry on in two-man exhibitions.

The Bluecoat Chambers was the hub of the art collective outside the Art School. James Cliffe had a studio at the Bluecoat. He was a successful commercial artist working with cinema advertisements. I thought it was terrible that the Bluecoat failed to give him a memorial exhibition after his death. His wife hated the fact that he was an artist. James and I used to get on really well, and I would always bring him back, red silk-lined, berets from Spain whenever I went. We used to laugh, because I said it must have provided his inspiration, as wearing one he looked the archetypal artist. All he needed in addition was a striped tee-shirt and a moustache and he would don the aura of an artist from Montmartre.

One of the teachers, Jim Weston, trained at Leeds, but worked in foundation studies at the Liverpool College of Art. He was a Prix de Rome prize-winner with his sculpture. Jim was a friend of David Thistlewood when they were in Leeds. Jim was at foundation studies for about eight years during my time there, and had particularly well organised and disciplined classes. This always produced good results from his students who were encouraged to complete pieces and set targets.

Not all the successful artists followed the straight and narrow path through the Art School. Many striking characters have been attracted by the bohemian life. One such is Yan Kel Feather, an interesting man. When I first saw him he was a struggling local artist with no money. He did not have any formal training but learned to paint when he lived in London by attending classes part-time while working. He was born in Liverpool but after his mother died, moved to London, probably only 14 or 15 years of age. After the war he returned to Liverpool around 1946, just before I started work as a model. He did not have anything to connect him with the art circles in the city and made his living selling second-hand goods.

Yan Kel became a bit of a wanderer and spent some years in the south, in London and Cornwall. He says that he was attracted by the artists of St Ives and wanted to learn more about them.

I first became his friend when he opened a night club in Liverpool in the late 1950s. Before going south ten years earlier Yan Kel had lived in

Cambridge Street and tried very hard to get in with the 'in' crowd which included Roy Cross, Josh Kirby and Ted Atkinson, all of whom went to Wivenhoe in Essex and did well for themselves. I was a member of this group and 'in the crack', as we say. Yan Kel was a funny man with a great sense of humour and was always exceptionally well dressed in his brother's clothes. His brother, Ashe, ran the Feathers Hotel in Mount Pleasant. Yan Kel had a lot of talent and produced very skilful and decorative flower paintings and portraits. His style was soft, gentle and appealing.

He was always successful in finding jobs (not as an artist in these early days), one in Penzance as a waiter. He spent the summer season in a hotel about two streets away from the house he owned. I gather that his hotel was one of the best in Penzance, overlooking the sea and cliffs.

As an artist he was regularly unemployed and penniless, and in an attempt to make ends meet he secured a job as an electrician at the Liverpool Playhouse. He knew absolutely nothing about electrics and ten minutes before curtain up he had the house in darkness when he fused all the lights.

A hasty retreat to London followed. He got a job as a telephone operator there, working on the night shift taking alarm calls for the stars. He was not on the ball at that either. He put the wrong call through to Gilbert Harding, the television personality, and he missed his rehearsal altogether!

Back in Liverpool Yan Kel managed to get a job at the Adelphi Hotel as a kitchen supervisor. He sat in a big glass-domed room checking in the food and sundries. At that time I was a visitor about three or four times each week after the night classes for cocktails. Yan Kel had the staff organised to suit him, from the bell-boy upwards. The parties in the kitchen were livelier than the ones upstairs and Yan Kel presided over them all with great aplomb.

He was still painting and trying to be an artist. He decided that he liked LS Lowry's paintings very much and discovered that he had a knack for making skilful reproductions. These he could sell at a handsome profit, as they were very convincing, until someone brought one back and said: 'This isn't a genuine Lowry.' 'I never said it was,' Yan Kel replied. 'But it is a genuine Feather!'

Through all of this Yan Kel managed to survive. He went on to open a very popular night-club. He called it the Basement Club, located in Mount Pleasant. After a shaky financial start he made a small fortune. It was a drinking club that he managed to run in good order. People came just to talk with him, as he had an engaging personality. He decided to go on a world cruise with his fortune and returned to live in Penzance and buy the beautiful house near the place he worked as a waiter. Yan Kel's is truly a success story.

He made Cornwall his permanent residence around 1977 and settled down with his companion, Bill King. Sadly, Bill died in 1993, but their life together has left Yan Kel with a deep affection for, and gratitude to, his partner. Bill helped Yan Kel improve his artistic style and technique, especially his ability as a draughtsman. I would not have said that Yan Kel was technically proficient at drawing in the early years. His ability to manage his hand/eye co ordination with a brush was far more exacting. Yan Kel has developed into a naturally comic but charismatic personality, epitomising the Liverpool character who does everything with a wink in his eye. His art does not illustrate his sense of humour, but could be categorised as Yan Kel's observation of others and their surroundings. Perhaps his next phase will be to look more at himself and his own experiences, capturing those on canvas.

When I came back to Liverpool from London I began to work for George Jardine in the early 1960s. George Jardine is the second of my artists of note whose paintings are especially distinctive. Jardine came to Liverpool from a teaching post in Yorkshire. He was working in an independent school when he was appointed as a teacher in the graphics department at the Liverpool School of Art. His work is particularly striking for its surreal nature. George is a very private person with the capacity to develop a whole world of imaginative, fantastic imagery in a single piece. Each is self-contained, but at the same time conjoining to appear like snapshot images of a mysterious landscape. His early designs that proved most popular were etchings with a modernist feel. They have a visual flatness and a structured, formal line. Even at that stage of his career, his work was minuscule in detail, and fine line has remained present in his work.

His period studying at the Royal College of Art gave George the opportunity to explore graphic art to the full, emphasised in his etchings. His surreal landscapes draw the spectator into a hidden world that at first is not seen. Each visit to his work reveals another secret, such as the iris of an eye that reflects an image, that shows a detail at first overlooked. The beasts that reside on the canvas may be real or imagined but there is narrative that compels the spectator's attention. His work is a sort of still-action, a snapshot in time of another world. Perhaps it is the world of our inner selves or a dimension of our real world, only the spectator is able to decide. His early work used pattern and form mixed together but, as his work developed into maturity, George has included new areas of development.

Midway through his career he produced a large collage, part of the collection of the Walker Art Gallery, entitled Sea Change (1960). I am featured in the painting as the central figure, surrounded by a myriad of items defined by their detail. There are nautical themes, coins, buttons, jewels, watches, clocks and painted images. Advertising material is included in the eclectic design with a masterly use of irony relayed through the visual image. George has the skill of the eighteenth-century miniaturist, almost like Hogarth in his exposure of human characteristics, but in George's case he used the image to accentuate the fantastic, the world inside the mind addressing the sexuality of humankind in relation to feelings and emotions. He once said that he found the female form more appealing to work with – and who wouldn't, he would joke!

George's experience of the world of art seems more personal and unique than that of most other artists. Certainly, he is capable of using his fantastical imagery as a new form of language. His figurative work looks like elfin or fairy caricatures. Whereas the Surrealists changed the representation of things known to us, George steps beyond this to create a separate, other world, rather like an alien environment.

On a personal level, George is a very private person, difficult to know, but entertaining. His stories are amusing.

Other aspects of his work, rarely seen, are his nature studies. Plants, flowers and bird life feature strongly, transformed frequently in his surreal painting, but deftly and gently portrayed in his representational work. George has a very disciplined approach to his painting, even though he is now retired from teaching. The upper floor of his home is given over to studio rooms which contain nothing to distract him from his task. He has studios at the front and the back of the house, to catch the best light and allow him to paint at every opportunity

I have two particular favourites. The first is a line drawing of me in profile, a head silhouette that is simplistic and linear in black on white. It exposes my sense of self almost like a mirror image of me – although it measures only 9 x 10 inches. I am instantly recognisable and my character is well portrayed. The second is a small oil painting measuring no more than 12 x 18 inches. I have my back to the spectator, holding an oval mirror in which I am reflected back to the audience. It is a bit like me watching you, watching me. I find it difficult to express the reasons why I like this piece so much. The colour is discreet, using a predominantly green and grey palette. The brush-strokes are loose and fall downward like rain washing over the scene, but yet there is still a distinct line to the outline, although not in the least hard-edged. As a professional model I do mirror the artist's intention through my physical form. Yet the artist can only ever grasp a reflected image of me.

Completely different in style and technique is the work of David Thistlewood, who arrived in Liverpool from Leeds. He is definitely a formalist and has written an introduction to the aesthetic beliefs of Herbert Read (Formlessness and Form, 1984). He came to Liverpool to teach whilst studying for his doctorate at the University of Liverpool around 1975. As an artist and academic, he recognised the benefits of the study of form for all his students. He started to bring his students of architecture from the University of Liverpool to the Polytechnic for study groups on a Monday afternoon. He wanted to teach them visual appreciation. He was himself a fine artist, producing excellent drawings of me from sessions in the life classes. I presented his work in an exhibition at the Royal Liverpool Hospital which proved very popular. David sadly died in the summer of 1998, a couple of years after becoming a professor and director of studies in SES Combined Honours at the University of Liverpool. He was a personal friend who taught me the fundamentals of exhibition organisation, for which I will always be grateful.

Another great organiser is the artist Ray Fields. Ray was an excellent teacher in the graphics department, who had been teaching since about 1965, after teaching night classes in Chester. These were organised to sharpen the reactions of artists by introducing a moving model. This would enable them to capture changes in light and landscape in outdoor painting as well as helping them bring a canvas to life. It made students work at a faster pace. It was always possible for people to fall asleep in the conventional life class, where many drawings too easily ended up wooden, with no life in them at all.

One idea, in particular, designed to enliven a student's work was the series of exercises that I would perform for the moving figure. I would perform the same series of movements up and down in a limited amount of space, then I would repeat the same set of movements. I would usually stop at intervals and hold the pose for less than five minutes at a time. The results were usually excellent providing a whole new perspective to a familiar situation. Ray introduced flashing lights and colour transparencies so that the figure gained interest as the tonal changes became dramatic. Differences in flat light and colour changes would enhance different parts my body, and shaded areas presented new challenges for the students to capture. It was a bit like chasing a moving shadow at times, making them nimble at drawing and adept at observation.

Ray aimed to teach his students 'how to analyse movement and motion in space and light and to disturb visual habits'. He wanted them to 'seek out the essence of a moving figure from a repeating repertoire of body movements and rhythms'. Ray said that most of his students were proficient in working in line, moving on to use colour and tone for particular reasons or effect. This encouraged students to tackle animation. Ray and his students won international acclaim for their work. He said that if a model were totally involved in the creative process, then the student too would be totally involved.

The results that Ray and his students produced were so successful that his sessions became quite popular. His work moved systematically in and out of graphic illustration and especially animation. He was a demanding teacher but his classes were fun.

Ray once said that I could be described as 'part of a visual spin', that is, there has been a change of approach to the visual arts. No longer are they simply painting, but we have media, graphics, newspapers, magazines, all broadening our experience of art and movement.

One of the associated areas of interest to me was the design of textiles and fashion. Charles Metcalf and I met in London, as I mentioned earlier, and I was thrilled when he was appointed to the dress design department at Liverpool. He had trained in dress design at the Liverpool College of Art and I remembered him from 1948. In London his designs certainly helped me to look elegant in original creations for prestigious parties and events. I remember wanting a dress for a party at the Royal College of Art and went to see Charles, who was then working at Dickins and Jones. He straightaway sketched on the back of an envelope, coming up with a show-stopping dress in contrasting satin trimmed with a little grey mohair jacket.

I remember saying: 'How much? If I went to Bond Street, I wouldn't have to pay that much!'

Off I went to Bond Street, but could not see anything as exquisite as his design. The next day I went back and he set to work. It was soon finished and I paid for it in three instalments. As I recall, it was mid-calf length, with an overlapping straight skirt in a satin bond with a tiny jacket with a horseshoe collar. With my grey shoes from Rayne's in Bond Street (the Queen's shoemaker) and my silver-grey pale French grey bag I felt really rich and looked great. This was just as well as the party was a huge success spent in the company of Lord Methuen and his son David (a student at the college) along with many other now-famous artists.

My other favourite outfit was made for an evening dinner at the Slade. It was in olive green wool, sleeveless and with a little blouse of the same soft wool. I would spend every penny on my clothes. I had no money but loads of clothes.

In the early years in Liverpool, around 1948, I remember buying a run of purple brocade which was shot through with a silver thread. There was only one yard available. I was very slim and thought that one yard would be enough to make me a dress. Charles said I would never get a dress out of that small amount of fabric. He was, however, an excellent cutter and had a go. He produced a sleeveless, mandarin-collared dress and included a contrasting velvet bodice. It was very tight and had a zip up the back. I was wearing it to a big party at the Adelphi Hotel with the town boys. Part way through the evening the whole lot split from top to bottom – it was about a 24-inch zip. I popped out over the top and into the soup. My friends shouted, 'Whoops, there she goes!' Being gentlemen, they were quick to hold me into the dress while I went to the ladies' powder room and the safety of an assistant. The place was, unfortunately, packed but it was such a good night that I ended up spending the rest of the evening in my black velvet coat with the satin lining, a bit hot, but safe and comfortable. The panache learned at my grandmother's knee was to prove useful.

When I was again working in Liverpool, Charles designed and made some very special outfits for me. There are a number that leap to my mind, in particular the party and cocktail dresses. I like to dress well and was complimented on my clothes by the fashion designer Jean Muir. I rarely dress up nowadays. In this part of Liverpool it is more sensible to keep a low profile and not dress up on the streets if you walk everywhere as I do. When there is a grand occasion I make an exception, though.

I particularly liked the end-of-year shows at the Polytechnic. Charles Metcalf designed the regal and ceremonial gowns for the Chancellor of Liverpool John Moores University and, without a doubt, the ceremonial occasions were embellished by his contribution. He also staged the College's fashion event by making it into an entertaining spectacle, an event that people eagerly anticipated. He emphasised the way the girls wore their designs and voiced-over their presentations by talking about the fabrics and styles of the creations. The quality of his shows was excellent.

Charles was indirectly responsible for dramatic changes to the textile department at the Liverpool Polytechnic in the late 1960s. He appointed Michael Hatjoulis who trained at the Royal College of Art. When Mike came to Liverpool Polytechnic in 1968, aged about 30, he revolutionised the department. He brought a lively, cobweb-clearing freshness, being on the same wavelength as the students. He stimulated their designs into a new 'up front' approach. A superb artist and designer, he often exhibits work in the Major Merseyside Artists exhibitions, helped and encouraged by his old art master Jack Shore, who was head of art schools in Chester and Blackpool, but now retired.

His colleague, Mike Knowles, born in St Helens was to be at the helm of the Polytechnic during the turbulent years leading to its change to Liverpool John Moores University, and another artist whose work I admire very much. Mike was taught at the Slade by Frank Auerbach, which explains the stylistic influence of Auerbach's work becoming evident in the work of Liverpool students.

Knowles drew me as a student before going to London. He returned after his degree to teach in fine art and eventually was appointed dean. He helped steer the new university through many crises as an excellent manager as well as artist. To be at the helm as the funding and infrastructure changed, as well as art itself, was an unenviable position. He was sympathetic towards my situation when my uncle was ill and knew that I had to rush home for lunch. However, he would always keep the pressure on to ensure the department worked efficiently. He was almost obsessed with time-keeping. Nevertheless, I gathered from his students that he was an approachable and supportive teacher, held in high regard. He continues to paint and contribute to the management of art and cultural activities across the region.

The teaching staff at Liverpool John Moores University has always been of high quality, showing commitment and dedication, often at times of great financial pressure. John Holden is head of fine art, noticeable for his elegant and charming demeanour. He is always first to help his students, often at his desk at 7am. His degree shows are of exceptionally high standard. Roy Holt, a fine practising artist himself, assists him. His students seem able to produce work that appears to be from established and mature artists.

One of Mike Knowles' talented associates is Richard Young. It was Mike who encouraged Richard to get into the formal structure of art education. Richard achieved a first-class degree and would joke that as a mature student he would get his bus pass at the same time that he graduated. His sketches are lively and full of personality, his use of colour belonging to the English tradition and drawing influence from Sickert in particular whom he obviously admires. A particular favourite of mine is his self-portrait. Seated, facing the spectator in the interior of his home, his self-depiction captures his personality, introspective and comfortable in his own domestic setting. The brush strokes are loose and are stating: 'This is me. I am familiar in this space, it is defined and yet expressive.'

I often wonder if the use of colour on Dick's shoes is light dimly reflected or paint splashed. It looks as if he has exhausted himself painting and has slumped into his chair only half interested in his surroundings and the spectator. I also found his line drawing of me intriguing. It was shown in a touring exhibition in 1985-86 called Merseyside Artists 2 and it picks up on Dick's use of shading and blurring, often used to the right side of his sitter's face. I feel as if he only wants a part of a character to be available. The other sides he recedes or melts into the background. It always leaves the spectator with an unfinished impression of the text of his paintings. It is a sort of specific narrative, suggestive of something other or darker in one's character.

The artist who had a similar penchant for this style was Sam Walsh. Sam arrived in Liverpool at the same time as Adrian Henri in 1957. He was from Wexford in Ireland, but had spent a number of years in London before coming to Liverpool. He had a flat around the corner from Falkner Street in Huskisson Street. He was charismatic, charming and well liked. I would describe him as the last starving Bohemian artist. He had no financial support so decided to get his teaching degree and qualified at Warrington, Padgate College as I remember. From there he moved to foundation studies at Liverpool Polytechnic in Myrtle Street (then in the original setting). Sam was a heavy drinker, eventually to die of sclerosis of the liver. His funeral was like a clip from a film, full of pop stars and celebrities, the church so full that you could not get inside. The service was full of Sam's favourite music. In particular, the song The House of the Rising Sun, by the Animals, was played. I was too upset to go to his funeral as I had many fond memories of Sam from when he was in good health.

He came to Liverpool when the city was starting to steal the limelight a little from London. Much creative talent was drawn to the city on the back of the Merseybeat fame. Sam had been working in London but had not achieved great success, so instead brought his ability and talent to the College. Sam produced a breathtaking portrait of Ivon Hitchens (1974); it was officially called Head of Man, and showed how Walsh effectively used cross-spraying onto a crumpled canvas to etch depth into the face. I have not seen such original craftsmanship at a stage when airbrushing was in its infancy. His traditional handling of paint was quite static. On a small landscape painting in my collection, Sam has used tonal developments in green with quite hard-edged imagery.

Mentioned previously was the hard-edged, quietly influential painter Roderick Bisson. Roderick wrote the reviews of my exhibitions for the Liverpool Daily Post & Echo. He lived locally in Percy Street. When he reviewed an exhibition he would never have a note in his hand. He would concentrate on the artists that he knew, not really giving newcomers much chance. For example, in one show at Senate House at the University of Liverpool I had about 120 artists on display. I decided to make sure that he had plenty of notes available, handing them to him if necessary, so that he would have biographical histories to hand and would get them right. Bisson endeared himself to everyone and did not get any criticism, only affection for his support of the Sandon, both artists and musicians.

Bisson's own style as a painter was quite modern and refreshing. He began painting in the 1930s, joining the Sandon in 1931 and producing work in a naïve style, which was very French and quite different from the Sickert-esque nature of the Sandon's early products. Many of his pieces are lost in private collections. They would prove immensely popular today with a 'retro' feel to them.

I was recently watching young people waiting for interview at Liverpool John Moores University for the forthcoming academic year and thought back to those who had already passed through on their way to the London schools. In particular, I had in mind the most prestigious schools such as the Royal College, Slade or Royal Academy. When it came to the history of art some did not have a clue, and often thought nothing had ever happened before they came on the scene. I remember one fine art student attempting to get into the Royal College, where the competition has always been great and where few places are available. One question that he was asked at interview was: 'Who is Sir William Coldstream?' (the then principal of the Slade School of Fine Art). The reply given was: 'One of the Pre-Raphaelite painters'! Needless to say he did not get in.

One of the last successes who worked on the National Diploma in Design course was Ray Walker, a Liverpool artist as tough as they come. His father was manager of a huge Liverpool pub in Smithdown Road and was very dubious about art. Ray was known to fight his way out of a disagreement. When Ray went to London for his interview the art staff had someone move his paintings all around the room. Ray told me that he looked at a chair that had been placed in the middle of the room and he thought: 'Is that where I am supposed to sit?' He decided it was and sat down to face questions from some of the biggest names in British art. All the time he was thinking: 'Make one wrong move and I've had it!', so he criticised them when they asked: 'Analyse that painting over there, Walker!' Ray replied 'Which corner would you like me to start from?' Ray said that he stuck their questioning for about twenty minutes and then kicked the chair to the other side of the room saying: 'They are not my ******* paintings, bring mine in and we will start again!' The work on view had been copied from Ray's own. The staff knew that, but wanted to test his reactions. Afterwards, Ruskin Spear came up and said: 'You did very well in there Walker,' and as a result they offered him a place.

During the first days of term it is traditional for the Royal College to hold an evening introductory soirée for students and staff. One student had the misfortune of asking Ray in a rather derogatory manner: 'Where does that accent hail from then?' To that Ray replied, 'This is where it is from' and then promptly smashed a bottle over the poor chap's head, knocking him out! The next day Ray was hauled in front of the principal. It was decided to let Ray carry on with his painting, but prudently not straight away. In order to separate the two students and avoid further conflict, Ray was despatched to parks and gardens for a year before being allowed to continue his studying the following year. When he eventually arrived back to study he had to put up with the jokes from staff about his imposed absence. Nevertheless, he went on to do extremely well.

Ray once said to me, 'the only thing which stops me from going to the dogs completely is going into my studio, locking the door and getting on with some painting.' He did a lot of figurative work and captured the seventies pop era and fashions in animated style. His work in mural captured the stereotypical images of gender, character and race. Not necessarily flattering, he used striking colour and hard-edged definition, which patterned his work, making a narrative clearly understandable. His work did not follow an obvious tradition, but his skill in portraiture was uniquely stylistic and graphically orientated.

In 1984, Ray died an early death aged only 39. His art master (who also trained at Liverpool College of Art), David Copestake, taught at Hillfoot High School and said that Ray was the only real success he had. Today his name is carved in gold letters at the old school, one of a list of outstanding students. Professor Carel Weight also thought Ray was a fine artist.

Another artist whose drawing skill reflected that of Ray Walker is Paul Cousins. I first met Paul as a student at Liverpool from the Bluecoat School, after moving here from Honiton, Devon. His line drawing is animated and detailed and his painting is quite innovative. Working in oils he produces vibrant landscapes by blacking out the base canvas before applying his pigment. In this way he enhances texture and relief and his work explodes into intense colour. He was a member of Liverpool Academy and exhibits widely. In particular, Paul kindly painted my Courtyard Garden for his one-man show at the University of Liverpool. In addition to his landscape pieces, he has produced some outstanding line drawings and cartoons showing Liverpool life that captures the humour and enthusiasm of the city.

On a more personal level, I have admired Julia Midgley for her great enthusiasm, which she always manages to pass on to her students. She teaches in the graphics department at the Liverpool John Moores University. When she worked in the life class she would often not only tutor the students but would manage to make drawings of me at the same time. Her commitment to teaching is outstanding. When she takes students off-site for a different visual experience, in such places as the police headquarters, they produce innovative results with a high standard of figurative skill. Her own pieces have sold well. In addition to my Major Merseyside Artists exhibitions, her work can be seen in art galleries across the region.

Adrian Henri is possibly the best known of the local Merseyside artists, with his professionalism and excellent management of his own affairs, in his art, his poetry and his art criticism. I got to know Adrian shortly after he arrived in Liverpool. He lives quite nearby in Mount Street in the cosmopolitan city centre. I admire the way he has progressed and find he is never side-tracked away from the end-product. His work has a very contemporary feel and his landscapes often focus on the form and line of the image within their formal structure. He has a vibrant use of colour, seen in Sunset Heights (1985). Working in acrylic Henri explores colour and form in landscape. He regularly produces multi-part narratives in that his work gives a continuous image when shown in sequence. It is as if he is not producing just one fleeting impression of what he sees, but a panoramic view of the whole vista. He also paints a landscape with his words. One amusing example is the poem written to commemorate the Tate Gallery Liverpool anniversary.

Quite different to Adrian is Julia Carter Preston who entered the College of Art after a couple of years working in another field. She had inherited the family talent of precision and commitment to creative work. As a ceramicist she creates original pieces that are a modern version of the arts and crafts designs of William Morris. Very desirable and highly sought after, her work features in many private collections. She works from her studio at the Bluecoat Chambers where her popular pieces can be seen. Much of her work is to commission, producing plates and bowls in earthenware and decorated with sgraffito and lustre in shades of blue, black and green. Lloyds Register was presented with a selection of pieces based on Liverpool ship bowls and more recently, her 1999 Retrospective show at the Walker Art Gallery was a huge success.

Sculptural work in the city is of an exceptionally high standard. One of the most controversial of the Liverpool artists was Arthur Dooley. His sculpture was distinctive and linear in form. He was born in Liverpool and was self-taught, his talent greatly promoted by his own terrific personality. I first met Arthur when he worked at the Dunlop factory. He had a taste for the art world, which he saw as a way of earning a living outside factory work. He was inspired when he had a bronze crucifix accepted by the Walker Art Gallery in the 1960s. As a striking and loud character with a positive attitude he was given almost revolutionary status. He did most of his own casting and his work stands out in its originality as part of his identity. He received considerable criticism when the Crucifixion sculpture was placed outside the Methodist Church, Princes Avenue. The image was definitely radical. Arthur captured the real sense of an agonising form of death and the work both shocks and disturbs the spectator into really addressing the issues surrounding the Crucifixion. The image drew national attention, acclaim in some quarters, effrontery in others. Set against the usual bland religiosity of church sculpture, it stood out from the crowd. Relatively small in size, the imposing nature of the piece, skilfully crafted, pulls the spectator into the message, the intention of the act. Thus, the piece works on a particular level and brings the 2000-year story right into the present to confront the viewer.

As a complete contrast, Arthur was adept at creating more personal interpretations of religion in brass. Most of these pieces are in private collections, but the public can see an example at the Swedish Church in Liverpool. These pieces are formal in structure and curvaceous. They offer harmony and a sense of stillness, weighty and solid. I think Dooley was exploring a different side of religious faith in these pieces to that of his public sculptures, a devotional image spilling forth from a modernist camp. Considering these two pieces of his work side by side, it could be argued that Dooley has a complete grasp of the diversity of religious faith. In the Crucifixion we see deep chiselled lines, ingrained into the piece, writhing out in every detail. His lines in the brass are smooth and sweeping, enveloping the bountiful promise of everlasting peace, a softer image from an ex-guardsman, a hard man.

Much kindlier and approachable is Sister Anthony, Liverpool's forerunner of Sister Wendy Becket, the television art critic. With a desire to see art become part of as many lives as possible, she is ever-helpful and informative. She was trained at the Liverpool College of Art graphic design department, helped and encouraged by George Jardine between the years 1948 and 1954. She was head of art at Notre Dame College of Further Education in Maryland Street, Liverpool. Part of her present duties is advising Liverpool Metropolitan Cathedral on its collection; she has been with the Cathedral since 1982, when Notre Dame closed. When Liverpool received a visit from the Pope, Sister Anthony was responsible for putting together the work of Liverpool schoolchildren for display. His Holiness was very impressed by the beauty and vibrancy of the exhibition. Sister Anthony continues to manage the cathedral collection and is never far from the art world in some form or other.

An associate was church artist Robin McGhie. He painted the murals in Philip Neri Church in Catharine Street around 1950. They covered approximately 800 square yards and took three and a half years to complete. Robin trained at the Liverpool College of Art between 1946 and 1950. His creations can be seen across the city. His Easter candlestick is on permanent view in the Liverpool Metropolitan Cathedral.

Also to be seen at that cathedral is the work of Sean Rice. Sean came to Liverpool in 1963 from London to take up a teaching post at the Regional College of Art, where he eventually became head of sculpture. His work was consistently of a high standard and he is one of the city's most notable sculptors. Rice used bronze in the sculpture and was a master of fabrication. His work is reflective of Italian Mannerist sculpture, both ornate and decorative, one example being the Noah fountain at Chester Zoo. The late Bishop Derek Warlock, for the Metropolitan Cathedral, commissioned The Fourteen Stations of the Cross, which proved to be his last work for he died suddenly in 1997. Peter Davies, wrote his obituary for The Independent.

Sean Rice has left a rich legacy of bronze work for us to admire. A ceiling bronze can be seen at the Atlantic Tower Hotel, Liverpool. His London dealer was Denys Alwin-Davis, of the Alwin Gallery, in Grafton Street. Sean gave up his teaching post as head of sculpture to work on his art full-time. During the economic recession of the late 1980s the art market was severely hit, and Sean's last years were blighted by worry. He married Janet in 1984, after they had been together for fourteen years. Janet, too, is a sculptor and was trained in her early days by Sean when at the Liverpool College of Art. At the recent inauguration of Sean's work The Fourteen Stations of the Cross at the Metropolitan Cathedral, Janet announced that she would continue with the work they had planned together.

I have not as yet given much space to the local watercolourists. Many spring to mind, but I can mention only a few who sell very well in local exhibitions and who have produced excellent work of a consistently high quality. The first is George Drought, born in St Helens in 1940. He studied art and graphic design for six years, first at St Helens School of Art, then Liverpool College of Art. He won a John Moores Scholarship at the LCC Central School of Art in London. He worked mostly in printing after leaving his studies, his painting and etching blossoming when he retired from full-time work. George has shown in many exhibitions throughout the United Kingdom, including the Royal Academy Summer Exhibition twice and the Royal Institute of Painters in Watercolours, the Royal Society of Marine Artists and the Royal Hibernian Academy.

His friend and associate Eddie Scott Jones is another who has gained national acclaim. Eddie trained at the Liverpool College of Art, prior to taking up employment in the advertising industry from 1938 to 1962. He served in the Royal Air Force during the war years and has, since 1962, worked full-time as a freelance artist. He has been involved in both solo and group exhibitions across the country. His work is highly sought after and held in many private collections, both in the United Kingdom and Europe.

One of the more regional successes is David Shiers. David currently produces the exhibition posters and flyers for my exhibitions, as well as painting and exhibiting his own work. David was born in Liverpool in 1945 and undertook his training at the Liverpool College of Art part-time for four years. He works full-time as a graphic designer and illustrator in a Liverpool studio, but exhibits widely across the northwest and North Wales.

Another artist strongly associated with the graphics and printing industry is Edgar Shakeshaft. Born in Merseyside, Edgar has always been connected with the printing industry, mainly employed as a lithographic artist and designing exclusively for a large American packaging company. He has always been interested in producing paintings of Liverpool, these indicating the changes that have taken place in the city over a period. Edgar has held many private exhibitions throughout England and Wales, including one at the Boat House, Laugharne, where Dylan Thomas did much of his writing.

In architectonic terms, we also have Rodney Warbrick who has a mixed selection of work in a wide variety of collections. Warbrick has in his own collection examples of some of the best architectural compositions I have ever seen. He has developed the landscape of the street and recorded in great detail some of the most magnificent buildings, the medieval, neo-classical and Georgian facades and church buildings, all part of our heritage. Much of his skill has been developed through close observation and descriptive recollection of architecture. The man-made environment he depicts is engaging, without figures. His other work, produced in the 1950s, captures the same detail but relates it to the human form, using gentle colour as part of the composition. Warbrick's work is rare, with each piece highly prized by private collectors.

Finally, I am aware that I have not recorded the work of Harold Critchley, more famous for his exquisite glass design. He has worked more broadly across the northwest and overseas, latterly producing large landscape pieces exploring themed issues of tranquillity and the natural world. Contemporary colour tone and frequent inspirational visits abroad have broadened his subject matter and his experience is evident in each of his paintings. Harold was born in St Helens in 1925 and gained his National Diploma in Design (painting) followed by his Art Teacher's Diploma in 1949. Initially working as a stained glass designer for some three years, he moved into teaching and became a lecturer in drawing and painting in schools across the northwest. Between 1974 and 1986, Harold was principal of St Helens College of Art & Design and was accepted as a member of the Manchester Academy of Fine Art from 1970. He exhibits widely in the United Kingdom and Europe, most recently showing in both France and Belgium.

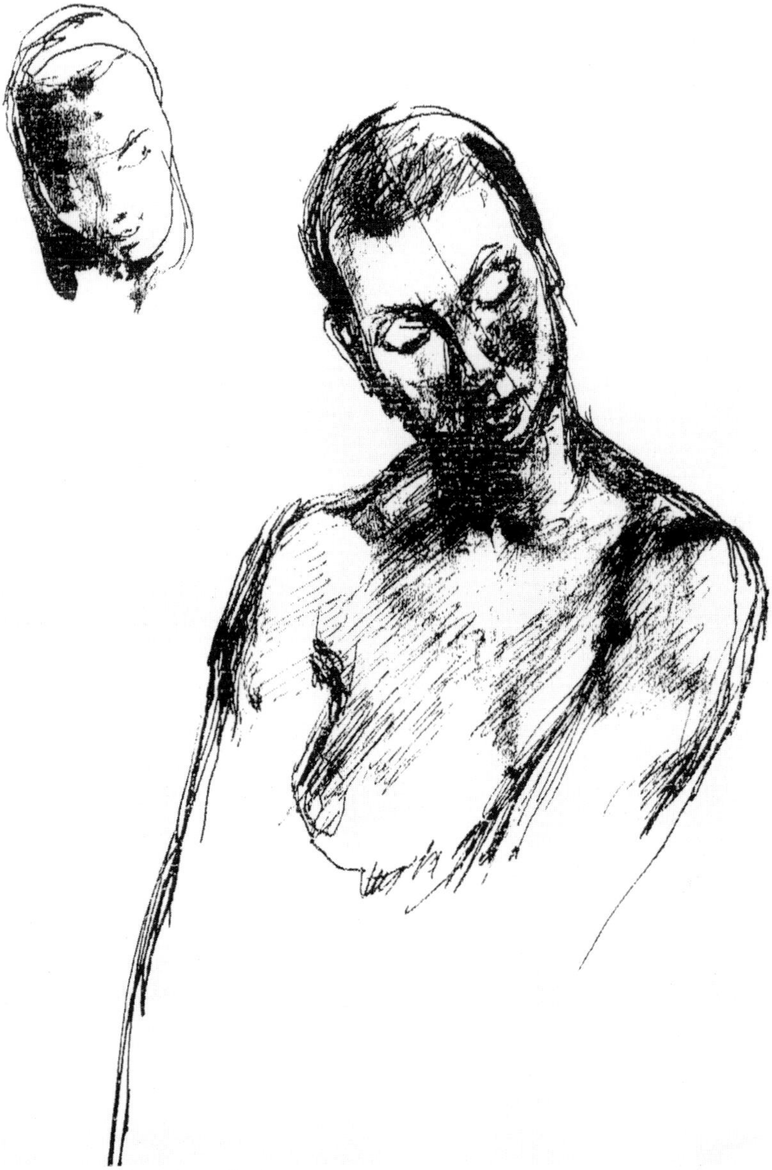

June Furlong, Pen and ink. Arthur Ballard.

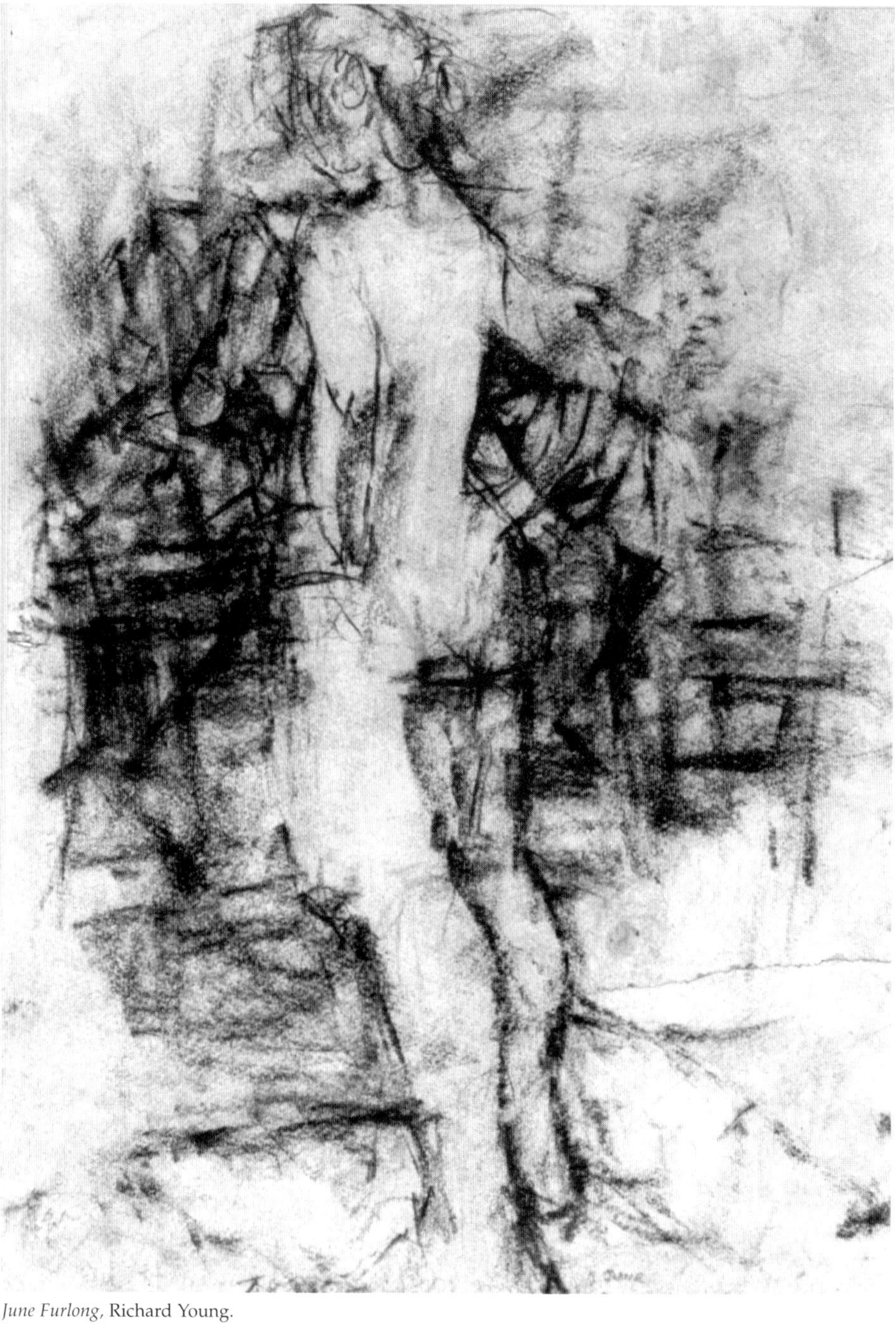

June Furlong, Richard Young.

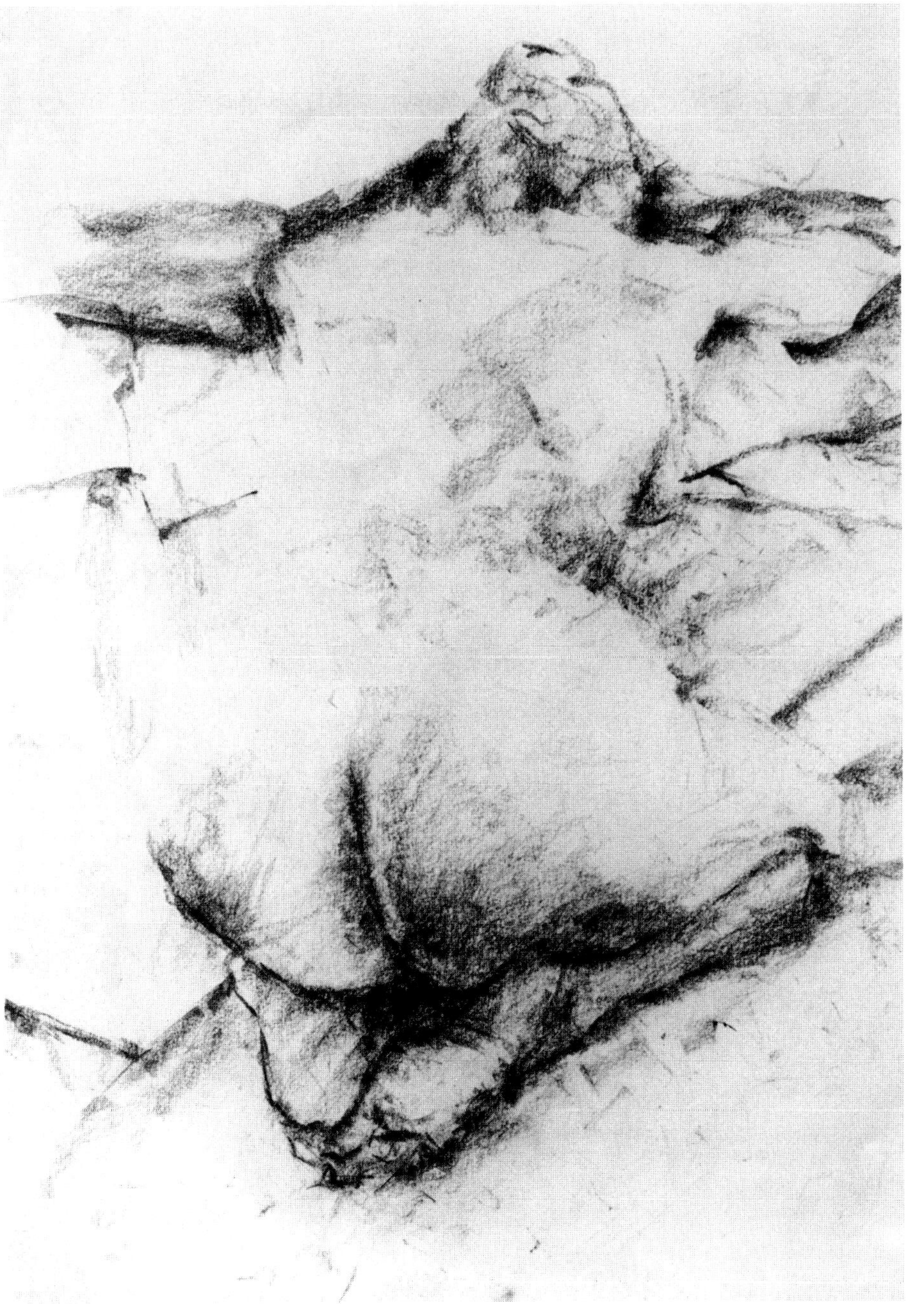

June Furlong, Richard Young.

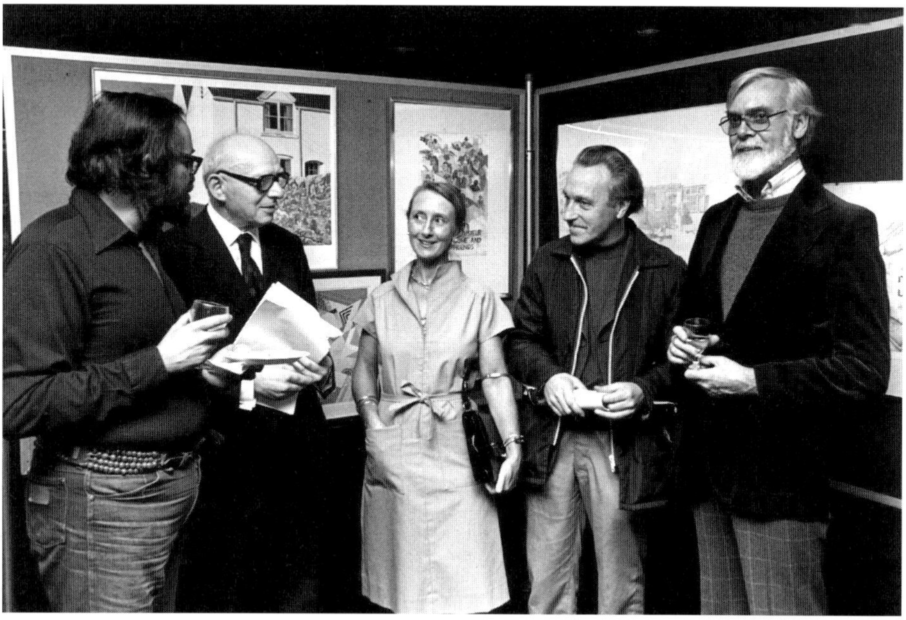

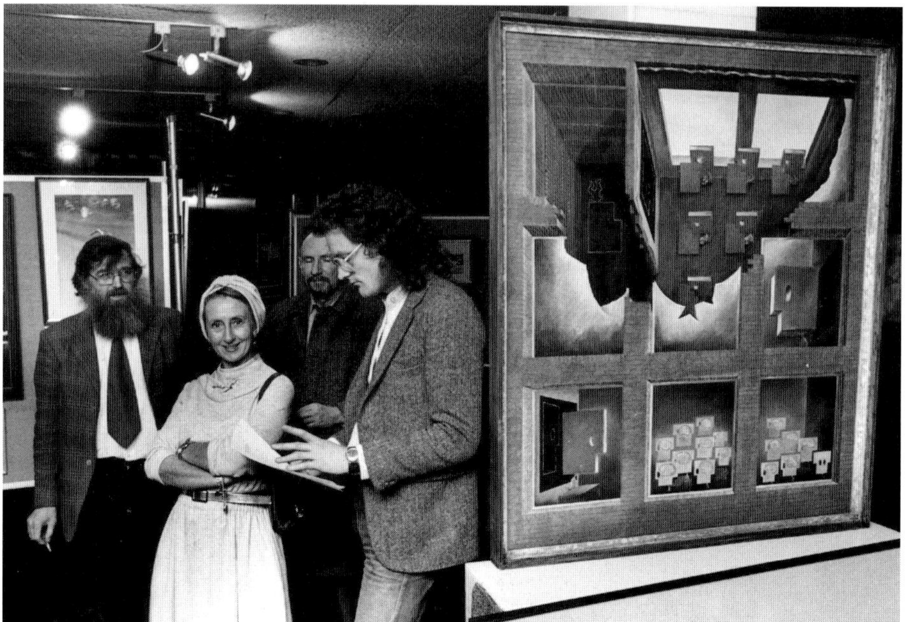

Top, Major Merseyside artists exhibition. Adrian Henri, Abraham Newman, June Furlong, Fred Corbitt and Ted Atkinson.
Bottom, Major Merseyside artists exhibition. Ulrich West, June Furlong, George Jardine and Paul Cousins.

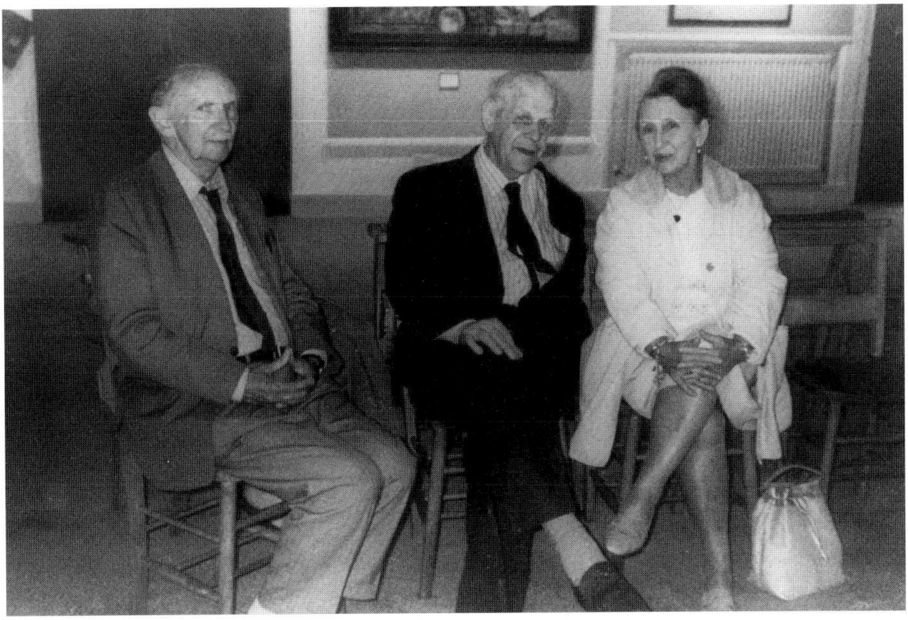

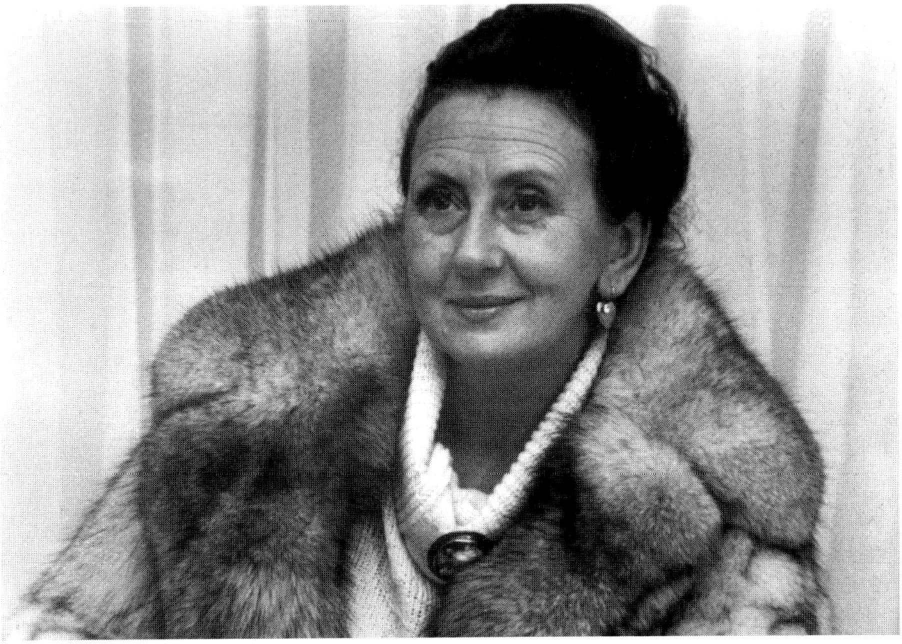

June with George Jardine, Professor Carel Weight.

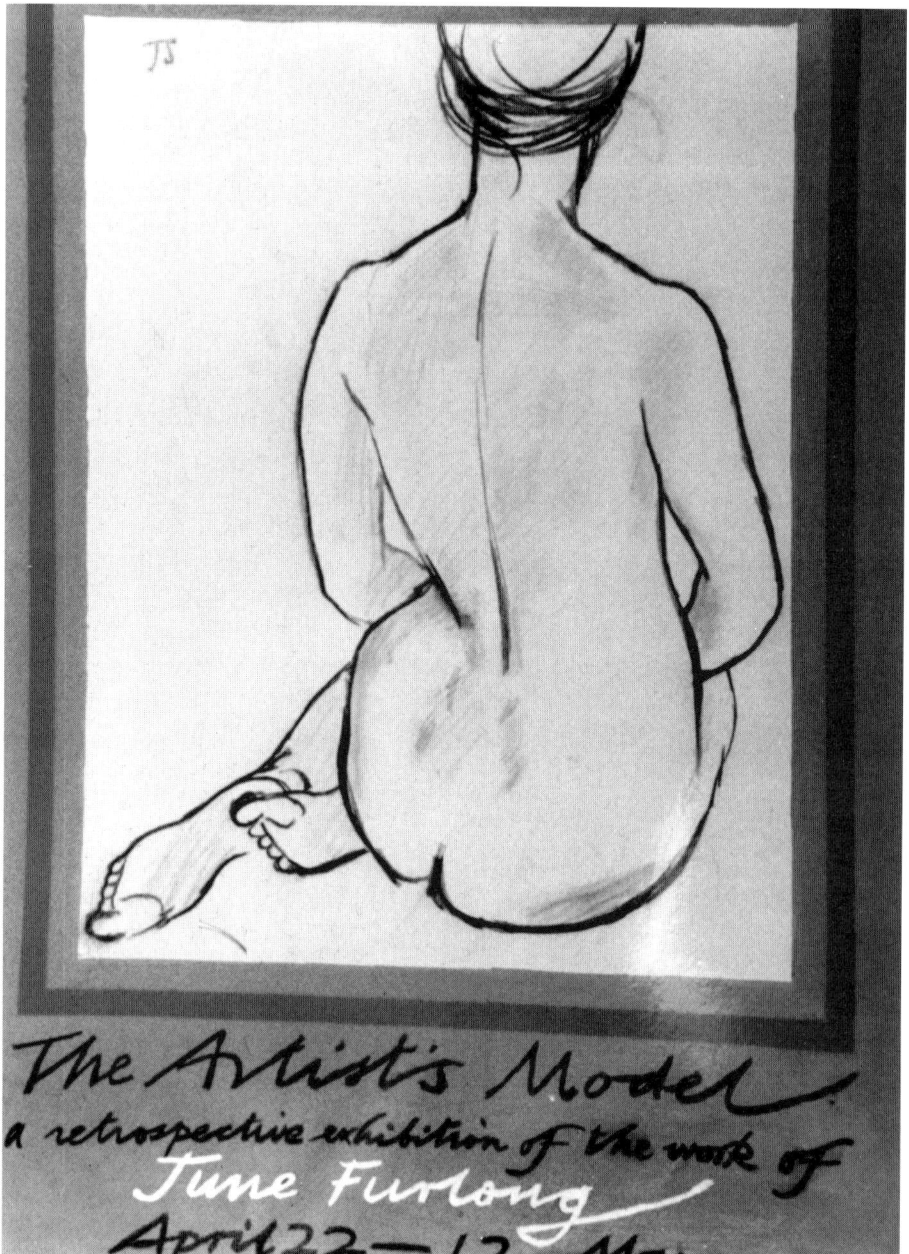

June, retrospective poster designed by Jack Shore.

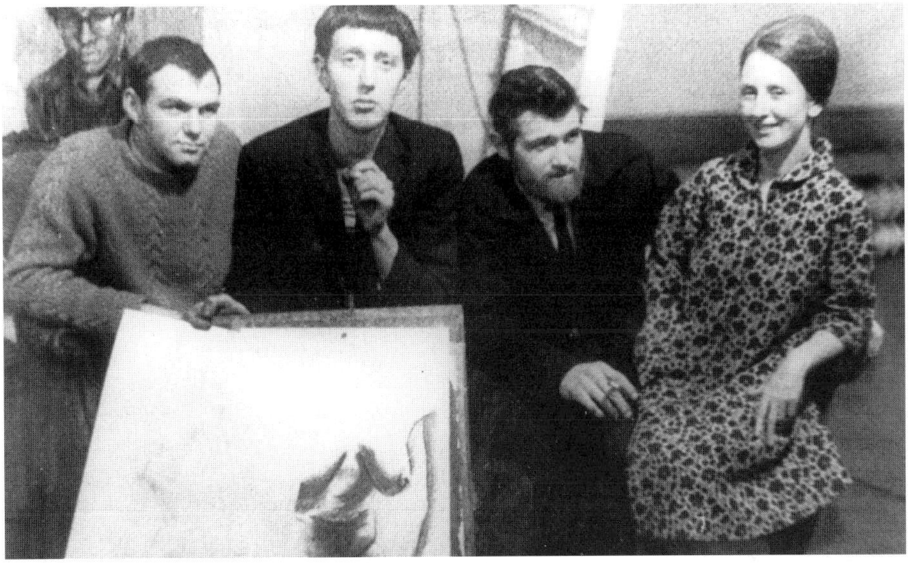

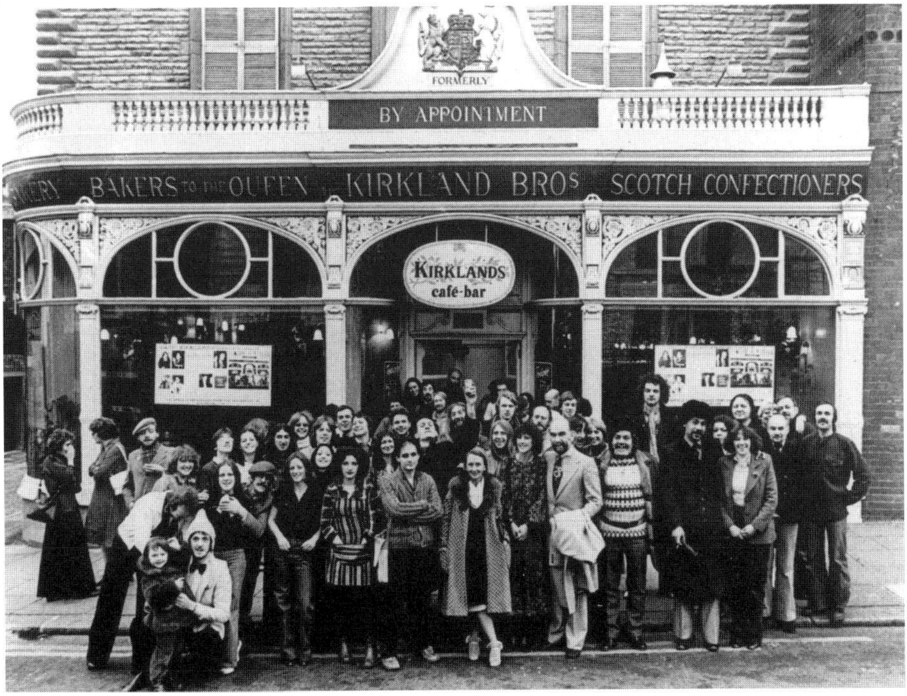

June with Ulrich West and friends.
June and friends outside Kirkland's Wine Bar on the anniversary of it's opening.

Merseyside Artists on Show

I had always maintained good contacts in Liverpool between the art students and their teachers. I eventually realised that I also had good contacts in the business world. The two have been hand-in-hand through the various gentlemen's clubs in Liverpool for over a hundred years. The possibility of organising a show of art from the Liverpool school soon became a reality, leading to a secondary occupation which has given me over thirty years' experience of organising exhibitions.

Initially, I was invited to put something together for the Racquets Club, then located in Liverpool 8 in Toxteth. It was a beautiful old building and gentleman's club on Upper Parliament Street. In the rioting of 1981, Toxteth was ablaze with the heat of revolution and, regrettably, the Racquets Club became one of the casualties. Razed to the ground, it has left a hole in the collective memory that has not been filled. Only in 1996 has the site received some care and attention and is presently being redeveloped.

The regeneration of the Albert Dock was the panacea offered to the people of Merseyside to compensate for the downturn in that part of their once wealthy neighbourhood. Liverpool 8 has the grand Georgian terraces, now fallen into disrepair, which give a glimpse of the gentrified occupants of bygone years. These houses were as elegant as were their inhabitants. The professional class gave provenance to the local artists and offered their support and encouragement through clubs like the Sandon, the Artists Club and the Racquets Club. This community supported the social circle within which I moved and made contacts. It was a natural progression to make the link between business and pleasure to be able to facilitate contact between the production and consumption of art in Merseyside. John Willett overlooked this aspect of art patronage when he studied Liverpool. Nevertheless, it has been a good starting point from which to progress.

Although I have a sentimental attachment to Liverpool, I started to organise exhibitions to help out my artist friends and with my eye for an opportunity, I decided to broaden my career from modelling to incorporate promotion of regional art, especially Merseyside art and the artists based here. That very first exhibition in the beautiful Racquets Club was full of pomp and circumstance but there were no sales, much to everyone's disappointment.

The other art-and-business link had been forged many years earlier at the Artists' Club in Ebele Street. Following the success of my exhibitions, and some years later, the Club president at the time, John Francis, asked me to present Major Merseyside Artists exclusively for their members, mostly businessmen. It is an exclusively gentlemen's club. The decoration is Edwardian with some Victorian fittings and is well worth a visit. The exhibition space is of fair size. In addition to a dining room full of members' paintings, the lounge and boardroom areas are comfortable and of good size for fixing screens.

It was Glenys Davies, of the Liverpool Academy, who first suggested that I stage a show. She went on to give me support in planning exhibitions, and is a person I would trust at all times.

The Academy itself has seen some changes of direction over the years and has had its fair share of disquiet amongst the membership. There has been a competitive division between members of the Academy and members of the Sandon since the inception of the Sandon all those years ago. Stimulated by the avant-garde, the Sandon came out top of the innovative arts, whereas the Academy fell back on tradition and official patronage. Nevertheless, I was friendly with the members of both associations and thereby was able to present work from a wide variety of Merseyside artists.

The Academy was not always able to stage exhibitions on request; a need for a committee decision delayed progress. It was far easier for me to reach a decision and put together a show quickly as the opportunity arose. Hence, when Glenys told me that there was an opportunity at the Racquets Club I thought I would try it out. At that time I knew nothing about curating an exhibition. But as I had been part of the art scene for thirty years, I thought I must have absorbed some of the required skills. The problems of getting work, hanging it and collating sales was learned on a trial-and-error basis. I have since discovered that skill in hanging an exhibition is not easily transferable, and many simply do not have it. I am grateful to my many artist friends who support the exhibitions and assist with the actual hanging of their work.

The appearance of exhibitions can really be determined only when all the paintings and sculptures are received and seen in situ. Nuances of colour, style, size and image must all be taken into consideration. A good written plan may look dreadful when the pieces are actually in place. Thus, flexibility is important, although my familiarity with the style and content of an artist will give me a fair idea of how the exhibition will shape up in rough terms before the event.

In 1983 I decided to take stock, to work out how best to use my time: I was sitting with Uncle Fred around the fire and it was freezing outside. I was working very long hours and my mother had died of cancer. In future I would concentrate on my exhibition work and drop modelling in colleges in the suburbs, working solely for foundation studies. By dropping some of the modelling I would be able to take a more serious view of my exhibition work, maximising my effort to make sales.

There are a number of different approaches to selling works of art. Permanent gallery owners and art shops can specialise in the more intellectual (and expensive) works. I, on the other hand, want to encourage the general public to buy original pieces rather than the standard department store run-of-the-mill photographic prints. There is great pleasure in looking at any original piece of work. Unlike cheap prints which both fade and date, a painting is a more permanent possession and investment. Collectors frequently tell me that they find many of the works that they purchase still appeal years after their purchase. This, to me, is the sign of good quality in a work. It is important, therefore, for me to stipulate a certain type of painting, which I know will attract purchasers. This in turn promotes the artist into the public sphere and introduces new collectors.

I see my exhibitions as an added aspect of an artist's work. The artists themselves will be promoting their work and seeking both national and international recognition. However, regional support can feed these wider ambitions by giving new artists exhibition experience to quote in their biographical notes. This is increasingly important when an artist begins to attract a following. Moving from showing on a small scale as part of a large exhibition to achieving a joint-exhibitor show and eventually having a one-person show evolves gradually over an artist's career. My exhibitions offer new artists an opportunity to get on the first rungs of the ladder.

The exhibitions are extremely hard work. Artists are notoriously unreliable and will promise the earth for an opportunity to show, but getting them to deliver demands almost obsessive persistence on the part of the organiser. I have learned from experience to gauge the potential output of an artist in order to determine whether or not they are likely to meet the deadlines being imposed upon them. Some have this ability, some do not. Over the last twenty years I have developed a mental list of those who can be relied upon, and who can be reasonably prolific to supply pictures or sculptures to more than one show running consecutively. I am also aware of those who might produce one tremendous exhibit that will be snapped up at the private view, then have nothing available for ages afterwards. When Timothy Stevens, now at the V & A, was at the Walker Art Gallery he was particularly supportive. He often said that I had great success with the local artists and liked to see artists exhibiting their work in more public spaces, such as the Royal Liverpool Hospital.

In order to attract as wide a buying public as possible, I have split my exhibitions into three main types. By far the most significant have been the Major Merseyside Artists exhibitions, running since 1976. I also have Young Artists introduced to highlight the regional contribution that Merseyside is making to the national scene. In this exhibition I try to focus mainly on the student body and artists below age 30 who are beginning to make a name for themselves. Finally, there have been the celebrated '100 +' exhibitions, covering a broader range of creativity. A smaller number of offshoots have also sprung into being. These include shows such as Let's Hear It for the Girls, with women-only exhibitors, or general exhibitions at traditional venues such as the Port of Liverpool, Women's Hospital, Liverpool Daily Post & Echo or the Artists' Club.

The most popular purchases by far are traditional watercolours and landscapes. Varying treatment of the theme of landscape usually attracts attention and sells well. There are Jardine's worlds of fantasy, West's Cubist interpretations as well as Cousins' imposing tempestuous colour topography. Local scenes prove commendable, with Shakeshaft and George Drought selling well, too. Dave Shiers' waterfront pieces are popular as are Harold Critchley's large landscapes painted en plein air.

Over the years many artists of talent have provided items for exhibition. It is regrettable that all that remains are listings, rather than photographs. Work that is held in private collections is now, of course, inaccessible. One of the best ways to appreciate the local stylistic developments is by looking at the John Moores Exhibition held in Liverpool. In addition, the Walker Art Gallery collection features many of those artists who have been associated with the area and have left their mark.

In 1977, the year of the Queen's Jubilee, there was a burst of activity in Liverpool. Part of the cultural melée were eight of my exhibitions included in the Hope Street Fringe Festival. Displays were held at the Everyman Theatre, Philharmonic Hall, solicitors Shufflebottom & Shield, Streets, all the restaurants in Hardman Street, the 43 Club, and so on. I had eight simultaneous shows. The solicitor John Shield was a keen collector of Maurice Cockrill's and Dave Tayborn's paintings.

In 1979, I was offered a retrospective exhibition of images of June Furlong. Organised by the artist Ray Fields, it was a tremendous success. It was held at the Royal Cambrian Academy gallery in Conway, North Wales where George Jardine, Peter Prendergast and Eddie Scott Jones were members. It was decided to include painting, drawing and photography. The exhibition revealed what a great pity it is that artists do not photograph all their work for record purposes. Many pieces are lost or altered, especially early pieces when artists are still searching for their own style and identity.

Liverpool Polytechnic was probably the last in the business to allow such freedom of creativity. Now new breeds of non-artist managers are forced to cut budgets and modularise everything. Liverpool students have always been good at drawing, allowed to continue with enough time to practise their skills to make sure they get them right. The evidence of drawing in my retrospective was testimony to the talent that we have had.

This region is particularly prolific artistically. I would suggest that the only equivalent area might be Cornwall. There has certainly been a distant similarity between the two even though one is rural and the other industrial. Liverpool has been linked to the Cornish coastal towns by sea for two hundred years, of course, importing china clay for the pottery industry. While Cornwall and St Ives have fostered modernist painting, Merseyside and Liverpool have encouraged modernist architecture and sculpture as well, inspiring generation after generation of artists. Again, both attracted interest and attention from well beyond their own borders. I feel that my exhibitions are testament to the keen interest in art that Liverpool can rightly claim as a defining feature of the city.

Listed overleaf is a brief summary of the effort I have made to contribute to the Liverpool art scene.

HISTORIOGRAPHY

Title	Location	Value	Date
Major Merseyside Artists	Liverpool Daily Post & Echo University of Liverpool Williamson Art Gallery Atkinson Art Gallery	£12,000	1976
Contemporary Artists Racquets Club	Upper Parliament Street	£4,000	1976
Contemporary Artists Queen's Jubilee Year	Major City locations Philharmonic Hall Empire Theatre Playhouse Theatre	£3,000	1977
One Man Show David Thistlewood	Royal Liverpool Hospital	£2,000	
100 + (No. 1) (MMA & YC)	University of Liverpool Senate House	£13,000	1978
100+ (No. 2) (MMA & YC)	Williamson Art Gallery	£13,000	1978
Major Merseyside Artists	Shufflebottom, Webster & Shield Streets Winebar	£5,000 £5,000	1978 1978
Major Merseyside Artists	Hope Street Fringe Festival Philharmonic Hall Antoni's Restaurant Streets Winebar Everyman Theatre Hardman Street Restaurants	 £3,500 £800 £5,000 £3,500 £2,000	1978
Retrospective June Furlong	Royal Cambrian Art Gallery Conway	£10,000	1979
Major Merseyside Artists	Liverpool Daily Post & Echo Atkinson Art Gallery Bootle Art Gallery	£11,000	
Young Artists	Liverpool School of Architecture	£16,000	
100 + (No. 3)	University of Liverpool Liverpool Artists Senate House	£34,000	1980
Major Merseyside Artists	Empire Theatre, Liverpool	£2,500	1984
Major Merseyside Artists	Royal Liverpool Hospital (Rolling three year exhibition)	£15,000	1987
Major Merseyside Artists	Port of Liverpool Building, Mersey Docks & Harbour Board	£20,000	1989
Visions & Topography Figurative Artists	Pilkington Glass Museum	£4,000	1990

Major Merseyside Artists	Ullet Road, Unitarian Church	£11,000	1990
Major Merseyside Artists	Liverpool Polytechnic,	£6,000	1990
Lets Hear it for the Girls Jacqueline Bayley & Barbara Davies Joint Show	Albert Dock, Liverpool	£4,000	
Major Merseyside Artists	Albert Dock, Liverpool	£11,000	1991
Colour & Imagination	Pilkington Glass Museum	£10,000	1992
Pictures & Craft Work (Part contribution to larger show)	Crosby Hall	£2,500	1992
Liverpool Seen (Part contribution to larger show) June: 45 years in Art	Williamson Art Gallery	£35,000	1992
Major Merseyside Artists & Young Contemporaries	Artists Club, Ebele Street	£11,000	1994
Art Exhibition (Part contribution to larger show)	Crosby Hall	£53,000	1994
Seven Artists Pilkington Glass Museum		£12,000	1996
Major Merseyside Artists	Liver Buildings, Liverpool	£12,000	1997
Major Merseyside Artists	Artists Club, Ebele Street	£20,015	1998
Major Merseyside Artists	NMGM Conservation Centre	£56,000	1999
	Total	£439,815	

Exhibitions undated

These are exhibitions that I can recall producing in addition to those listed above, but for which there remains no documentary reference or catalogue.

Major Merseyside Artists, Three Welsh Libraries
Major Merseyside Artists, Walton Hospital
Major Merseyside Artists, Adelphi Hotel
Ladies Only, 26 women artists, School of Architecture, University of Liverpool
Major Merseyside Artists, Playhouse Theatre, (6) Royal Liverpool Hospital, Empire Theatre (12)
Artists Under 30 Years, School of Architecture, University of Liverpool
Major Merseyside Artists, Port of Liverpool, Three Exhibitions
Major Merseyside Artists, Pizza House, Hardman Street, Streets Winebar, Baltimore Street
Young Contemporaries, Liverpool Polytechnic, Rodney Street
Major Merseyside Artists, Anglican Cathedral
Major Merseyside Artists, Liverpool Daily Post & Echo
Major Merseyside Artists, Empire Theatre (3)
Major Merseyside Artists, Everyman Theatre (2)
Major Merseyside Artists, Artists Club, Ebele Street
Major Merseyside Artists, Central Library, William Brown Street (3)

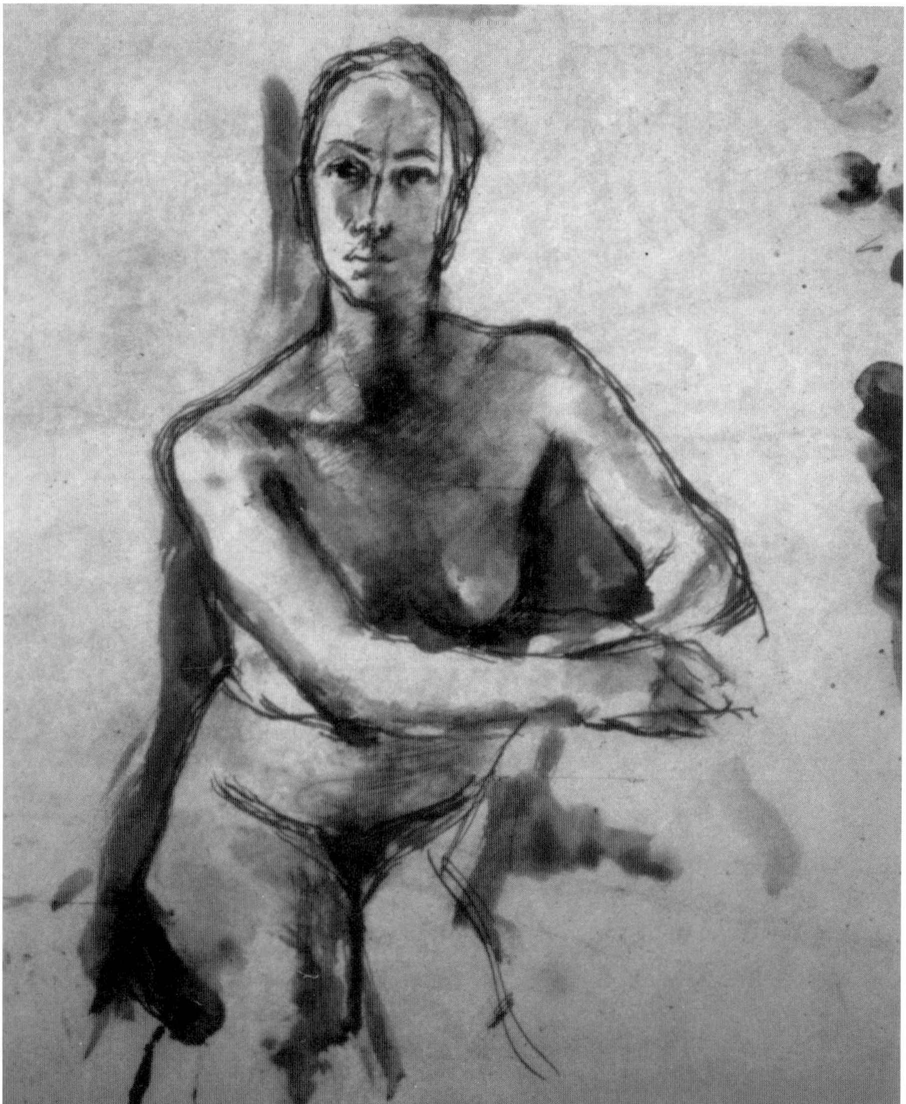

June Furlong, pen and ink on paper. Ballard.

Impressions of June
by artists and friends

From Lionel Burman

There are episodes in life which linger in some recess of the mind, like packets of Japanese paper flowers which unfold into blossoms only when engulfed with water. Such is the flow of memory, which from time to time float to the surface a faithfully realised experience of the past, like a perfectly formed blossom.

An image of June Furlong, from a long-dead era, is one such. Prompted by some undiscoverable association there germinates lucidly in my inner vision a picture of June in the life-room. I see clearly the shiny pale viridian paintwork of the walls and the steel roof-trusses and against them, bathed in the luminosity of the cool light descending from the roof, the figure of June, in one of her natural, relaxed-looking poses. The simultaneous contrast of the wall colouring enhance the cream and rose tints that bloom across her flesh, and fill its shadows with a subtle pale malachite tone. But above all it is a memory of June herself, and her lively inquiring mind and effervescent personality which resonates. The enclosed hermetic atmosphere of the life-room, its silence enfolded by the painstaking sobriety of the class intent at their easels, nevertheless seemed to become dominated by the radiance of June's personality. At the regular breaks between sittings June would emerge from her booth in her robe and walk around quite critically examining our labours, or, sitting on the throne, chat amicably with staff and students, her enquiring mind ranging over a diversity of topics and betraying a devouring curiosity about the world of art, and the manners and customs of its practitioners.

How distant those past years now appear: it seems uniformly to have been a grey cold era, in which it felt as if an oppressive gloom had settled over most aspects of life. The background of our lives was shadowed by the grinding tyranny of the great power systems in conflict, whilst in daily life one encountered frequent petty frustrations, in the fag ends of the age of austerity, reinforced for us, as students, by the discipline of college life, pursuing a curriculum virtually unchanged from the early years of the century, and a constant awareness of the exam system looming over us, on success in which our grants depended. So, from time to time, an outbreak of rebellious high spirits, in which June usually featured, was an inevitable release.

June's radiant disposition unfailingly lifted the spirits in what in retrospect

I cannot help but recall as the desperately intense strivings in the life-rooms. I think too, in looking back, that our responses to June's enthusiasms and questionings, in contrast to our usually more reticent and inhibited relationships to the quieter models, was an awareness that she had what nowadays is called a hinterland – a network of friendships, associations and experiences which enriched her life, beyond the self-absorbed rituals of art school, and one which some shared in, though not I, as I had other preoccupations and interests. Thus, whenever June was posing there was a more charged atmosphere in the room, whoever the lecturer in charge happened to be: Martin Bell, whose abstruse asceticism evoked echoes of the Euston Road School, John Keats, whose military bearing inherited from his war service gave him a slightly intimidating air, and Teddy Griffiths, a painstaking and serious man who produced works of great charm. (Years later, I happened to be in Llanrwyst, visiting the church, and as I stepped out I saw down by the river's edge a figure seated at an easel. It turned out to be Teddy Griffiths, employed on a watercolour landscape, executed in a very traditional English manner. Just for a moment, I felt transported into the century of Cotman and Sandby.)

But of all those doyens of the life-room, and the one with whom June seemed to have the closest rapport, Arthur Ballard stood out. Sparks seemed to fly when those two occupied the room. Ballard had as much the air of a student as an instructor. Indeed, he would often paint alongside us, impressing us with his constant air of striving toward an ever difficult to attain ideal. Arthur Ballard possessed more strongly than any of our lecturers (until, in later years George Mayer-Marton similarly entered on the scene) a generosity of outlook, seeking to share with us our common hopes and ideas: in this way he entered markedly into all our lives, becoming a significant influence, not least I am sure on June.

It is difficult to say which of these two distinctive personalities more dominate my recollections of those bleak 1950s years. The same conundrum, like another unfolding flower opened up when I returned some fifteen years later to Liverpool. Within days of my arrival I attended the opening of a Liverpool Academy Exhibition at the Walker Art Gallery. As I entered the picture gallery I found myself face to face with the ebullient figure of Arthur Ballard, surrounded by fellow painters, Don McKinley, Adrian Henri, and others. No sooner had I engaged in conversation with them than I was startled by a deep contralto voice echoing over my shoulder, 'Boris!', the nickname bestowed on me at seventeen, and which I have never entirely escaped. Turning round, I once again found myself in the company of June, on this occasion accompanied by George Jardine, her by then close friend.

As a student, for a year I had spent a day a week studying illustration under Jardine. Our relationship was one of mutual wariness: both of us highly introverted, I masking it under a display of brazen aggressiveness (acquired in my pre-college experiences), he, reticent seemingly to the point of embarrassment, which I put down to the influences he had encountered when a student in the Lake District, and already producing fascinating paintings of distinctive character. By the time of my return he was an established figure, and June, I rapidly learnt, a moving spirit in the contemporary art scene, regionally and nationally. Ever since it has been virtually impossible to attend any art event without encountering the vivacious presence of June, usually the focus of a group engaged in lively discussion, with June often having had a hand in the staging of the event herself.

I hope her biography will provide us with some measure of the contribution she has made on behalf of the wide circle of artists whom she counts as friends, and to contemporary artistic life. Having long memories of the entertaining autobiographical sketch she once wrote for Ark 14 I have often suggested to her that her full biography should be written, and now am pleased it is to appear. We should all be glad that she never became a professional skater instead.

Lionel Burman 1996

From Jack Shore

1 August 1996

I can't recall when I first met June but I drew from her when she came to Conwy to pose at the Royal Cambrian Academy which put on an exhibition of works by artists for which she had posed. I did two posters for this based on photographs June provided and thinking that the Conwy yobbos might make additions I used back views. Len Mercer, the curator of Plas Mawr knew the reputation of some of the local youths & decided not to display the posters on the street, relying instead on a local signwriter's skills – those used to advertise chapel anniversary services. In consequence the poster's when given to June were in a better, though perhaps less interesting, condition than if they had the attention of the Conway graffitists.

For a time after retiring from my post in Chester I taught Life Drawing to Graphics students at Liverpool on Thursdays. I knew when June was arriving as her voice preceded & heralded her entry into the drab, long narrow room that had to be used. The decrepit dreariness was only enlivened by the use of props & putting the day's work on the walls – Good models such as June showed a perceptive interest in the drawings, based on years of attentive observation of artists & teachers. They had an insider's understanding and knew from the tensions experienced in a pose whether these were expressed in the drawings.

June had a particular fad; she like to retain her shoes when posing, saying she feared stray drawing pins, and only with persistence could she be persuaded to take them off. Imagine the Rokeby Venus in platform sandals – I have a drawing of a rather prim conventional post on an upright chair which is a profile view of a pair of thick-soled shoes with June above them like a monument on a corbelled plinth.

J.S.

From Maurice Cockrill

I remember June being a strong force for good at Liverpool foundation course, much more than the usual inert model who sat like an apple and left when the class ended. She always made her cheerful presence felt in a most positive and direct way, encouraging students and tutors alike and generally contributing to the spirit and flow of the School, commenting on students work in the breaks in a most astute, perceptive and articulate way, getting to know them, their work and their problems and acting in every way like an ally and art-hungry fellow enthusiast.

She has very high standards and a keen intuition for who or what was good in drawing and painting and one always had the feeling that here in provincial Liverpool was someone who had known artists of real distinction and commitment and could still recognise these qualities and commend them. All this was carried by her extremely attractive personality, good-humour and a certain style that was refreshing in the drab, mean times.

She was kind to me and supportive and taught me a few things about tenacity, perseverance and self-belief and I'm very glad to have known her.

Maurice Cockrill

From John McFarland

Dear June,

Thank you for asking me to write about you for your book. You said, backing off a couple of inches and raising your voice three decibels, 'I've never been short of a word or two. So don't you be shy. You can have a page of my book. Say what you like'.

So here I am aware of a greater responsibility than Mark Anthony, for this subject is ALIVE – VERY MUCH SO, and whenever I see you which, in my case, is always with your clothes on I know I am in for some LIVELY CONVERSATION and some GOOD ADVICE.

You have given your life as a distinguished model to ART and those who have enjoyed the symbiosis of painter and painted have been enriched by its fruit.

As friends we go back a long way and in spirit even further for we are true Liverpudlians both, born round the corner from each other and not far apart in time. For a good while it was a happy chance that we were close enough neighbours for voice power to be our option for greeting

'Good evening June, have you had a good day?'

'Yes thank you, VERY NICE'

Your book is the nicest of evening events. No need yet to prepare to shed tears.

With love John McFarland

From Josh Kirby

10 May 1996

I met June in my last year at Liverpool City School of Art, as it was then. That was in 1948, she lived 'round the corner' from the Art school and joined in with the hectic student life style of the time, tracking from pub to café to pub! Don McKinlay, Arthur Ballard, Max Eden were always there, we seemed to go around in crowds everything being in walking distance. 'The Crack' in a little back ally was nearest pub to the Art School 'The Philharmonic' next in line, just over the road from the famous Philharmonic Hall where we saw foreign films in a film club there.

George Jardine taught at the art school then as did Martin Bell and we art students were sent out sketching around the city streets to get material and notes for paintings. So we were to be seen on the Pier Head sketching the ferries as they came and went, amongst boxes of vegetables in St Johns, market, recording elaborate ornate Victorian pub fronts perched on bollards as the cart horses went by. We thought the fun would never end...

Little did I know that then that June would years later be organising for me a big retrospective exhibition of my work at the newly refurbished Albert Dock complex in 1988. June had been gaining a reputation as an organiser of exhibitions and had mounted various mixed exhibitions of Liverpool artists over the years to which I had contributed maybe one or two but the Albert Dock idea was a quite a different scale about a hundred paintings and turned out to be a huge success having crowds of visitors day after day.

The gap between student days and the Albert Dock exhibition June and I had gone our separate ways, me making my way painting covers for science fiction paperbacks in London, June modelling in London also, but the only time I recall our paths crossing in that period was when I turned up at a private life class in Hampstead and low and behold June was the model.

Josh Kirby

From George Jardine

I first got to know June when she first came as a model. I would sometimes draw in the Sandon Studios Life Class at the Bluecoat Chambers.

June was very reliable as well as good looking. When it was known June was to come, the place would be packed out. Other models usually amateurs, obtained by advertising in the Liverpool Echo, were liable to come late, or not at all having panicked over having to appear nude. So a handful of people who had come to draw would wait for a time in conversation (often very interesting conversation) and then eventually drift off one by one. Some well known characters attended the Life Class – Stanley Reed who had accomplished many portraits of Lord Mayors now in the Town Hall, and was also an amateur astronomer who built his own telescope in his garden was knows as 'the banana man' owing to his eating bananas in the interval or rest period. He used to say – 'Tennis in the summer – life class in the winter'. The Belgian ambassador, – an elderly man with a monacle, and Roderick Bisson who drew large robust nudes after the manner of Frank Dobson. Even if the model happened to be thin, he would draw with circular flourishes of the arm, voluptuous nudes which he afterwards coloured pink.

June was the mainstay of the Sandon Life Class and in great demand at other colleges and Life Classes, even at the Lever Art Gallery in Port Sunlight, where the Life Class was held in a Freemasons room, with their symbols carved in the wooden panels. And all this as well as her full time work at the School of Art.

In the early days, Antique drawing was still in use. The students would say June far outclassed in perfection the Venus de Milo or any such Greek models. As my teaching in graphic design never included drawing classes. I seldom saw June at work in the College. Mr Penn, nearing retirement, a vigorous draughtsman of the John Singer Sergeant school of thought held enormous evening classes for part time students which depended on June for attendance.

Eventually the College grew and was divided into different departments, and June became the Fine Art model.

A visit to London with June brought out reminiscence of well known Artists she had known such as Lucien Freud, – even Jacob Epstein and Augustus John, when at one time she went to live and work in London.

How June escaped being a leading fashion model, I don't know, for she had the most elegant and fashion conscious dresses to wear. She introduced me to holidays in Mallorca and Spain and we have been going every summer for the past 20 years. A most companionable person. She learned to speak Spanish and has many friends among the local people and artists.

She works for Liverpool Artists where there is a lot of talent is remarkable. Creating exhibitions at different venues, such as the Albert Dock, St Helens Glass Museum, the offices of the Liverpool Post and Echo, and the University have been invaluable to local talent.

June has always been one of the greatest assets for art and artists in Liverpool.

Yours George Wallace Jardine A.R.C.A.

From Adrian Henri

June Furlong seems to have been an integral part of the Liverpool art scene since I settled here in 1957, a constant in an ever-changing world. Not only has she never quite retired from modelling, but from the late 1970s she had devoted much of her time to finding venues to show the work of artists of the regions, notably in a series at the Royal Liverpool Hospital, then at the Pier Head and elsewhere. 'Indomintable', is, I suppose, a word that might have been invented to describe her. Even though she does less of this activity now, and spends more of her time travelling, no Liverpool private view is complete without June's unmistakable voice and laugh in the crowd.

Galleries may come and go, art colleges become polytechnics, then universities, new artists appear, old artists die, ambitious artists leave for the greener pastures of the south, but June is still here, constant as the Liver Birds. Long may she remain so.

Adrian Henri

From Rod Dickson

7 February 1997

I remember arriving on my own from Ireland into Liverpool. A couple of hours later I was starting off my life as an artist by attending my first day at Liverpool Foundation. I soon met June who immediately let me feel at home with her warmth and good humour. From then on we continued to become great friends as she entertained us all with her stories. These often included Auerbach, Kossoff, Lucien Freud etc. and I think we were all intrigued to hear of such people and many of us became fans of their work.

June was really very much more than a model at Art College. She was a Key figure in the course and best friend to many of the students. She seemed to have tireless energy and also organised exhibitions around Liverpool. The first time I every exhibited my work was when June invited me to show a painting I had just finished during the first term on Foundation, in one of her exhibitions in Streets Restaurant, behind Kirklands on Hardman Street. I exhibited beside David Liddell also for the first time and shortly afterwards we became great friends and taught each other how to paint.

I think that Liverpool Art College, now called JMU owes a lot to June Furlong as do many of us who drew her during our time there. Also she has worked with most of the artists in Liverpool and I am sure that we have all been charmed by her at one time or another.

My very best wishes to you June

Love Rodney

From Julia Midgley

June Furlong has modelled in the life room at the School of Art here in Liverpool almost since time began. When I first started teaching in the life room, there were three models Sue, Marie and June, serving the three life studios.

During my first week of employment the then photography lecturer Reg Cox showed me some photographs of June taken, perhaps, thirty years earlier. It could have been a Hollywood still. Even today on her retirement the poise, hairstyle and involvement in the arts are the same.

She continues to organise exhibitions around Merseyside, organises the artists to commit work, and tirelessly embraces one project after another.

It is different, not to be drawing her, but she had not really gone. Hope Street and Falkner Street bear witness to her busy walk, the art school buildings are visited by her and in some ways because she is a member of the art community, she will never leave.

From Ron Scarland

21 May 1996

I sat in Liverpool's Philharmonic pub, enjoying a quiet pint, with my newly married wife. I was approached by a young woman who asked 'did the Liverpool City College of Art need an extra model?' I explained the current situation. Next week, June Furlong was employed. June's long and dedicated service to the Authority, as a Life model has now been some 45 years. She quickly learned by trial and experience about the often tiring, strenuous and disciplined craft of posing for life classes.

June developed a dedicated, professional approach to the task which over the years has rarely been bettered.

Always reliable, often taking the initiative, choosing or suggesting a pose, or spacing time spent between poses, she could hold difficult and demanding ones with alacrity and poise.

June's instinctive understanding of the difference between being an Artist's model and a photographic one was appreciated, techniques being so different.

Life modelling requires real stamina, tenacity and application. Initially, underpaid and overworked and often lacking appreciation of skills employed she developed a personal insight into the lives, attitudes and qualities of current practising draughtsmen, painters, and sculptors, often working day and evening sessions until 8-9 pm

Sometimes complex situations arose during the routine running of the life class, with helpful, tactful advice and understanding she helped to resolve the matter.

She developed a genuine interest in the visual arts as a whole, encouraging good, bad and indifferent abilities alike, when appropriate.

I would like to thank June for the stoic resilience and tenacity, over such a protracted period to time as professional Life Model.

Ron Scarland

From Jagjit Chuhan

10 May 1996

June Furlong with her perennial enthusiasm and love of art and culture, combined with an indomitable spirit, is an inspiration to Liverpool's art world. Indeed, she has been a contributor for several years to the cultural scene, as a Life Model of distinction at the Art School (along with her erstwhile colleagues Sue Lee and Marie Slott), and as a veteran organiser of exhibitions on Merseyside under the aegis of 'June Furlong Productions' I am sure that many students and lecturers will recall with great fondness, grappling with the complexities of drawing, painting or modelling with June Furlong as the life model – who posed well and seemed always to be surrounded by a kind of echo or shadow consisting of her long and rich experiences of working with numerous artists. So, in this way, as well as being an excellent physical presence, she was a generous source of cultural history, fascinating anecdotes, and considerable charm, with and spirit.

Jagjit Chuhan

Artist and Lecturer at JMU

From Yan Kel Feather

24 November 1996

She must have been only sixteen when I first me her at Peter Andersons Cave Café in Catharine Street she was so pretty and looked deliciously edible with the plumpish figure of Monroe, and the face of the then famous Gorgeous Gussie.

It was predictable that she was and would be a model. With June there was that added interest not only in modelling for artists, but in art itself. From friendships with various artists such as Weight, Jardine, and Ballard etc. she has gleaned enough knowledge to become a well informed useful arts promoter. All this she has accomplished without the help of lottery money, 50 years of modelling will not get a Turner Prize but possibly a place in the Guinness Book of Records.

One fine summers day in the early fifties we walked the length of the Kings Road. By the time we reached Sloane Square I had collected many addresses for rooms to let and she had collected three or four dates for modelling.

She modelled for me when I was in Upper Parly and tho' we were friends it wasn't a favour – she charged me the going rate, like the true professional she has been from the start.

Yan Kel Feather

From Mike Knowles

My wife Veronica and I enrolled at Liverpool in 1959 – I think that June was then in her prime, and a fine figure of a woman. I was 18 and maybe a slow developer for June was the first woman I saw wholly naked (I was still in a school uniform, having decided to enter the college late in the term on impulse). We gradually learned that June worked hard to keep herself in trim for what is certainly an arduous job – an all over tan from summer visits to Majorca/Ibiza and regular visits to (I think) a masseur. At that time she was heavily involved in the student social life, ever-present at parties usually with the pick of the new students in harness.

When eventually I moved on to London to study at the Slade I was slightly surprised to find that June seemed to be as well-known there as she always 'boasted' a roll call of the best known artists. Auerbach (my tutor) who remembered her with a carrier bag full of fivers, Skeaping, Freud, Carel Weight etc.

When eventually I returned to Liverpool, Veronica, Ken and myself hired June to pose for us for week or so – my painting is long gone, but Veronica's is still in existence, about 4' x 3' and an excellent likeness of June in her prime.

Eventually I went back to Liverpool to teach and for some years was in charge of models – not a task to be envied. There was always fierce rivalry between June, Sue (in particular) and to some extent Marie. It has to be said that following the loss of a kidney June was a somewhat subdued character, naturally nervous of her health, less stoic about the kinds of pose she would hold. She was very much an art-school institution and escaped the retribution which her cavalier spirit might have invoked from a strict regime. Criticism was like water off a duck's back and in any case she was always a major contributor to the ambience of the place.

June has always had instincts about painters and will encourage anybody who is half-way serious. She is usually fairly uncritical when it suits her purposes (i.e. if artists are prepared to show with her!) but probably has a secret list of artists whom she really respects. I made a small portrait of June in the early '80s which I gave to Richard Young, and which he in turn donated to the Williamson Art Gallery.

I don't see a lot of June these days but regard her as a personal friend, and value my many memories of her.

From Mike Kenny

JUNE FURLONG: Notes, April 1996

June was very much part of the Bohemian life of Liverpool 8 at the time when I first met her in 1959 when I started as young student at Liverpool College of Art. The Liverpool 8 area was very close-knit; the 'arty' area covered only several blocks around Canning Street, Hope Street, Gambier Terrace, when I moved in to 645 Canning Street, a famous house in the area owned by the MacKinlays, I became much more part of the life of Liverpool 8.

I first drew June Furlong in my first year at Art School. I was required to work with the other first year students in the rather austere Life Classes of Mr Wiffen. At that point Life Study was a chore to me. It could not compare with the excitement of the avant-garde. In those first months in Mr Wiffen's class I saw nothing in it but a mindless discipline, perhaps rather analogous to learning Latin at school. I remember, when you drew a standing figure in Mr Wiffen's class, you started the head half an inch from the top of the paper and the feet finished one inch from the bottom of the paper. Any deviation from this was considered to be pretty bad! As time passed I began to discover the importance of drawing, throughout the route of my awakening interest in sculpture. I worked on figurative sculptures and so the importance of the figure and understanding of the figure became clear to me. It was at that point that I began to work seriously in the Life room and began to appreciate the professionalism of June Furlong. She was able to strike a pose which was both refined and elegant, and above all had the amazing capacity to keep completely still for long periods! It was during this period later in the first year and into my second year at Liverpool College of Art that I drew from June increasingly. I mentioned earlier that I moved into Canning Street at the beginning of my second year and so I also got to know June as a person who frequented the pubs and parties around the area, in particular a pub that the students and tutors frequented called The Cracke. It was there that June would be seen at weekends with her then boyfriend…? I was often there talking to friends, whether it was Rod Murray and the girls Diz and Duckie (Margaret Disley and Margaret Duxbury) and also Rod Jones, Adrian Henri, Stuart Sutcliffe, John Lennon, Arthur Ballard, etc.

I remember being struck, when I look back on it, by the dichotomy between knowing June in the ambience of the formal Life Classes at the Art School and meeting her in the more relaxed social atmosphere at evening and weekends in the local pubs, etc.

In the autumn of 1961 I left Liverpool and started life as a student at the Slade School of Fine Art in London. It was there that my drawing was to develop and take on the pivotal role that it has for me today in my work as a sculptor. That early grounding in Liverpool, and particularly in the Life Classes where June modelled, was to have a crucial significance in my later development.

Michael Kenny

From Augustus John

20 September 1954

Dear Miss Furlong,

Thanks for sending the photographs. You have a very good physique and I would like to do some drawing when I can.

I sometimes come up to London for a short visit for I have no studio there at present but could draw in an ordinary room. I will let you know when this can be arranged shortly.

Yours sincerely,

Augustus John

I'm sending the photographs back

From Terry McDonald

I have known June since 1947. From that time until she retired in 1996 June posed for well known artists. She posed at the Liverpool College of Art, Hope Street, while I was a student there. I well remember working long hours at the college studios and modelling rooms while June posed for us. She had an innate sense of fun. I can remember one occasion when she was posing in the modelling studio for me and another apprentice of H Tyson Smith, a well known Liverpool Sculptor at that time. June was in a half-reclining pose and James (the other apprentice) had just taken a measurement from her – when he went back to his model June winked at me and reversed her pose so that when James turned his attention back to her he could not at first understand what had happened.

I can remember her posing on Friday evenings at the 'Sandon Studios', Bluecoat Chambers and on Saturdays in James Cliffe's studio. While she posed she recounted her experiences as an artist's model – with many an amusing anecdote.

I was privileged to draw June from life along with the masters of the College of Art – Messrs Jardine, Bisson, Keats, McPhearson, Tankard, and Stanley Reed of the Liverpool Institute who were all long time members of the Sandon Studio together with my employer and mentor H Tyson Smith/

June had a superb figure, like a miniature Venus. Speaking for myself and I am sure all the other artists, we will miss her posing.

Terry McDonald

Liverpool Sculptor

From Richard Young

Dear June,

I'm replying to your recent note. I must tell you I'm not a very good writer. However, I am moved to say you have been a great influence to many students including myself.

The unflagging effort in organising exhibitions, you have made a considerable contribution to the arts over a wide area.

In spite of having to retire from the Art School you are carrying on with the work of encouraging reluctant artists, long may you continue.

Yours with affection

Dick Young

From Peter Prendergast

12 November 1996

Dear June

I had Peter Davies here last week and this Friday just gone I went and saw Arthur Ballards exhibition in Birkenhead, he was the first person that I worked for, I could never quite understand why I had so much respect for him, on seeing the best of his work at the Williamson Gallery made me realise why, – he obviously had it all, what a pity that he didn't find the will to keep going and do something important. I remember having lots of arguments about teaching and drawing in particular, yet he never really seemed to disagree with me! On seeing his work I know why, he obviously believed in the same things as myself and in the probity of drawing.

I remember at that time, June, you were the model for the class that I taught. It was October 1970 til the Easter of 71. I made quite a few drawings of you, that I still have. In fact one of the best drawings I've made I gave as a gift to Mike Knowles, and hangs on their wall in Amwlch.

What I remember best is your professionalism and the way you helped me to get the students on my side. I remember you showing me the photographs of yourself when you were a Beauty Queen in Hampstead. I think it was the time that you also posed for Frank Auerbach at the Royal College, and do you remember those lovely etchings you have that Frank made, the most sensitive of images of yourself. I think, what I remember most about you June was that you took being a model as seriously as I did teaching and painting, I remember that first year on the foundation course, the atmosphere in the life room was electric and even on Friday afternoon, we worked right up until the end, and you were very much part of the scene, encouraging students to look harder and to listen to what I had to say, the drawing that Mike has of you, sitting on the floor on a mattress with your back against the wall. It's the kind of drawing that I wouldn't be able to do now – we are organic and change, through all these years later you've only just retired and I'm still painting and still teaching drawing two days a week. My eldest son is 25 now and teaches sculpture. Bronwen, my eldest daughter did a painting and now has a baby and my two others are 20 and 18 also making their way in the world. Lesley my wife did a degree in psychology and now works at the university.

I was showing at Agnews for 6 years, but this summer changed galleries and am with the Boundary Gallery in North London – after all these years I think my work is at last developing!

Well June I don't know if I've made any sense or whether I've said anything that will be useful for your book, I suppose my real memories are in the drawings I made of you all those years ago.

If you come this way ever with George Jardine don't hesitate to give us a ring. I would love to have a chat.

With many best wishes Peter

From Don McKinlay

Extract from letter to Jill Block, 26 March 1996

You will of course, know how June met me in Liverpool in the late forties. She started modelling at Liverpool School of Art, where I was a student around 1947 (June's memory of the date will be more accurate). Whilst I was a student I painted her many times and she was the model I painted for my N.D.D Exam. She was a delightful, reliable and beautiful model. Once she moved to London she continued to model at several prestigious Art Schools there.

Although I don't know the date, I can tell you that she returned to Liverpool to model. This was where she proceeded to develop her interest in the business of the Visual Arts by organising exhibitions to promote Merseyside artists like myself. She has been committed and enthusiastic about Art since I first met her as a student.

The paintings and drawings I did of June were done during the late forties and as far as I know all N.D.D. paintings were destroyed. I do knot know the whereabouts of any of my other student work and shortly after leaving College I was drafted into the Army for a couple of years.

I wish you well.

Yours sincerely,

D McKinlay

Interview with Nicholas Horsfield

After working in Manchester for the Arts Council. Horsfield painted June for a few years previous to the appointment Liverpool. I have many drawings labelled June, but few manifestly recognisable as June. Horsfield taught life drawing as part of his job one did everything in those days. I remember I had difficulty in painting June's head, few success satisfactory. My view of June as a model is coloured as I moved from painting to art history in 1963 and then retired after a marvellous job – half retirement really – as faculty tutor in life drawing which meant that I could draw for all comers that was probably 1977-82, which was of course, late in June's career. Her body was always in good trim. I remember from my own days as a student, the professional model always imposed a discipline on a class. I remember the star model at the RCA in the 1930s was Connie Swann – June and Connie are very similar.

From Charlie Metcalf

In 1959 I returned to Liverpool to teach in the Fashion and Textile department. June had also returned and more clothes were made. The last garment I made her was a changing robe that she wore when she was resting between poses. The design was very simple; a beautifully cut trapeze shape in a heavy furnishing fabric with a long zip down the front and a ruffle at the neck and elbows. This became a classic and was made in many fabrics. June also wore it out of the Life Room.

In 1995 I organised the design and making of the robes for the Chancellor and Honorary Fellows of the new Liverpool John Moores University. Perhaps June's simple robe was an excellent trial garment culminating with the sumptuous vestments worn by the University dignitaries.

In 1995, my wife and I sat with June and her friend at the Convocation Lunch when her Cousin Trevor Furlong, Managing Director and Chief Executive of the Mersey Docks and Harbour Company had received an Honorary Fellowship from the University. It is a pity that the University has not shown any appreciation for the work that HIS cousin has undertaken to benefit the artists on Merseyside.

In 1949 I completed my Intermediate course in Art and started the National Diploma course in Dress Design. June became a client. Her main request was that her dresses should be close fitting! We both agreed on the importance of using good fabrics. One of the fabrics was so expensive that she challenged me to make her a dress out of one yard. I did. She wanted it tighter. I obliged. She had an important date. It was a huge success. The long zip in the back of the dress split and the rest is history.

After my National Service in 1954 I worked in Dickens and Jones in London. June had come to London and was the toast of the town. More dresses were made. My wife remembers meeting June in Fitzjohns Avenue in Hampstead. I said "There is June, she owes me some money for a dress." we crossed the road and June suggested we met the following week in the new coffee bar in Hampstead. We dutifully called-in to the coffee bar, one of the first in London. When I asked the Spanish guitar player where June was, he replied: 'I took her to a party on Saturday and she is still there."

Yours Charlie

From Paul Cousins

24 April 1996

I first met June as a fresh young Art student of seventeen years on the Foundation Course at the Hope Place Annexe in the Autumn on 1968.

She was the first 'Life Model' I had ever seen and was certainly the first naked lady I had ever drawn. I remember being very nervous on that first encounter but also recall how professional and friendly June was, who without moving a muscle, would say just enough words of re-assurance to put everyone at their ease. (I still have that very first life drawing of June).

Throughout my degree years studying Graphic Design at Liverpool I sketched and painted June a great many times and grew to know her as a friend. I remember, with affection, the times in the Life Room when she would sit and discuss our paintings over a mug of tea during her 'breaks' and how I was interested in the many stories she would tell of her early days as a life model for the numerous, now very famous, artists she had posed for throughout the 50's and 60's.

I began exhibiting my paintings having joined the Liverpool Academy in the late 70's and met up with June again at about that time when she was organising group shows for 'Major Merseyside Artists' in venues throughout the city as far ranging as the Empire Theatre and Walton Hospital or the Post & Echo buildings and the University School of Architecture

In 1985 she organised my first 'one-man' at the Royal Liverpool Hospital and three years later presented my second and considerably more prestigious and successful show at 'Mercury Court', the then, recently re-developed, Exchange Station

I also worked with June on producing a number of posters, signs and programmes for some of the exhibitions and, as with many other artists, helped whenever possible with the hanging of the work.

Later exhibitions have included several small group shows at Pilkington

Glass Museum in St. Helens with a number of artists including Anthony Butler, George Drought, George Jardine and Ulrich West Recently Ulrich West and myself have been working more closely and have exhibited in a number of 'two-man' shows as a result of June bringing us together.

Since the early 80's I have been involved in over twenty 'group shows' and two 'one-man shows' organised and presented by June Furlong and without a doubt my artistic career would not be where it is today, nor would I have gained such professional confidence, without her tireless and ever optimistic support.

We continue to be very good friends and recently, as a thank you to her for all her professional help over the years, I presented her with a 'pastel' picture of her very own and very interesting 'yellow courtyard' garden which was part of my most recent 'one-man' show at Liverpool University's Senate House Gallery

Paul Cousins

Opposite June Furlong, Plate Sculpture. Ted Atkinson

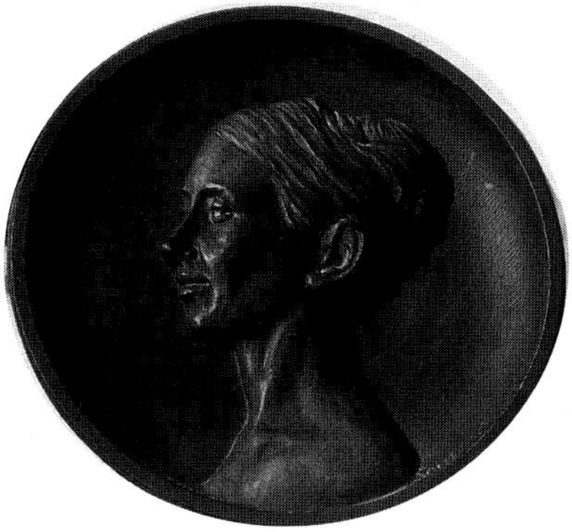

Books by Belinda

Belinda E Edwards moved to Yorksl
a lifelong people watcher and storyteller, but it took her a long time to settle down long enough to write things down. The only consistent thing about her writing habit is the dog at her feet.

She isn't content with simply observing behaviour; she has a deep-seated need to understand the why!

Love comes with the job. A series of interconnected feel-good standalone stories. Falling in love at work is never a good idea, but sometimes people cannot resist.

Batting for Charlie

When a face from her past turns up in a photo on her desk, India knows she'll need to protect her heart when working on her first solo project.

Presenting with Daniel

A professional sports star and farmer tries his hand at shopping TV, not expecting to fall in love. But then he meets his perfect co-presenter.

Designs on William

A heartbroken interior designer moves in with her best friend's brother to help him save his business. Neither accounted for how much they had grown up since they last met. Can they work together?

When Joe Met Matilda

Matilda is trying to escape her family when she takes a job on a Mediterranean yacht. Despite the sparkling location, a heartbroken Joe just doesn't want to be there.

His Perfect Block novella

A heartwarming and romantic introduction to Belinda's volleyball world.

love comes with the job

designs on WILLIAM

Belinda E Edwards

This is a work of fiction. Names, characters, businesses, places, events, and incidents are the products of the author's imagination or are used fictitiously. Any resemblance to actual persons, living or dead, or actual events is purely coincidental.

Cover created by Sparkling Creatives featuring photography by M B Worsnop.

ISBN: 978-1-917169-13-4

Sparkling Creatives.
Oak House, Beverley, UK. HU17 8XJ

Dedication

This book is for my son; he will probably never read it, but he inspired the story by introducing me to the world of millionaire homes on YouTube.

<<Hello, my name is Star. I am the home computer system designed by the technology guru William Thoresby. You will spot me talking in this story>>

Prologue

Damn, Damn, Damn! Stella balled her fists at her side as she slammed the door to her London flat. *This was my dream! Now what?*

Her shoulders sank as the music and voices filtered down from upstairs. After today's drama at work, she hoped Dan and Tasha wouldn't mind if she skipped their party. Who was she kidding? They'd only understand if she explained, and she felt too embarrassed to do that. *How didn't I see it happening right under my nose?*

The weight of what she'd done sat heavily in her stomach. With one slap to his face, she'd walked away from her dream job as soon as she realised how blind she'd been. It was simple; her boss had taken advantage of her in more ways than one. She could see it as clear as day now. He'd flattered Stella to manipulate her into working long hours, making her believe he not only loved her work but also that he cared deeply for her, too.

She tried to sort out her hair, but the anger boiled in her veins. Stella wanted to scream at herself for being so stupid as she pictured his face after she slapped him, and finally, the tears began to flow. The silent tears turned into sobs as she wrestled with what to do.

Knock, knock.

"Shit!" Stella stared at the mirror. *Pretend you're not here.*

"Stella, Stella, are you alright?" Knock, knock. "I can hear you crying. Let me in."

Well, there's no point pretending now. It was her cousin India. The one person she thought might understand. She'd left her own dream job for a lot less, but then India had something else to run to.

Resigned to having to tell at least one person, she opened the door.

"Stella, what's fudging wrong?"

"I quit." She walked away from the door, and her cousin followed.

"Thank God!" India hugged her.

"Really? That's your answer."

"Stella, you were here when I quit working for Bentley & Bentley. It's one of the best things I've ever done."

"Yes, but you had Charlie. I don't have anything or anyone. I've been such a fool." Stella slumped onto the sofa, and India sat beside her.

India took her hand. Stella couldn't look at her. She stared outside at the rain washing over London. *What do I do now?*

"I honestly believed Jackson cared about me." She frowned at India.

"I've been so blind. Why did it take me so long to work him out?" It was almost a whisper.

"Wait a minute, Jackson?" Stella watched India's face twist. "Stella, tell me, Jackson who?"

"Jackson Wilde, my boss, he … I thought he cared for me."

"Fudging 'eck, not Jackson Wilde!"

"See, even you knew. How could I have been so dumb?"

"What happened, Stella?"

"I found him all over the new girl. She only started a couple of weeks ago. I heard him telling her how rubbish I am at the job and how she had far more talent in her little finger," Stella let out a scoff.

"He said the same things to me when I started. I was so mad, I stormed in. I couldn't stop myself. I found him with no trousers on; they were neatly folded on his chair. I wonder if he trained her to do that, too."

"I'm so sorry, Stella. You don't deserve that."

"Do you know him?" Stella narrowed her eyes at her cousin.

"Not that well, but I've met him. He offered me a job. Tilly's dad saw him, and he rescued me, so I guess he suspected."

"Well, now I know. What the hell am I going to do?"

"You don't need to decide today." India smiled softly. "You weren't planning this. It's OK to take some time if you need it. Your dad will be pleased to have you home again for a while."

"Is that what you would do?"

"Fudge, no! But that's me … and my parents' problem. You need to do what is right for you. Take your time. But come to the party, please."

Upstairs, Stella found the small flat bursting at the seams with friends. Daniel looked ecstatically happy. He'd started making another round of pizzas when a quiet Stella arrived with India.

Wandering aimlessly over to the food table, Stella cringed when she heard them discussing her.

"Ha, you found her." Daniel frowned.

"Is she OK? She looks like she's been crying."

"She will be. Tasha, you won't believe what I've just worked out."

"Go on." Natasha encouraged.

"Her boss. It's Jackson Wilde. Or should I say it WAS Jackson Wilde? She quit this afternoon."

"I'm sorry, she loved that job, but Jackson Wilde! I can't help but think it's for the best. Explains a lot, though. The big money budgets and the stupid demands on her time. He hasn't …?"

"She isn't saying." Stella watched as Natasha and India shivered.

"Have I met him?" Daniel asked, and Stella's heart sank even further. *Does everyone else know about Jackson?* She wanted to leave, but India would only follow her and insist on talking about it.

"You might do. He's the creep in the car park in Leeds."

"Tilly is the only one I know who got the better of Jackson Wilde from the start. She is very much her father's daughter."

"Probably because he found out she's Maxwell Sykes's daughter."

"How is Tilly?"

"Fed-up. They're pretty sure she'll have this baby by Christmas."

Stella walked away. She wasn't sure what was worse, talk of Jackson or talk of babies. She silently studied the food on the table until her phone lit up with the face of her best friend.

She stood back to talk to Sarah, still watching as Daniel fussed, putting more snacks into the bowls on the table. She tried to assure Sarah that she'd be fine despite feeling like her whole world had collapsed. Her dream and the man she thought was a dream, too.

"It's fine. I'm not alone."

"Stella, I know how important all this was to you. You've been giving this guy twenty hours a day."

"Sarah, I said I'm fine. I'm at that party. It's just in the flat upstairs."

"The flat that India had?"

"Yes, she's here too."

Daniel watched her, watching him. He marched over and stood beside her, looking poised to take the phone from her. Eventually, Daniel touched her arm and whispered to her.

"Your friend can come here if it helps."

"Thanks, Dan." She slipped out of the room, away from the party buzz.

"Look, Sarah, why don't you come over? Then I won't offend my neighbours and my cousin."

"Are you sure?"

"Yes. I admit it, I could do with talking this through out loud. At the moment, I can't think straight."

"Is there food? I haven't eaten yet."

"There is plenty."

"On my way then."

Back in the room, Stella kissed Daniel on the cheek. "Thanks, Dan, my friend's coming. Her name's Sarah."

"I hope she isn't a troublemaker." Daniel teased.

"She is a lovely girl, though I'm sorry to tell you, but when we get together, we are known for causing trouble."

"Not that, Sarah!" India said, her eyebrows pulling together. A frown hit Daniel's face, but India couldn't hide her smile. "I haven't seen her since school. Is she living far away?"

"Her brother is in the U.S. She's staying in his London flat for now."

"I don't think I ever met her brother. Is he older than you guys?"

"Four school years older than us, but he didn't go to our school. A long streak of nerd. He didn't come down to the pub much either."

They fell silent until Stella blurted out, "I feel like a fool for falling for all his lies. Do you think he simply wanted me to work longer hours?"

"To be totally honest, I don't think the guy can help himself. I guess he thinks being surrounded by beautiful women is a power thing, or maybe he thinks he can flatter them into doing whatever he wants. I'm not sure he does it consciously."

"That makes sense. Do you think he means what he says?"

"Actually, he probably does. He seems to do well with his business, and you were happy working for him at first, weren't you?"

"Yes, the hours were terrible, but I was so keen. I enjoyed the work. I feel so foolish. How did I miss it, if you all spotted him straight away?"

"London is not like Hursts Bridge. I suppose back there, we were all protected by Granddad's name. Then, when your mum left, your dad struggled, and his new wives didn't help, so the rest of the family, led by Grandma, moved in to shelter you. She meant well."

"I guess she did." Stella dug her toes into the carpet.

"Even the set-up here: Our Grandparents owned this building, so we had somewhere to escape to London in … it made life easier for us. It was more of Grandma sheltering 'her girls'."

"So, you think I've been spoilt?"

"Not spoilt but sheltered. We all have," India sighed, "except the boys don't see it."

As the party wore on, people started to dance, and Stella retreated to the wall by the door, waiting for Sarah. She struggled to watch as Daniel whirled Natasha around and gently kissed her. Wrapped in Charlie's arms, her cousin swayed slowly. His smile lit up the room, and Stella was happy they'd found each other. Sadly, tonight, watching them made her heart feel heavy in her chest. Tonight, she felt destined to stay only meeting men like Jackson Wilde.

Sarah's arrival came as a huge relief. A big hug from her best friend seemed to make everything that had happened that week go away. Finally, someone she could talk to who she knew would never judge her. They'd been so close from the moment they met. Their parents were friends, and their lives had been meshed together forever.

As an only child, Sarah was the nearest thing to a sibling Stella had.

"Are you going home?"

"To Hursts Bridge? I could, but how do I explain this mess? I think my best hope is going to see my Mum in New York?"

"Ah, Christmas in New York sounds fun. I'd come with you, but I'd never get time off from the restaurant at this time of year. Now, where is the food?" Sarah fell on Daniel's pizza.

"Come dance with me," Zach Mitchell held out his palm.

Stella took the offered hand, and as they moved slowly to the music, his arm tightened around her waist. She sighed as she rested her head on his chest.

"You looked like you've had a difficult day. I hope that sigh means you're relaxed now."

"Let's just say I'm getting there."

"Is it a work thing or a guy thing?"

"Bit of both, really, but I quit my job today, so no problem now."

"So, you don't need to work on Monday?"

"No, I guess that's one thing."

"Do you have a new job lined up, or is it time for a holiday?"

"Well, I don't have another job lined up, so I'm not sure what I'm doing next."

Zach bent his head down until Stella could feel his breath on her neck. She shivered as he whispered in her ear.

"I'm flying back to Aus on Monday. Come with me."

"Thank you, but I think I need to go spend time with my family."

"I take it they don't live in Australia."

"No, my dad lives near Hursts Bridge, which is close to my grandparents and my uncle, that's India's dad."

"Ah, well, I've met your uncle and your granddad. I'm guessing you aren't rushing there." Stella laughed and shook her head.

"Hmm, I'm the youngest, so they all love me. I'm just worried about what they would think about this mess. I guess that's why I'm thinking about going to see my mum instead."

"And where does she live?"

"She lives in New York with her new husband."

"New York? No wonder I can't tempt you to the outback." Stella smiled. Zach was lovely, and being in his arms felt safe.

"And there I thought I'd got myself a pocket-sized Barrington Jones," he said with a wicked smile. Stella laughed.

"A 'Barrington Jones' after you've met the men of the family?"

"I guess you're right there. I do rather like India, though, and you look so alike. I suppose I know now that doesn't mean you are like her that much."

"Zach Mitchell, I thought you were smooth."

"I guess I should just stop talking. But the offer to come back with me still stands." He pulled her closer and danced her a little faster.

"When will you go?"

"As soon as I can get a flight."

Chapter 1

"She has such an amazing sense of colour. She keeps finding so many wonderful new makers. Of course, she gets all her taste from me."

Stella squirmed in her chair, hoping she hadn't just rolled her eyes.

"How long is she going to be here, Judy?" *Hey! I'm right here, can't you ask me?*

"I have two more bedrooms to decorate, so I hope she stays long enough to do those."

"Is she looking for a job or a husband?" *Hello. I'm still here.*

"Why get a job? Get a husband and let him do the work stuff. "

"I'll drink to that." *How much do they drink?*

"My daughter has sense. I'm sure she will find a great husband, eventually."

"Excuse me, I must go to the toilet." *Before I say precisely what I'm thinking.*

Whilst away from the table, she checked her phone to find a menacing text from Jackson.

BOSS: You are going to regret your actions.

She turned off her phone and angrily pushed it deep into her bag. *I regret starting. I don't regret leaving.*

Back at the Manhattan apartment, Stella's mum fidgeted with her bags, not looking at Stella. She walked towards her studio, and Stella followed her through the door. The room was drenched top to bottom in intense, bright colours.

"You were quiet today. I hope you didn't take all that chatter to heart. They all mean well."

"You haven't been in here since I arrived, Mum."

"Well, it's been Christmas, and I had you here. Maybe it was something I didn't need to escape from."

"Do you only paint to escape?"

"Good lord no. I do it because I can't not paint. It's in here." She patted her chest.

“Don't rush to find what you do next, Stella, it will come. I'm so sorry for what you've been through with that man.”

“But how … I didn't say …”

“Stella, you don't get to my age without realising that at the root of most problems is a man.”

“I guess the banter today hurt a bit because I feel so lost right now.”

“Isn’t it about time you told me what happened?”

“I feel so naïve. I was so excited about that job. I couldn’t wait to move to London and work with such amazing clients. Jackson couldn’t have been more encouraging. He said I had a wonderful style.”

“Well, that’s because you do.”

Stella’s lip twisted.

“The flattery extended to me. We worked late, and he would take me to dinner. He bought great wine, and champagne was always around. I fell for his sweet words hook, line and sinker.”

“Darling, we all make mistakes, especially where men are concerned. You can’t let it define your future. It’s a lesson. Learn from it and move on.”

“The problem is Jackson owns the London scene.”

“Does he? Or is that just what he told you?”

India had assured her he was a well-known sleazeball. Why hadn’t she asked more questions before she took the job? She suspected that his reputation was somehow linked to that. She couldn’t help feeling threatened by his comments as she left. ‘You be careful, little girl’.

Stella couldn’t imagine going to London and trying to exist in the interior design world without bumping into Jackson Wilde. *What will he be saying about me?*

“Now, when are we going to talk about you redesigning the master bedroom?”

“The primary mum. We don’t say master anymore.”

One thing was certain in Stella’s brain: she couldn’t stay with her mum much longer. First, she had to figure out where to go next. Was she ready to go back to London and try again?

“Why didn’t you have a studio in Hursts Bridge?”

“Do you think I could have had a studio like this? Do you think I could be myself?” Judy shook her head. “I'm far too loud. I wore a pair of pink trousers and a yellow shirt once, just to run to the shops, and

several old ladies nearly had a heart attack. I had to get out of there, Stella. I had to come back to the U.S. It's where I was born. It's where I belong, and it's where Mike was waiting for me."

"Did you know Mike before?"

"I didn't leave your dad for Mike or any other man. I left your dad. No, maybe I didn't leave your dad. I left the life that was strangling me so that I could be myself." It was only a few sentences, but it was the start of understanding her mum leaving her. She looked up at the vast canvas on the wall, colour and texture springing off its surface and filling the room.

"I love this one full of orange."

"I painted that after we visited Mike's sister."

"Maribeth? She lives in northern California, doesn't she?"

"They live in the south. She seems to prefer it to the East Coast."

"You're so clever, Mum, I wish I had your talent."

"You have your own talent. But if you'd like the painting, it's yours."

It was a relief that her mother was going to yet another gala dinner tonight, so she had the apartment to herself. She took her snacks into the bedroom and devoted some time to her blog. She'd lost count of the photos she'd taken since she arrived. Being in New York had given her so many opportunities to meet new designers.

When she grew tired of working, she turned to the video blogs she loved. *Hidir has a new one AGAIN!* This was probably her favourite channel. She watched in awe as he toured yet another millionaire's home. Today's video was from the south of France. The way the sunlight sparkled into the interior lit something inside her, and she grabbed a notebook, making sketches as she watched.

Stella had been making notes on designers she would like to use, but tonight she'd finally decided to consider a plan for her own business. She didn't have the working capital that Jackson had, but there must be a way to use what she'd started to save. She hadn't spent the money she had been given at Christmas from either of her parents. The money she'd earned doing jobs for her mum's friends would help. Her savings were adding up. Maybe one day she could do this on her own.

When Sarah's name flashed up on her phone, she sat back on her bed and crossed her ankles. *Just what I needed.*

"How's New York? Have you been enjoying the January Sales?"

"It's great." Her flat tone didn't match the words.

"From your blog, I thought you were having a wonderful time, and yet you don't sound too excited."

"I guess I've just been busy doing things with Mum."

"So, you aren't enjoying it?"

"I know I needed to escape, but I'm not sure coming to New York was the best idea."

"So, is it New York, or is Judy being her normal self?"

"Well, as always, you're right. Mum has me working for free – flaunting it all in front of her friends. I don't mind that so much, but she's still my mum. It's not like working for a client I don't know. If I had a job to come back to, I would have an excuse to leave." Stella sighed and lay back on the bed. "Tell me, Sarah, how am I going to find a job in London, stuck here, running around after my mother?"

"I might have the answer. That's why I rang."

"A job? In London?" Stella's heart lifted.

"Ah! No … It's in California."

"I'm not sure …"

"Stella, I want you to do this for me."

"For you?" Her brows pulled together.

"Yes. It's for Will. He's got into some sort of mess."

"For your brother, Will? I thought he was earning mega bucks in that business of his."

"He is. Or do I mean he was? I'm not sure I understand it." Sarah sighed. "His tech company has been focusing on home installations. You know, the stuff that turns on your lights or opens the garage door."

"I thought it was more technical than that."

"It probably is, I'm a baker. What do I know about technology? Anyway, he got excited when a major player in property development approached him to provide all the technology for the showhouse. It's a new development of ten houses outside Los Angeles. The idea was that as they sold each of the properties, Will's company would be awarded the job to do all the bespoke work on the other plots. I think he told Will it would open doors to the right sort of publicity."

"Sounds like an amazing opportunity." Stella mindlessly smoothed the elaborate bedcover.

"You know what Will's like, completely brilliant and not a clue at the same time."

"Do you remember when he tried to make pancakes for us?" As Stella said the words, she saw a skinny Will, scratching the back of his head, his dirty blond hair hanging in his eyes and covered in flour.

"His glasses were covered in batter. He had no idea what he'd done wrong."

"I've so many memories like that. I guess he had to look out for us so often. So, you want me to cook him some pancakes?"

"He needs your fabulous interior design skills."

"Well, I've seen that flat of his you're living in. It's very black and white. But surely this developer has a designer."

"I have to say I don't understand the details, but somehow this fancy developer hit a hurdle and then another, and Will bailed him out. Now, this guy's gone missing, and Will's been left holding the can. Poor Will needs to sell the units to get the money back into his tech business."

"I see. Are you sure I can do something?"

"Will hates fuss, as you said. His whole life is black and white, but he needs to show these units."

"So, are they built?"

"Will's staying in one. It's not finished, but he needed to sell his old place out there. He says he can work on it more easily if he's there, but I'm not sure he had much choice. I'm thinking if you go down now, you can work on styling to be ready to go as soon as his team finishes."

"What did Will say?"

"Please, Stella. I'm worried about him. Can you do this for me? I need someone who understands him."

"I don't know him that well anymore."

"OK." Sarah let out a long sigh. "Stella, I need someone I can trust."

"I guess I owe both of you a few favours. Do you think he'll be OK with me taking a few photos for my blog and my portfolio?"

"Of course, he won't mind. I think he wants a lot of publicity for this project; maybe it can help you, too."

"I'll do my best."

Chapter 2

The flight had been bumpy, so she was relieved when the plane landed bang on time. Stella didn't want Will waiting for her too long. Bright overhead lights in the arrival hall cast a glow over the scene in front of her, spiking the excitement she'd felt since she'd booked her ticket.

Despite her shaky legs, everything went smoothly as she came through baggage claim, and when she came to customs, she had a fun chat with a tall customs officer with a twinkle in his eye who wanted to know all about her plans for her trip to Los Angeles. She avoided telling him about working for Will and focused on staying with a family friend.

"Is this friend a girl or a guy?"

"It's a guy."

A cough from the man's supervisor made him blush, but he winked at Stella as he passed her back her passport. Life could be more fun here.

Outside, the warm air hit Stella. It was definitely winter in New York, and she hadn't realised how much warmer California would be.

Her heart skipped as she frantically searched the faces in the crowd, looking for Will. Her brain whirled with a myriad of questions. Would he have changed? She felt sure she would recognise him with his glasses and mop of hair. No matter how hard she looked, she couldn't see him. Maybe he's been held up? I'll get a drink and call him.

Stella settled down with a coffee to stay awake and tried to call Will. His number went straight to voicemail. Well, if he's driving, maybe he won't be able to answer. I guess that means he's on his way.

Making the most of her wait, she posted on social media to announce her arrival, leaving comments on posts and searching for ideas for local designers and suppliers. She also messaged Jenny, one of her favourite vloggers, to let her know she'd be in Los Angeles for a while.

Two hours and three coffees later, and still no sign of Will. The anticipation she'd arrived with had disappeared, and her confidence was starting to wane. Stella had tried calling him several times, but still, there was no answer. Concern for him sat heavily on her stomach.

Maybe if she just hired a car from the airport, she would be sorted until she flew home. As soon as she entered her age in the online form, the price doubled. She could see the money she'd been saving for her

business dripping out of a big hole in the floor. With a sigh, she picked up her bags and made her way over to the shuttle buses.

Stella couldn't believe just how hot it was on the second bus, considering it was January. The long journey gave her too much time to worry. When another aggressive text bounced in from Jackson Wilde, she blocked his number.

One more bus and a taxi, and finally she stood in front of a large mud-splattered black gate. A tall, dark-haired man with the darkest eyes opened the gate and waited for her to explain that she was looking for Will Thoresby. He watched her suspiciously.

"This is it. I'm Grigori, the works manager." The man finally smiled at Stella. "Is Mr Thoresby expecting you?"

"Well, yes, I thought he was picking me up from the airport. I hope he isn't there trying to find me."

"No, he's been here all day. If you go through that door and down to the big windows at the end, you should find him." The warm smile was still there, and Stella picked up on the European accent.

Stella filled her lungs, hoisting her heavy tote bag onto her shoulder, and pulled her case towards the door Grigori had pointed out. The sound of hammers and power tools echoed in the almost empty space.

She left the case just inside the door, making her way tentatively down the corridor and into a large room with just one simple two-seater sofa in it. The rather sad sofa reminded her of the one Will had in London. There was still no sign of William Thoresby.

Stella's eyes swept the unfinished room, finally settling on the expanse of glass and the breathtaking views of the hills. The whole day had been one of contrasts. She may still be in the States, but it wasn't just the time zone that had changed.

Eventually, she spotted another worker with his head inside a wall panel. Long jean-clad legs extended out into the room with a pair of enormous feet on the end. She looked away from the stretched tanned torso above the jeans and tried phoning Will again.

A phone buzzed in the pocket of the jeans. The jeans kept working inside the panel. Stella stamped her foot.

"William Thoresby! Is that you? Ignoring my calls!"

"Stella? What the …?"

He scrambled to pull himself out of the panel until his whole body lay on the floor, looking up at her, banging his head in the process.

"What day is it?" A stunned Will rubbed his forehead.

"It's Tuesday!"

"That's what I thought, so why are you here? I wasn't expecting you for two days. Why the change of plans?"

"It's always been Tuesday, Will."

"Are you sure?" He stood up, looking at Stella, still with the same confused look on his face.

"Actually, are you sure you are little Stella? I mean, you look a lot bigger. Not taller, I guess, but definitely more rounded." His eyes landed on her chest. Stella was annoyed to feel her cheeks heating. She'd come here to work, not flirt with Sarah's big brother. Nevertheless, she found herself checking out how he'd changed, too. The thick, black-framed glasses were gone, and his body … he was taller and broader, and his hair! It still flopped in his eyes, but there was no doubt it was blond now.

"I guess we've both changed."

Will scratched the back of his head. "Wasn't I supposed to pick you up at the airport? Shit, Sarah's going to kill me. Is there any chance you can forget to tell her that bit when you report in?"

"Report in?"

"Come on, Star, my little sister's going to expect you to report on my life here, isn't she?" *Star, no one's called me that since ... well, since Will last called me it.*

Stella froze, her whole body felt heavy, and that one word triggered something. Whatever had been keeping her going left. Will must have noticed the change.

"Are you OK there, little one?"

"I'm just tired. It's been a long day."

"Oh, and no one picked you up. I'm sorry." Will wrapped his arms around her and pulled her close. After a long day travelling from New York, it felt like home. A single tear slipped down her face, which she rubbed away. If Will saw it, she was grateful he didn't mention it.

With a squeeze, Will pushed her away, stroking the short black hair from her face.

"I think this calls for a cup of tea. That will pep you up."

He walked her into an area that contained a kitchen section. Stella's eyes swept the room, her brain looking for what still needed doing. It was clearly not finished, and just a few items were focused at one end of the room.

"How do you like your tea? Still two sugars?"

"Milk no sugar, please Will."

"Sit down." The only place to sit was three mismatched barstools that stood next to a makeshift breakfast bar. Stella reminded herself that this unit wasn't finished, and that's why she was here, to help Will make it look wonderful. The whole place, though vast, was devoid of any character or warmth. The scale of the rooms was staggering compared with the compact spaces she worked on in London or New York.

"I don't think I've ever seen you so quiet. Are you OK?" Her eyes were now back on Will, observing this man who had replaced the boy from her childhood.

"As I said, it's been a long day."

"How long did you wait for me?"

"Two hours, then I caught a bus, well, the first bus."

Will placed a mug of tea in front of her and sat on the stool next to her. Leaning forward on his arms, he studied her again.

"Where are you going after here?"

"Oh, I haven't really thought about it. It depends on how long it takes us to complete this project. Do you have any idea of time scales?"

"Time scales? For what?"

"Getting this on the market. That's why I'm here. Sarah said you needed help."

"Ha."

"Will?"

"Sarah said you needed a place to stay, something about your old boss."

"Oh, I see. Well, I guess she's right, to some extent. I did leave my job." Stella looked out at the men working outside.

"I've been staying at my mum's, doing some bits of interior design in New York, but it's time to move on."

"So, you think you're here to do the interior design on this project?"

"Does that mean you don't need me?"

The silence that followed her question hung heavy in the room.

Will's hand rubbed the back of his neck. It was a pose Stella recognised from the past. The weight of Will's confusion was displayed across his face. When he didn't speak, she felt compelled to keep talking.

"This is what I do. I understand this isn't London. I know what's done out here." Stella waved an arm at the views out over the rolling landscape and the houses that twinkled on the hillsides.

"Vanessa, my business manager, has been using this designer."

"This designer," she looked at Will, "is he someone I've heard of?"

Will cleared his throat. "His name is Valentin LaRoche – he's French. I'm told he is important in L.A."

"Well, it's a new name to me."

"I guess he hasn't heard of you either," he smiled. "I do know he seems expensive. Some fittings have been ordered, but I'm not sure the budget can stretch to everything on the list.

"Hmm, so it's a tight budget."

"Sadly, yes. But it can't look like that, quite the opposite, in fact. I'll be here, for what good I'll be." Stella's heart wanted to melt at the sad look in his eyes, but was this too much for her to take on?

"Why Will? Why is the budget so tight?"

"I had an agreement with the original developer. I would fit the tech package for the show house, and then we would use that to sell the other houses. Somehow, I agreed I would like the show house."

"And you didn't want to live here?" Will sighed.

"Oh yes, I did, but in signing the documents to buy that, I undersigned the whole development. And then he just disappeared, and the bank got in touch. I had two choices: take over the entire project or walk away and lose all the money I'd put in."

Stella covered his hand with hers. Will offered her a half smile.

"Sarah was right. I'm in a mess. I do need help. I'm just not sure if we aren't both out of our depth here, Star."

Stella squeezed his hand as that name slipped out again.

Chapter 3

How did I end up in this mess? And now I find myself accepting help from Stella, of all people.

Now here he was sitting on a wonky stool with her hand clamped over his. Turmoil spread through his body. It had been there since she arrived. When Sarah asked him if she could stay, because she was in trouble, his protective big brother sense had kicked in. The thought that someone could upset her was something he didn't like to think about. The hand covering his felt so soft, and he couldn't sit there any longer.

"You look tired." He said, standing up.

"It's been a long day."

"Where are you staying?" As soon as the words left his mouth, Will realised he'd done it again. Of course, Sarah had wanted her to stay here, and he still only had one bedroom finished. Will forced a laugh out to cover the mistake.

"Just joking, Star. I'm just so embarrassed I got the wrong day, so I haven't changed the bed. I think we need to get some food, and I'll get the bed sorted."

One glance inside the fridge had him slamming the door shut again before she saw how little food he had in there.

"Do you still eat pizza?" When she nodded, he swiftly ordered three pizzas to be delivered.

"Would you like another cup of tea, or do you want something stronger?"

"If we're waiting for food to be delivered, I'm going to say tea. I would be asleep before it gets here otherwise."

"Right, help yourself, and I'll go and sort somewhere for you to sleep."

"I can take the couch, Will."

"As if! Sarah's going to kill me for leaving you at the airport. If she found out I let you sleep on the couch, she would finish me somehow."

"You'll never fit on there. When did you get so tall?"

"Me? You are the one who has grown up."

Stella paused with the teapot in her hand.

"I guess we both grew up, hey?"

William wasn't sure why he felt quite so off-centre. This whole project was getting so out of hand, and now he had Stella to take care of, too. Deep inside, he was pleased she was here. With clean sheets in his hand, he looked around the bedroom he'd been using. His bedside table was clear, the entire room was clear because that was how he liked his life, ordered. On the other side of the bed, a lone bottle of hand cream. *Vanessa, every time Vanessa. Why does she keep leaving things?*

His mood shifted back and forth between thinking of Stella's arrival and Vanessa's place in his life. One thing he knew, he needed to tell Vanessa in the morning. If she found out about Stella some other way, he wasn't sure how she would react. In his head, he went over the words he would use to explain how he was doing a favour for his sister's friend.

The room looked pretty basic by the standard he knew Stella had back in Hursts Bridge. There was nothing he could do about that tonight.

He changed his bed and collected clothes for the office in the morning, along with his swimming gear. He couldn't think about starting a new day without his swim. The pool had been the first thing he'd finished, even before anything inside the house. It was where he did his thinking. He might just swim later.

"This is the room I've been using. It's the only one anywhere near finished at the moment. I'll get the team on it tomorrow. In the meantime, I insist you take the bed." Will looked down at Stella; she looked exhausted, and it made him want to protect her again. She didn't answer him, and he lifted his hand to her cheek. Every inch of him wanted to hold her, and it felt so wrong. Fortunately for him, the pizza arrived. It stopped him from doing something he would regret later.

He lifted the pizza boxes and looked around him. Shit, where do we sit? It's back to that tiny sofa. What is wrong with me? I've known her for years. I can manage to sit next to her long enough to eat.

"I'm afraid there's only the sofa." He placed the boxes on the floor. "Can I pour you a drink? Wine or beer?"

Stella's tired face looked at him. He didn't remember her ever being so quiet.

"Maybe you want more tea?"

"Can I just have a glass of water now and maybe a cup of tea later?"

"Of course." He fetched her the water and himself a bottle of beer. Lifting the first box, he offered her a slice.

"I hope you're hungry."

"Are you telling me, you couldn't eat all three pizzas these days?"

"I try to eat a bit better."

"Is that another sign you've grown up?" She grinned at him as she took another bite. Relief spread through Will; she was back. It had been nothing serious; she just needed food and probably the water. He remembered that she'd flown from the other side of America, and her body clock would be off.

"Probably. What was life like in New York?"

"You've met my mum," Will nodded, and Stella continued with a smile.

"Her new husband is 'an important man'. So, take what she was like in Hursts Bridge and multiply by ten. Every day involved shopping and lunch, unless she was at the salon. Most nights involved a dinner of some sort."

"How did that go for you?"

"It wasn't as bad as it sounds because whilst she had me there, we mostly shopped for the apartment."

"Does that mean what I think it means?"

"If you mean she was using me as an interior designer for her and her friends, then yes."

"I'm sorry, Stella."

"Actually, I think I enjoyed it. It was nice that she trusted my judgment. It's not like she doesn't have a good eye for colour."

"I get that. It took ages to get my dad to let me do anything at his house."

"You don't mean they don't always get that we've grown up?" She laughed and dropped her head to his shoulder. And then she froze.

Will froze, too. It all felt very strange.

Chapter 4

Stella woke to an alarm. Her eyes stayed tightly closed as a mechanical voice said.

<<Good morning, William.>>

<<Today is Wednesday 30th January.>>

<<There are four things in your diary today.>>

William? It took her a few moments to understand where she was, but William?

She blinked open her eyes and closed them again, luxuriating in the enormous bed. *How kind of him to let me have the bed. Wait a minute. Where did he think I was going to sleep?*

The soft music stopped playing, and Stella stretched her arms out over her head. Her eyes flew open when the shower began to run.

Cautiously, she crept towards the noise, her brain full of confusion.

Her bedroom door burst open.

"I'm sorry … I forgot …Oh!" Will was wet, dripping on the floor.

Stella tugged her T-shirt down.

"I'm sorry, it's just. I didn't think."

Stella's eyes sprang to the tight swimwear, black, of course. She slipped back into bed, pulling the white sheet up to her chin. Will stared at her, his hand on the back of his neck.

"I'm such an idiot." He sighed. Stella smiled; she'd heard those words before. "See, I do my thinking when I'm swimming, and this morning … well, I've a solution to a problem with the pool cover for Marco."

"Marco?"

"My neighbour, Marco Martelli." Stella dropped the sheet.

"THE Marco Martelli?"

"Take that look off your face, young lady. Don't be getting ideas." Stella reeled at the speed and force of his reaction.

"Will … I …" Her brain had too much to process. Marco was next door, Will knew him, and Will was telling her to stay away from this Italian sensation.

"Sarah would kill me."

"Because?"

"I like Marco. He's a good bloke at heart, but I wouldn't trust him with my sister, and you're like a sister to me."

Well, if it wasn't clear before, it was now. William Thoresby stood in front of her, almost naked. Every muscle defined and glowing from his morning swim. He thought of her as a sister. Stella was speechless.

"Are you OK if I go shower?"

"Yes. Of course. It's your bedroom."

When Will disappeared into the bathroom, Stella lay back, pulling the sheet over her head. *How the hell did this happen? Why are you so bothered? You told your mother he was a gangly nerd. Well, I think he might still be a nerd, but that's considered a thing these days. He's certainly filled out a bit. It must be all that swimming. SHUT UP! Look, just come up with a plan and go home.*

Slowly, she pulled the sheet down and looked around the room. The shower was still running, and she reached out her hand to find the small, grey-knitted dog she slept with every night. She kissed his pink nose and tucked him away under the pillow.

"I'm sorry, Spike, but I don't know if Will knows I have you, and after all these years, I'm not about to give you back."

Once the water had turned off, Will appeared with a towel wrapped around his hips, his hand holding the back of his neck again.

"Look, I'm going to have to go to the office today. I don't know what you can do here. I wasn't expecting you until tomorrow."

"Look on the bright side; you don't have to pick me up now. And don't worry about me. If you have paper and a tape measure, I can be working on a plan."

"Sure. Help yourself to anything in my office." And he left.

The silence felt painful. In slow motion, Stella dragged herself out of Will's bed and into the bathroom, all too aware she was in his space. The scents filled her head, and seeing his wet toothbrush made her shiver. She smiled at the way the few items left out stood in straight rows.

Dressed and in the vast kitchen, the silence sat there too. She peeked into cupboards. The first two were empty. The third one looked like a cupboard from her childhood. Cornflakes, Ketchup, and Marmalade.

She found a bowl and ate her cereal slowly, trying to avoid thinking too much. The house was big and empty. Sarah was right. This place needed some personality. As she washed her solitary bowl and mug, Grigori walked in, and she at last relaxed.

"Good morning, Stella. Have you seen Will?" Stella blushed at the memory, and Grigori raised just one eyebrow.

"He said he'd found a solution to a problem and had to go to the office."

"Shit!"

"Is it a problem?"

"No, sorry. No, I can work around it. It's just when he goes to the office, I can't reach him about any decision."

"I can ask him anything when he gets back."

"Good luck with that." Grigori looked so serious, Stella looked away. "Oh, I'm sorry. It isn't your fault. It's just when the boss is there … forget I said anything." He smiled at her, and Stella smiled back.

"Where are you working today? I'll need to get some measurements and ideas ready to show Will. Do you have any plans I can look at?"

"I'm not sure I have a lot of time." The usual smile had gone from the tall man's face. His dark eyebrows crowded his even darker eyes. She needed him on board. Stella plastered on her brightest smile.

"Grigori, if I'm going to be working on this project and living here, then we are going to be working alongside each other. If I know what your time plan looks like, we can work together more easily."

"But…"

"Oh, I know things change. This isn't my first job." *It's the first one with no supervisor, and at this size,*

"I just thought she was overseeing all the design stuff."

"She?"

"Vanessa, whenever she's here, she talks as if it's her house. She has some strong ideas, but those ideas seem to change on a daily basis. But if you are living here, does that mean he's finished with her?"

"What … no … I know there is only one bedroom, but Will slept on the couch. He can't keep doing that."

"I can look at getting someone to finish a second bedroom."

Chapter 5

"The primary and junior are in that wing. The other four rooms over this way are the closest to being finished. So, can we start by looking at these bedrooms?" It sounded like a question. Stella needed to get busy, being still wasn't working. It made her itch.

"Sounds like a plan to me."

"Why don't you pick out the one that you like the look of best, and we can get that finished?"

Looking around the bare rooms, Stella tried to select which one was closest to being ready.

"Is there a reason these rooms have been left unfinished?"

"Yeah, that would be Vanessa. I think she likes the fact that there is only one bedroom available."

"Will said she's his business manager. Is she something more?"

"She acts like she's more than someone who …" Grigori was stopped by his phone. "Speak of the devil," he said. Stella held her breath.

"Morning, and what can I do for you today?" Stella couldn't hear what was being said, but when Grigori smiled, it was a relief.

"Well, yes, I agree. Today is a good day to finish the bedrooms."

Grigori was silent, but he covered his phone so that any laughter that spilt out wouldn't be heard on the other end.

"Oh yes, we can't have Will sleeping on the couch. What time can I expect the new bed to arrive? Oh, I'm sure that will be just fine. I can have it erected this afternoon."

Grigori ended the call and laughed.

"Vanessa heard that you've arrived and that you are staying here."

"What is she like?"

"Oh no, no, no." Grigori shook his head. "You don't catch me like that. This is my job, and I know how to be diplomatic. So, Stella, where would you like your bed put? Is there a room you would prefer?"

"Let's just focus on getting a bathroom finished and a bed. I can work around that. Is there any paint yet?"

"We've plenty of paint as long as you like white."

"You mean Will hasn't bought any black paint?"

Grigori snorted, “Ha. How long have you known him?”

“Quite possibly all my life, but I only really remember him from when I was six, maybe seven. We all went on holiday together; that was before the divorce.”

“The divorce?”

“Yeah, my parents, not his.”

“Will’s sister and I have been friends all our lives. Certainly, since we started school, our parents were also quite close. Until the split.”

“Do you have any brothers and sisters of your own?”

“No, perhaps that's why Sarah and Will were so important to me growing up. They were like my siblings, and from what Will said this morning, I guess he thinks of me as his little sister.”

“So, do you want this bedroom next to Will’s?” Stella paused for a moment too long, and Grigori laughed. The rooms were all the same. The question was, did she want to be near Will?

“I wouldn’t want to sleep next to him and the ice princess, either.”

“Do you mean Vanessa? Is she … his girlfriend?”

This time, Grigori’s smile didn’t quite meet his eyes, and he offered no answer. Stella made a quick decision.

“I’ll take the one at the other end.”

“Good choice.” Grigori nodded in approval and moved into the room.

“Do you need my help?”

“No, my team will do this.”

“Can you help me, then?”

“What do you need?”

“The plans, a tape measure, and some paper.”

Stella pored over the drawings on Will's desk. The challenge arose from the fact that all measurements were in feet and inches. She found herself trying to convert them to metres.

The all-white surfaces of Will’s office were clear, with very few things left out, so it would have been hard to miss the photo of the three of them on that famous holiday. The one when she finally knew who Will was. It must have been a happy memory for him, too.

As she'd already seen, each of the bedrooms included a good-sized en-suite bathroom and plenty of storage space. The main living spaces she'd seen last night were a great size and flowed well. Now it needed colour and texture.

Stella created lots of lists and ideas to share with Will. At last, it was time to explore the spaces themselves. She reached for her coffee to find it stone cold. She drank it anyway.

As she walked to the kitchen to look for lunch, she took in the scale of this project. A full house, and for Will, someone she knew so well. Someone who seriously needed help.

The kitchen was empty and quiet. Stella opened the fridge, hoping Will wouldn't mind. She found one large steak and a carton of eggs. She wasn't sure what else to eat, so she poured herself another bowl of cereal.

She munched away, making more notes and trying not to get too excited about this project. Despite so much to think about, she found herself wondering about Will and Vanessa, and when she thought of him, it wasn't the reclusive 13-year-old in the photo she pictured but the awkward yet well-built man who had stood in her bedroom that morning.

Not your bedroom. You were sleeping in his bed.

Having eaten, she went in search of Grigori again. It took her almost half an hour to find him in the bedroom they were working in for her.

"There you are?"

"Ah, yes. I should have given you my phone number because the computer is off this morning."

"Pardon?"

"Has Will shown you the computer system?"

"No. I'll ask tonight."

Stella couldn't read the look on Grigori's face, but it wasn't the smile she was getting used to. He looked away, then turned back, smiling again.

"How do you like your bedroom?"

"Well, it's a little plain, but I'm sure it will serve a purpose until I get some fabric."

"Are you sure you don't want a coat of paint or two on these walls before we put the bed in here? It's arrived with some bedding."

"It's probably not a great idea to sleep in a room you've just painted," she smiled. "I've been wondering where I can work, set up my laptop

and that? Is there a desk other than Will's? I don't feel right working in there."

"I'll look to see what I can do tomorrow."

"OK, I'll go and work on the sofa for now."

Stella settled down on the battered sofa with her laptop and the pile of paper she was beginning to build. The challenge was to soften Will's cold, yet clean, lines of black and white into something that would resemble a home and help sell this concept so that Will could save his company. *No pressure then!*

It was dark when Grigori shook her shoulder to wake her.

"Sorry, I must have nodded off."

"Your bed is ready now if you want to get some sleep."

"Is Will back?"

"No, but when he's working, it's not unusual. You should get some sleep."

"I guess it's midnight in New York."

"Give your body a chance. Don't try to work the hours he does. Have you eaten?"

"I'm fine."

"Shit, I bet there's no food in that kitchen. Hang on."

Grigori picked up his phone and spoke hurriedly in a language Stella couldn't identify.

"Let's go to the kitchen, Stella."

Stella silently followed him back to the kitchen area. Grigori pulled a plate and cutlery and placed them neatly on the breakfast bar. He filled a glass with water and ice and placed it next to the plate. Just as he finished, the door opened, and the painter, she thought was called Paulo, appeared with a foil tray.

"It's nothing special, but it's hot food, so eat."

Stella didn't want to argue, so she perched on a barstool and dug her fork into the red stew. She wasn't sure, but thought it could be goulash. She looked up to ask Paulo, but he'd gone.

"Paulo's shy. Just eat the food, Stella. I'll see you in the morning."

Whatever the spicy dish was, it was soon eaten. It didn't take Stella long to get into the bed in her new room. She carried her suitcase through and looked to empty it in her new space. There were just two problems: no drawers and no coat hangers, so she pulled out a shirt to sleep in and

her tiny, knitted dog. She stroked his pink nose and hugged him, then carefully put him back in her case and closed the lid.

Stella sat on her new bed, her phone in hand, as she picked out more designs to show Will. She was delighted when a message popped up from her online friend, Jenny.

Jenny: Hey, are you enjoying SoCal?

Stella: It's good so far. Hitting the shops tomorrow.

Jenny: Without me?

Stella: Can you join me?

Jenny: Not until Saturday.

Stella: I have to go tomorrow, but I'll still need your help on Saturday. Can you take me to meet the glass guy?

Jenny: If you mean Eric, yes, we can do that. How long can I have you for on Saturday?

Stella: If we're meeting designers, as long as you like.

Jenny: Send me an address, and I'll pick you up at 9:30.

Stella: You're a star.

Jenny: I thought that was you. I hope you will be tagging me.

Stella wrote the arrangements in her calendar and lay her head back. Having Jenny to guide her around the designers was going to be a bonus. She went back to her phone and her list-making, happy and excited. Her eyelids were so heavy, but she desperately wanted to talk to Will, so she sat up on her bed, listening for him to come back to the giant box that was currently his home.

Chapter 6

It was dark when William Thoresby returned to his building site of a house. It wasn't just dark, it was late, very late, even for him. He worked long hours all the time. After all, he had nothing to come home for, or was that no one to go home to? Except today, he did, he had Stella, his Star.

Tonight, even Will realised he'd stayed later because he'd struggled with how his body reacted to Stella and the grown-up body she'd arrived with.

The house had been in darkness, but his phone triggered the arrival mode when he was just a mile away. Now that the exterior lights were lit, as he walked through the building, the lights should have turned on. He kicked himself when they didn't. How had he forgotten the computer problems? He would sort that as soon as he'd eaten.

He muttered under his breath as he tripped over the leg of a stool left away from the breakfast bar. *And that's why I don't like people in my space.*

The spicy smells in there had made his stomach rumble. *Shit, what did she have to eat?* He pulled open the fridge, remembering how empty it had been the night before. No food seemed to have gone. *I need to get another food delivery. That steak is still there, so I could have that tonight, but first, I'd better find Stella.*

When the living areas were empty, he tried the bedrooms. In the hallway, the smell of paint hit his senses. All the doors were open except one.

Lights and music spilt out under the closed door. A gentle tap got no response. He hesitated and then, sighing, tried knocking louder. Eventually, he opened the door slowly, peering around to find Stella asleep on top of her bed amongst a sea of paper.

Trying not to stare, William collected the papers and stacked them. Then he laid the pile neatly on the floor because, quite simply, there was nowhere else to put it. *She needs more furniture.* He shook his head. *She needs sleep and food, you fool. You knew that at fifteen!* He stood up straight. *Tomorrow I'll get back in time for dinner. Oh, I will, Star, I promise you.*

William stood close to Stella's new bed and looked down at her in an expanse of white. He closed his eyes, enjoying the floral scent filling his head. Her black hair shone in the lights that filtered through the blinds. He'd seen her sleeping many times before, but never in so much white. Plain rooms might work for him, but not for Stella. He placed her phone on top of the paper and then very gently lifted her into the bed, covering her with the white duvet. *Definitely too much white.*

He might have been back in his own bed, but William Thoresby didn't sleep well that night. He had a few different dreams, and yet they all seemed to feature the new-look Stella. In one, she was fading away because he hadn't given her any food. In another, she was dancing at a party with Marco. He woke up having dreamt she'd painted his entire house in shades of pink, and none of them pastel. The pink vision was the last straw; he threw back the covers and got ready to swim.

Surprise stopped him when his phone rang before he could leave his room. His heart stopped when he saw his sister's name.

"Sarah, it's five a.m."

"It's lunchtime here, and I bet you were up."

"I was. I'm just going for a swim."

"Is she OK?"

"She's here, and she has a bed of her own now, so she won't have to sleep in mine."

"William?"

He swallowed. Sarah was going to struggle with all this, and she couldn't even read the thoughts in his head.

"When she arrived, I only had one bed. Don't worry, I slept on the floor. She slept in my bed."

"Look after her, Will. She needs it, and I need her."

"I always do. You don't have to ask." He shook his head. "But her timing is off this time."

"Are you crazy?" his sister's voice rose. "The timing is perfect. Stella's an amazing interior designer. She can make that place look like a home. Stella is just what you need right now. Tell her to call me."

"I will."

The sun wasn't up yet, but William had never needed a swim more. He had so much to process. Length after length, his arms pulled him through the water as his legs kicked. He needed to think. An hour later, he'd made no decision other than to be back for dinner. And of course, he wanted to get Stella's room sorted. Remembering her childhood pink bedroom didn't help.

Grigori met him in the kitchen at seven thirty, like he did every day.

"How did yesterday go?"

"For obvious reasons, boss, we focused on the bedrooms. I'm thinking that with one more day on them, I could have them ready to hand over."

"And Stella?"

"Oh, she's fun, isn't she? She seems to think she's the designer now."

"I know." He shook his head.

"And V?"

"I'm working on it. Actually, I've had an idea, but maybe I'm being a bit of a dick." He stood, taking his dishes to the sink, and began washing them.

"Go on."

William looked over his shoulder at the site manager.

"If I say to her, 'do your bedroom first', that way she gets the room she wants, and I get to see her work." He picked up a towel to dry the few pots he'd used.

"Sounds like a test to me."

William flashed Grigori a warning frown.

"Well, don't use those words. Let's focus on saying I want her to have a space that's more her. One thing I do know is, that blank white room isn't Stella, so give her any help you can."

"OK, boss."

"Anything else you need from me?"

"The computer?"

"Yes, I realise that needs doing, but I'm going to go into the office now. I'll be back this afternoon, and I'll sort that." Grigori laughed, and Will rushed to reassure him. "I know I've said that before, but today I have to be."

"Why? No, forget I asked." Grigori shook his head. "Look, I'm glad she's here, boss, and if it gets you to come back earlier, she has done one

good thing. And you do need to talk to her about this job because she isn't Vanessa. She's going to want your input."

"You think she needs my help?"

"Hell no, but she'll want to consult you. She asked so many questions yesterday that I think you should be the one to answer. This is going to be your home."

"But V just does it for me."

"Does she do it for YOU, though? Or does she just do what she wants?"

Will's eyebrows pulled together as he puzzled over that.

"I know my tech. I need Vanessa for the other stuff. I wouldn't have a business without her." He frowned. "Look, I want to get off so that I can get back again."

"She needs food, too! And I'm not sure she has California clothes. Sorry, boss, I know you've a lot on." Grigori looked at the ground before looking squarely at William. "I do think she could be the pair of eyes we need on this project. The only question is, how do we handle V?"

"I'll keep her busy at the office."

"So today, bedrooms, and you'll be back early?"

"If she needs a car, show her the Jeep."

"Can she drive a shift?" William's grin was the only answer Grigori needed.

Chapter 7

When Stella woke, she found herself tucked up nicely in the new bed. Her phone sat on a pile of papers she'd been looking at last night. Next to that stack lay another pile of sketch pads and coloured pens. Will had left a note.

Star,
Sorry, I was so late. Work stuff.
Don't work too hard.
Here's a bank card; please use it for anything you make.
I'll see you for dinner tonight.
Will x

Stella swallowed. *Did Will put me to bed? When can I talk to him about my ideas? Is he hiding from me?*

It felt strange having these feelings for Will. That wasn't new. But this isn't the boy she knew when she was younger. *And it isn't just the way his looks have changed; he's grown up in so many ways. But if he isn't here, how will I discuss my ideas?*

It was a big, empty house to be in on her own. There was a shadow of Will everywhere she looked, but it certainly didn't feel like his home. Today, she intended to get out and find suppliers because she wanted to change that.

"Morning, Stella."

"Morning, Grigori. Have I missed Will?"

"You need to get up early to catch him, I'm afraid."

"Oh. What's the plan for you today?"

"The focus is on bedrooms still. The boss wants you to focus on your own room.

"My room?"

"He said white wasn't your colour." She laughed. *So, he has been in my room.*

"As much as I want to do my bedroom, I need a space to work."

“I could rig up somewhere for your laptop.”

“Thanks, but I’m thinking more sewing machine and screen printing. I need space, Grigori. Access to a sink might be good, too.” Grigori’s face didn’t move, and he made no comment. Stella tried again. “We could look at space and then talk to Will when he gets here.”

“Don't hold your breath, little one.”

“He said…” Stella felt her stomach drop.

“I know, and he means it, but he gets busy, and then he forgets. Anyway, let’s think about what I can do to help you in your space. What do you need in that bedroom?”

“Well, a space for a laptop wouldn't be a bad idea. Maybe we could combine it with a dressing table, something with a mirror, and coat hangers would be useful. Do you have any mirrors or any fabric picked out?” Grigori shook his head.

“What about the side of your bed?”

“Do you have anything already organised for the bedside? Drawers? Lamps, anything like that?”

“I think that’s up to you.” Stella nodded as she started making a list and then looked up at Grigori.

“Oh, wait a minute, is this some sort of challenge?”

“Why did you say that?”

“It just makes sense. I mean, it’s an expensive project, right?”

“Have you any idea how much land costs here?” Stella went white. Of course, she was familiar with the local land and house prices. *How could I be so naïve?*

“Oh, gosh, yes. Question in that case, why doesn’t he just sell the land?”

“Because … maybe I think… well, I think he can see that the publicity … the inroads into the industry … could really take his business not to the next level, beyond that. It could be incredible the way Vanessa talks about it anyway.”

“She’s probably right. But how many people have this much tech?”

“In this area, most people, but look how much technology is growing in everyone's home.”

“I digress. Will knows me, but the last time he saw me, I was playing with my paints. Why would he trust me for this job?”

"I would trust you over Vanessa any day, but then I wouldn't trust her to make me a cup of coffee."

"So, if I do a good job in the bedroom, it's going to help him to trust me with the rest of this project." Grigori smiled at her. "And in the meantime, I can get my ideas onto mood boards. Then I can present to William just like I would to any other client." She looked carefully at Grigori. "When's your next break?"

"In an hour."

"Would you meet me in the kitchen and go through where you think the project needs design solutions?"

"Really?"

"This isn't my first gig. I know my design skills can be useful in the construction field."

By the time Grigori joined her in the kitchen, Stella had a list of questions. She poured him a black coffee and sat down to show him her ideas. She was surprised when he pulled a scribbled list out of the back pocket of his jeans.

Time flew as they exchanged questions and answers.

"Thank you. I should go shopping for this bedroom."

"Will said if you needed a car, you could use the Jeep."

Last night, Stella had carefully planned her route around the shops in a logical order, and she told herself she needed to stick to that order to make the most of her time. At least she had somewhere to start.

She parked the Jeep and prepared to walk around the first three places on her list. She needed to focus on the soft furnishing for the TEST, as she was calling it in her head. That would be her jumping-off point, and from there she would find a colour for at least one wall and some art. She had the feeling that if she talked to Grigori, he would come up with an answer to her furniture problem.

She found the first store filled with some of the most amazing baskets and cane furniture she'd ever seen. The place had a narrow front window, but when she entered, it opened up and then continued to expand backwards. Stella liked everything she saw, but she couldn't help thinking about Sarah. Her best friend would love this place, and she took a photo to share with her. She was about to cross the road to the next store on her list when the shop next door caught her eye. It seemed to be exactly what she was looking for.

Elisa's Vintage Fabrics sounded like just the place to find something a little more exclusive. Her eyes bounced around the rolls of fabric and bins of trimmings, not knowing where to look first. Stella rubbed her arms, trying to rub away the goose bumps. She loved shopping, probably something she inherited from her mum, who would shop every day if she could.

The owner found her towards the back of the large room, trying to get enough light to take photos on her phone.

"Can I help you?"

"I'm sorry, I should have asked. Is it OK to take some photos to show my client?" *Just look how I'm dressed., She is going to think I'm weird.*

In her nervous state, she kept talking. "I didn't even know this place was here. But then I've only been in town myself since Tuesday."

"We only opened after the holidays, so not many people have found us yet. Now, what is the project?" The woman, who turned out to be called Susan, became keen when Stella told her she had a whole house to work on.

"But today is about one bedroom … oh look, Sarah would adore that!"

"Sarah?"

"She's the sister."

"And the bedroom is for her?"

"No, but maybe it could be." As Stella's eyes wandered again, a plan began to form. Why not make this a bedroom for Sarah? She was more likely to use it than Stella. And what was the challenge in selecting things you liked? This way, Sarah became the client, and if Will hated it, Sarah could maybe have the throws and things anyway.

Stella pulled out the rolls of printed velvet that had first caught her eye. It was full of peacock colours, and Stella had her theme. Together with Susan, she pulled out and bought four different fabrics that would complement the velvet. She added ribbon and tape, plus buttons and thread. The ideas were starting to flow. She'd been wondering about a sewing machine, and now she had her answer.

She said goodbye to Susan, who had given her some fabric samples for other ideas, and walked back to the Jeep. Stella promised to include the shop in a blog post soon. She loaded up her parcels and looked for somewhere to have lunch. A quaint café on the corner looked inviting

and appeared to have Wi-Fi, so she went there for a sandwich and a long coffee.

Settled at a corner table, she used her colour reader to select paint colours to coordinate with the fabrics she'd bought. She added paint to her next shopping list. As doubt nagged at her, she reached out to Jenny.

"Sorry to bother you, but I'm out here trying to work out the practicalities of buying a sewing machine. Just something basic but strong for soft furnishings and stuff."

"OK, I'll do my best."

"If I were going to buy a sewing machine, where should I go?"

"So robust, but not fancy?"

"I guess so."

"I'd just go down to one of the craft barns. There's bound to be a choice, and you'll get what you need there."

"You think so?"

"Yes, I wish I could come with you."

"Will I be able to get some foil in there, too?"

"I'm pretty sure you can find almost anything in there."

"Well, that's my afternoon planned, then."

The bright colours of the Craft Mega Store lit up Stella as soon as she parked up. Jenny had been correct; this was much larger than any craft store she'd seen in the U.K. Excitement bubbled through, but she needed to focus and avoid distractions if she was going to get everything she needed. She searched her bag and pulled out her list, checking it carefully and trying to estimate how much she would need to spend. She was convinced that money was a major issue for William at the moment, and she knew she didn't want to add to his problems.

She decided to take the time to walk across all the aisles to get her bearings, and then she started loading her cart. First, the sewing machine, and then an electronic cutting machine and blades, before she went in search of paint that would work with the fabrics for Sarah's room.

Stella thought she needed two litres of paint to cover the area she wanted, but she needed to check the coverage suggestions on the tin. Then came the realisation that the paint came in pints and not litres. In New York, she selected the colours and her mother's decorator had done the rest. She'd spent so long changing the measurements from the plans

to metres, and now she needed to know square yards and pints. Her stomach dropped. She'd been so confident just minutes earlier.

"Are you just going to stand there, girl?" A large woman pushed her out of the way to get to the counter, making Stella retreat to a quiet corner and pull out her phone to do more calculations. It was such a relief to realise that the paint manufacturer's website worked in both imperial and metric units. She squared her shoulders; she could do this. This was only the beginning. She resolved to spend a bit more time on the U.S. website instead of the U.K. site.

She was pleasantly surprised at what it all cost her, and that made her relax as she filled her cart with paint and materials, mostly for her best friend's room, but she treated herself to some extra touches.

As she handed over her card to pay for everything, she mentally relaxed. This was significantly cheaper than she was used to in the U.K. It took her some time to get everything loaded into the back of her vehicle and make her way back to William's house.

Chapter 8

When the computer didn't greet him, Will called out. "I'm home!"

"Lovely!" He wasn't expecting the answer to come in a gruff voice.

"Oh, it's you, Grigori. Where's Stella?"

"Shopping, I think, for the bedroom."

"How did it go this morning? Was she mad?"

"No. She seemed happy with the idea." Grigori shrugged.

"Really?"

"Really, boss."

"What have you got there?" Grigori nodded towards the brown bag.

"Dinner for tonight, you're right. I need to feed the workers."

"And there was me, going to take her to dinner," he said as he left the room, "there's always tomorrow." *What?* Will's stomach clenched. *Is he joking?* He still couldn't read Grigori.

William walked up and down in front of the huge glass doors. He'd sorted the computer issues and pushed dinner in the oven, so all he had left to do was worry about how Stella felt about his challenge. In reality, it wasn't his only problem, but it was all he could think about. *I do want her to have a room that's more her. I hope she understands.*

William checked his watch once more, still pacing. I hope she's OK driving that Jeep. Downtown L.A. isn't sleepy Hursts Bridge. Maybe I should have driven her. Sarah's going to kill me.

<<Welcome home, Stella. William is in the kitchen.>> *Thank God, she's home. Home? Is it really?*

Listening, William lifted the hair from his forehead. He could hear her walking in heels, down towards her bedroom. It seemed to take forever for her to come back. His body still couldn't relax.

By the time Stella found him in the kitchen, the noisy heels were gone. He was setting the breakfast bar for them to eat. Will stared at her a little too long before speaking. *God, I've missed her.*

"Something smells good," Stella said.

"Lasagna. It's just a lasagna," he shrugged. Stella smiled, and his simple heart skipped.

This was better than eating alone. I need a drink. She needs a drink.

"Wine or beer?"

"I'm going to say wine if you're opening it."

He tested out a smile.

"Stella, just say what you would like."

"Thank you," she murmured.

This is awkward. And it's my fault.

"Take a seat. It's nearly ready." Stella perched on the barstool, pulling down her skirt. William didn't miss the movement, but he kept his eyes fixed on the wine as he passed over her glass. He felt her eyes on him as he moved around the kitchen.

"This is a long way from when you used to cook beans on toast."

He smiled and watched Stella withdraw into her head again.

"You're quiet? Did you have a good day?"

"Busy, but I've a busier one planned for tomorrow. May I use the Jeep again?"

"It's yours for as long as you want it. I bought it when I first came here, but V hates it." Will realised he'd said the wrong thing yet again. Stella seemed to steel herself. He watched her fidgeting with the hem of her skirt. When she lifted her piercing blue eyes to his, he wanted to melt into them.

"So … is Vanessa your girlfriend?" Will shook his head.

"She's my business manager. She's in charge of the brand and things like that. She's the bit between me and all the other businesses. That's why we end up going to a lot of events together. I know the technology." He sighed, "I struggle when it comes to selling, especially to big companies and particularly in the USA."

"In what way?"

"I don't know. It's so hard to put into words. If I could just design things and solve problems, I'd be happy."

Sitting next to Stella, Will felt comfortable being close to her again. She seemed relaxed, too. *Maybe it's the wine.*

"This is tasty."

"Thank you, but it's only reheated." Will looked away.

When Stella reached over and touched his thigh with a gentle squeeze of reassurance, surprise was written on her face. Will broke the silence.

"Swimming."

"Sorry, what?"

"My thigh. It's the swimming."

"Did you always swim? I don't remember."

"Not really. I could swim, but who had swimming pools?"

"True."

"When I bought my first apartment, there was a pool in the basement. I figured I was paying for it every month, so I was going to use it."

"Obviously!" Her smile was a welcome relief.

"I found it helped me to think. The fitness has been a bonus."

"And the glasses?"

"Laser treatment. I have reading glasses still if I'm working a lot."

"Well, you look good." Stella teased. Will leaned over to nudge her with his elbow.

"You look pretty good yourself."

Stella leaned into him. "Thank you. I guess we've both grown up."

They ate on in silence. He watched as Stella pulled at the neck of her sleeveless top.

"Is it me or is it hot?" she puffed.

"It's warm. I guess I'm acclimatised now. I'm a host." He pulled out his phone, and with a few swift taps, cool air flowed across the room.

As they cleared the plates, Will's phone buzzed.

"Hey, Marco."

"I've got some friends over to play pool. Come over and join us."

"Sorry, no. I have a guest."

"Vanessa?"

"No. A friend from home." Stella perched on the edge of her chair. He realised she knew the name, and judging by her face when it came up the first time, she had a crush on him. This was Marco Martelli. She'd said she watched him play on TV. He was more than a tennis player, though; his family had amassed a fortune from oil, so for Marco, tennis was just a game. One he could afford to indulge in. He had a wicked smile and a reputation to match.

"Brilliant, in that case, bring him over." Marco's voice boomed out of Will's phone.

William reluctantly looked at Stella, his brows pulled together.

"I don't think so, mate." Stella's face fell, and she nudged Will. Hard.

"Hang on. I'm getting a dirty look from my friend."

"Just bring him over. It must be boring in that empty house." Stella's face lit up, and he knew he would have to face this one day. "We're in the games room, but I've no British beer, so bring some with you if you Brits want some."

"Ah! I understand now. Is John there?"

"He might be." Will knew she was watching him, her excitement written all over her face.

"You could have just asked." More laughter boomed out. "We'll be over." Finally, he agreed, unsure of the look on Stella's face.

William finished the call and looked at Stella with his big brother stare. He had to get things straight.

"Before we meet Marco, I'm going to repeat what I said about him."

"OK, big brother."

Don't remind me. "Look, I know you've some sort of fancy idea about him, but don't."

"You said you liked him."

"I do, but he's an incorrigible flirt. So just watch that."

As he left her at her bedroom door, he started again.

"We're playing pool, so jeans and trainers will work fine, and no low necklines if you're going to play."

"If?"

"Star!" *She's killing me.*

"OK, I'll dress like one of the boys." *And now she is pissed off with me.*

Walking over to Marco's, Will carried the beer, and Stella used her phone as a torch. He watched, his heart in his mouth, as she tiptoed across the rough ground outside of his house. *I need to do something about this side of the grounds. The list is endless.*

"Do you see him often?"

"Marco?" She nodded. "I think Marco would have me over every night I wanted. He claims he likes the accent, and he has a taste for British beer." Will scoffed. "And he can always find me a job."

Marco's house was, as usual, lit up, and music drifted out of the open windows. Will led Stella down into the basement, where they found Marco. Stella was delighted to discover John was, in fact, John Kingston,

a British tennis player that Marco knew from his days on the circuit. Stella had seen him play and recognised him straight away. A shy look flittered over her face.

“Ah, Will, my man. Come in. Good, you brought beer.” Marco’s smile was wide, and his dark eyes sparkled as he reached and took Stella’s hand. “And this, this is the Stella I’ve heard so much about.”
“What? Marco knew?

“You already knew she was there?”

“Come on, Will, you couldn’t keep her all to yourself.”

“You keep your hands off her.”

“Understood.” Marco’s smile widened as he kissed the inside of Stella’s wrist. The sparkle in his eyes made Stella smile.

Marco maintained a delicate grip on her wrist as he introduced her to the others in the room. He managed to tease everyone, including Stella. Will’s heart beat faster. Stella’s face lit up, but then who wouldn’t enjoy a bit of attention from someone like Marco?

William found himself talking to Patrick White most of the night. Watching Stella from a distance as she enjoyed playing pool with them. Patrick could be shy, but the other men flirted as they played. John, in particular, enjoyed himself once Stella announced she’d watched him play at Nottingham. He liked it even more when she admitted she’d never seen Marco play in the flesh.

Will usually loved a visit to Marco’s, but that night, he hadn’t relished watching Stella take photos of all the guys to send to India who had been to tennis matches with her. He didn’t even enjoy the tapas that Gabriella, Marco’s housekeeper, had served.

Stella seemed so happy playing, but she looked over to Will as he sat with Patrick. She mouthed over to him. ‘OK?’ Will reassured her with a nod, even though he was struggling to watch her with Marco.

Chapter 9

Stella woke to a pounding deep inside her head. She groaned when she opened her eyes to discover another note from Will propped up against a glass of water and two paracetamol tablets.

Star,
Gone to Marco's to do a couple of jobs.
Help yourself to t-shirts.
Don't work too hard.
Dinner at 7
Will.

Slowly sipping her water, she flicked through her phone to see what she'd missed. *Damn, I missed Dad again. I'll call him back when I work out what time it is.*

Dressed sensibly in jeans and trainers, she dragged herself and her lists to the drab kitchen space. Groaning inwardly, she hoped Will intended to take the kitchen out and start again. By the time she hit the halfway mark in her tea, ideas were whizzing around her head, and she scribbled more notes and sketches. Stella was still capturing ideas as she crunched away through her cereal. Her mouth was full when Grigori found her.

"I hear you met Marco last night."

Stella swallowed hard.

"Yes. He's so…"

"Loud?"

"Alive, might be a better word. Does he ever stop?"

"Good question. I think having endless money does nothing to put the brakes on. He gets an idea. He does it."

"The contrast between his place and here is pretty extreme. Marco's house is so opulent."

Grigori offered her a smile, which softened as he said, "But today is about you, little one, getting started on this room for you."

"For Sarah."

"Will has another woman?"

"No. Sarah is Will's sister. I thought I could design a room for her."

"You know her?"

"She's my best friend." Stella took a deep breath. "I need some help, though. Can you help me with some wood?"

"That should be easy enough. What do you need?" Despite the encouraging way he spoke, anxiety gripped her as she shared her ideas.

"I thought if we could run a floating shelf all around the room. I mean as narrow as four inches wide in parts, with wider areas, like next to the bed or deeper for a desk area, with smooth curves between all those different spaces. Like a wave." The words came tumbling out.

"I think we can do that. I just need to figure out how to join the sections if you want it to look like one piece."

"I also want to make a padded headboard with panels like this." Stella lifted her notepad to show Grigori the shape of the panels. "What do you think?" Grigori scratched his head but did not comment.

"I was thinking of varying the width of the panels. I've never done this before, and I thought maybe if the panels were a different width to start with…" She looked at Grigori for some indication that he thought the idea was workable.

"It'll add more interest to the project anyway, but have confidence, Stella. Maybe we could make a paper template for the headboard and shelf idea. Do you want that made from wood?"

"The shelf, yes. I'd love it to be a dark wood, certainly not a blonde one. I'll show you the fabric." Stella's excitement was building again, and she couldn't wait for Sarah to see it.

"If we draw the templates and then take a drive down to the lumber depot, you can pick your own wood."

Stella enjoyed working with Grigori. Her biggest worry was Will. She really hoped that he'd like her work. She knew Sarah would love it.

For as long as she could member, Sarah had loved these colours. Going to see the peacocks in the park at Carlton Magna was one of her favourite things. At school, every notebook, comb, and pen had to be blue or green. The cover of each notebook featured a doodle of her initials entwined into a monogram usually in gold.

Chapter 10

Will walked back from Marco's to have lunch. After watching three other men flirting with Stella the previous night, he'd decided his strategy of avoiding her wasn't working. *She's my guest. I should be here for meals when I can. Eating together last night felt good.*

<<Welcome home, Will,>> the computer announced.

"Star, where is Stella?"

<<Stella isn't in the house.>>

"Star, where is Grigori?"

<<Grigori isn't in the house.>>

"Star, are they together?"

<<I don't understand that question.>>

Will was accustomed to being alone but today felt different. *She's only been here three days. How can I miss her?*

He took his time making a set of sandwiches to share with her. Cheese and pickle. He remembered she liked that, although he wasn't sure what she'd make of the cheese here.

When there was still no sign of Stella, he reluctantly put the sandwiches in the fridge and made a cup of tea. He stirred his mug, trying to make sense of everything he was feeling. This was Stella, his sister's best friend. Perhaps the feelings rushing through his body this week were just a reminder of a simpler time in his life.

When the computer announced her return, he took the sandwiches out of the fridge and put them on the breakfast bar. The sound of her heels as she laughed with Grigori vibrated through him. Will had to tear his eyes away as he focused on making a new pot of tea.

"Help yourself to a sandwich," he said over his shoulder. "Sorry G, do you want one too?"

"Sorry, boss, we already ate."

"I'm sorry, Will, I didn't realise you would be home." Stella's voice was small.

Now, I feel bad for making her feel bad. That's weird.

"That's OK. Why would you?" William tried to force a smile.

"I'm getting off, boss. See you on Monday."

Stella sat down and drank the tea Will had passed her without asking.

"What are your plans for this afternoon?" she asked quietly.

"I need to get back to Marco's, if that's OK?"

"Sure, I want to work on a headboard for Sarah's room."

"Sarah's?"

"I meant to say. I thought I'd design something for Sarah. She's more likely to be using a bedroom here than I am. I'll be back in the U.K." The emptiness Will felt when he arrived at the house an hour earlier washed over him again like a cold shower. Of course, she'd be leaving. *And if I don't give her the project, she'll go quicker. Maybe I can get her doing other things. Do people still make quilts? They take forever, don't they?*

Eventually, Stella disappeared, talking animatedly with Grigori. *Will, you can't go there!* He took himself back to Marco's house. It might have been a mistake because Marco wasn't going to let his brain rest.

"What's up? Didn't she like your sandwiches?"

"She'd already eaten with Grigori."

"Ahh." Marco shook his head and then looked sideways at Will. "So just how long have you been in love with her?"

"Don't be stupid." Will frowned.

"Don't say you don't have feelings for her? Remember how transparent your face was last night every time someone spoke to her."

"She reminds me of home, that's all."

"I thought that's why you buy Yorkshire tea. To remind you of home."

"She's like a sister to me."

"Then my friend, you're in trouble because you're in love with her, and I suspect it's not new." Marco grinned at him. *He's enjoying this, damn him.*

"You must have started drinking early today."

"I might come across as a mindless Playboy, but the key to making money is understanding people." Will sighed as Marco's grin widened.

"I won't deny I have feelings for her, and my feelings for her may have shifted, but I think she is interested in Grigori."

"Then you are crazier than I thought."

"She's going back to the U.K."

"When?"

"I guess when this project is over."

"So, keep her on the project."

“Come on, Marco, you more than anyone know how important this project is to me. You’ve got a business head. I can't just let her do it. If this were my place, all paid for. I’d keep her busy.”

“So, what’s the plan?”

“I’ve told her to decorate her bedroom, so I can see if she’s as brilliant as my sister says. Even if she’s great for the London market, will that translate to Southern California?”

“And did you ask her to do her bedroom, so she feels at home here?”

“She wouldn’t be happy in a white room, and it needs furniture.”

“Does she know it’s a test?”

“I don’t know, but she says she is doing it for my sister, as she is the one most likely to use it.”

“Oh … and how’s the glamorous Vanessa taking this?” Marco’s smile was tight as Will played with the multi-tool in his hand.

“She’s asking a lot of questions.”

“Like what?”

“How long have I known her? Why doesn’t she have a job already?”

“I think you have a problem with that woman,” he frowned at William, “but I’ve told you that before.”

“I've been keeping her busy. But let's just say this, when she heard Stella had arrived, she okayed the bedrooms being finished and ensured a bed was delivered the same day.”

“Ah! She's keeping her out of your bed. Mind, I’ve eight beds in this house, and it doesn't keep anyone out of my bed.” Marco's eyebrows waggled to emphasise his grin. “What’ve you got planned for the weekend in that shed you live in?” Will's face was blank. “Look, come over here on Sunday and I'll give you my opinion.”

“I'm supposed to be attending an open house with V.”

“And Stella? You're going to leave her on her own again?”

“No.”

“Don’t go with that woman; come here, and I'll invite people you need to meet. Now, how long before my TV comes out of the floor like yours?”

Chapter 11

The A/C was off again. It was too much for Stella, so she took her newly acquired fabric scissors and hovered over her jeans. She'd only packed her favourite pairs with her, and she couldn't decide which pair to cut. In the end, she picked the pair she had the most hope of replacing. The new scissors sliced through the heavy cotton with ease. She clutched the shorts as she returned to where she'd slept that first night.

Her stomach tumbled at the thought of going back into Will's room. She knew it was silly because he'd let her sleep in there three days ago. A pair of his tiny swimming trunks lay on the end of his bed, and even that made Stella blush. She found his older t-shirts where he said they would be and picked one she remembered him wearing when he came home from university. Cal Tech. in blue. She always liked Will in blue, as opposed to the black he wore these days.

With Will working next door, Stella could get on with making the headboard. Beginning with the smallest panel might not have been the best idea, but by the time she started work on the third board, she found a rhythm and hoped she'd have it finished by the time seven o'clock arrived, when he'd said dinner would be ready. She set her laptop up on the side so she could watch YouTube as she worked and catch up with her favourite vloggers. It reminded her to take plenty of photos of today's project for her own blog. The number of comments had started to go up since she'd arrived in the U.S. New York had caught people's attention. She couldn't wait to catch up with Jenny the next day.

Looking out from the window of her makeshift workspace, Stella spotted a sleek red BMW glide up to the house. It parked abruptly in front of the door. The driver's door flew open, and Stella watched transfixed as a pair of long legs swung out. The red-soled shoes told her this was someone who cared about labels.

Vanessa? God. It's worse than I thought.

She looked down at her newly cut-off jeans and Will's T-shirt. For a moment, she considered getting changed. If this was Vanessa, as she suspected, why did she want to impress her?

Except she is important to Will. Perhaps this woman would realise that Stella posed no threat to her and back off, not just Stella, but everyone on the project.

She wiped her hands down the denim and went to meet the newcomer.

The front door swung open wide, and a cold shiver ran down Stella's back.

<<Welcome, Vanessa.>>

Stella's heart thudded as the tall woman clipped in heels from the front door towards her. The woman's white, blond hair swished in a ponytail high on her head as her lips curled on the right. Stella tried hard to take in all of this woman striding towards her. The bold red lips matched the nails. Her steely gaze looked Stella up and down.

India's words, 'just be yourself,' bounced through her head as the heavy perfume hit her.

"William?" The newcomer raised an eyebrow.

"No, only me, I'm afraid."

"Where is he?"

"He went to Marco's."

"I thought he said he was working?"

"This is Will, of course, he's working." Stella tried a smile and held out her hand. "I'm Stella, by the way."

"Sorry? You're Stella ..."

"Yes."

"Not one of Gerry's crew?" The puzzled look on Vanessa's face made Stella smile. She didn't know what to say, so she focused on putting the kettle on.

"I guess I'm both."

"I didn't realise you were actually working here." Vanessa swiped at one of the barstools and sat down. "I can see why he thinks of you as his little sister!" Stella swallowed. There was no answer to something that was a statement rather than a question. At 5ft 2 in, she'd been accustomed to digs about her height. So why did this one hurt so much more? Why did she care what this woman thought?

"Can I offer you a cup of tea?"

"Why has the actual coffee machine broken?"

"No, I'm not sure how to use it. Will might have instant."

"Oh, my God! What sort of use are you?"

"I'm sure Will won't mind if you make your own coffee." Stella was still trying to understand the shocked look on Vanessa's face when a very sheepish Will walked in.

"There you are, William."

"Hello, Vanessa."

"William, you haven't been answering your phone again. I can't keep dragging myself out to this hole to sort out my weekend with you."

"Ah, about that."

"Yes?"

"I'm not going."

"I'm sorry, what?"

"I've had some food delivered, so we can all have steak here tonight rather than going out. And on Sunday I'm going to an event at Marco's."

"Not going out for dinner on Friday night? Are you actually ill?"

"No, it's just that we had a late night yesterday, and I thought we could be a bit more laid-back tonight."

"You told me you were having lasagna last night. At home, I might add."

"We did."

"We?"

"I ate with Stella, then we went over to Marco's." Stella thought Vanessa would explode. She anxiously edged her way back towards the door of her room.

"William, I've told you about associating with that man. He doesn't have the best reputation. I'm working hard on making sure you actually meet the right people, and that's what Sunday is about: meeting the best people. If you won't go, then I'm still going. If you don't want to meet these people, I do."

Stella watched Will's face fall. She struggled to watch this woman talk to him like a child. She opened her mouth to say something, but the slight shake of Will's head made her bite her lip. He'd kept her out of trouble so many times when she was younger by helping her see when it was best to say nothing.

"I'm sorry you feel like that, V. Now, if you are stopping for dinner, would you like to make the salad whilst Stella and I finish work?" Stella thought she would choke on the laugh that threatened to erupt from her throat. She'd only just met Vanessa, but she was pretty sure she wouldn't be interested in making the salad. *Is Will doing this on purpose?*

Vanessa regrouped in the swift bat of her long eyelashes. "Actually, I still have jobs to do, but I'll be back for eight, and we can eat then."

"Seven."

"Sorry?"

"Dinner is at seven tonight. If you'd like to eat with us, be back for seven."

"Right!" Vanessa spun on her heels and left the building.

Stella fought to keep her face straight. Still unsure what had happened and what these two meant to each other, her insecurities flicked through a Rolodex of questions about what she'd just watched.

"How's it going?"

"I've got nine out of twelve panels made. So, I should finish soon. Can I make anything for dinner?"

"Stella, you're my guest."

"Will, I'm a friend, and you know I love to cook."

"There's steak and salad stuff. Not sure it needs anything else."

"Garlic bread? Herb butter? Dessert?"

"I know you've only just met V, and you haven't been here long, but…"

Stella flexed her hands, fighting the confused emotions that could overwhelm her after the long week of work and decisions.

"What about you?"

"Me?"

"Would you like those things? You made garlic bread yesterday."

"I put it in the oven, it's hardly the same."

"Would it upset her if I cooked for you?"

"I've lost track of all the things that 'actually' upset V." He shook his head. "You look better in my t-shirt than I do, by the way."

"You always looked good in this one, blue suits you."

"V says it isn't very professional," he said with a sigh. "Now, do you need any help?"

"That would be nice, but I'd prefer you to see this whole room when it's put together."

Will frowned, and she rushed to explain.

"There are some bold pieces, but when you see them as a whole, I think you'll like them."

"What about Sarah?"

"Oh, Sarah will absolutely love them. It's great working for a client I know so well. Which reminds me, I need to make some calls."

When Stella had covered each of the panels, she laid them out in order. Taking photos as she worked slowed her down, so she had to rush to shower and look decent for Vanessa's return. She struggled to shake off the nervousness that had been circulating in her stomach since the woman had left in the swish of a ponytail.

Determined to have Vanessa reconsider those little sister comments, for the first time since she left New York, Stella wore a dress. Standing in front of the new mirror, she took the time to think about her makeup and perfume, torturing herself over every decision.

Who am I doing this for? Yes, I want him to notice me, but then what? Maybe I simply want everyone to stop thinking of me as a little sister.

In the kitchen, Will looked like he'd wanted to make a point, too. The black clothes had disappeared. Instead, he wore a soft chambray blue shirt and some stone-coloured chinos. He looked wonderful. His hair still looked damp and fell onto his face. It made Stella's heart stutter as she fought the desire to run her fingers through it and push it off his face. She had been determined to look special for him. She hadn't expected him to dress for Vanessa, too.

"V isn't coming, so what do you say we take this outside? Let's be honest, the space out there is more finished." *Not coming? Is that why he feels he can wear blue?*

"I noticed that."

"The pool was my first priority, and I had the grill and furniture at my old place. I guess it'll all be replaced soon."

"Well, if it is, it will be to hone it for you. Unless you are going to sell this place."

"I don't want to sell it." Will gestured for her to follow him outside. "You look amazing. Can I pour you a drink whilst the grill gets hot?"

Stella's designer eye checked out the space. The furniture looked worn, yet comfortable, and arranged around a table. A fire had been lit, and when Will said, "Star, open the bar", a marble panel slid to one side and displayed an array of bottles.

"I'm still warm."

"There will be plenty of ice. But you might want a jumper soon." He smiled. "I've got some sparkling wine that's well chilled."

"Don't tell me, V likes it." Will looked down at the bottles in the fridge, avoiding an answer to that.

"Sparkling wine will be fine."

He smiled, opened the bottle, and poured two drinks. He offered his glass to hers, and they clinked them together.

"Here's to family."

They were the words his dad would use whenever they gathered together. It was a memory for both of them, another thing that drew them closer. 'Family' was the word that stopped them from being more.

"I'm fetching jumpers. We're going to need them." Will said in a croaky voice.

Stella sipped her wine, looking out at the sparkling lights of the bustling city. She'd come so far from those days in Hursts Bridge, and it had happened so fast that she still felt unsteady. She couldn't help but wonder what the story was with Vanessa. Why hadn't she come back to eat? Sarah wanted Stella to help Will, but what if she could cause more problems for him?

"Penny for them," Will said softly as he passed her one of his jumpers. Stella pulled the jumper in to hug it close. A scent of Will washed over her, and she closed her eyes to enjoy the moment.

"Will, I'm sorry. I came because Sarah thought I could help. I never wanted to …"

"Stella, I'm pleased you are here. I'll admit the timing's a bit, well … awkward, but I'm still glad you are here." He patted her head. "Now, how do you like your steak?" That conversation was over; she knew the signs. She comforted herself by pulling his jumper into a hug; she knew Will well enough to know he would never complain about her being there, even if it didn't work for him. It only renewed her resolve to be as helpful as she could.

By the time the steak had grilled and rested, the air had cooled enough to pull on the jumper. Will sat next to her, and their knees touched under the table. There was still something special about sharing a meal he'd cooked just for her. Did it remind Stella of home, or did she feel a sense of being home whenever she shared a space with Will?

The fire provided a welcome light, and the friends talked and talked. The twinkling town below them mesmerised Stella as she enjoyed the bond building between them again.

The more they talked, the more they laughed. Stella leaned into Will, and his arm went around her shoulders. The talking had stopped, and the two friends sat together enjoying the peace. The stars seemed so close tonight. Will bent his head and softly pressed his lips to hers. A gentle whisper of a kiss, and Stella leaned into it. Will kissed her a second time, this time still soft but more sensual. The kiss was only just getting started when a shrill voice called out.

"Where is everyone?"

It was a brutal end to their kiss, and Stella's hand shot up to cover her traitorous lips.

"Vanessa!" she gasped.

"Oh, shit, I'm sorry, I don't know why I did that. Sarah will kill me."

"Well, I'm not going to tell her," Stella's eyes flicked to an approaching Vanessa, "or anyone else, so you don't need to worry."

She stood up, gathering herself before moving back to the house.

"He's over here, Vanessa. I'm off to bed."

Chapter 12

When Saturday morning came around, Stella decided to wait outside for Jenny to pick her up. She wanted to avoid Will. That kiss last night really confused her. It was Will's words after that which cut her deeply. *"Oh shit, I'm sorry, I don't know why I did that. Sarah will kill me."* Stella replayed that one sentence all night.

If Vanessa hadn't turned up, she wondered what would have happened. She needed to talk to Sarah about the project, and guilt was rocking all her rational thoughts. Deep inside, she knew it was time to have that conversation with her best friend. Stella wanted the room to be a surprise, but she still needed her help.

The phone rang a little longer than Stella expected. As she waited, her thoughts ran riot. *Don't mention the kiss. What if she already knows, and that is why she hasn't answered?* Stella stopped straightening her jeans and clutched her stomach. Eventually, Sarah replied.

"Hey, you. How's SoCal?"

"Good. I'm enjoying it."

"Have you started?"

"Not quite."

"Is Will looking after you?"

"He's busy, but he has cooked my dinner for the last two nights."

"That's good for him. Have you met any nice men?"

"Did you know he lives next door to Marco Martelli?"

"The tennis guy? No! Tell me more. Have you met him?" *A safe topic ... I think.*

"Yes, we played pool there on Thursday night."

"Who was there?"

"Marco, a guy called Patrick, Marco's cousin and a British tennis player, John Kingston. Marco said something about how he'd been his mentor at one point."

"So, four guys, you and William. Did you win?"

"I played it cool."

"Oh, hustle time. What are you up to today?"

"I'm waiting for Jenny to pick me up to show me some artists she knows. She could be here any minute, so I want to ask you a favour."

“What?”

“I could do with photos or pictures of home; you know, Hursts Bridge, that sort of thing. I want to get them on canvas.”

“Won't that need to be a good-quality photo?”

“Possibly.”

“I'm there this weekend. It's the party for your gran tomorrow.”

“Damn! I forgot.”

“OK, so I’ll look at what we have, but I'm guessing India will be there for the party. You should ask her.”

“Yes, that's an idea.”

“I do have them every now and then. So go on, ring India.”

“I will. Talk soon. Thank you.” Stella rushed to call India whilst she still had time.

“Hey, you. How is it going?”

“Good, I think.”

“You don’t sound sure. Don’t give Mr Wilde any headspace.”

“Easier said than done.” Stella closed her eyes to stop her thoughts. “Hey, sorry, India, I don't have much time, and I need a favour.”

“OK, so tell me what you need?”

“Are you going to Hursts Bridge this weekend?”

“Yes, aren’t you?”

“I'm in L.A. I presume that's why my dad has been calling.”

“I guess that explains the photos online. Was it John Kingston? Why are you in L.A.?”

“I'm staying with Will Thoresby and doing interior design on a huge house in the hills. That's why I need your help. I'd like to add some art that's personal to Will. Could you possibly take some arty landscapes this weekend? You know the bridge, the green, their house, and the river. Sarah will help. I want to print them on canvas.”

“I'll do my best. Do you want me to get photos of his family, too?”

“Yes, take anything you can, thanks. I guess I need to ring Gran and explain where I am.”

“Yes, do that!”

“Got to go; my lift’s here.”

“Talk soon.”

“Yes.”

Jenny beamed a big smile at Stella as she pulled up to Will's gate in a small red SUV.

"This place looks amazing."

"I think it will be when it's finished."

"Let's go. I can't believe you're finally here. Where do you want to go first? What do you need to look at today?"

"Lighting and somewhere that sells decent paint."

"I've got you, girl." Jenny smiled as she swung back onto the road.

Now she wasn't driving, Stella didn't know where to look as they drove into town. Enormous walls covered with colourful images that seemed to shine under a brilliant blue sky. As they stepped out of the car, Stella encountered a myriad of spicy aromas. Life in L.A. was so different, not just from Hursts Bridge but from London too.

At their first stop, Stella fell in love with Eric's glasswork. He had some amazing pieces that captivated Stella's imagination. The colours achieved in the glass were striking. She spotted some intriguing pieces she thought could be made into lighting and lamps with a bit of help from her technological friend. The artist knew Jenny and seemed excited to discuss the entire house project with Stella.

"I saw your post, the one where you made that peacock headboard. It's amazing. I'd be honoured to work with you."

"Thank you. I can't get over how colours look in the light here in L.A. And the street art is so inspiring."

Together, they drew up designs for glass to be turned into lamps. The wave in Sarah's shelf inspired him, and they decided it would be a great place to start. Stella couldn't believe how open he was and how much he seemed invested in her project. Realising Eric could tailor colour and size to suit her created a wonderful feeling that anything was possible now, lifted her shoulders. That inspired Stella, especially when Eric reassured her that things could be made quickly. She took a lot of photographs and brought a couple of pieces for Sarah's room.

"I think you made a new friend there," said Jenny, "and now it's coffee time."

"Great idea, and I really need to ring my Gran."

Whilst Jenny organised coffee, Stella made the call she'd been dreading.

"Hi, Gran. I'm so sorry, I won't be there this weekend. I'm in L.A." Stella bit her lip.

"I bet that's a bit nicer weather than we've got here. Are you with friends?"

"I'm staying with William Thoresby."

"Are you indeed. And how long are you staying there for?"

"That depends on whether Will agrees to my designing the whole house he's building."

"Well. I think he's lucky to have you. I know your granddad and I really appreciated having you in London doing our flat."

"Yes, but Gran, he doesn't know my work."

"I'm sure you'll find the answer to that. What are you doing now?"

"I'm out shopping and just having coffee with a friend."

"Well, go and enjoy your coffee and ring me next week, and I can tell you everything you missed at the party."

"Thanks, Gran. Have a lovely day."

Jenny rushed over, waving her phone, and put a tall Americano in front of Stella, a puzzled look on her face.

"Did I hear you say that this Will guy is dithering about you doing the work on his house? Has he seen your post? And the reaction it got?" Jenny thrust her phone towards Stella.

"It's an important project, and he doesn't know my style."

"Well, why not?"

"Great question. Anyway, I'm doing one room, and I'm hoping he changes his mind."

"And if he doesn't?"

"I don't think I can watch someone else do it." She closed her eyes to consider that possibility. "I need to go home and get my life started again at some point."

"You sound sad about that."

"I do want this job. I feel like this needs more colour. I mean, look at the colours out on the streets here."

"It's more than that, though, isn't it?"

"Like?"

"Like … most sentences this morning contained the word Will." Stella's eyes closed again, and she thought for a moment before she answered Jenny.

"I guess I wasn't expecting to find Will had grown up into something quite so special in the last ten years."

"You must have grown up in that time, too."

"Jenny, Will is my best friend's brother. Oh, and he keeps putting me in the little sister zone."

"Ouch. But surely when he sees this post and the attention it's getting, he can see how bringing you on to the project can only help."

"Let me see." Stella pulled out her own phone. "That must be a record. For me, that is. I know other people get better, but for me, that's the most reactions I've had to a post."

"So far. You just keep posting. Watch those numbers rise."

Stella stared at her screen, struggling to process what this could mean for her. Was it possible that the idea of having her own business could be real? She needed to get back on track.

"So, this afternoon, can we look at ceramics and metal? Can we get food? I want to cook for him tonight. I don't want to forget the paint."

"And I'll try not to point out that everything you're looking at today, including the food," she paused and looked at Stella, "is for William Thoresby."

<<Welcome home, William. Stella is in the kitchen.>>

Stella's hand went to her hair when she heard the computer announce his arrival. She'd changed since she got back from shopping. *Why are you doing this? It was just a kiss.* She'd made bread and a chunky chicken and vegetable soup. Jenny said there could be storms this week, and she still wanted to give him a feeling of home.

"Something smells wonderful."

"That will be me," she laughed.

"You always smell wonderful, but tonight I smell something … bread and maybe something herby?"

"That will be the sage in the chicken soup. Jenny took me to the farmer's market. It was wonderful. It smelt amazing."

Will looked at the breakfast bar as Stella had tried to set the places.

"I hate that we're eating at a makeshift breakfast bar. I'm ready to get this place sorted."

"Didn't you have a table at your last place?"

"I hate to tell you this, but I didn't spend a lot of time there. I certainly didn't have guests over for a meal."

"When do you plan to do the kitchen?"

"I've been waiting for Vanessa's designer to have the time."

"I see." Stella studied the room, her designer's eye scanning for colours and shapes to include in a wonderful kitchen space.

"What would you do in here?" He asked.

"That all depends on whether it's for you or for sale," she said, observing Will's reaction. She needed clues.

"Does it make that much difference?"

"You're very particular, Will. You like things clean and simple. We can dress it with art."

"Every time someone says the word 'art', I hear the word money."

"Go look in those boxes. There are some things I picked out today. I need your help to add a light to this glass for Sarah's room."

"Now?"

"No. Tomorrow or Monday. Tonight, we're having dinner. Will Vanessa be coming? I made plenty."

"I don't think we will see her before Monday now." *You said that last night,* Stella thought as she served two steaming bowls of soup.

"This soup is amazing. When did you learn to cook?"

"School … my mum can't cook. She says she only has a kitchen in New York because it came with the apartment. I've got a long way to go to be as good as your sister, though."

"Oh yes, I spoke to Sarah today."

"So, did I. You didn't tell her, did you?" Stella saw the darkness in his eyes. "About her room. I'd like it to be a surprise."

"But will you be here when she sees it?" Will's voice was soft and slow, his eyes now distant and unfocused. It made Stella shiver. She didn't know the answer to that question.

"What did she want?"

"Mainly to find out what was happening with you," he laughed. "She's not interested in me."

“That’s not true. She wanted me to come because she was worried about you.” *And I kissed you. How am I helping?*

“She hasn’t told Dad, has she? I asked her not to.”

“If you asked her not to, I’m sure she won’t.” She tried her best to reassure him.

“Are you sure about that?”

Stella’s face tilted as she considered her reply.

“She might, if she gets more worried.”

“We'd better work on that then.”

Will kicked the makeshift breakfast bar.

“On Monday, I'm going to see about a table and some chairs.”

“Shall we do something temporary until you've decided what else we're going to do? Maybe you have something at the office.”

“Stella! You're a genius. There's a huge room at my place full of redundant furniture. Vanessa redid the conference room only last month.”

“But I thought money was tight?”

“Oh, it is. However, Vanessa assures me that we need to stay up to date. Speculate to accumulate is her favourite phrase.”

“Will, it's your money.”

“I know.”

Chapter 13

"Stella, are you awake? Will's head appeared around her door.

"Huh, yeah, yes." He walked in and sat down on the end of her bed.

"Can you ring your dad?"

"My dad?"

"Yes, he just rang me. It seems you haven't been answering his calls."

"And you do – 'Mr what phone', the man who never answers his phone, you actually answer when my dad calls."

"I was concerned when I saw his name. He's worried as it's his mum's party today."

"I spoke to Grandma yesterday, so I know she's OK."

"Just call your dad." He insisted, patting the bed by her feet.

"I will."

"I'm going to swim before we go to Marco's."

"Oh! I want to work first. Is that OK?"

"Of course, you do want to go, don't you?"

"I do. It sounds fun. I'm just so anxious to get on with Sarah's room so I can show you."

"Stella, you know I wanted you to make a room for YOU."

"Thanks, and I'll enjoy using it whilst I'm here."

"Good, because I'd like you to be happy here." He patted the bed again, and the look in his eyes made her stomach tumble. She still wasn't sure how she felt about that kiss.

"Right." He stood up. "I'm off for that swim."

Picking up her phone to call her dad, she absent-mindedly opened her blinds and watched him walk to the pool. She still found it hard to believe that the Will she knew now looked like that. So distracted watching him, she missed her father answering her call.

"Stella? Stella, are you OK?"

"Sorry, Dad, I'm here."

"Why didn't you tell me you were in Los Angeles? I had to hear it from Jayne Thoresby."

"Sorry, it was rather a last-minute thing."

"I was expecting you to be here this weekend. It's your grandma's event today."

"I forgot about it. I'm sorry. India reminded me yesterday, and so I rang Grandma and apologised."

"What did she say?"

"She was fine about it."

"So, I won't be in trouble when I walk in without you?"

"Yes, Dad, you'll be fine."

"Thank God for that. So why are you there? Because I know that was what Jayne was trying to find out when she mentioned it to me."

"I'm just doing some interior design stuff. I'm working on a bedroom for Sarah. But you can't tell her that."

"Who, Jayne?"

"No, Sarah. It's supposed to be a secret."

"But I can tell Jayne?"

"As long as she knows not to tell Sarah. Can't you just be vague and say I'm doing some decorating?"

"Darling, I've no problem being vague. In fact, that is possibly the best answer because I'm sure I will get it wrong, anyway."

"Thanks, Dad."

"Are you having fun, though?"

"I'm working, but yes, it's fun. Today I'm going to a Sunday brunch thing at Marco Martelli's house."

"Do I know him? Is he the guy who sells cars in Nottingham?" Stella chuckled.

"No, he's just William's neighbour. I'd better go. I want to do some work first."

Completely engrossed in painting boxes to match the fabrics she loved, Stella became completely distracted and lost track of time. When Will came looking for her, she wasn't at all ready.

"Sorry, Will. I need to shower and change. You go. I'll catch you up."

The opulence of Marco's stylish house came as a vast contrast to the monochrome simplicity of William's. Everywhere she looked, the finishes and artwork were over-the-top ornate. Someone had used extravagant marble throughout.

The sound of laughter and the lively atmosphere Stella associated with Marco filled the sunny morning as Stella approached the pool area. Stella wiped her hot hands on her skirt. Her heart thudded faster as her eyes searched for Will. But it was Marco's eyes that found her, from where he stood talking to a tall, dark-haired man in a white shirt with smart black trousers. Stella made her way over to Marco, confident he would know where to find Will.

Marco's eyes lit up, and the dark-haired man turned to see what had caught the big man's eye. Stella's stomach dropped when she realised it was Hidir from the Million Dollar Property YouTube channel. They'd connected online, but it would be a stretch to call them friends. She was stunned when he recognised her.

"Stella?"

"Hidir, how lovely. I didn't know you would be here."

The two exchanged air kisses and the briefest of hugs.

"I knew you were in California. Jenny's posts from yesterday looked like you were enjoying it."

"It's good to see you, but what are you doing here?"

"I'm trying to persuade Marco here to let me in with the crew."

"And he isn't saying yes?"

Marco shrugged. "Do I need the publicity?"

"Have you seen the guys who have been on his channel?"

"I hear you have some wonderful tech in this place."

"Mostly Thoresby Technology."

"And that's who you're working for, Stella?"

"Yes, and he's here somewhere."

"Fiddling with the TV," Marco laughed.

"That makes sense," Stella muttered.

"Davey's got the drone up at the moment. Could we get some shots of your tech when he gets back?"

"Say yes, Marco … for Will."

Marco smiled as his eyes softened. "I'll say 'yes, Marco', but I'll only say it if you say yes to doing a bedroom in my house."

"Of course, I'll say yes, but why?"

"So, I've something to remember your face by when you're gone."

"When I go?"

"If you won't stay for William, what chance do I have?"

Hidir raised his hand and waved. “Davey, over here. Look who I found.”

“Stella? Wow.”

“Don't disappear; I’ve more people for you to meet, Stella,” Marco muttered.

“Thanks, Marco.”

“And get something to eat.” He called as they walked away.

An excited Stella led Hidir and Davey to find Will. Her heart skipped when she saw him lit from behind, his sun-bleached hair falling into his eyes as he slipped a multi-tool into his back pocket.

“Is it ready for a demo?”

“I think so. I haven't tested it yet.”

“I thought it was already working?”

“It was. I thought it could be smoother, though.”

“This is Hidir and Davey. They'd like to film some of Marco's tech, and I guess you are the expert on that technology.” Will locked eyes with Stella. He looked lost, and when his hand went to the back of his neck, she knew she would have to step up.

“Why don't you tell Hidir about the magic in here? And I'll help Davey.” The filming went well, and Marco took Will off to meet more people.

“So, am I right in thinking you are working for William to get next door ready for the market?”

“I’m working there on one room at the moment, and yes, it’s coming to the market.”

“You are just doing one room? Who is doing the rest?”

“It could be me. Just one step at a time.”

“We’ve got time next week. Could we shoot some ‘in development’ stuff? We can use it for teasers and come back when it's done. Get the drone up, etc.”

“I’d love that. I need to explain it to Will, though.”

“Friday? What about we film your work there and here? If Marco and William don't get it, let's make this about you.”

“Friday? I should have a room done at Will’s. I don't know what Marco wants yet, but it could be a quick job.”

“If Marco is around, he could maybe film before that.”

“Come on, Davey, let’s go find him.”

Worried about William, Stella found him over by the pool.

"You OK?"

"I hate this stuff."

"What Barbecue?"

"No, making small talk with people to further the business."

"You looked fine talking to Hidir."

"He seems to know his stuff. He asked me how I knew you. And he congratulated me on getting you to do a whole house. He seemed excited to see it." Stella felt a much-needed inner glow that came from someone like Hidir recognising that she had skill. After Jackson Wilde's comments, it felt good.

"What did you say?"

"I told him I got in early." They both laughed, leaning in to touch heads. Will stood with a glass in his hand, taking in the party.

"I'm sorry about this," he said, waving his hand with his glass in it and sloshing the wine.

"Sorry about what?"

"Barbecue for Sunday lunch," he sighed.

"Do you miss it, proper Sunday lunch, I mean?"

"God, yes, and Sunday tea at my Gran's with homemade scones."

"If I cooked you some food from home, would it help you sit down with me and look at my ideas?"

Before he could answer, Marco swooped over to them both, draping an arm around each of their necks.

"How is the golden couple?" Stella blushed. She wasn't sure what worried her most, the word 'golden' or the word 'couple'. Will didn't speak, either.

"Come on, more people want to meet Stella. I should invite you more often. I'm not sure what impressed people more, reclusive William or stellar Stella."

The chatter was exciting, the food exotic, and the wine filled in any gaps. Stella had contact details of people she followed, but living in London, she'd never expected to meet. As people drifted away, she found herself in a sleepy haze, still on a cloud-like sofa between Marco and William. Her eyelids were heavy, and she fought the urge to let her eyes close.

"It's time to take you home."

"Stay," Marco commanded.

"No. Stella is not on our time yet."

Back at his own house, Will brewed a pot of tea and carried it over to the sofa on a tray.

"Damn, I need a table. Since you arrived, I keep seeing what is missing in this house."

"That's just the thing, Will. Living in the house, you can see what jobs you need furniture to do. You just need to look for a style you like."

They sat quietly drinking their tea. Will looked pensive. *What is he worrying about? I've so many ideas, but I know this isn't just about making Will happy. His priority is attracting buyers.*

Will interrupted her thoughts.

"When are you going to be ready to show me what you've got?"

"I beg your pardon?"

"Your designs. Look, if it's not finished, I think I can have vision."

"Can you wait until I speak to Grigori in the morning?"

"Sure."

Chapter 14

"Boss, we got a problem."

Will looked up at Grigori as he stood in the doorway to the kitchen. "I've just had a notice to close down construction. Seems some paperwork hasn't been filed for the next stage."

"I thought …"

"So did I."

"Vanessa said she'd take care of all that. So why …?"

"Didn't you see her face on Friday?"

"She wasn't happy, I guess, but she came back later. So why this?" *Had she seen the kiss?* Will wiped his mouth. Grigori shook his head.

"Let me ask you this, Boss, what is your usual response to something like this?"

"I'd ring V."

"That's how she makes you need her. She solves all the crises. Have you ever thought she created the problems in the first place?"

"No, I don't think so, it's probably because I've been keeping her busy." *And away from the house.*

"Do me a favour, let me sort this paperwork issue. I need to learn all this, and that way, she isn't rescuing you." Will thought about it, Grigori wanted his support. Was he right about Vanessa? He hadn't seen her since she'd left in the early hours of Saturday morning. She wasn't happy about him going to Marco's on Sunday, but he felt it had been a good move. He nodded to Grigori.

"How long are we going to be down?"

"Three or four days at least."

"Look, give the guys the week off and let them know we'll be making this time up as soon as we can. That gives us time to look properly at Star's … I mean Stella's suggestions. I can compare the two proposals so that next week …"

"Next week, we can crack on. I get caught up on supplies."

"Marco has some jobs if they work. He asked Stella to do a room."

"I'm not surprised."

"Yesterday at Marco's, everyone was talking about her." He smiled. "Someone asked me how I managed to get her to agree to do a whole house. It made me look online."

"And?"

"It's good, it's very good. How do you feel about working with her?"

"Are you kidding? She's a dream to work with. Have you seen the room?"

"No, she wants me to see it when it's finished."

"I don't think you will have to wait long. Now, are you OK with me picking up this paperwork issue?"

"Sure, it is probably best we work on this project as much as possible without Vanessa. If my sister and everyone else are correct, and we go with Stella on the design front …"

"Then we can probably get this job done a lot quicker and a lot cheaper … and with a lot less drama."

"I just don't know what I'm going to say to V." He shook his head. "For the time being, can we try not to talk to Stella about V too much? If her designs aren't up to what we need, she is going to find that hard to take, especially if V is doing things to hold the project up."

"That's OK with me, boss. Getting between two women fighting over you is a job I can do without."

"Fighting over me," Will scoffed. "You are joking, right?"

"Deadly serious, boss."

Vanessa is pushing more and more to have a relationship. I didn't think I had the headspace for a relationship with anyone. That kiss on Friday made me see things a little differently.

The men stared at each other for a moment too long before they left.

Wandering back to his office, Will had to fight the urge to open the door to Stella's bedroom. He could picture her curled up in his shirt and probably holding that grey dog of his. He'd been surprised when he spotted it in her bed. He knew she'd taken it all those years ago, but to see that she still slept with it came as a surprise. *Maybe she hadn't changed that much after all.*

With a deep breath, he passed her door and entered his own office. The pool outside his window was calling to him. He'd swum for two hours this morning, and it still hadn't been enough to sort through his thoughts.

As he settled at his desk, his thoughts drifted back through the mess this house had created for his business and his personal life. What should he do about Vanessa, especially after Grigori's suggestion that she was the problem, not the solution? *Thank God I didn't sleep with her. I don't know why she is pushing so hard. I'm clearly far from what she thinks is acceptable. One thing my dad always made clear; don't get involved with people at work.*

At the side of his screen, his phone vibrated.

STAR: Tomorrow night? Presentation and dinner.
Will: It's a date. x

Why did I type that! And why a kiss?

At last, tomorrow, he would know whether to switch the design to Stella or not. Maybe he should just wait until that decision is made. If he stuck with Vanessa and her designer, then Stella would leave, and he wouldn't have to think about that bloody kiss anymore.

When her dad called yesterday, he felt sure the news of the kiss had reached Hursts Bridge. The last thing he wanted to think about was what everyone back home would think. His sister was the biggest issue.

Stella walked past his door, and when she spotted him, she stopped to speak. William swallowed as he took in her smart trousers and cream blouse. It appeared to be made of silk as it draped over her curves. His hand itched to reach out and stroke it to check if it was as soft as it looked. Instead, he drummed his fingers on the edge of the desk.

"Morning, Will. I'm going shopping for things to finish that room. Can I pick anything up while I'm out?"

"No. I've got dinner sorted. Seven o'clock?"

"Lovely. I should be back fairly soon. I still have so much to do."

He rubbed his palm down the side of his jeans as he watched her leave and walk down the hallway. *She has grown up so much. That kiss was so real.*

Chapter 15

Shopping for fabric was never a chore for Stella. Today, the rolls of cloth excited her as she trailed her fingers across the bolts, taking in the textures and colours. She wanted this room to be special for Sarah, not just to impress Will, but because she loved her friend. She collected a few items from the various designers she had met so far and then made her way back to the farmer's market.

Walking the colourful stalls, she realised how much she wanted to feed Will. From the things she'd heard, he was working long hours, and the contents of his kitchen suggested he wasn't eating. Everywhere she looked, there was something exotic she hadn't seen before. But fresh ginger and lemongrass wouldn't remind him of Hursts Bridge. Instead, she bought a fresh chicken and plenty of eggs.

Am I just desperate for Will to say yes to my work? It's more than that, obviously; doing a design project of this size could be a significant boost to my portfolio. She moved to pick out trimmings. Will was our guardian angel when I felt like I didn't have a home. Now it's my turn to help him, not just with this room.

No, I want him to have a sanctuary, a place to return to each night. And that's what cooking a meal was all about.

I'm not going to worry about that kiss. It'd be madness to think it could be anything more. I'm not repeating mistakes. It was simply a silly lack of judgment.

Stella had the sewing machine running smoothly, even with the thicker fabrics. With the cutting machine clipping away in the corner, she was flying through the projects. If Hidir was going to be filming both rooms on Friday, it wasn't only Will she wanted to impress. The exposure on his channel would be amazing for her online profile and hopefully her business. *Who do you think you are kidding? You didn't last a year in your first job.*

The excitement of finally seeing her textile designs finished for Sarah's room took over, and she forgot to stop to eat or even drink. She was pushing hard to get all the sewing finished that day so that in the morning, she could complete the painting in the best light.

Only when Will came to find her did she realise how late it was.

Knock Knock.

“Come in.”

“Are you sure I’m allowed? Isn’t it secret?”

“Hang on.” She threw a sheet over the pile of things ready for Sarah’s room. “You can come in now.” Will’s face appeared around the door.

“Have you eaten?”

“Hm, no.”

With a sigh, Will walked in. “Have you got much more to do?”

“Another thirty minutes should do it.”

“Are you going to be finished tomorrow?” He reached out to squeeze her hand, his eyes soft.

“Yes. So, you'd better get ready to look at all my designs.” She narrowed her eyes.

“You said you’d cook me some real food if I did, so, yes?”

“I guess you’ll look at it because you really like your food … I just hope you’ll have an open mind.

“I will, Star.”

Stella’s heart missed a beat. Star! It still stopped her heart when he called her that.

“Oh, Will.”

“Sorry. Do you hate it … when I call you that?”

“No. It feels good,” she blushed.

“You have thirty minutes. Then I’m coming back to get you.”

Stella trimmed the threads on the last piece with minutes to spare before Will’s deadline. In the kitchen, she found Will putting out food on a black table surrounded by ten metal-framed chairs. She stroked the vast table.

“Is this from your boardroom?” She asked. Will nodded.

“It’ll work for now, won’t it?”

“It’s brilliant.” Stella ran her hands over the smooth surface.

“It was your idea,” he laughed.

“Could I alter this table a little?”

“We can talk about it after I've seen your plans.”

“I'd like to do it for dinner tomorrow.”

“In that case, knock yourself out. It's just a temporary fix, after all.”

Over their meal, they spoke about life in Hursts Bridge. Will talked mostly about what he missed: family and food, mainly. Eventually, they spoke of the TV they'd enjoyed growing up. For Stella, it brought up images of the three of them curled up on one sofa with at least one dog. She must have drifted away, because she was shocked when Will said.

"I've got some recordings we could watch." His voice was low and sounded very tempting, but Stella wasn't ready to sit on that tiny sofa with Will's body so close to hers. When her phone buzzed, the sight of Zach's name brought a new flush to her cheeks.

Zach: Are you back home yet?
Stella: Not yet.
Zack: Still in NYC?
Stella: No, I'm near L.A.
Zach: When are you coming back?
Stella: It could be this week, or it could be a couple of months.
Where are you?
Zach: Brisbane.
Stella: Cool.
Zach: Have a great day, Stella.
Stella: And you, Zach.

As a smile warmed her face, she looked up and caught William watching her.

"Is that my sister?" he frowned. She lowered her chin, looking into his eyes over the top of her phone.

"No, it's not Sarah, it's Zach."

"Zach?" The frown was still there.

"Zach Mitchell."

"I know the name. Is he from Hursts Bridge?"

"No, Brisbane. But he plays cricket for Yorkshire."

"Does he indeed. I didn't know you were a cricket fan."

"I wouldn't say I am. Zach lives with my cousin. Do you remember India?"

"So, the guy your cousin is living with is sending you texts that make your eyes dance?" Stella smiled a half-laugh.

"I can see how that sounds bad. But you see, India lives with Charlie Robertson, that's the love interest. Zach just lives there when he's in the U.K. So, there's nothing wrong with him sending me a text." William didn't look convinced.

She stood up and left the room, hugging her phone.

"I want to do a bit more work. Before tomorrow, you know."

He nodded. "That's OK. I've got plenty to do."

Stella thought he looked sad, but she couldn't help thinking it was for the best. Walking back to the workroom, she wished she could talk to someone about that kiss. But how could she speak to her best friend about such a moment with her brother?

Settled in her workroom, she found an e-mail from Jackson Wilde. Her hand trembled as she clicked open.

My Dear Stella,

I hear you are visiting your wonderful mother. I hope she is well. I wouldn't want her upset by all the naughty things you did in London.
Be incredibly careful, little one.

JW

The threat was clear. As much as she had worried about what he would say about her, more importantly, what he could say that would impact the rest of her family.

A second email arrived from India with the photos from the weekend. She used it as an excuse to phone her cousin.

"Stella, I just emailed you."

"I've got it. That's why I called."

"Does it make sense? I've sent the original images in a file, and well, I played with a few."

"They're amazing, India. You even included Jack's Landing."

"That was Sarah's idea. How's it going?"

"Fine!"

"I hope you aren't thinking about Jackson. The man is a menace."

"It doesn't help when he emails threats. He was clever. He listened to me. He acted on my ideas. Little gifts, a Hermes scarf for working late. A bottle of perfume for running a personal errand. A dress, he said, that I needed to wear for a work event. We had intimate dinners always related to work. Always paid me close attention. Always champagne.

"Then, one night after we worked late yet again, he took me back to his apartment. He was my boss, but neither of us were married. I thought he respected me. I'm worried about what he thinks he has to threaten me so much."

"The man is beyond words. He belongs in another decade."

"But that's the thing, India. You knew that, and I fell for it. How can I trust myself now?" Stella paused, but India didn't reply. "Am I going to keep making the same mistakes?"

"Has something happened?" India's voice was soft. It was tempting to share, but how could she?

"Not really? Not something I can talk about anyway."

"Why can't you talk about…? Oh fudge! Will? Is it Will?"

"India, please. He's my new boss. It's crazy."

"Life has a way of being crazy now and then. So is Will your new boss?"

"I'll find that out tomorrow, and I'm going to be doing a couple of days for Marco Martelli."

"Marco? Is something happening with him then?"

"Oh, he's lovely, but no."

"I thought you said William Thoresby was a skinny nerd. And yet you're more interested in him than the Italian stallion?"

"I know it's mad, but Will has changed. A lot! Oh, I don't know, maybe I'm just homesick?"

"If you like Will, what's the problem? It's not like you'll be working for him forever. Is he single?"

"Ah, that's another thing! There's this woman. She works for him. I think he's been sleeping with her."

"Is it serious?"

"I don't know. The people around him don't like her."

"Does that include you?"

Stella sighed. "She believes Will sees me as another little sister."

"Is she right?"

“Sometimes I think so. It certainly gets mentioned.”

“But something happened?”

“India … I…”

“OK. Another question, do you want something to happen? Is this a physical thing, or could you live with this guy?”

“Physical, definitely, more than that? I think so.”

“So, what's the problem?”

“What would Sarah say?”

“Ah, so that's why you're having this conversation with me?”

“I guess so.”

“If it helps, at Gran's birthday do, Sarah talked about you and William a lot. That you would make such a fabulous partnership, I presumed she was talking business-wise, but maybe she is hoping for more.”

Stella’s heart lifted. “Do you think so?”

“I don't know. I wasn't listening for that. But I can tell you what Auntie Patricia told me when I was overthinking being with Charlie. She basically said, whatever you do, you can't please everyone, so you might as well do what pleases you.”

“Well, that's something to think about.”

“So, do you know what you're going to do?”

“I'm not deciding anything until after I present my ideas to Will tomorrow. If I'm staying longer, then I can take my time.”

“And if you don't get the answer you want? What are you going to do then, Stella?”

“I'm doing a room for Marco and filming with Hidir on Friday.”

“Listen to you.”

“I know it seems unreal.”

Stella showered and slipped into bed. Cuddling down with Spike, she checked her lists for tomorrow. Jenny was coming to help. She had two separate time plans, one for the room and one for the meal. After several long, hard days, she fell asleep quickly, but not peacefully.

Chapter 16

Will had been tossing and turning for what seemed like forever. Stella was going to show him her work tomorrow, and she'd made every effort to ensure he'd seen nothing of his sister's room. He'd done some work towards it. He'd added LED light to the glass art that she'd bought down in the Arts District, and he knew she wanted him to add more light to the project once her part was done. Adding lighting effects was one area where Thoresby Technology excelled.

Tomorrow, he'd have his answer. Would he be able to ask her to complete the entire house? In his heart, he felt Stella was the one who could create a home for him. Hell, Stella made it home just by opening a door with that smile on her face.

If he couldn't agree to her doing this project, she'd leave. One thing William knew, he needed to sell as many of the plots as possible as soon as they could get them on the market. This house had to appeal to the sort of people who were prepared to pay over twenty million for a house, and they had very particular tastes. Marco tried to assure him that these people wanted unique homes. If he could combine architecture with his understanding of technology, personalised to the client, and match it with the designer who could deliver for that very particular client, then Will would hit on the magic formula.

Marco was keen for Stella to do a room in his house, and that's what she was going to do next, so at least she'd be here for a few more days. Thinking about her leaving and going back to the U.K. was something he just couldn't do. Stella was very strong-willed and had been all her life. He didn't think she could be persuaded to stay if he didn't have enough faith in her work to do the whole house. He had toyed with the idea of asking her to do some other minor pieces. *I've told you before that you can't possibly expect her to sit around making quilts that you can bury if you don't like them or create artwork that you can take down to sell this place. I could tell her I want to keep it for my house and then buy a home that doesn't matter so much.*

He'd said to Marco just the other day that if it were his house and he wasn't trying to sell it, she could paint it whatever colour she liked.

William had the impression from Grigori that the paint she was going to use in his sister's room was far from white. He had also called her fabric choices interesting. *What the hell did that mean?*

“Star, turn on my shower.” Kicking off the sheets, Will walked into the bathroom. He had to do something to clear his mind. Naked in the shower, his thoughts turned back to Stella. *This was a mistake.*

His body reacted to the memory of her body next to his, the sweet smell of her shampoo over dinner, and finally to that kiss. His hand reached down to hold himself. Maybe that would help him sleep.

Lying back in his bed, busy thoughts still ran around his head, and he had no idea what the answer would be the next day. If he hadn’t known before that kiss, he knew now that he wanted so much more with Stella. He couldn’t help but worry about what his family would think.

But mostly, he worried about Sarah, his sister. Stella and Sarah had an unbreakable bond. He couldn’t be the one to destroy that.

The silence was getting too loud, and he considered putting on some music until his ears detected another sound. Being alone in this house, he wasn't accustomed to the sounds of other people. *It must be Stella.* He lay still, trying to pick up the sounds she was adding to his life.

The sudden realisation that she was crying lifted him from his bed as he sped down the corridor to her door. Blindly, he burst in. Stella was fighting with the sheets, thrashing in her bed, in the full throes of a terrible nightmare. He pulled her from the pillows and held her close. Her crying stopped, shifting to gentle sobs.

“Hush hush. It’s OK now. I’ve got you.” He stroked her silky hair, taking a deep breath to enjoy her floral scent.

He held her as close as he could, whispering softly. Her sobbing slowed.

“It’s OK, Star. I’ve got you. I’m not going to let anyone hurt you.”

Stella slowly opened her eyes and looked into William's face.

“Oh, I’m sorry, it all felt so real.”

“Dreams can be like that.”

“It’s since that problem in London. I dream about when Mum left. Why can’t I let it go?”

Let go of what? Her mum leaving? Or whatever happened in London?

He pulled her closer, needing to surround her. Feeling her warm body next to his skin felt good. Too good.

Shit! I have no clothes on.

Stella’s eyes opened and looked up into his.

And now she knows I'm naked. Can she feel that poking into her?

"I'd better go."

"Will, don't go. Please don't leave me like she did." *Her bloody mother.*

"I told you then, I would never leave you."

"But you did leave me, didn't you, Will?"

"Only to go to university. By the time I got back, you'd grown up."

"I missed you." It was a whisper, but Will didn't miss the pain in her voice.

William pulled up the throw to cover himself as he sat up in her bed beside her, gently pulling Stella into his side.

"Are you worried about tomorrow?"

"Not so much. I'm happy Sarah is going to love the room. If it's not right for you, I don't want you to feel any pressure. I'll live. I'm more worried about the filming on Friday."

"If I don't ask you to do the entire house, would you still stay here?"

"No." *Well, that's clear, then. There was no hesitation, just a straightforward no.* He had to respect what she was saying. After a few moments, she said more.

"Will, I'm not Vanessa. I'm not just going to steamroll you. If I do more work, I won't keep you in the dark. I'll talk to you. I'll work within any boundaries you set."

"I know." He squeezed her shoulder and kissed her forehead.

"I'm just hoping you can cope with a bit more than flat black and white." She chuckled.

"Go to sleep. You've got a busy day tomorrow."

"Yes. And I'm cooking for you, too."

Sitting next to Stella on a bed whilst he was naked was not a good idea. He crossed his legs and tried not to look over at his companion. He could control his eyes, but he couldn't control his brain. Everything that had been keeping him awake before was still there. And now it was complicated by her body breathing softly next to him. Her dark lashes fanned out across her cheek.

At two a.m., when he was sure Stella was sound asleep, he slipped out of her room to put on a pair of boxer shorts, hoping that might help him control something.

He collected his phone so he could at least work on that while he lay awake guarding Stella.

Without thinking too hard, he called his sister.

He wanted to know what had brought Stella here and if it would be safe for her to go back.

"Sarah."

"Hello, brother, how's it going? Have you finished that house yet so that I can have my friend back?"

"I haven't decided if I'm going to use her yet."

"Oh, brother!"

"I know. Look, I need to know why she left her job?" he paced the room, unable to sit down.

"What has she told you?"

"Nothing, but she had a nightmare tonight, and she mentioned she'd had a few since she left London."

"And she still didn't tell you?"

"No."

"I'm afraid it's not my story to tell."

"If I'm going to employ her, I've a right to know about her last post."

"One: If you don't employ her, someone else will." A vision of Marco sprang to his brain.

"Two: She left her job. It had nothing to do with the quality of her work."

"But Sarah!"

"If you don't like her style, Will, that's one thing. We all know you struggle with that, Stella included. But you know her well enough not to question her ethics. Talk to me when you've made your mind up. YOUR OWN MIND, WILLIAM." And she hung up on him.

Will shook his head and took himself and his phone back to Stella's room. He very carefully slid back in place next to her. He stroked her hair off her face and smiled as he spotted Spike's pink nose sticking out. *Still looking after her, Spike. Good Dog.*

Chapter 17

Stella woke to find herself curled into Will's side. A memory of last night drifted through her brain. Jackson's email and its veiled threats, and Will's rescue. *He hasn't been for his swim.* She nudged him gently. She didn't want to make him late, and she had a busy day ahead.

"Good morning, Star." His voice was croaky, and his hair was even more ruffled than usual. Stella swallowed.

"Did you want your swim before going to the office?"

"I guess I should. It sets me up for the day."

"I'm sorry."

"Sorry for what, Star?"

"Ruining your night's sleep?"

"To be honest, I couldn't sleep until I got into your bed," he smirked. "Right. Time to get this day started." He pushed off the bed. Stella closed her eyes quickly, covering them with her hand. Her stomach clenched; she wasn't ready to see him naked again.

"It's OK, Star, I'm decent." She opened one eye.

"When?"

"Once you fell asleep."

"And you came back?"

"I promised you, didn't I?"

"Yes," she breathed.

He closed the door quietly behind him, and Stella fell back onto the bed, pulling the pillow he'd used into a hug. She filled her lungs with his citrus scent. Then she reached under her pillow and pulled out Spike, the dog she'd stolen from him so long ago.

A couple of hours later, Stella was putting the lid back on the paint when Jenny arrived.

"Tea?"

"Sure?"

"You don't sound very convinced."

"I never really got tea, but I'm happy to try again."

Stella made a pot of Yorkshire tea and set it on the new table.

"Lovely table."

"I think it needs something, maybe some wax? I'm hoping I've time to do that before tonight. I'm cooking a meal for Will."

"Is that a romantic or a business move?"

"Oh? … oh, business. Will is going to struggle to make choices. I want him to be as relaxed as possible."

"Have you got wine?"

"Yes, but I'm not sure."

"If you want to use this table, we'd better get started."

"Follow me!"

"Oh, Stella, I love how the wave runs around the room," Jenny gushed as she stroked the smooth wood. "I can't wait to see the rest."

When Stella showed her the workshop, Jenny clapped her hands.

"I knew it would be wonderful."

"I've been promised help to move all this, so I'm just going to text Grigori to remind him while you have a look around."

"I love this room," Jenny sighed, stepping inside, her eyes sparkling at Stella's workspace.

"I've got a few more plans. It's a great space. Eventually, it will be used as a utility room, hence the big sink."

"That's useful. And so much light." Jenny fell on the pile of fabrics on Stella's table.

"These peacock colours are for the room I've just seen," she sighed as she stroked the fabrics. "So, what are the dark reds and golds for?"

"That would be for Marco's sister."

"Oh yes, the neighbour."

Paulo arrived, grinning, by the door. He wasn't tall, but he looked powerful. It was hard to judge his age. His long silver hair was fastened in a neat ponytail that reached to his waist. And that smile was wide.

"I am here to help you today."

"Good morning, Paulo. I want to ask a couple of questions. Are you busy?"

"No, I can't do build this week. So, I help you with next door."

"Is the plaster finished?"

"No, it takes work, Venetian plaster, you want a good job, not a quick job. Is there anything I can help with other than lifting today?"

"I've been looking at that table."

"Yes."

"I'm thinking, sand it, paint it flat black, then wax?"

"I can do that."

"Could you do it today?"

"If Grigori helps you lift instead of me. You'd better ask him, not me."

Stella laughed.

"I'll do that."

Paulo left to start work on the table, and Grigori arrived to help.

"Tell me, is this going to get you the big job? Because I don't think I can work with the other option."

"What do you think?"

"I think Will wants it to be you, too, but he panics when it comes to anything involving colour."

"I've done this for Sarah. It's not how I see the rest of the house, but I'm hoping that he'll see that, even when I use bold and colourful options, I can make it look aspirational. I realise Will is going to find this hard, don't worry, I've plenty of mood boards."

"Vanessa doesn't do that. Will just trusts her."

Stella stared at Grigori. *What do you say to that? Why does he trust her more than me?*

No more words were spoken as the job got started, transforming the bedroom for Stella's best friend, Sarah. Jenny helped Stella make the bed whilst Grigori unwrapped the chair and ottoman.

"Don't you think we should get the rug down first?"

"I'm not thinking straight." Stella bit her lip.

"Just relax."

Stella tried to stay calm, but it wasn't easy. So many emotions were flooding her body. Seeing the different fabrics and materials coming together in the room helped her see how her ideas were working. Smoothing out the bed cover, memories of starting the day in this bed, next to Will, washed over her. It all seemed so impossible. *How can I compete with someone as sophisticated as Vanessa?*

It was a late lunch, but the room was almost ready. Stella nibbled a sandwich while applying pewter-coloured wax to the table. She kicked

herself for not organising flowers. She had candles in her workroom, but they would be lost without flowers. The grounds were still completely bare of plants, but it was worth a try. She sent Grigori a text.

> Stella: Is there anything growing out there? I could use something to put on the table.
>
> G: Unless the ivy growing outside the gate would work, no.
>
> Stella: That will do nicely.

She took her scissors to cut several long lengths of ivy and used them along with some ribbon and candles to decorate the centre of the table. Stella spent two hours preparing dinner for William's beloved seven o'clock. The table was looking so much better. The chicken was in the oven, and the vegetables were ready to go. With nothing left to do, Stella went to have a shower and dress to meet her potential new client. Doing a presentation always gave her a surge of adrenaline, but today Stella was feeling the effects more than usual.

She felt embarrassed that William had seen her so distressed the night before, and that she'd begged him to stay. It would hardly be the way to start a professional relationship, and the thought of that and Jackson's email added to the churning in her stomach. She'd changed her mind on and off all day about what to wear for this dinner. She wanted to get this job on her own ability and not because Will liked her more than Vanessa.

But what did he feel? He still hadn't mentioned the kiss, and she hadn't seen Vanessa since that night. Stella had no idea how often she usually came to the house before all this started, so how could she judge? *Was it just Fridays? Is that why she got so upset about not going out on Friday nights?*

She finally decided on smart trousers and one of the tops she'd bought in New York. She tried to play everything down the middle: clothes, makeup, perfume. Heels were the only exception. She wanted, or maybe needed, to look grown up. She just wanted no more references to being a little sister.

Chapter 18

Back at her workbench, Stella flipped erratically through her mood boards as the panic once again began to rise in her stomach. There were still two hours to go until the seven o'clock dinner.

<<Welcome home, William. Stella is in the workroom.>>

Will's early arrival did nothing to quell the feeling inside. The computer had told him where she was; he would find her. *Do I need to get the vegetables on now? And what about the Yorkshire puddings? Why did I try to prepare a meal and the presentation? Because you were hoping it would help him be calm about making decisions. Because you know how difficult this will be for him.*

She could hear his hurried footsteps down the corridor. The door bounced open, banging against the wall.

"I'm sorry, I didn't mean to do that. I had my hands full."

Stella looked up from the spreadsheet open on her screen. A pink-faced William Thoresby, in an immaculate black suit, stood nervously clutching an arrangement of orange roses.

"Flowers?" Is this to soften the blow, his idea of a consolation prize?

"I just thought a dinner at the table called for flowers."

"Me too. Thank you. I still need to do things for the meal?"

"Seven o'clock, I know. I couldn't wait. Sorry." He looked down at the bouquet. "If you're not ready, I understand."

Stella smiled softly. "Shall I show you Sarah's room?"

"Yes, please. I know there's blue in there."

"Oh, because of the glass art I gave you?"

"And the paint on the back of your arm." He laughed as Stella checked to see if it was clean now.

"And there I was trying to look professional."

William was still holding the flowers.

"Shall I leave these here?"

"Let's put them on the table, and I'll check the oven. You arriving early has thrown me."

"I'm sorry. Please don't let it upset you. I can wait for my meal, but…"

"…but you want to see the room."

Stella placed the roses in the centre of the table, adjusting the ivy around them. The sun was approaching the horizon, and the combination of colours awoke warm feelings in Stella's centre. Will's attention was on her face; she blushed as a smile licked her lips.

"What happened to this?"

"You said I could paint it; if you don't like it, I can…"

"It's not that. How did you have the time?"

"I've had help."

"From?"

"Grigori helped with the shifting, Paulo helped with the table, and my friend Jenny helped with the rest."

Stella paused, her back to the door, her hand on the handle.

"Remember, this is for Sarah. So, I do hope you keep this house."

"I would love to live here. Let's hope we can sell the concept." Stella looked at Will in his immaculate suit, waiting for him to see her work. She swallowed, opening the door, gradually revealing the room.

William stepped through, his eyes taking in every inch. He didn't speak as his hands swept along the wave shelf, feeling the smooth curves. He sat in the chair, stroking the velvet armrests. In the wardrobe, he examined the monogrammed hangers. Tracing the lettering with a finger, he found it embroidered on pillows and robes, etched into glass, and embossed on the hangers. Blues, greens, and gold spread throughout the spaces. He stood in front of the canvas prints of their hometown. Stella couldn't even see his face, let alone read it. Finally, he turned to Stella and hugged her without a word. *God, he hates it!*

"I'm sorry. I did my best."

"Stella, it's wonderful, all of it. I don't know where to start. It's so, Sarah. I remember the day she first saw a peacock." Stella nodded as he spoke. "I can't wait to see your ideas for the rest of the house."

"Where?"

"My office?"

"The workshop might be easier. I have a bigger table and the extra samples, if we want to consider alternatives."

"Fine, your workshop."

My workshop? *He called it mine*. The excitement was bubbling. *Stay calm, don't blow it now.*

"Take a seat," Stella said as she moved a pile of fabric from the spare stool next to her table.

"The main open spaces will need continuity throughout. Talking to Grigori, you have birch pocket doors, and the blonde wood picked out for the floor. I'd love to make the doors in the primary and the junior primary a bit more interesting. It'll give them some more scope for personalisation." Stella studied his face to check he was still with her. "I realise you like simple, high-contrast designs." She passed him the first sample board. "Any of these can be tweaked. I want to understand the things you love and the things you hate."

William's eyes roamed the boards, his panic obvious. She realised the one he held carried over twenty samples of materials and photographs. It was too much for Will. She slowly took the board from his hand.

"We should do this one step at a time, one decision at a time. It gets easier as the project moves forward. We could make some global decisions, too." William didn't speak, and Stella continued. "Could I take you to a kitchen showroom so you can see materials …?"

"With salesmen! I don't think so, thank you very much."

"I want to show you combinations."

"Maybe we can do it online."

"We can use some choices you've already made. Do you like the marble you've used in the bathrooms? Do you want to use the same or something similar? Did you see another you liked when you chose that?" *Shut up, Stella, you are overloading him. One question at a time.*

"The bathrooms? Nobody asked me. I didn't know I had a choice."

"I don't understand."

"Some things had been ordered already."

"By whom?"

"The original developer. I thought if he'd bought it, I should use that. He had way more experience than me."

"Was Grigori working on this with him?"

"Yes. That is the one thing about all this. I like him. I think we can work together on so many projects."

"I obviously haven't asked enough questions. If the bathrooms were ordered, maybe the kitchen is." The optimism drained from her.

"I still can't find the guy to ask."

Stella frowned, angry that he was so in the dark.

"What has Vanessa been buying then?"

"Just the art."

"You need to know what has been bought before we go any further."

"I'll chase the paperwork and talk to Grigori, and I must speak to V."

"I'm going to …" Stella waved in the direction of the oven, "I have things to do with the food."

In the kitchen, Stella cleared the work surfaces, trying to wipe away the negative thoughts and berating herself for not asking enough questions. Will said he liked her work, but she still didn't really know if she had a job or, if she did, what that job was. She couldn't believe that Will had lost grip on all this.

When Will didn't reappear, she pushed on with preparing the dinner.

It was five minutes after seven when the Yorkshire puddings were finally ready to crown the plates.

"Star, where is Will?"

<<William is in the office.>>

"William is just here," he said with a smile.

Stella turned around to face him, the tray of hot puddings in her hands. Will's eyes lit up.

"Well, if you didn't already have the job, you do now." Stella dropped the puddings onto the breakfast bar.

"I've got the job?"

"Yes. How did you not get that?"

"It could be because you didn't say I had the job."

"I'm sorry. Come here." William wrapped Stella in his arms. "I guess we've both been a bit vague. Last night … I mean… I knew then that this was not ideal. I need you to understand. I wanted to ask you to help me with this from the start, Star." Standing with his arms around her, all Stella's fears fell away. Her body relaxed into his solid chest.

William gently pushed her away to check her face. "It's not just money I've invested in this, it's my business, and well, my business is my life."

"I do understand. I wouldn't want this job other than on merit."

"Stella, before you say yes," he dipped his head to look into her eyes. "I need you to remember we must keep a grip on the costs and the timescale."

"Because time is money – I know."

"I sound like my dad, don't I?" They both laughed. It was another sign they'd relaxed. "But this is serious, Stella."

"I understand. I need two days to finish this job for Marco. Filming with Hidir will help in the long term. It doesn't matter how good we say your technology is; it'll have more weight if someone like him says it."

"I get it. I don't like it, but I do get it." Will released her, and Stella immediately missed his arms.

"Do you have time tomorrow to put a few of your tricks into this room for Marco?"

"If we start early, and it doesn't take too long. I left a few things unfinished on my desk today." He grinned. "It was the pull of Yorkshire puddings."

"The puddings! They've gone flat."

"They'll be fine. You have gravy, right?"

They ate the meal, relaxed friends at the end of the day. Stella enjoyed watching William eat the food he missed from home. Her homemaker instincts had kicked in.

Be careful; you are not here to play house with William Thoresby. You wanted a job, but it wasn't to be Mrs Thoresby.

It wasn't going to be easy, but something had shifted. They could start to move forward as soon as Grigori had obtained all the necessary permissions. But Stella still had so many questions buzzing around her head.

When it came time for bed, Stella felt alone, having the bed to herself. Will had hugged her tonight, and it was wonderful, as if she had found where she wanted to be.

She pulled Spike out from under her pillow and hugged him.

What would Will do if he knew I had taken his dog?

Chapter 19

"Star, open my blinds."

Stella looked out to the terrace. Her memory flicked back to Friday night by the fire. Will appeared walking towards the pool, that trim body on full display, and today, she didn't take her eyes away. *I thought I was up early, but Will is already up.* Her eyes lingered far too long as he powered through the water.

Despite the effort she'd put in this week, there was still a lot to do. Today, Stella needed to start work on the textiles for the bedroom at Marco's. Paulo was over there already working on the plaster feature wall she'd asked him to do.

"Coffee?" Will offered her a travel cup.

"You're up early?"

"I am, and I've had my swim, so now my head is a lot clearer."

"That's good news."

"What did you want me to look at over at Marco's?"

"As I understand it, it's one of the spare rooms and doesn't have much in there yet. Can you do the blinds and some lighting?"

"Of course."

"This is the headboard." She looked sheepish at William as she showed him the piece on her phone. "Could you add some lights behind this?"

Will stared at her and raised an eyebrow.

"I know, it's a silly question."

"Do you have time to show me this room?" he asked. Stella looked at the work piled on her table.

"Yes, have you got your tools?" Will laughed and left her workroom. Stella ran to catch up with him.

That morning felt so different. The weight of the last few days was lifted, and she was confident about this bedroom makeover. The weak February sun blinded her as she tried to keep up with Will's long strides. He reached out and took her hand. Stella felt her heart expand. It all felt so normal. Like this was what her life should be, walking hand in hand

with Will to work on a bedroom for an international sports star. She wanted this to last.

"Come on, slowcoach." His smile was soft, and Stella thought he was going to kiss her again. But he didn't; he turned his head away as Stella's smile fell into a frown. A coldness gripped her chest. *Have you really started considering a relationship with your boss the day after you got the job? Focus.*

The morning went quickly, with so many things to pull together for Marco. As Stella tried to concentrate on which colours to match the fabric swatches she had, her mind began to wander, thinking about the whole project at Will's. Once the filming was over on Friday, she wanted to order more prints from India's photography. She was still juggling ideas in her head as she painted. She needed to get them out of her head and write them down.

She'd just stopped to scribble one more thing on her scrap of paper when Grigori arrived at her workroom with a sandwich and a couple of bottles of water.

"Thank you. I think I might have forgotten breakfast this morning."

"I look after my team." It was his trademark smile. "Now, do you need any more help next door? The rest of the team is off on another site until Monday, but Paulo and myself are available."

"Has Paulo finished the plaster?"

"Yes, and he has prepared that dresser."

"Brilliant. I'll be over there doing the decorative layers on that after this." She waved her sandwich. "I'd like to get that bit finished tonight. Can Paulo seal it tomorrow?"

"I'll tell him."

After lunch, Stella moved next door. She felt the normal rising emotions as a project came to completion. She needed to take a deep breath as she settled down with her paintbrushes to add details to the dresser. She had been working on it for about an hour when Gabriella, who worked for Marco, popped in with coffee for her.

"That is so pretty, Miss Stella. All those tiny flowers. How long will this take you?"

"I hope to be finished with the painting tonight."

"Will you want some help in making up the bed?"

"If you've got time tomorrow, that would be great." Gabriella still hovered in the doorway. She shifted from foot to foot.

"Sure, I can do that. Can he come and see it? Now, I mean, he wants to know if he has to wait like Will did."

"Do you mean Marco?" Stella asked. Gabriella nodded.

"Sure, tell him he's welcome any time he likes." Gabriella hadn't left the room before Marco burst in.

"I won't ask why you are treating me differently to William; I guess you have your reasons." Stella didn't make eye contact with him as she puzzled over that statement. Marco was undoubtedly attractive, and he made her smile, but it wasn't the same feeling she had when she looked at Will.

"That room was for someone I know very well. I've only just met you, so getting feedback as I go, could be useful."

"You know Will's sister? I think he told me that."

"She's been my best friend since we were six."

"And you know Will from then, too? I am right, aren't I?"

"Yes."

"Is that what makes it all so hard between the two of you?"

"I'm sorry?"

"You obviously love him." This wasn't a question. Stella turned her attention back to the tiny flowers she was painting. She needed to change the subject.

"Do you like the flowers?"

"I won't be adding them to my room, but for this room, they look great. I didn't realise it would all be so bespoke. Is that why the guy on Sunday was so keen on your work?"

"I hope it's more than that. I can't customise every piece of furniture I put in a room. But if I can add in something I've made, it is harder for someone else to copy the style."

"How do you match the colours so well? That paint doesn't look the same as the parts that are dry."

"That's part of what you are paying for." She looked at him with the most serious look she could conjure up, then burst out laughing. "To be honest, I have a colour reader that helps to match the colour of anything to a paint colour. Not only that, but some paint companies will match a colour for you. They have scopes in the shop."

"Good, good. I wanted to see you and the room. I was flying out to Switzerland at the weekend, but a friend is taking his jet in the morning, so I'm going with him."

"Oh!"

"Look, I could pay you now. Anything else you need?"

"I'm not sure." Stella's brain scrambled to think through the project and what she might need to ask Marco.

"Stella, you've got a bit of a challenge helping out our mutual friend. Personally, I know you are the right person for the job. But if I can help, would you please tell me? Gabriella will be here when you come to film. If you need anything, and I do mean anything, let me know."

"Thank you, Marco, you've been really kind. When will you be back?" Stella thought she would miss knowing he was next door. She knew Will needed him there.

"I'm not sure. You never know what might turn up. Why?"

"Nothing." She focused back on her painting, not daring to look into his dark eyes a moment longer.

"What will I be missing? Your birthday or something?"

Stella focused back on her work. She didn't answer.

"Damn, I'm good. So, when is it?"

"Not for weeks."

"I'll be back."

Chapter 20

Stella’s anxiety was mounting like a storm inside every vein. Today, they were going to film the two rooms she had completed. This had the potential to showcase her style and elevate her profile. It could be exactly what she needed to launch her own business on both sides of the pond. She was struggling to rein in all the ideas for a future that constantly danced across her mind. This could trigger a fundamental shift for her.

Don’t get so excited, girl. I know the possibilities, but this is your first full house. She ran a hand over her hair. *I can’t wait to start.* Dinner yesterday with Will went much better than she could have ever imagined. They appeared to have survived whatever that fumbled kiss was last Friday night. *I think that’s good, isn’t it? It can’t go any further. Just focus on the job. Be excited about that, not a kiss.*

The boys from Million Dollar Property wanted to look at Will's latest technology, too. She was still trying to persuade Will that it would be worthwhile. She knew the team's reach online, and their YouTube channel had over two million followers.

As she ran the steamer over the headboard, Stella stroked the fabric, enjoying the feel of the velvet. She walked around, inspecting and adjusting each piece that made up this room for her friend. She had put everything she had into each inch of it, and she was proud of the results, but what would others think? *At least we can breathe after today and then come up with a sensible plan for what comes next. I can work with this team.*

Grigori's voice echoed down the corridor, calling her name. *This is it!* With a quick check in the mirror, she opened the front door to Hidir and Davey. Hidir was as smartly dressed as Davey was laid back.

They both looked weighed down as they carried huge black nylon bags of equipment into the kitchen area.

“Tea?”

“I have some here.” Hidir passed her a pack of green tea.

“He's always prepared,” Davey laughed.

“I need to be. I’ve a lot of talking to do today.”

“Can we look at the space here first, then go over to Marco's?”

“Marco is away in Europe. Switzerland skiing, but I’ve got his permission all signed.”

“See, I'm not the only one who's prepared.” Davey grinned.

“We're off to the Alps on Sunday too.” Hidir plucked a tiny piece of lint from the jacket of his black suit.

“Filming?”

“Some of the time.” Davey laughed.

“Let's see this room, I'm excited to see your work this side of the States. I hope you remembered we want to do a sit-down designer interview with you, too.” Stella tightened her lips and nodded.

“This way, gentlemen.”

“Oh, gentlemen! It's like being in London.”

Stella pushed open the door, revealing Sarah's bedroom.

“Wow.”

Relief spread through her. *They liked it.*

“I'm here with interior designer Stella Barrington Jones, who is in Los Angeles this week working with the technology genius William Thoresby.” Hidir smiled at the camera. “This is a space they worked on together for William's sister.”

“Sarah is my best friend from school. When I visited some of the extremely talented artisans you have here, I saw so many things I knew Sarah would absolutely love.” Stella waved her hand out to show the rest of the build. “This house is going to be so fabulous and quite exclusive, but right now it's pretty much a blank canvas.”

“A blank canvas with some amazing bones and wonderful views.”

“The views are important up here in the hills, aren't they? This house features some incredible technology built into it. Working with someone like William Thoresby, who is at the cutting edge of the latest technology, is making this job a dream.”

“And this is just the first of ten? Is that correct?”

“There are ten proposed plots out here. Will wanted to get this one finished first.”

“This house is for William himself?”

“I don't think that decision has been confirmed yet, for the right price, maybe someone could persuade him to take one of the other plots.”

Stella showed them some choices she had made in putting the room together. Making a point of showing carefully where technology had met creative design.

The filming at Marco’s followed the same pattern. They filmed her interview by the fire near the pool, with Stella answering a stream of questions about what inspired her designs. As the light began to fade, Davey wanted to record some drone footage. Stella took Hidir back into the house to get started on the meal, whilst he spent some time with Will.

“I'll put the kettle on.”

“I could do with checking my emails,” Hidir said. Stella opened the door to her room.

“If you want the Wi-Fi code, it's on that painting.” She pointed to a painting of a small fishing boat.

“Clever.”

“I'll find Will. Star, where is Will?” Hidir raised an eyebrow.

<<Stella, William is in his bedroom.>>

“Don’t worry. William can show you how it all works.”

Stella knocked on his bedroom door. “Will?”

“Come in. I'm having trouble deciding what to wear. Black or blue?”

“You know I like blue, but why not ask the guys? They do this all the time.”

“Good idea.”

The computer announced a new arrival.

<<Welcome, Vanessa. William and Stella are in the bedroom.>>

Shit!

“What now?”

They walked out of the bedroom together to greet Vanessa.

At least she'll see that we're both dressed.

“Good. I've actually got you together.” Will and Stella exchanged glances. “You can thank me later, but I’ve an open house sorted for the 12th.”

“Which 12th?”

“February, of course.”

“That's Tuesday!” Stella stuttered.

“V, we aren't ready. There's no way we can be ready by Tuesday. We've just lost a whole week of construction.”

“Oh, why is that?”

“It doesn't matter. Look, it's simply not possible.”

“Well, we must. The invitations are out, and the replies are coming in. I can do it. I can have a team in here over the weekend. It's going to cost, but it can be done. Then Valentin can be here on Monday, and he can be here Tuesday for the filming.” Hidir walked out of Stella’s room, looking puzzled.

“Yes, I've managed to get the top influences here.” Hidir looked at Stella, still puzzled. “Even that Million Dollar Property king is coming.” Will looked concerned, but Stella started to smile, and Hidir laughed.

“I take it you're Vanessa.”

“Yes,” purred Vanessa, “and who are you?”

“I'm the Million Dollar Property King. You can call me Hidir, and if you check your e-mail, you’ll see that I declined your kind invitation.”

“Could I persuade you to change your mind?” her voice a low purr.

Stella laughed louder. “I think you'll find this is not the week for an open day with influencers as they’ll mostly be in the Alps from Sunday.”

“How do you…”

“Because, Vanessa, this is my business. A full open day now is not the answer.”

“I think you’ll find I've already sent the invites.”

“I asked you to work on the exhibition stand for March.”

“I've done that,” she said with a wave of her hand.

“Good. Bring it here.”

“When?”

“That would be now, V.”

“It's Friday.”

“And the new Friday dinner is here at 7 o’clock.”

Davey walked in, waving his phone. “Hey, I just got an email about this place. Who's Vanessa?”

Between them, they tried to explain what had happened to Davey. He shook his head.

“Can we film Will now?”

“William, if you're being filmed, please get changed.”

“I don't think so, V.”

“Hidir looks so good in black,” she purred again.

Hidir laughed and smiled at William. “I prefer him in blue, anyway.”

They left to film William in his office.

Vanessa stalked behind Stella, following her into the kitchen. It was time for her to focus on the meal, but she quickly texted Grigori to come over for dinner. They would need him to sort out this new event.

Stella rubbed at her arm and the goose bumps that had erupted there when Vanessa sidled up to her. She swallowed as she closed her eyes to try to settle the jumbled emotions of the day. She felt relieved by Hidir's response to her designs and even more relieved that her part of the filming was finished. Now, if only Vanessa would go away, she could start dealing with the bombshell she just dropped. She forced her eyes down the carrots, taking a small side step away from Vanessa.

"When did you arrive in L.A.?" Vanessa asked as she wiped at the makeshift breakfast bar.

"Two weeks ago?"

"When did this get arranged?" She drummed her long nails on the hard surface.

"This what?" Stella kept her eyes on the vegetables she was peeling.

"This filming with the Million Dollar Property guy."

"They were at Marco's do last Sunday. We made a lot of contacts."

"I'm impressed. How did you persuade Will to agree?"

"Hidir knows his stuff. I simply let him talk to Will alone for a while."

"You've actually known William for a long time." *Was that a statement or a question?* Stella wanted to stay polite.

"Yes, they live near us. Our parents were friends. His sister is my best friend."

"And that's why he treats you like a little sister," Vanessa snarled.

"Sarah is four years younger than Will; he ended up looking after us quite a bit."

"What's their house like?"

"It's nice. Amanda, his mum has great taste."

"The money's actually from her side, isn't it?"

Bile hit the back of Stella's throat. Was she reading this right?

"I don't know."

"But they have lots of it, don't they?"

Stella's skin itched. She focused on the vegetables in her hand.

"I couldn't possibly say."

"The table looks nice. Who did it for you?"

"You're joking, right?" The orange roses that Will had brought had opened now and brightened the display. This might be a simple meal shared with friends, but Stella always liked the table to look welcoming.

"No, I actually have a wonderful girl; I'll give you her number. She could do a better job than that. What about caterers? This looks good, but my guy has a bit more finesse."

"Vanessa," Stella sighed. "I'm sure you're really good at what you do, but haven't you realised why Will likes to stay here at the weekends?"

"But how will he ever meet anyone?"

"Maybe that's why he employs you."

"He has always needed me … until recently." She stroked the table, watching Stella cook. "Stella, why is that guy here today?"

"He's been filming my work."

"But you're actually nobody … I mean, how?"

"We've known each other online for a couple of years, but we didn't meet until Sunday. It was a lovely surprise. Hidir wanted to film Marco's place, and he asked if he could see my work here and next door."

"Why would he want to film Marco?"

"A well-known international personality? Hidir makes a living from his channel; he plans months in advance, sometimes a year ahead. He's good at what he does, too. Here, can you put the bread on the table?"

"Where did that come from?"

"The table, it's the conference table you replaced last month."

"But…!"

"It's had some work," Stella smiled.

"The chairs still look worn."

"It's only temporary." Stella shrugged. "I was tempted to do something with them, but whilst we're all working, it seemed a better idea to focus on the new stuff."

Over dinner, the voices ran together as Will poured more wine. Stella thought they would be feeling totally relieved now that the filming was over, but they now had Vanessa's bombshell to deal with.

"Davey's driving, and to be fair, I think we should be getting back." Hidir sighed.

As they gathered their bags to leave, they each hugged and thanked Stella.

"I'll be in touch when we are back in the States. Have fun on this project and don't work too hard. I know you. I don't want to hear you've burnt out again."

"I won't, I'll be watching your adventures."

When Davey hugged her, he said softly, "If I can get anything edited, I'll send it before Tuesday. It might help. Good luck with that one." Stella could see that his eyes were on Vanessa, where she had shifted to sit next to Will. Stella had been trying not to watch her constantly touch Will. He didn't seem to notice, and he wasn't touching her. It still annoyed Stella. *You don't own him. You would be mad if he complained about Marco touching you.*

When they disappeared to look at something in his office, she sighed. Grigori leaned over and touched her arm.

"Are you OK?" he muttered quietly. "It's been a long week."

"It's going to be a long weekend."

"She's quite something. I wish I could have seen her face when you told her he'd be in the Alps."

"Why does she hate Marco?"

"To be fair, you can see why someone who doesn't know him might not like him. Plus, I don't think she can manipulate him."

"Well … not everyone gets to see how big his heart is. Thank you for stepping up this week."

"I'm hoping this is enough for him to see what she's doing after our chat on Monday." He tapped a rhythm on the table. Before Stella could ask about that, Will joined them in the kitchen.

"I've messaged some of my team, so we've extra hands tomorrow to see how much tech we can have a show by Tuesday."

"Where's V?"

"She's gone."

Did he send her? Or is she scared of work tomorrow?

"She's coming back Sunday night with the presentation stuff. I think we can use it."

"I'm off too, boss. See you in the morning, Star." Grigori had never called her Star before, and her first reaction was to check Will's face. He didn't say anything, and his face barely moved, but it told Stella he wasn't comfortable with it, and in a way, neither was she. She did like Grigori, but 'Star' was something between her and her childhood friend. She had to say something.

Stella stepped forward to hug Grigori. Speaking softly into his ear.

"Thank you for working so hard this week, Grigori. We couldn't do it without you." Will walked away before she could continue. Grigori whispered back to her.

"I shouldn't have called you Star, should I? It's only the boss who called you that, not everyone back home, like he said."

"He said that?"

"I heard him explaining to Marco, whatever. Don't worry, I won't do it again."

"Thanks for understanding."

After Grigori left, Stella stood alone, feeling flat after the excitement of today's visitors. *What do I do now? I need an early night if we are going to work this weekend. I could just check my room and maybe pull out the fabric I want to start on.*

"Has he gone?"

Stella spun round to see Will holding two glasses of wine.

"I don't have any flutes, but V likes me to have champagne in the house. She claims it's to celebrate the business milestones. It's her theory that if you're always ready to celebrate them, you will attract them to you. I'm not sure I get it. But she does keep finding reasons to celebrate."

"Do you think she just likes champagne?"

"I don't know. I admit it feels good when we open a bottle."

"And you feel we should be celebrating tonight?"

"I do. Don't you?"

"All morning, I was looking forward to tonight. When we started the day, I felt so anxious about the filming, but I knew we had two great rooms. It's been hard work, but we managed it. I was ready for the weekend to simply breathe. But thanks to your business manager and her latest bombshell, we must work all weekend on something we didn't need to be doing now."

She took a long drink from the glass, and the bubbles hit her nose.

"I'm sorry. Look, if you walk away, if you need to go, I wouldn't blame you. This is my mess, and it's not your responsibility."

Stella knew as soon as the words were out of Will's mouth that the last thing she wanted to do was leave him with that woman. She'd promised Sarah. Stella didn't know how to explain her frustration to William. She shook her head.

"Look, Will, I understand that you need to get this on the market as soon as possible. However, this is the sort of job where rushing too much can only make it take longer. I've seen it before. People doing floors then realise that they need to re-plaster something. Folks trying to paint before the surfaces are ready. Trying to rush painting and not letting things dry properly. It just adds more costs and more time to a project." She could see the frown on his face, but now that she had started, she wanted to say what she had been bottling up since she arrived.

"Selling houses is a seasonal thing. The magazines need stuff for those seasons, months ahead of when they hit the newsstands. But right now is not the best time. I guess what I'm saying is, please think about how much power you give her. Ask more questions."

"Vanessa has been working closely with me for the last two years. Since she joined the company, she has helped me reach new markets and having her lets me focus on creating new and better products." His voice was hard, and his words clipped.

Stella put down her glass. "I think an early night might be helpful. I'll see you in the morning."

Chapter 21

William lay awake in his bed, trying to work out what to do first. It felt like it was up to him to solve the problem of this damn event. He knew how important it was, but he couldn't begin to think about it until he had spoken to Stella on her own. He knew she was annoyed last night, and who could blame her?

I was so relieved on Tuesday when I saw her work, and we got started on ideas for the whole project. How did things get like this with Vanessa? How did I not see it?

He rolled over, looking at the blank white walls of his room. *What will she do for the main bedroom? I like the colour in Sarah's room, but I couldn't sleep in there. I need to sort this with her, and I need to do it before I do anything else. How early can I wake her?*

He rolled over again. *What if she goes home?* His stomach tightened. *Maybe I should just let her go.*

A gentle tapping on his door made him turn over fast. It could only be Stella.

"Come in."

"I didn't know if you would be awake." She said softly.

"I couldn't sleep. I need to talk to you."

Stella slipped through the door and sat on the edge of Will's bed.

"I'm sorry." She wasn't looking at him, and he had to wonder how he could get through to her.

"Why should you be sorry?"

"I know this event isn't your fault. Being mad at anyone isn't going to solve the problem."

"I guess so. I'm sorry, too. I'm totally unable to see anything until I have this sorted with you. Maybe now I can start to think about what on earth we can do, which doesn't involve throwing money I don't have, to solve all this."

"I've some ideas about that."

"Really?"

"I think we focus them in one space and give them snapshots into what we can do. The technology, the art, the options. We make attending this preview their ticket to advanced access when we go to market."

"Where?"

"Downstairs."

"The basement? It's bare."

"Precisely. We can use it like an exhibition space. And give them glimpses of what can be achieved with our team."

"It could work."

"I can't see another way at the moment. What about you?"

"I couldn't see past talking to you." William looked deep into her blue eyes. "But if I have you, I think this might work."

Will's time in the pool this morning had been most useful.

It's marvellous what a deadline can do for your focus. I wanted to have so much more done before any agent saw the place. Obviously, I can blame Vanessa for the tight timescale. Grigori is correct; in the past, I would have panicked and let V take care of it. Now that he trusted Grigori more, he felt what he'd said about Vanessa was worth considering. Together with Stella, Grigori had persuaded him to ask more questions. They both seemed to have a different view of the industry.

Stella had said a few things last night that had filtered through his brain as he slept. To stand out among the sea of open house events in Los Angeles, they need to make this one different. It would be impossible to finish the whole house before Tuesday. They needed to give them enough to get them interested and talking about it.

Before showering, he created a group chat and asked everyone to meet him at the table at eight a.m. He connected his laptop to the huge television and then made jugs of coffee and one pot of tea. By the time everyone had settled around the table, he had the beginning of a plan.

"If we take them to the basement and create something like an exhibition space with samples of technology and finishes that people can select from for their build – a menu sort of thing."

"An à la carte menu. How will that affect prices?"

"It'll raise them, of course, but we'll have a basic package. The thing is, we aren't talking specifics this weekend. We are just giving a glimpse of what is to come. The idea of an à la carte list is to highlight the bespoke nature of this project."

Will looked down the table at Stella. This was scary when Vanessa had announced it yesterday, and yet with Stella at the table, Will felt it

could be done. Maybe it was the way she had handled yesterday, but he couldn't help but feel the way she looked at him now made him invincible. Well, that's how it felt.

"Stella, I know you have mood boards and samples, but what else?"

"We've got the polished plaster samples that Paulo made for Marco. I'll speak to Marco to see if we can use the things I made for him." Will liked the smile she gave him. He knew she wasn't happy last night, and he was relieved that today she was back to being ready to work. She would enjoy the challenge of this. It gave him more confidence for today to work.

"Grigori, can your team work on the entrance to the lift? That polished concrete floor is going to save us a fortune." Grigori nodded, and Will turned to the guys who had turned up from the office. "I want LED screens on at least two of the big walls. Then, I want a list of products we can showcase. Then we need to get them here."

"If it would help, I could contact the artisans I've been working with to see if they can support us. I'm sure they'll see the value in that. But I guess we need to start with working out how we are going to use the space." And there she was again, reminding him to think of the bigger plan. She's done so much already.

Will took Stella and Grigori down to the basement to mark out the space.

"Shit! I forgot how much we've been storing down here."

"We can soon clear it, boss. Let's put some tape down and divide the space up."

With decisions made on where things were going, they marked the areas out with tape. Everyone had their tasks, and they'd dispersed to get on with it. Will was left sitting at the table, looking at the lists in front of him without reading them. Deep down, he knew he still needed to talk more to Stella.

Her words at the end of the night had given him things to think about. He needed her to know he appreciated her input.

He knew she'd be working in her room. She'd muttered something about staying out of their way. He made a pot of tea and took her a cup plus their favourite shortbread biscuits.

"Thank you for that. And whilst you are here, can you go through this pile of fabric? Just do a spot of yes/no ing," He stood flicking through the fabrics, pulling some out to reject. Then stopped.

"What am I doing? There is nothing terrible here, and having seen Sarah's room, I know it's in how you combine them that creates the whole thing. Use what you think is best, Star."

"Good. I've messaged all the artisans I can think of. Now we wait for them to decide whether they want to display stuff. I'm hoping Jenny will have some time to help."

Will pulled out a chair and settled to drink his tea with her. He still needed her to know how he felt.

"Star, I want to thank you for what you did yesterday." He reached out and touched her arm to make sure she heard him. Stella's eyes lifted from her work and landed on his face, and his heart melted.

"What did I do?"

"You stood up to V. Probably something I should have done."

"Why don't you?"

"She's good. She has brought in clients and opened doors for me."

"For example?"

"She introduced me to this developer." Stella looked away.

"Grigori says she creates half of the drama." She said quietly.

"He could be right. I do need her at the moment."

"What does that mean?"

"Star, trust me on this." Will affectionately squeezed her arm, but the magic had gone.

The day went fast for William. He loved the way his team from the office was on board with giving up their weekend to join in. It helped that their minds worked like his, and they loved finding solutions to problems. The work in the basement had moved on at a pace which made him happy.

William missed Stella's calming voice. She'd wanted to stay out of the way.

He was comforted by the hum of her sewing machine, even though he was concerned that she didn't join them for lunch. Grigori had taken her a sandwich and reported back that she was making progress. His sister's voice *Look after her Will* danced around his head.

When the pizzas arrived, and she didn't show her face again, he went looking for her. The sandwich from lunchtime sat on the side with just two bites missing. It was the first thing that Will saw when he walked in. Stella didn't seem to want to make eye contact with him.

"Stella, what the hell! You need to eat. I hope you've been drinking." The hard tone in his voice came as a shock to both him and Stella. She turned to face him but said nothing; she simply stared.

Shit, what is wrong with me? She is only trying to help. His heart sank, and he tried again, this time softer.

"Pizza's ready. It's gone seven."

"Could I just have a slice?" *Nope, that is not going to work for me.*

"You can have what you like as long as you take a break and join the rest of the team."

"I really want to get this out of the way."

"Stella, look at me. You need to eat, and you need some time out of this room. Now come and join the others. If I can't persuade you to break, I'll struggle with everyone else."

The buzz at the table told Will the rest of his team was excited. The result was that the voices were loud as they talked about ideas they had come up with since the morning. At either end, Stella and Will sat quieter than usual, watching the group, and when they caught themselves looking at each other, neither looked away until Stella's phone buzzed with a text.

She smiled when she read the text. William wasn't about to ask who it was from today.

Chapter 22

Stella's stomach tumbled as she stood in the shower, trying to focus. It would be too easy to rush around for this damn event and lose track of what needs doing. *Three people are bringing their work for you today. You've got this. Just breathe.*

Over the last few days, she had felt that old connection with William, as a friend she could discuss anything with. Anything that is, except the way her body responded when he was around. She found it hard not to fixate on that kiss. She had spent the past week avoiding a situation where that might happen again. However, they were living alone in this house, sleeping in rooms down the same corridor.

The night he'd heard her dreaming had been interesting; he slept next to her and not kissed her unless you count the one on her forehead. He'd simply been a friend to hold her and help her relax. *Maybe I'm reading too much into that kiss. He's with Vanessa after all. He said she'd be back tonight. Is it any of my business? Just focus, Stella!*

Stella realised it made sense to ensure the work she put into this preview would contribute to the final reveal. They needed a solid time plan for the full open day. She wanted to talk to Will, and they would need Grigori to confirm it was possible. *Time to get something on paper.*

Her excitement drove her out of the shower, and still wrapped in a towel, she pulled out her laptop. When it looked like she had a plan, she rushed to get dressed for the day ahead. She strode quickly to Will's office to print off some copies.

The view from his window stopped her. She stood transfixed; no matter how hard she tried, she couldn't drag her eyes away from the sight of William Thoresby having his morning swim. Seeing him wet and practically naked didn't help. It had been a persistent problem since she arrived. She appreciated that the daily exercise had created that body he hid under a wardrobe of mainly black clothes.

The distraction mounted as Will began to get out of the pool, it meant she wasn't watching as she pressed print. As she continued to watch him, the large TV that hung on his wall swung out.

THWACK!

She landed on the floor.

Outside, William swam length after length. Today, he had a lot of thinking to do. He needed to decide whether to sell the London flat. He did like it, but it held no real emotional attachment. Since Stella landed in his life, focusing on his business seemed impossible. Why?

She had amazing ideas.

She worked hard.

She was diligent.

She focused on the job.

She should be making his job more straightforward.

One glance at his window told him she was watching him again. Why did that unnerve him? He swam faster, harder, and further than before, but still, it made little sense. Eventually, Will lifted himself from the pool, drained of all energy. The water cascaded down his body as he paused, arms locked on the poolside, still trying to make sense of what was wrong.

"Aghh!"

A high-pitched scream left the open doors of his office.

"Stella!"

A new energy filled Will's limbs as he raced to her. The long white voiles Stella had fitted the day before, fluttered out towards him. They clung to his wet body, wrapping around his torso as he burst into the room. Stella sat stunned on the floor as the TV moved in and out from the wall. Will laughed, a reaction to the fear that had driven him forward as he sprinted to the rescue. He tapped on the phone, which he'd left on the desk, and the TV swung back against the wall. He held out his hands and pulled Stella to her feet, still laughing.

Stella wasn't laughing. She hit out at Will, thumping at his chest with both fists. A confused Will gripped Stella's wrists to stop the battering. He searched her face for the problem, but he still felt lost. Nothing in his life prepared him for what he felt, looking down into Stella's sapphire blue eyes. Time stood still for him. Words had left his brain. He felt something deep inside his chest turn somersaults; it was a new feeling for Will. Stella had stopped shouting now and stood still, her arms limp in his hands.

He let go of her wrists, pulling her into his chest. He felt her relax.

"Are you hurt anywhere?"

"Does my pride count?"

"Of course it does. Shall I kiss it better?" William wanted to bite back his words. It was a sentence from their childhood. He didn't know where from exactly.

He looked down into her face, her eyes settled on his, as she gave him the slightest nod. He dropped his lips to hers, pressing so gently, waiting for her to respond. Stella leaned into his kiss and returned the gentle pressure. The kiss deepened as she clung to him. It felt both new and exciting, yet familiar and reassuring, all at the same time.

What am I doing? She is kissing you back, though. But where can this go? My family will not be happy. Sarah will kill me if I hurt Stella. Then don't hurt her.

William kissed her again; the passion stirring within him couldn't be hidden in such tiny swim trunks, and he pulled away.

"I'm sorry, I'm wet."

"I think I am too." She mumbled in a voice he could hardly hear. The pink in her cheeks told him he'd heard correctly. The computer announced Grigori and Paulo, and they quickly stepped apart.

"I'd better get showered before breakfast. Can you fire up the coffee?"

"I'm not sure … how… it scares me."

Will laughed at this confession from the very capable Stella.

"Star, start the coffee." He commanded.

"Why didn't I think of that?"

"I'll get you a list of commands she knows."

"I do feel weird calling her Star."

"You'll get used to it." Stella didn't look like she believed him. "Or you could just learn how the coffee machine works."

"Have I ever told you how much I like tea?" She smiled.

They left the room together, laughing again, as they always seemed to end up doing.

Once the team arrived, Stella and Will were never alone.

She kept catching him watching her, and each time she did, her heart skipped a beat. This was an important day in her career. A move towards developing her own name in this business. Things were starting to pull together, and each achievement was putting more spring into her step.

The artisans trusted her and wanted her to showcase their pieces.

Grigori, Paulo, and the rest of the team were so easy to work with, they contributed ideas and helped make sense of the timelines involved.

And Will, it had been a relief when he liked her designs last week. She wasn't sure of the reasons behind his shift in attitude towards her. She couldn't help but think that the confidence that Marco and Hidir had shown in her had helped.

Her brain jumped to the kiss! Or did she mean kisses plural? And what did those kisses mean for their friendship or even her friendship with Sarah?

Stella was focused on opening boxes containing the glass from Eric. His work was so intricate that she needed to take care to unwrap the paper from around each of the prominent sections. The first time she knew Vanessa had arrived was when she heard her kissing William very noisily. Stella looked up to watch her patting his arm and calling him, darling. Stella cringed.

Maybe she is like that with everyone? Grigori caught her eye. Vanessa wasn't like that with him. *Is it just William? How would she react if Marco were in the room?*

From everything that had been said. She understood Vanessa disapproved of Marco. But would his vast wealth and his strikingly attractive body mean that Vanessa would kiss him? Call him darling? Did she suck up to him? Because that's what Stella felt this was. Sucking up to people that Vanessa believed had power or money*? Perhaps if Will lost all his money, Vanessa would lose interest in him.*

Maybe she needed to play down how much money his family had. And how powerful they were back in the U.K.

Stella dropped her eyes back to the box, willing herself not to watch the woman who insisted on touching William as often as possible. When her eyes flicked up for a brief second, she caught Vanessa staring at her. A threatening stare. A stare that said, 'He's mine. Leave him alone'.

Stella wanted to say, ‘I saw him first!’ in a very childish voice. It made her want to rush over and lick him and say, ‘mine now’. You can't eat him. Hands off.

I don't remember feeling territorial about any of the men in my life. Maybe with my dad’s second wife. Certainly not the third and fourth.

Vanessa carried her laptop and the smallest purse. She'd brought the presentation to show William. And he took it to one side to help her set it up on the tiled screen that now filled the end wall. The slides were slick and professional, and although intended for the exhibition, they would be helpful for this project too. Stella doubted it was all Vanessa’s own work; however, she had a fantastic video, ready for the event.

Vanessa turned to face the room and raised her voice.

“Great, I have you all, you know what time to be here on Tuesday. I’ll be here, and I expect you to be here dressed as smart as possible. Those of you who will be meeting customers, could I ask that you wear black suits and white shirts? But then her eyes lingered on Stella.

“I don't suppose you have something more professional than that?” Stella looked down at her shorts and T-shirt. “Yes, I’ll be appropriately dressed. However, I will not be in a black suit with a white shirt. I'm the designer. And if I look like the designer, I don't think it's a problem.”

“All right,” said Vanessa very slowly and not looking at all convinced. “But please, can you promise me you're going to look smart and professional?” Her lip curled as she eyed Stella's cut-off jeans.

“I'm here today working. I've been moving boxes, painting, and doing some dirty jobs. I don't have an extensive work uniform with me. But I came over for Christmas with my mother. And I can assure you that in the Watson household, the holidays are a very formal affair. I do have suitable clothes with me. Did you want to vet my wardrobe?”

“No, no. That won't be necessary. Actually, I was wondering if I needed to pick something up for you. But I'm not sure I could get anything in your size so easily. That's the problem.”

“Being a size zero is not a requirement for my job. So, I can promise you that I’ll look smart enough to do the job on Tuesday.”

Vanessa turned away. But Stella could see her raise her eyebrows to William. William just smiled.

Chapter 23

When Stella's confidence wobbled enough to make her feel sick, an early morning call with her cousin was supposed to help her survive the day. India's voice was calm and uplifting.

"Where's the Stella I know? Where's that Barrington Jones confidence?"

"I think it is sitting on Jackson Wilde's office floor, where it fell that day I found him with his trousers down."

"Come on, girl, you've got this."

"I can still hear his words, India. The emails don't help."

"Forget him, you are better than that. Don't let him steal the rest of your life."

"Thanks."

And yet when she stood in the shower later, Stella's thoughts were bouncing again.

Are you going to do this every morning now?

Stay calm and breathe slowly.

You have until two p.m. before anyone comes.

Someone could come early.

We need to eat.

Jenny will be here.

But what shall we eat?

Just get out of the shower and make a start.

Stella took a long look at the dress she intended to wear today. "Not until you've eaten, young lady," her mother's voice said. Painting clothes would do for now.

A text in the group chat from William read,

Breakfast at 8:00.

At the table, Stella still felt sick. Picking at a pastry, she watched an animated Will talking to everyone and making sure they each knew what they were doing. She hadn't seen Will quite so focused and energised

about the build before. It suited him. It seemed to add a sparkle to his blue eyes. Stella squirmed in her chair as she studied him.

Will sent the team to the basement, and then he pulled up a chair and finished drinking his tea beside her.

"Star, I want to touch base with you before it gets heated today and especially before Vanessa arrives." Just the mention of her name upped the feelings Stella had been fighting since she woke up.

"Wasn't she due to be here for the meeting?"

William didn't answer her question; he ploughed on.

"Let me thank you for the work you have done with Grigori and the tech team, making all the magic stuff look good, too."

"Will, I know that a few pretty cushions won't sell the house. The house might sell the artwork."

"Your work is still important, though. Sarah's room shows a real-life example of what we can do as a team. What I'm trying to say is, don't let anyone's remarks get to you today. These guys are pretty catty."

"Is it all men?" William looked confused. "Has Vanessa only invited men?" she clarified.

"Well, I wouldn't have thought so…"

"Did you look at the guest list? It looked like all men to me."

"Oh? I guess we'll know when they all turn up."

"If they all turn up."

"I think the email that went out yesterday about needing to be here to get in first for the big reveal will make a difference."

"Davey posted some footage last night, too. That should help."

"Really?"

"They were here when she dropped the date on us, remember?"

"Of course."

Almost all of Stella's work was organised, allowing her time to help the others. As two o'clock grew closer, Stella could feel the tension rising amongst everyone. It made her feel a little better about constantly needing to wipe her hands. No one in the basement had experience with this sort of event. There was a collective sigh of relief when Vanessa arrived. Stella was pretty sure the group had never been so keen to see her.

Will looked stunning in his suit, and even Grigori was well-dressed, so Stella felt relieved she'd made an effort to look her best. Vanessa was something else. Still in her trademark black, she'd really ramped up the style and the height of her heels. It was clear that sales were where Vanessa shone most. She even smiled when she saw Stella's work.

"Stella, that's amazing." *What?* "Such wonderful colours. They're probably actually a little too loud for some people's tastes, like me, for instance. But I'm sure it will catch the eye of those looking for a more unique experience today." *Ah, that feels better, a little dig and her favourite word... actually.*

"Now, let's actually get this straight. I'll bring the individuals in as they arrive. And I'll stress to them, as we did in that update yesterday, that they are very, very privileged to be here today. And that by actually attending this, they've secured their invitation to the big reveal and that they will have privileged access when the time comes." Vanessa surveyed the room, looking at each person. "When it's completely ready, that is, and you've given me a date now, of course. Gentlemen. When you mess up, and the house is not ready when it should be, it will be on your heads." Her smile was there, but so tight.

"Now! Try to sound accommodating. Try not to use the word 'no'. If you're not sure whether we can do something, then defer the question …Oh, we might do it ... most things are possible, if the price is right. Isn't that correct? William." The smile was wide, but it made Stella's stomach clench.

"I've scheduled people to arrive at five-minute intervals. So that they can have some personal time with me." Vanessa's eyes fluttered as she paused. "And in that way, we can establish what it is that a particular agent is looking for. Remember, we will not be meeting buyers, and we're not meeting those 'influence' people, whatever they do. Today we will be meeting agents. We're looking for people who sell and people who buy, and we're particularly interested in those who have a large number of buyers on their list. So, talk to them about their buyers. Would your buyers like this? Do you like this? Okay, it's a question. But would your buyers like this? is an important question. It's also important that they understand this team can tailor the property to meet almost any need their buyer may have. The one thing that's fixed is the location. And that's what's going to make people bite."

Stella had to smile. Will was right, Vanessa's good for business. *And a salesperson is precisely what we need.* The rest of the group was aware

of the projects. They understood the technology. They knew the design or the construction. But it would be hard to suggest that any of them would be natural at selling. This is obviously Vanessa's strength. And Stella had to be grateful for that.

Her assumption about Vanessa had been correct. All twelve guests who had been invited were men. And she'd been overly familiar with all of them. That is, except for the last guest to arrive.

Stafford Johnson arrived with his wife, Maribeth. Vanessa managed to hold back from gushing over him; no hugging or kissing for Stafford. Her face twisted as she tried to talk to him without Maribeth being involved in the conversation. Stella's smile widened. She was beginning to understand Vanessa more. Not only that, but Stella knew Maribeth; she was her stepdad's sister.

As soon as Maribeth spotted Stella, she left her husband and rushed over to hug her. She hadn't become her aunt until Stella was fourteen, and as she lived so far away from her brother, they had only met a handful of times.

"Stella, I'm just back from New York and saw your work there, but this is amazing." Maribeth stroked the upholstered chair that Stella had finished the day before.

"Thank you, I'm glad you like it. Did you get a drink yet?"

"I'm too excited. It's been so long since you've been over to the States. I thought you were in London until Mike told me you were responsible for all the updates in their apartment."

"Yes, I came over for Christmas."

Maribeth looked behind her and lowered her voice.

"I heard about London. Are you OK now?"

"I'm fine." Stella spotted William watching them carefully as Vanessa tried not to stare when Stafford left her to join his wife. Stella couldn't read William's face. The mention of London had unsettled her, and she was worried William would hear about it. With great effort, she pulled her eyes away from him to focus on her aunt.

"I've got a couple of clients I believe might be on the right timeline for some of the later builds. Is this one going to be for sale?" Stella relaxed. Stafford was the last agent to arrive, and she had already met him. She liked him, and she loved his wife.

"I know William would love to live here himself, but for the right price, I'm sure he would sell it. Why do you ask?"

"To be honest, I'm interested in all the plots; I simply want all the information at hand when I'm talking to clients."

"Of course. What else can I show you?"

Stella took the Johnsons to see Sarah's room. They both seemed excited, and that was a major relief for Stella.

As she was showing them out of the house, Maribeth gripped her arm.

"Do you think you could get your aunt in before the official opening?"

"I don't think I can, but I could maybe invite you over for dinner a few days before, as long as you aren't expecting the full presentation."

"That would be wonderful if we could be in a position to make an offer on the day the plots are released… well, I'm sure that would be good for you too." Her aunt's voice was just a whisper. It left Stella with a great deal to think about.

Waving off their car, she realised that Vanessa had already left. Certainly, her car wasn't outside. Together with the conversation with Maribeth, that news made Stella feel so much lighter. This event was over, and now they should have a real action plan to get them to the full launch day. Stella took a deep breath before turning back into the house and toward William Thoresby.

Chapter 24

The feeling amongst the team the next morning was one of relief to be back in building mode. Stella hurried to join William for breakfast and to be there when Grigori arrived to discuss the day's jobs.

"I want to crack on with the cinema. I want to get it finished today."

"Sure, boss, do you need any help, Stella?"

"How much have we already got for the kitchen?"

"We have cabinets and the appliances. You won't like them."

"I guess I'll look at what we can do. When were you planning to start on the build?"

"I thought if we finish off the service kitchen, you guys can use that, then the main one can be left unused … in case."

William's brows pulled together, and he tightened his lips before speaking.

"In case we have to sell this. I get it. I hope it doesn't come to that. In fact, I'm going to talk to my sister about selling my place in London. I've been putting it off. I don't like to kick her out, but if I don't …"

"Sarah will understand. My flat is empty anyway. She can go there until I … I don't know if I'll ever move back to London …"

"Stella, you can't give up your flat."

Why, because you want to get rid of me?

"It's not mine, actually; it's my grandparents', but they wouldn't let it out until I knew what I was doing. There is no reason Sarah can't use it. I'll talk to them." *For God's sake, what is wrong with him now? I know he doesn't want his sister homeless, but if he needs the money, Sarah will want to help, and I'm not using my flat. It's simple.*

Will left the room with a scowl on his face. Stella decided to try to forget his mood and focus on the jobs she needed to do. She found Grigori to check out what she had to work with to create a property-selling kitchen.

"I've emailed you the current layout. These are the doors."

"Oh, a bit dark, aren't they?"

"You could paint them."

"Maybe, but that's a lot of work. I'll think about it."

She made notes and took photos. The marble for the counters was pretty simple and possibly the most expensive thing to change. She settled down with her laptop to look for solutions to make the kitchen less generic. She began to work on ideas for a one-of-a-kind island that she felt Grigori's team could build. An hour had gone by when she heard Will calling for her over the computer system.

<<Stella, Will would like your help in the cinema.>> *What now?*

Despite her reluctance, she knew that whatever he needed, she would be glad to help. Whatever had caused his mood earlier, it was a smiling Will that greeted her. He took her wrist and pulled her to a wall panel.

"How big is your hand?" He held her wrist and laid her palm over his. Her small hand sat neatly on his, palm on palm. Stella felt a small charge of heat coming from his hand. Will must have felt something, too, because he pulled his hand away quickly.

"Just what I need. Could you help me with this job? There isn't enough space for me."

"Sure." Will needed help, and she was more than happy to provide it. That was what she had been trying to do earlier when she offered her flat. The truth was that she didn't know if she ever wanted to move back there.

The success of yesterday meant she would be here for a few more weeks, or, actually, two months, if Will let her stay until the launch. A successful launch could mean she might find work on the other plots. It would also mean Will could not only save his business but also live in this house - it could finally become his home. That was her biggest motivation.

"Are you busy? Or can you stay here and help me?"

"I could stay if it helps." Stella swallowed.

"Please, I would like that."

"Did you talk to Sarah?"

"Yes, you were right. She was happy to do something positive. I think she has a lead on another place, but if not, she knows to get in touch with you. She asked me to thank you."

She watched intently as William's nimble fingers worked with the cables in front of them. Her body tensed as she watched him grip the pliers, exposing the wire.

"Can you just flick that switch?"

"Doesn't Star do that?"

"She will when it's all connected."

"Sorry." She flicked the switch.

"Pass me that screwdriver, Star." He held out his hand, his head down. Her fingers lightly brushed his palm as she slipped the screwdriver into his hand. Stella froze.

"Any news from your Australian friend today?"

"Zach? No." Stella picked up the pliers, turning them over.

"Does he message often?"

"Why do you ask?" She put down the pliers and studied Will.

"Nothing, just making conversation. Sarah said he's a big guy."

"I guess he is." She remembered dancing with Zach at the party.

"Did you say you met him at your cousin's?"

"No. We met at Dan's party."

"Who's Dan?"

"He's another cricketer."

"Does he live with India too?"

"No, he lives upstairs from me." She laughed.

Will said nothing, clearly trying to make sense of it all. Stella continued, trying to help him understand.

"I suppose when India moved in with Charlie, we met the whole team." She rattled off the ones she'd met. "Charlie is fun, wears a kilt, great legs. Dan is, well, tall. His brother captains England. They have a farm in Malton." She paused and looked up. "I think I know Dan best."

"Because he lived with you."

"Because we did TV together."

"You what?" Will banged his head.

"Well, he did the TV. I dressed the set." Stella thought a little more as Will rubbed his head. "That's where he met Natasha."

"Pliers."

"I presume that means I've said enough."

"If Sarah moves into your flat … how safe is this, Dan?"

Stella laughed at the idea of Dan being a threat.

"Dan is a one-woman man."

"Pro sports star, really?"

"Actually, they are. I'm not sure about when they were younger. What about you?"

"Me?" He looked up in surprise.

"Are you seeing anyone other than Vanessa?"

"I'm not seeing Vanessa." He looked at the wires, his brows pinched.

"Does she know that?"

"She should," he muttered, still not looking at Stella.

"And are you seeing anyone else?" Will looked at her for a long time before he answered.

"Sadly, no."

Stella swallowed. *Is that what you wanted him to say?*

They spent an hour finishing the wiring behind the panel. Stella wasn't sure what help she'd been. Will had her passing things and employing her smaller hands. She couldn't help but think he could have managed without her. It felt good to be together, though. Stella enjoyed the effortless way they chatted when it was just the two of them.

"Have you chosen the seating for in here?"

"Yes. The developer had already bought them among the other fittings before he disappeared. It's been at Thoresby Technology for months, and we have nearly finished them, which is why I wanted to get on with this. Having a room finished would feel great."

"Have you tried to find him again? The developer, I mean."

"I've given up. There doesn't seem to be much point now."

"I see." She said slowly. Will smiled, and she returned his soft smile.

"Thank you, Star, I think it's lunchtime."

Stella and Will shared lunch at the table. The flowers from yesterday's event brightened up the room. It felt like things were finally on track, and they were back to being friends. The memory of his kisses hadn't disappeared, nor had the feel of him touching her hand this morning.

Chapter 25

Yay, it's Sunday. Why do I love Sundays here? Is it because it's just the two of us?

As the electronic blinds rose, she saw him lifting himself out of the pool. The water dripped from his hair and body, his muscles glistening in the darkness on his skin. It was an image that would stay with her for a long time.

In case you forgot, how much Will has changed. Stella exhaled. *I know I always cared for him before, but why am I so attracted to him now? Be honest, Stella, when you were kids, you were more in love with ponies than boys.*

The laid-back nature of their Sunday found Stella counting eggs. *I could make omelettes, and we could have a slow breakfast together. It would be a surprise.* Stella licked her lips. *But does Will even like surprises?* Stella closed her eyes and pushed out a breath.

"Star, start the coffee."

Stella pulled out the few pans she could see, but she couldn't find anything that would work. It was frustrating, but this wasn't her kitchen, and it might not be Will's much longer. She really hoped he could stay here, given all the effort he had put into it. *It's no good cooking eggs until you find Will, now is it? It's time to stop dreaming of being the little housewife, too! I don't want that.*

The starkness of the clinical stainless steel in the service kitchen was as far from feeling like a home as anything she could imagine. *Maybe I can get some plants, even some herbs, for that windowsill.*

Still pondering solutions, Stella poured a coffee and took it to her workroom. The corridors were empty; the whole house was eerily quiet. A sudden noise made her jerk to a stop. A loud buzzing sound filled the peace as it spilt out from the plant room. She'd seen through the door just once. It was usually firmly closed with a keypad lock on the frame.

Today, the door was ajar, and inside, she could see William in a white Tyvek forensic suit.

"Don't come in here!"

The sharpness in his tone took Stella completely by surprise. She swallowed.

"Sorry." Stella walked away, her good mood gone. She stalked down to her workroom and flopped down.

There's a reality check for you. He has a lot on his plate, I guess.

The lead feeling in her stomach made her push her drink across the table and pull over her laptop. *This will only take a few more weeks. This isn't permanent. You need to think about what you do next.*

Stella picked up her coffee again as she got lost in the mood boards for her dream home. She'd been working on them for longer than she wanted to admit. *When I have my own design studio, with my own style, people will come to me for that look.*

Her coffee empty, she wandered back to the kitchen for a refill. It made her smile to see that Will had been in, and every surface was once again clear. The eggs and pans she had left out had been cleared away. *I wonder if he wore his hazmat suit. I guess that is William Thoresby. I always knew he was like that.*

The sun was shining, so Stella took her fresh coffee outside. *You don't have time for a break; you haven't done anything constructive so far today.* Reluctantly, she stood up to go back to her workroom when her phone rang. It was Sarah.

"Hello there." She sat down on the soft sofa.

"Good morning, Sarah."

"Sadly, it's Sunday night here, and I'm trying to avoid thinking about work tomorrow morning. I'm hoping you can distract me."

"I have to admit I'm outside, avoiding work myself."

"It is Sunday there, too?"

"Yes, but Will and I usually do some work whilst no one else is here. The peace and quiet is nice."

"I'm a bit worried about Will. I mean, he's selling the flat here. Is he going to be OK?"

"Money is tight, that's all, and I don't know for sure, but I think he needs it for Thoresby Technology."

"What about the building project?"

"He must need some, but there are a lot of things already here. We are making the most of what we have. I've got enough cash at the moment for what I'm buying. I can wait until he sells something."

"Do you think it means he isn't coming home?"

"I think he just needs the money, in the short term, you know. You're OK with it, aren't you? My flat is empty."

"Does that mean you aren't coming back either?" Sarah huffed.

"I can't see I'm staying here." *How could I?*

"If it's only money, why doesn't he ask Mum?"

"I think that's obvious; he is desperate not to tell them, if it can be avoided." *I can understand that.*

"And is that brother of mine avoiding work this morning, too?"

"Nah! The last time I saw him, he was in a hazmat suit doing something in the plant room."

"Sounds like William."

"He didn't want me in there. You don't think he was dealing with a body, do you?"

"No, that isn't his style."

"No, I guess it isn't," Stella sighed.

"I have to say I expected to hear you a little more excited. Your blog sounds much more upbeat."

"Ah, I've told you, social media is a bit like that. Then, to be fair, I've only been like this today."

"Any reason?" *Not that I'm going to share with you, no.*

"No, I can't say there is. Possibly because I realise I still have to work out what I want to do after the situation with Jackson. What must people be thinking about me?"

"Well, I would think the people you told will only be thinking badly of him. I don't see him telling anyone, do you?"

"I don't know." Stella closed her eyes. "He emailed me. It sounded like a threat. You haven't told Will, have you?"

"No, I think you should tell him, but I'll leave that to you."

"I feel so stupid, especially as it was my job. I'm working for Will … promise Sarah."

"Of course, we all make mistakes. Do you remember when we started at St Hilda's? I wanted to be a veterinary nurse, and you wanted to be a scuba diver?"

"Life changes, doesn't it?"

"I guess I'm saying, do you still want to do interior design?"

"Yes, I do; I know that bit?"

"OK, let's dig a little deeper. Do you want to work for someone again?"

"I'd like to work for myself at some point. I'm not sure if I'm ready yet." Stella bit her lip.

"And have you decided where?"

Stella shook her head.

"No, that's the part I'm most stuck on."

"I'm sure you'll work that out. Will is going to keep you busy for a while, and when you finish, maybe you and I can go away for a week or something. I need to get out of this restaurant soon."

"I'll look forward to it."

"Don't let Will's ways get to you. And remember, I'm counting on you to look after him. Got to go. Bye."

"Bye." That last sentence revolved in Stella's brain.

'Look after him. I'm counting on you…' She's counting on me. Stella murmured as she looked down into the city below. A shiver ran down her spine despite the warm sun that bathed her face. She wiped a silent tear from her cheek.

"Stella?" *Shit, he's found me.* "Stella, are you OK? … Stella."

Stella pulled her shoulders back and forced a smile to her lips before she turned around to face him.

"Hi Will, yes, I'm fine. Sarah just rang."

"Shit!"

"It was nothing bad, just girl-talk, you know." Her stomach clenched. *Where had this morning's light mood gone? So much for enjoying Sunday.*

Will screwed up his brow as he looked out in the same direction as Stella.

"Shall I make some tea?"

"Thanks, Star, that would be nice."

"Good, because I want to show you my ideas for the kitchen."

"Is this going to cost me money?"

"It's going to cost you time, but I think you're going to enjoy it."

Stella gathered up her laptop and sketchpad and led Will to the kitchen. She laid out her designs in front of Will and moved to make the tea.

“I’ve been trying to figure out how we can make this kitchen more interesting than simply installing the units that are already here. It’s like no one cared about this part of the house.” Will looked away, but Stella didn’t give up. “Will, a great kitchen can really sell a house.”

“I thought you said this wouldn’t cost me money.”

“Just listen, I’ll explain. We have the best technology team ever on this.”

“Kind of you to say so.” His face had softened, and Stella saw that as a sign to push on. “Grigori is amazing with wood. If we combine your tech with his skills, we could build a bespoke key feature for this area. That will free up some cabinets, which gives us greater flexibility with how we fit the rest of the room.”

“What do I need to do?”

“Either you or one of your team needs to work with Grigori to build all your magic into something that will look like a vast block of driftwood. And William, I really hope this is something you can let go to the team.” She pushed the tea towards him, spilling a few drops.

“Hmm, lovely tea.”

Stella slapped her hand on his arm, and he caught it. Frozen, they looked into each other's eyes for too long. His eyes pushed deep into her soul, and Stella pulled back. She tugged her hand away from his skin. *He’s my boss. There is no way I’m making that mistake again!*

Chapter 26

Monday afternoon, after a solid week of things going according to plan, it felt like they were moving at a pace. Stella was with William, looking at plans as they ate lunch. Things felt better, and yet William still wasn't relaxed, and that concerned Stella.

"Do you think the flat will sell quickly enough?" Will said on a sigh.

"Is it that important?"

"Probably, I don't know any more. Am I clutching at straws?"

The weak winter sun smiled through the window, lifting the fragile mood in the room until a dark cloud drifted over it. The shadow changed the feeling in the room as the computer announced a new arrival.

<<Welcome, Vanessa, William and Stella are in the dining room. >>

"I'd better go see what she wants now." Will rose to find Vanessa.

Just tell her to fuck off. Stella thought, possibly because it felt like the newcomer had stolen the sun and plunged her day into darkness. She picked up the plates from their lunch and went to clear up, rather disgruntled. Her mother's voice pierced her thoughts. *Stella Barrington Jones, that woman, saved the day at the preview. It looks like Will is correct, and he does need her. You might want to save him single-handedly, but it will be better if you all work as a team.* Stella knew it would take all of them pulling in the same direction to make this happen.

Stella was pouring herself a cup of tea as Vanessa strode into the room, with William trailing behind her. Stella puzzled over what attracted Vanessa to Will because he didn't seem to be her style. Although it seemed like something she was trying to change. Today, she'd arrived clutching a fine black knit high-necked jumper. Will had changed into it, along with a pair of black jeans. It seemed to wipe out all his personality.

"Ah, Stella." Will coughed, an embarrassed smile drifting across his face. "I have to go to an event with Vanessa. I'm not sure when I'll get back. Will you be OK? I can order some dinner sent in."

"Will, I'm fine. You get off. I've more work to do, so I won't be very sociable anyway."

"It's business. I'm sorry for ditching you again, Star." Will looked like he meant that. His eyes were soft, and he didn't take them off Stella's face.

"It's OK, Will." He walked away, leaving her sipping her tea, but Vanessa stayed. Her eyes drilled into Stella so much that it made her look away.

"Did he just call YOU, Star?" It felt like Vanessa used the word YOU like a weapon.

"Yes, he's done it since we were kids."

"But he calls his computer Star." Stella wanted to smile, but she forced her lips to stay still.

"I'm sure it's just a coincidence."

Vanessa's face twisted as she stalked away, and Stella went back to her room and her painting. It was her happy place.

Cleaning her brushes in the workroom sink, her mind drifted back to the conversation with Vanessa. She wasn't sure about the connection with her name being the same as his computer. It wouldn't do to make it any more than it was. But it certainly rattled Vanessa. She was so lost in her thoughts that she was startled when Vanessa burst into the workroom without knocking. She'd never been to the workroom before. Vanessa had clearly come to say something, but took some time to study the contents of the room before she spoke.

"I thought this was the actual utility room."

"It will be. The plumbing is sorted, so when the kitchen is fitted, the team will fit the cupboards in here, too."

"You actually think you're clever, don't you?" *There it was again. YOU.* "But you're not. You're a silly little girl who could ruin everything for William. And I'm sure you don't want to do that. I'm the one with connections in this town, and without me, he is nothing. He can mess around in his laboratory all he likes, but without me to sell what he creates, he would have nothing. If you don't back off, young lady, I will make sure that he has just that. Nothing. You're meddling could cost him Thoresby Technologies, and he won't thank you for that even if you are his Star." Vanessa turned on her heels and left once again. As she walked down the corridor, the click-clack of her heels receding into the distance, Stella could hear her calling William's name.

She watched Vanessa usher William into the car. You didn't need to be an expert in body language to pick up on his mood. It wasn't good.

She felt the urge to run out of the house, stand in front of the car and stop whatever that woman was trying to do. Vanessa's cutting tone had bitten into Stella like a sharp sword. Of course, she didn't want to create

any problems, let alone so many issues that William lost his business. She knew it was his whole life. It was written in the hours he spent at the office and in his home.

The one space she knew she really needed to be special was the main bedroom. She wanted this to be a place where Will could be himself and where he could remember his roots.

The canvases had arrived with views of Hursts Bridge. Selecting a fine brush, she touched in detail on the images with size, ready to apply gold leaf in small, discrete areas. Investing in some gold leaf had been a big decision, but it was going to be put to use on the artwork for the hallway to the primary suite. She was soon lost in her painting. The computer brought her back to the present.

<<Welcome, Marco. Stella is in the workroom.>>

What? Whatever he wants, I'd better go and find him.

“Hi, Marco, I’m over here.” His new tan lit up his face as he strode towards her, kissing her cheek.

“I’m back. I thought I’d better check if I missed your birthday.”

“No, you didn’t miss it,” she laughed.

“Tell me when it is.” He pulled at her hand. “I could ask Will.”

“No, you won’t. He has far too much on his mind right now to be worrying about my birthday. He’s dealing with the sale of his flat in London. That’s stressing him because his sister is staying in it. But she can move into my old flat, so it's not really a problem.” Stella bit her lip, aware she had said too much.

“I told him to talk to me. I could buy that plot behind me, so he has some working capital again. I can expand on it or sell it back to him if he wants it later. If he doesn’t finish this project, it will give me a buffer between whoever takes over this development and whoever buys it. There’s no saying it would be someone I like.”

“Did you explain to him that you want that insurance?”

“Well, no,”

“Maybe you should explain it to him in terms of him doing you a favour; he might listen. If the flat doesn’t sell, he might need it.”

“I’ll try. I wanted to ask you about doing some more work for me.”

“Sure, but when? I need to help get this ready for the launch.”

“I get that. I can wait for you to finish this, but if things change…”

“Thanks, Marco. When can I come and see it?”

"I was going to suggest Thursday night, and I'll do dinner, but if you've something planned."

"No, nothing planned."

"Maybe Will has?" Marco's eyes twinkled as he teased her. *Did he know it was her birthday?*

"I very much doubt it. Look, Will's brain is full to overflowing, so I'm not going to create more worry. And you can't tell him either."

"Stella…"

"Marco, please don't add to his stress."

"OK."

"Promise?"

"I promise. Now don't work too hard, I'll see you at seven o'clock on Thursday night."

Concentrating with a tiny brush to get the effect she was looking for meant that after a couple of hours, her eyes refused to cooperate. She washed the brush and turned out the light in her workroom. Ready for a shower, she took one last look out of the window before closing the blinds. The swimming pool dominated the view, its tranquil water lapping gently against the brilliant, tiled walls. It was Will's happy place, the place where he could think. Maybe it would work for her. She wasn't expecting Will back for at least another couple of hours, and possibly he wouldn't come back at all. Stella was sure that was Vanessa's intention. It was time to stop musing. She pulled on the simple black costume she'd bought at Target. A swim would stretch out her stiff shoulders and might ease her aching back. Just twenty minutes, that's all she needed.

Stella paused at the edge of the pool; her toes curled as the water gently lapped at her feet. She was pleasantly surprised by how warm the water felt as it licked its way up her calves. When the water reached her waist, she pushed off and swam slowly to the other end. Will was right, the energy in this space was so liberating, and she swam length after length as she thought through the best ways to create the home Will deserved. Soon she'd be back in the U.K., and no doubt Vanessa would be the one to enjoy the work that Stella put in, but she still needed to do it. Would Vanessa even keep Stella's work? Or rip it out?

Sarah asked her to look after her brother, and Will had always looked after her. She knew she could do this. The big question for Stella was whether she could create something that would work for William AND sell all the other houses on a very restricted budget. William had told her

to use the credit card he had handed over. Stella had managed to avoid that so far, thanks to the fee she received from Marco. She intended to let William pay her back only when the other lots had been sold.

If she took plenty of videos and photos to fill up her blog, then this work for Will would go a long way towards creating her portfolio. Hopefully, with the input of Hidir, Jenny and all the other bloggers out there, she could launch her career after this.

There were times when Stella was sure she could do it. The only question in her mind was where. Her original thoughts had been London, but that had been before Jackson Wilde and his veiled threats. Hursts Bridge probably wasn't the place, but what about Los Angeles or New York? The time in New York didn't fill her with confidence that people were ready for her style, so maybe that wasn't the best choice.

It was peaceful in the water, and Stella stayed much longer than the twenty minutes she planned. Suddenly, the lights on the outdoor kitchen sprang to life, and the fire burst into flame. William Thoresby was home and had found her in his pool.

"What the hell, Stella, why are you swimming? Don't you know better than to swim in the dark and alone?" There was no hiding the anger in his voice; he wasn't even trying to disguise it. Stella touched the edge of the pool and looked up at William.

"You do it every day, sometimes twice a day."

"Precisely, I do it often enough to know what I'm doing; besides, it's my house. If I have an accident, I only have myself to blame. If you had an accident in my pool, the whole of Hursts Bridge would blame me."

"Oh my God! I can't believe you just said that!"

Stella pulled herself out of the pool. She'd heard enough.

"I still … I'm sorry, I was just upset. I'm tired. What am I saying? You must be tired, too. We're both working so hard."

"Well, at least you've had time for a night out," she said, turning away from him. William reached out and grabbed her arm to stop her.

"Stella don't, don't let's fall out, I've had enough of that tonight."

"Is that my fault, too? Because I know Vanessa will be blaming me."

"She is who she is. Even if you weren't here, there's always drama."

"So, she has been blaming me?"

"Did she say something to you?"

"I'm not going to start telling you tales. You clearly know what she is like or should. William, you are not a drama person. I don't understand why you're with that woman."

"I'm NOT 'with her' but I do need her. Right now, I need her too much. The last thing I need is more drama." Stella glared at him, unable to believe what he'd just asked. Will looked back at her, his eyes soft and pleading, and she felt awful for causing him all this trouble. Her eyes dropped to the floor, and Will placed a finger under her chin, lifting her face back up so he could look into her eyes.

"I don't want to argue with you, Star."

"May I suggest you stop calling me Star, especially around Vanessa."

"Is that what caused everything to kick off tonight?"

"Yes, I think it is. I could be mistaken, but I think it came as a bit of a shock to your friend. She certainly thought it was significant, so before you think I'm the one causing drama, maybe you should wonder what you've done that might upset her."

"Oh, Star, I'm so sorry." William's arms wrapped around Stella and pulled her into her favourite place in the whole world, William Thoresby's chest.

"William, I'm wet."

William chuckled. "And this time, it's my turn to get wet too. Fancy some hot chocolate?"

"Now you're talking. I'll just go and get dressed."

As Stella walked back into the house, she thought she heard William say, "There you go spoiling everything again."

She shook her head. Stop imagining he fancies you. You've made that mistake before.

Chapter 27

When Will saw his sister's name on his phone, he hoped it was news about the sale rather than Stella talking about what had happened the night before. He'd been so scared when he saw her in the pool, but holding her in his arms had been far more terrifying.

"Tell me it's good news."

"Well, hello to you, too, brother."

"I'm sorry, Sarah, life is a bit tense right now."

"I do have good news, as it happens. The agent received a call this morning from a cash buyer at the full asking price. He wants to move fast. But he is happy for me to lease back for a month, so I can take my time moving out."

"What's the catch?"

"I haven't found one yet. Maybe you should talk to the agent."

"I will. So, what's your other news?"

"Did my parcel arrive for Stella? I posted it to Thoresby Technology."

"Sorry, what?"

"For Stella's birthday, I sent it to your office so you can make sure she gets it on the right day. I'm worried because you hadn't been in touch to say it was there."

"Sorry, Sarah, I haven't seen it, but then I've been mostly working here."

"Could you check? I mean, it's tomorrow."

"It's her birthday tomorrow? I thought her birthday was 28th February?"

"Yes, and that is tomorrow. Well, it is here."

"I guess I'd better get busy."

"That would be great. She had a really rough day last year. Both of her parents missed it. Her mum was a couple of days late. She claimed it was the time difference, but I'm pretty sure there is nowhere three days behind."

"Damn."

"Her dad never remembers, so that's not a shock. But her boss was a complete bastard, too. He said he was taking her out for a really special meal, she bought a new dress, shoes, the works."

"And?"

"He flew out to Paris to meet a client and stayed there for a week, and he never mentioned her birthday again. He didn't even call to cancel." Will's vision of Stella dressed up with no one turning up to take her out hit his stomach… *How many times have I missed dinner with her?*

"And her new boss isn't doing much better. OK, I'm on it."

Will phoned his office and discovered that Vanessa had taken the parcel, telling Tina, his PA, that she would deliver it. Tina was very apologetic and explained that Vanessa had said that, as she was living there, she would take it home with her.

"She actually used those words. Living here and bringing it home?"

"Yes, she did. Have I done the wrong thing?"

"Was the parcel addressed to me?"

"Yes, but it did say it was for someone else, and could you give it to her on her birthday?"

"Stella? It's from my sister. Look, this isn't your fault, Tina. How would you feel if I said to contact her and ask her to bring it back to the office before ten o'clock tomorrow morning? I mean, I could do it…"

"If you wouldn't mind, I'd like to be the one to contact her. I take it she lied?"

"I can assure you she isn't living here."

"I'll get it back, sir, if I've to go find it and take it back myself." Will knew he was playing with fire, but he hoped that the more other people who called Vanessa on her bullshit, the more likely she was to acknowledge the truth. *Hell, she was here yesterday, and she didn't produce the parcel. It was the day she discovered Stella was my Star.*

Maybe it wouldn't hurt to let her know that he knew what she had done. He made a mental note to send a text later.

Knowing that the flat had been sold allowed him to relax a little about the budget. It was time to give Stella the good news.

"Star, where is Stella?"

<<Stella is in the workroom.>> Will took a deep breath. Spending time with her in a small space challenged him to behave appropriately, as shown last night. He really wanted to speak to Stella, so he braced himself to get through the next five minutes without touching her.

What do I say about her birthday? It's probably easier to focus on a pleasant surprise for her on the day. If I mention it to her, she will only build her hopes up—one last deep breath.

"Hello Star, how's today going? Are you ready for some lunch?"

"I'm fine. What do you think?" She held up a large square of fabric.

"What am I looking at? I recognise that pattern."

"I'm just printing up some fabric to match the patterns we built into the pocket doors in the junior primary."

William's eyes widened as he looked again at the design she had created on the material.

"Is it for a cushion?"

"William Thoresby, I don't just make cushions."

"Sorry. I know you do more than that."

"To be honest, I haven't decided; I wanted to see if it would work. I'm thinking light shades for a traditional lamp or a waste bin."

"I trust you to decide."

"Thank you."

"I've got good news. Sarah rang, and there is a cash buyer for the flat in London. She has a lead on a flat, but if that doesn't work out, she'll be in touch."

"I've spoken to my grandma, and it's fine, mainly because she sees it as my problem to get her out if I go back to London." She laughed.

"Thank you."

"Dan and Natasha have a key, so I'll call Sarah and let her know."

"The buyer has offered a lease-back, so she has some time."

"They did? Do you know who the buyer is?"

"No, some international property company, I believe."

"Really? And so quick."

"It means I can breathe a bit. Don't go mad, though, not until we get a plot sold."

"Have you thought about Marco's offer?"

"I have, but I'm hoping with the release of some capital from London, I can get to the next stage without any more help."

"I understand how you feel, but I think Marco would like you to sell him that land as some sort of insurance, in case someone else finishes this development."

"I suppose so. I'll think about it."

"Just talk to him, Will. He's a friend, he wants to help, and he wants to have that plot."

"OK, I'll talk to him. Now lunch."

Will enjoyed eating with Stella each day when one of them stopped working long enough to call a break. The conversations were easy. They talked about their childhood, but more often they talked about her ideas and plans for targeting niches in the market.

Today, she wanted to know more about the British expat community in the area. William told her what he knew, but he could tell that she would be doing more research on the subject. It made sense to use something they both knew.

"I'm just thinking the British would be happy to see some of the things you've done here, like have a 240-volt outlet for an electric kettle in the kitchen. My mum is convinced an electric kettle won't work with the 120-volt outlets."

"She's wrong, but I see what you mean."

"You've lived here for long enough. Why don't you come up with a list of things that you would do, and I'll see how big the market is."

"I'm going to Marco's later. Do you want to come with me?"

"No. You need to talk to him without me, and to be honest, I'm tired. When I've finished, I want to curl up with my laptop and do a bit more research."

"Don't work too late or too hard, Stella." He reached out and squeezed her arm. Heat shot up his hand, and he lifted it from her as quickly as if he'd touched a hot plate. She looked so tired, he wished he could get her to rest, maybe on her birthday.

He had an idea for some gifts that might help her relax and take a break. He knew she would love some new paints, but he wasn't going to be responsible for her working harder. And flowers, she always loved flowers.

Later, as William cleared up after their makeshift meal, he berated himself for not planning the food properly. He really needed to do something better than this, and on time if possible. He still needed to speak to his sister, but he also wanted to go and talk to Marco now that he was back from Europe. But he was concerned about leaving Stella alone again.

He sent her a text message.

Will: I'm going over to Marco's. Are you sure you won't come?

Stella: I'll pass. I want to finish this artwork. I'd rather not leave it at this point.

Will: Do you want me to stay?

Stella: No. I think you should talk to Marco. He could help.

Will: I don't like asking for help.

Stella: Who does? Marco wants to help. It's a good deal for him, too.

Will: No swimming whilst I'm gone.

Stella: Yes, Dad.

Chapter 28

Walking across to his neighbour, William was sorting through all his shifting thoughts about Stella. Working with her in the cinema had been fun, and if Vanessa hadn't turned up, he was going to offer to take her out, and not just because it would get him out of cooking. She'd worked so hard, and no one was more relieved than he was about how well the preview event had been. The only spanner in the works being it proved how much they all still needed Vanessa. Hopefully, Stella's birthday would be the perfect opportunity to spoil her instead.

He found Marco sitting outside with a glass of beer.

"Hello, friend."

"I didn't expect to find you out here."

"After Europe, I was ready for warmth, but I think it's about to change. Let's go inside."

William followed Marco, and together they took a seat on his sofa.

"I've seen some videos that guy did, and I hear the event went good! Well done, my friend."

"Thanks, yes, it's going well."

"So how are things with you and the bellissima Stella?"

William sighed. If he didn't know what was happening, how did he describe it to Marco?

"Have you got any easier questions?"

"She is a lovely girl; she obviously likes you. What's the problem?"

"Well, let's see, she works for me, she's my sister's best friend, who would kill me, oh and yeah! She gets texts from Australian cricketers that make her smile. What chance do I have?" He threw up his hands.

Marco just laughed. "And I thought you wanted to talk about my offer. Want a beer before we unpack all that rubbish?"

"Sure, thanks, and there is nothing to unpack. It is what it is."

Marco passed him a bottle of beer and sat down facing him. Will took the drink from Marco and tried to change the subject.

"So how was the skiing?"

"It was bloody glorious. How have things been going here?"

Will sighed. His friend wouldn't give up.

"Did you see the video of Stella's work? It's just amazing, isn't it?"

"She amazes me every day. I found her printing fabric today."

"And how are things between you? Have you admitted you love her yet? Or are you just taking advantage of having her around for a lot longer? Smart move there, genius."

"I've got extra time, and I'm really pleased to have it, but that's it."

"And nothing else has happened?"

"I've kissed her."

"You'd kissed her before I went away."

"Yeah, I've kissed her again. It got a bit more heated this time."

Marco raised his drink to Will. "Then why don't you look happy?"

"Where's it going, Marco? That's the question. And there's still V. And before you say anything, yes, I've talked to her. She's just not listening. She keeps playing down my attraction to Stella."

"I can't see Stella staying here if she thinks you're sleeping with V."

"I haven't had sex with Vanessa. She works for me. So why is it so hard with Stella?"

"I always got the impression V wanted you to. Like the night her car wouldn't start, and she had to stay over."

"I'm a grown man. I knew I couldn't get involved. What would she be like now if I had? But then Stella came to work for me."

"Mr Thoresby, you call your computer Star. You must have known something."

"She was 5,349 miles away, living in Hursts Bridge."

"That's very accurate." Will blushed and mumbled.

"It's where my family lives. That's how far away I live from them."

"So why is Vanessa still hanging around?"

"She works for me, Marco. She has done weird shit recently, though. I guess that's why they tell you never to sleep with the help. Not that I have, but it's gotten so complicated."

"Well, I never listened to that." He smirked. "Have you taken her out yet? Stella, I mean."

"I guess I've been focusing on the house. Time is slipping away."

"And she isn't?"

"Oh, she is; if anything, she works harder and longer than anyone."

"She's looking tired, mate."

"Tell me about it." Will sighed again. *Why did I come here?*

"As long as you know. Now, have you thought about my offer?"

"I have actually, and I understand your position. If things get tight again, I'll talk to you. But I received some good news today, which has lifted some of the pressure."

"Oh, what's that?"

"My flat in London is on the market and…Damn, is that thunder?"

"It was forecast, so what's the surprise?"

"Can we just open a door? Your soundproofing is too bloody good."

"What's wrong with you?"

"It's not me, it's Stella. She's like a timid dog during a thunderstorm. She'll be hiding under the bed, shivering. I'll have to go."

"Will, she's a grown woman. She must have survived a few thunderstorms without you holding her hand through the years."

"She's pretty burnt out at the moment, though; this could be the straw that breaks the camel's back. I'm going to go."

"You'll get wet."

"It's not far, and I can get dry when I get home. I can't sit here listening to it, knowing she's on her own." Will left his drink. He nodded to Marco, his lips tight. He ran the most direct route he could.

As the rain hit his face, he mentally made his way around the house, thinking about where to look first. He remembered finding her that first night he discovered her fear. Her parents were fighting, and her father had brought her over to stay with them. He probably thought it was for the best. Sarah was asleep, but he'd heard Stella crying through the wall.

He'd taken her back to his room to avoid waking Sarah, and he'd let her hold Spike because he thought it might help. The little, grey-knitted dog always seemed to help him. He'd tried to explain what thunder was and how beautiful it could be. It hadn't worked, but he had tried his best. The next morning, her mum had left.

The rain soaked him, leaving his clothes clinging to his body. Water dripped onto the new floor as he raced to find Stella. He gently opened the door to her bedroom, desperate not to startle her. But her room was empty. He checked the bathroom and then the closet—still empty. Where would she go?

He grabbed a towel and a dry t-shirt, drying himself as he walked. He couldn't stop until he found her. He tried the workroom, but that was

empty, too. He swapped t-shirts and dropped the wet things back in his room as his head rushed to work out where she would be.

Will felt sure she wouldn't be in the great room, as there were too many windows in there. He was wrong again. He found Stella sitting on the floor near the tiny sofa in the dark, staring out through the window.

"Are you OK? Do you want a light on?"

"I'm watching the weather. Someone once told me how wonderful it can be." She smiled up at him.

"I'm pleased it doesn't disturb you."

"Thanks, William, but I'm all grown up. I can enjoy it now." Will wasn't convinced. *It must remind her of that night.* Even in the darkness, Will could tell she was putting on a brave face. Granted, she wasn't as upset as he thought she might be, but that didn't mean she was fine.

"I've come back to watch a film. I've finished the cinema room. Do you want to join me?

"Are the seats in yet?"

"No, but we must watch it in the cinema, is that OK with you? Have we still got any popcorn? I fancy some of that caramel."

He held out his hand. "Shall we go down there and pick a movie, then I'll go get the snacks and drinks?" In the darkness, he could see Stella still sitting on the floor, hugging her knees. Spike was squashed in her hands. He waved his fingers at her.

"Come on, Stella. I need a friend tonight." He bent down and took her hand, gently pulling her to her feet. He wrapped an arm around her shoulder and led her quietly down to the cinema in the basement. Will could feel a slight tremor in her body under his arm, and it made him feel even more protective of her. Some people didn't understand why she should feel so scared. But he remembered how she was always afraid of thunder. Then, during the worst storm they had known in their young lives, her mother left, taking her dog, but not her daughter.

Halfway down the stairs, she froze.

"Snacks!"

"Snacks?"

"We need snacks."

"I'll get them." Will assured her.

"I'll get something to sit on." She turned away from him and ran back up the stairs. He hoped she wasn't running away.

His arms were full when he returned to find her sitting on the floor amid a pile of white. He opened his arms and dropped everything he had been carrying. It bounced onto the floor and scattered around her.

"Shit! I'm sorry. I didn't mean to do that." Stella just laughed at him, rolling onto her back. Looking down at her smiling face, his heart crumbled. He'd run back from Marco's, expecting to find her a mess, and here she was laughing up at him.

He knew she wasn't as comfortable as she'd said, but looking at her on the pillows and duvet now, it was hard to see any problems. Taking her down to the cinema had been the right decision. How did he now distract himself from thinking about lying straight down on top of her?

He sat down next to her, sitting as upright as he could. He needed to keep her mood upbeat, so he had picked a film he thought was funny, although he hadn't seen it before. From the title and images, he thought it was about a dog, a scruffy mixed-breed dog named Bobby.

Will knew how much Stella loved dogs. He hoped it would hold her attention so that she wouldn't be thinking about the storm, but what about him? What was going to stop him from thinking about her? He would just focus on keeping her laughing.

As the film started, Will realised it wasn't so much about Bobby, although the dog was cute. This film was not just a comedy; it was definitely a RomCom with an emphasis on Rom. The sexual chemistry between the people saving the dog was so strong that even he could see it. He could see how much she was enjoying it and how it made her smile, so he didn't care if it made him uncomfortable; he'd watch it with her.

In an attempt to distract himself from Stella, he opened a pack of chocolate balls and passed them to her. Stella didn't seem to notice as she snuggled down on the duvet. William lay down next to her and reached over to her with a chocolate, popping it into her mouth.

Stella turned to him, her eyes bright in the soft light from the screen.

"Do you do that with all the girls you lure into your cinema?"

"What girls?"

"Well, women then."

"You know perfectly well you're the only woman that's been in here."

"This one, yes, but at your last house?"

"My last 'house' was a small apartment, hence the lack of furniture to bring here. It didn't have a cinema. If it did, I wouldn't have been luring women, as you so delicately put it, into it."

"OK." And as simple as that, she turned back to the screen.

"Would you like some more?" He held out the bag, but Stella stayed still, just opening her mouth for him to feed her. William had to look away. The temptation to do so much more with her mouth was too great. He stared at the screen, trying desperately not to look at her, yet he was very much aware of her every move. Stella didn't seem to notice. Instead, she reached her hand into the bag and offered a chocolate ball to his mouth.

William opened his mouth, taking the chocolate and the tips of her fingers, kissing and sucking them. His eyes closed, enjoying the moment.

"Will." It was a soft sound that made him open his eyes. Had he gone too far again? Stella moved closer until her lips were touching his, and she offered him the gentlest of kisses. Her lips touched his, as light as a feather. It took every ounce of control he had not to return that kiss with the fire that was building inside him. His hands reached for her shoulders, holding her still as he slowly deepened the kiss.

A million thoughts rushed through his head. *Will Vanessa turn up again? What will Sarah say? What about my parents? Or her parents? How far is this going? Do I have any condoms?*

Stella pulled away from him, lying back on her elbows and reaching for more chocolate, her eyes firmly back on the screen. *What the…? Was that it? Does that mean I can kiss her again? Is it progress?*

William lay back, trying to focus on the film and not the woman next to him. When the dog ran out in front of a car, Stella curled up on his chest. His arms tightened as the dog was rushed off to a vet. He stroked slowly up and down her arms, and he felt her relax under his touch.

"Don't worry, I'm sure this has a happy ending."

Stella looked up at him.

"Do you believe in happy endings?"

"I guess … I live in hope." He kissed her hair, and she relaxed again. William was no longer watching the film. He kept his eyes locked on her face as her own eyes slowly shut. When her eyes stayed closed, he watched her chest as it rose and fell in a steady rhythm. William understood how tired she was, and he suspected that her falling asleep

was probably for the best. *Will we ever get past the kissing stage? Don't get me wrong, I'm enjoying the kissing, and it solves all my worries about going too far. It's her birthday tomorrow. I hope I can make it special this year.*

William mentally ran through everything he planned to do for her the next day. An early night would mean he could get off in the morning and be home quicker. He considered carrying her to her room as he studied the stairs, trying to decide if he could do it without banging her head.

He moved his body from under hers to get a better look at his path. Stella stirred in his arms.

"Will?"

"I was just working out how to get you back to your room without knocking you out on the handrail."

"You've put me to bed already this trip. I think I can manage."

"Sorry. I was thinking about how tired you are …"

"Sorry, I know you meant well, but if I need you to take me to bed, Will, I'll ask you."

Will couldn't be sure, but he thought he might be blushing. *Does she mean what I think she means?*

"I told you I'm grown up now. When are you going to work that out?"

She stood up and reached out her hand to pull him up, too. He took her hand, and together, they climbed the stairs.

"I know what you said about the weather and being grown up, Stella, but if it gets noisy or …" he shrugged. "You know where I am."

"Thanks, Will, I'll see you in the morning."

Chapter 29

It was early when her phone lit up with her mother's name. *She will never get the hang of time zones.*

"Good morning, Mum," she yawned.

"Are you OK, Stella? You sound, I don't know, not with it."

"That would be because I just woke up, I guess."

"Late night?"

"No early morning. It's five o'clock here."

"Oh, I'm sorry. I just rang up to wish you a happy birthday. I'm sorry you haven't got a card. I don't have your address." *If you'd wanted it, you could have found it.* "I've sent you some money. Buy yourself something nice."

"Thanks, Mum."

"I spoke to Maribeth. She was impressed by what she saw."

"I think she is hoping to get in early before the launch."

"That's good then. Why don't you ring her? I'm sure she would be pleased to see you."

"I might just do that."

"Well, I have to go. I'm meeting the girls for lunch. Have a nice birthday."

As it was early, she decided to take a shower and catch Will before he left for the office. Maybe he would remember what day it was. Combing her hair after the shower, she despaired at how out of shape it had grown. All things beauty had gone by the board since she arrived in California. As she did the best she could, she wondered who she could ask about hairdressers.

Stella checked her phone, but nothing from Sarah or the rest of the family. A niggling feeling that this year her birthday could go completely unnoticed sat in her stomach. Finding the house completely empty didn't help lift her mood at all.

In the kitchen, she found a note from Will. It didn't mention her birthday. It explained that he had left early so he could get back. So, there was hope there. She poured cereal into a bowl, but the milk was sour, so she made a black coffee and ate her cereal dry while she checked out social media. Grigori found her there.

"Morning, Stella. Oh, sorry, I forgot about milk."

"It's not the end of the world. And it's hardly your fault."

"Need anything from me today?"

"No, I've a full day in the main bedroom ahead. Can I help you?

Before he could answer, her phone rang, so he shook his head and left. Stella rushed to answer the call. It was from Zach.

"Happy birthday to you. Happy birthday to you. Happy birthday, dear Stella, Happy birthday to you."

"Thank you, Zach."

"I hope I didn't wake you."

"No, I was up, just about to start work."

"Working on your birthday? You should be having a day off. A day being treated. If I were there …"

"Ah, but you're not. I'm alone, so I might as well get on with this work. I might sound sad, but I get excited about projects like this."

"I hope you're going to be having fun later."

"I think I might be." *But are you sure? Will said he'd be back early, but when? Would he even make it at all?*

"Will you be in the U.K. for my birthday in June? We could make it a double celebration."

"Now that's a good idea."

After a couple of hours working in the bedroom she was creating for Will, Stella made herself another black coffee and called Maribeth Johnson. Maybe she could tell her where to find a good hairdresser. And maybe, as it was her birthday, she should go to the spa.

Checking her bank account, she saw how much her mother had given her. It seemed bad manners to spend that on the business. And right now, what she needed was a really good haircut, and maybe a manicure, looking at her hands. Maribeth answered after just two rings.

"Good morning. Stella, how are you? I was thinking of calling you today." Her voice was so cheerful that it made Stella smile. "I was talking to your mum last week, and she said it was your birthday." *Hmm. Yes. She's discussing it with Maribeth; she could have asked her for the address. Couldn't she?*

"Oh yes, it is my birthday. Listen, I was wondering if you could recommend a good hairdresser. Short hair is lovely, but it requires

regular cutting, and it needs to be cut by somebody who knows how to cut short styles.

"Sure. Why don't I pick you up and take you? I was going myself today. I'm desperately in need of a manicure."

"Yes, me too."

"That's brilliant. Let's have a nice girly spa day. I've always wanted a daughter for such things. I guess I'll have to make do with my niece. You don't mind me calling you my niece, do you, Stella?"

"No, of course I don't. I don't have that many aunts. I can always manage one more."

"How about forty-five minutes, and I'll pick you up? Or are you working today?"

"On this project, I could work 24/7. But I've decided today I'm taking time off. You know, I work for myself. So, why not?"

"Oh, I thought you worked for that wonderful William with the beautiful eyes."

"I guess I do. He's more the client. You know, I'm his interior designer. I'm not on his payroll. Anyway. I like the idea of meeting up today. I've got some questions I want to ask."

"Some questions?"

"Yes, you're local, and I need to understand the local market.

"Well, I do have a few insights. I'm sure I don't mind sharing. Forty-five minutes, Stella. I'll see you soon."

Stella made a note of the time and headed to her wardrobe. She looked at the New York clothes that her mum had bought. She wanted to make an effort for Maribeth's sake, if not for herself.

Maribeth was true to her word and arrived bang on time. Stella slipped into the leather seats of the sports car, a little silver convertible—the sort she had always coveted.

"Happy birthday, Stella, now haircut, manicure, what else?"

"To be perfectly honest. I think I could do with whatever they can fit me in for. I'm feeling… well… not quite myself."

"Are you having a good birthday?"

"Well. Mum rang at five this morning to wish me a happy birthday. She apologised for not sending a card, but she's sent me some money. Which is going to be useful for this spa trip, and that's it." She sighed. "I

haven't heard from anyone else. I guess it doesn't help being in a different time zone from my usual friends."

"I can remember that feeling when we moved here. And I was just moving from the East to the West Coast. My friends back in the U.K. found it even harder. It threw everything out of whack. I never seem to be in touch with my old friends the same." Maribeth shrugged and smiled at Stella. "But you get used to it, and you make new friends."

Stella's mind drifted with a vision of her family and friends back in Hursts Bridge. She didn't want to think about losing touch with them all. *I'll be back there soon. Focus. Get this project done, and you can go back sooner.*

"That was one of my questions. Are there many British people out here?"

"Oh, there's plenty, darling."

"I'm sorry if this is a delicate question, but are these expats a source of people with the money to buy into this development?"

"I think I know where this is going. And yes, many of the people on our agency lists are from the U.K. It's who we do our networking with, really, people we meet out socially, other people we know."

"So, do you think it would be worth my while to look at design features that would appeal to that community?"

"For example?"

"Well, for example, Will has an outlet for an electric kettle. Higher voltage, you know."

"Oh, definitely."

"Now, what other things would these people be looking for in a house design? What do they miss?"

"A decent-sized bath?"

"Oh yes, I get your point. A fireplace."

"True. You've just got me thinking, but yes, I'm sure through the day, we could come up with lots of things." She smiled. "I've rung ahead, there's going to be space for us at the spa. I'm not sure why. I think it's because there's a large group that has gone away. Their escape is our gain."

Once inside the spa, they were whisked away to start manicures and pedicures. They chatted throughout the treatments, with a string of ideas. Stella was desperate to write them down, but it wasn't that simple while someone was working so hard on her nails. She made notes on her phone

when they paused for a coffee before Maribeth insisted on paying for Stella's facial.

The ladies finished by having their hair cut and blow-dried in the main salon.

"Stella, your hair… I can't get over how much it shines. You must look after it very well."

"I'm afraid I don't. It's very much a Barrington Jones thing. We all seem to have very dark hair. Not quite black. But almost."

"But it's such a contrast with your blue eyes."

"You'll find the rest of the Barrington Jones family has them too."

"I've only met your father once."

"I don't suppose you usually meet your new sister-in-law's ex-husband, do you?"

"They seem to have been very amicable."

"I think that's mainly because Dad's like that. Of all the Barrington Joneses, he's the most laid-back."

"How's he doing? Did he remarry?"

"He's on wife number four. Gemma and I are polite but …"

"Oh, I see."

"Yes. He doesn't have time to remember my birthday. The second wife tried to be a bit of a mother whilst I lived with him. But she really didn't have … well, whatever it takes to be a mother. We got along fine, and she took me shopping, but I wouldn't have considered her anything like my mum or anyone's mother, for that matter. She tried, though. Numbers three and four didn't bother. To be fair, they were that much younger. That, and they had other things to do. I don't blame them."

"Really?"

"I already had my mum and my dad treating me on my birthday and at Christmas. Sure, usually a couple of days late, but you know, I've had a lovely day, Maribeth. I can't thank you enough for doing this."

"I've enjoyed it, Stella. And I do like your ideas for the development."

Stella smiled. "Maybe I need to do more research."

"Don't wear yourself out. I'm sure you'll find that the people are asking you for what they're looking for. I find that when I'm out showing houses, the best thing to do is ask lots of questions. Get the buyer to tell you what's really important to them. And then, well, it's easy to point out

those things. Even if you're only pointing out 50% of the things they asked for. Do you see?"

"Oh yes, I do. I know when I was in London, you couldn't ask too many questions."

"Ah, getting to know the client."

"Well, it's the most important part of the job, isn't it? Really? I mean, I love the shopping side of it. The understanding of which shops sell what, and who? And where is the best place to go for whatever it is you're looking for? But if you don't understand the client, you will just buy all the wrong things."

"Stella, I think you're going to go far."

Stella looked at her newly decorated nails, and a buzz of pride flowed through her.

"Thank you."

"Will you be ready for launch day?"

"It's going to be hard work, but yes, I believe we will be ready."

"Any chance of showing your favourite aunt before the launch?" Stella's head turned to stare out at the traffic. Had she just fallen for another Jackson Wilde set of flattery, designed to get Maribeth and her company a foot in the door first? *Will I ever learn?*

When Maribeth dropped Stella off at Will's house, it was after four.

<<Welcome, Stella.>>

No one was home, and Stella didn't know what to do with herself. The uplift of her trip to the salon had gone when she realised that Maribeth was just using her.

Chapter 30

In her bedroom, she intended to change into her work clothes but couldn't summon up the energy to make her way down to her workroom. *I'm an interior designer! Why do I spend so much time sewing?* She threw herself back on the bed and lay looking at the ceiling. *Maybe for Marco's next job, I need to ensure he sees a professional designer? Now, how do I do that?*

Stella was still ruminating on the bed when a text bounced in.

India: Happy Birthday. Is this a good time to video chat?
Stella: Sure.
India: Great. I'll send a link.

Stella fetched her laptop and settled down on her bed. When she clicked through to chat with India, she was surprised to see her grandmother's face too.

"Happy Birthday, Stella."

"Thank you, Grandma."

"I hope you don't mind my muscling in on India's call with you."

"No, I'm pleased someone remembered; it feels a bit flat."

"Should I ask why? I know your dad remembered because I reminded him last week, and India posted everyone's cards over together."

"Nothing's arrived yet. It'll be a lovely surprise when it does."

India laughed. "Well, hardly a surprise. So, other than your birthday, why are you feeling down today?"

"I don't know; maybe it's just old age."

India chuckled, and her grandma didn't hold back her own laugh.

"Your hair looks nice, though, so it can't be all bad."

"I took some time off, and I've just got back from the salon. I had a bit of a spa day with my step-aunt, if that's what she is. Look, nails," she waved her fingers at the camera. "The works, really. Mum sent some money, and Maribeth organised and paid for some extras."

"That was kind of her."

"I'm not sure of her motives, though."

"Oh?"

"She's an agent in L.A., and I think she would like to get in early on the project. I'm starting to believe she is just being nice to me because she wants something. She gave me this big speech about wishing she had a daughter to do spa days with. Then, when we got back, she asked about early access to Will's launch."

"If you think that, why did you go with her?"

"A few things, really. I didn't know where to go, so she offered to pick me up. I still get a bit confused on the roads here, so that helped. And I wanted to ask her about the local market."

"I see." Her grandma said slowly. "Did you have a good time?"

"I did."

"And did she help you with what you wanted to know?"

"I see where you are going."

"Stella, it's quite possible that she meant what she said. There is no reason why she shouldn't also ask you for help."

"It's just after Jackson, whenever someone says something nice, I start to wonder what their motives are."

India pushed her face in front of her grandma.

"Who else has got you thinking?"

"There is a woman who works for Will. I don't believe a word she says. Don't get me wrong, she is good at selling, but every time she speaks to me, I wonder what she actually means."

"Is that the woman you told me about?"

"Yeah. Tell me what I'm missing back home."

"India is going to Paris for Easter," Grandma announced, sounding impressed.

"How is Charlie?"

"He's away in the West Indies with the development squad and the coaching team. So, I've come over to Hursts Bridge. It's not as warm, but the company is great." India put her arm around their grandma.

"We'd better go. I'll call you later."

"Bye. Thanks for calling me. I miss you both."

"You'll be home soon. We will all go out together then." Grandma smiled and returned India's hug.

As they closed the call, Stella wondered about her grandma's words. Would she be home soon? She really wasn't sure where she wanted to

call home. With Gemma, her father's fourth wife in residence, she didn’t really feel that at home these days. The building was the same as she’d grown up in, but it no longer looked or felt like home. She had been so excited to go to London, but the shine soon wore off that dream.

Time for a coffee. It was only when she opened the fridge that she remembered the lack of milk. That's my life at the moment, isn’t it? *What do I want? I miss Sarah, I know that.*

Stella was sitting on the sofa, trying to enjoy a black coffee, when her phone announced a call from Sarah, making her smile.

“Happy Birthday.”

“Thank you.”

“How is it going?” Stella took a deep breath. The last few days had caught up with her. What could she say to Sarah? She wasn’t about to start talking about how confused she felt about Will. Last night in the cinema room had been wonderful, but she felt he was still pulling back from going further than a kiss.

“Sorry, was that a hard question?” *Be positive.*

“I’ve had a lovely day at the spa with my aunt. Hair, nails, facial, …”

“Did you get my parcel?”

“No, sorry, but I haven’t got the one that India posted yet either.”

“I sent it to Will. Is he there?”

“No, he said he’d be going into the office to pick something up, and he isn’t back yet.”

“That could be my parcel. I posted it to his work last week, so he could make sure you get it today.”

“Thanks. I’m sure he’ll bring it home. He tries to be here for dinner.”

“So, plans for tonight?”

“I’m going to look at a job. Re-designing a bedroom. It’s for Marco. He said he would ‘do dinner’. I don’t think he means he’s cooking.”

“Having dinner with Marco … on your birthday? Is that significant?”

“Noo … It’s just a job.”

“I thought you liked the great man. You didn’t stop talking about him after that great year at Wimbledon.”

“Oh, I do like him. He is fabulous. A great laugh, and he’s a good friend … especially to Will.” She added. “I don’t suppose you know who bought Will’s flat in London?”

"It's just a holding company, as I understand it. They've been very kind and have extended the time I can stay on. Why do you ask?"

"I get the feeling it could be Marco. I was telling him about it, then a few hours later, you had the cash offer. I don't know, I just think it's the sort of thing he'd do."

"It'll be a good investment, so I don't suppose he'll lose money on it. Why don't you fancy him anymore? Has he done something?"

"Not really, but Will gave me a long lecture on the way Marco treats women. It put me on my guard. Not that Will is in a position to talk."

"Will? Surely you aren't saying Will is a womaniser?"

Stella sighed.

"No, I'm not saying that. Something is happening with a woman who works for him, though. I think he was sleeping with her. He says he isn't, but she keeps turning up here."

"From the tone of your voice, you don't sound happy about that."

"She works for him. I get that. I don't know all the ins and outs. I just don't see them as a good match. I get the feeling she is trying to change him into the man she thinks he should be. She buys him clothes and tells him where to go. It's possible she sees that as part of her job. Let's face it, the Will we know would be in jeans and a tatty T-shirt and stay at home rather than get out meeting the 'right people'."

"Sounds complicated. What about you? If you aren't lusting after Marco, have you met anyone you do fancy?" *And what do I say to that? Your brother. Is that the honest answer?*

"Marco knows John Kingston; he was Marco's mentor from the Winners Club. He seems friendly, but he's showing his age. I haven't met anyone else." *Oh, that was sneaky. I don't like it, but at least I'm not lying to her.*

"They say never meet your heroes," she laughed. "Well, hopefully, my brother will be back soon and give you a birthday you won't forget."

Wait a minute, are we both playing games here?

"Look, Stella, it's late here. Catch up soon."

"Oh yes."

"Promise me you'll call me and tell me all about tonight."

"You mean going to Marco's? Sure."

"Goodnight, Stella, enjoy your birthday."

"Thank you."

As the clock ticked away, she meant to work on design ideas inspired by Marco but found herself selecting products for her own dream home and pinning them to her online mood boards.

The minutes turned to hours until her mum called again.

“Hello, Mum. Is everything OK?”

“I thought you sounded a little down this morning. I wanted to know if you felt better after your day out with Maribeth.”

“Oh, thanks, Mum. Well, I certainly look better than I did.”

“But do you feel better?”

“Yes, I do. I had a call with India and Grandma, then Sarah called.”

“Are you missing Yorkshire?”

“I think today showed me how much I miss my friends and family.”

“I know how that feels. When I was stuck in Hursts Bridge, I think I missed life back here, too. You know the food, things weren't so available in the U.K., and Hursts Bridge was very different from Pennsylvania, where I grew up. It was like living on another planet. My family and friends were all here in the U.S.

“Did you enjoy anything from then? Was it always so miserable?”

“I loved painting with you and watching you pick up your crayons. “

“I think we did that a lot. I'm sure you did some painting at home. I remember some postcard-size watercolours.”

“Again, I think that was my idea of being a British mother, watercolouring landscapes.”

“I do think your work is clever. Mum.

“Oh, thank you, dear, but you make your colours create a whole room?”

“How do you do it, Mum, balance the creativity and the life as Mike's wife?” Stella scribbled out one more dream on the list in her notebook.

“When I see you leave with him for dinner, it's like you're a different person.”

“That's because I’m a different person now. My creativity is just for me. I'm not trying to scratch a living from my painting. I'm not a struggling artist. I live a very comfortable life, one that allows me to come into the studio whenever I want. Sometimes I don't come in here for weeks, like this Christmas.”

“I see.” Stella looked out at the sun slowly approaching the horizon.

“Listen, would you like me to send you that painting you liked?”

"I don't really have a place to hang it yet, Mum." Stella sighed.

"Unless."

"Unless?"

"Unless you wouldn't mind my hanging it in the house for Will. I can see it in one of the rooms here."

"I wanted you to have it."

"Think of it as helping me get my business off the ground. I want to work with talented artists, and you are one of the best."

"Oh, flattery. I see you inherited something from your father. I can go along with that. Now, what are you up to tonight?"

"I'm not sure. William isn't here yet."

"And you don't have any options other than waiting for William Thoresby?"

"I've got options. I've got a job to look at and the promise of dinner."

"You know what my mum used to say. Never wait for a man. There will be another one along in a few minutes."

"I think that was never run after a bus."

"Oh yes. That makes more sense."

"Good night, Mum, and thanks."

As seven o'clock approached, there was still no sign of Will, so she put her notebook in her bag and set off for Marco's.

Chapter 31

<<Welcome home, William.>>

William froze, a bouquet in one hand and a gift bag in the other. The parcel from his sister was tucked under his arm. *Where was Stella?*

"Star, where is Stella?"

<<Stella is not in the house. >> William knew he was late, but where would she go? *It's her birthday, and you left her alone. It couldn't be helped, or could it?* Dropping the flowers and the gift bag on the table, he poured himself a glass of whisky before pulling out his phone. He felt guilty about it, but he checked where her phone was and hoped she had it with her. The app showed her to be outside, maybe on Marco's land. *Damn!*

He lifted his eyes to see that his neighbour was mid-party. He dropped his phone on his desk and walked towards the wall of glass that separated his office from the terrace. To be fair, if Marco was home after eight pm, he was rarely alone. *Why didn't you acknowledge her birthday this morning? Now she'll think you forgot. How could I forget?*

Picking up his phone again, he called Grigori, desperate to know she was safe. He fought to sound calm.

"Hey Grigori, just checking how today's gone."

"Fine. The service kitchen is ready. So, we'll start in the kitchen tomorrow if that works for you. We've dropped the island in there, ready to install.

"What about Stella?"

"She did some work in the primary this morning, and then that woman picked her up."

"Jenny? She has a small red SUV?"

"No. It was a silver Mercedes. I think she was at the preview."

"Did Stella come back?"

"Yes. She'd had her hair cut and I think her nails done and stuff. Isn't she there?"

"Yeah, I only just got back, and there's no sign of her, but you know how it is."

"True, boss. I think it's her birthday…"

"It is. But how do you know?"

“She got a call from someone singing Happy Birthday. I think he had an Aussie accent?”

“Shit!”

“So, you didn't see her this morning, and you were late for dinner? On her birthday? Are you sure you care about her?”

“It couldn't be helped. Crisis at the office.”

“Would this be a Vanessa-shaped crisis?”

“Not really.” William was shaking his head, his blood pressure rising the more he thought about today. Why did he think a woman like Stella would sit around and wait for him? *She's always been too good for you. But the last few weeks, the kisses and when I held her ... Sarah had asked me to look after her... and what have I done?* He'd kissed her … more than once. Then he'd abandoned her on her birthday, and now God knows what is happening at the party. He showered quicker than ever and hurried over to his neighbours.

Music spilt out of Marco's house, as did the people laughing and enjoying themselves on the terrace. *Why didn't he invite me?* He took a moment when he hit the edge of the patio to get his bearings, his eyes scanning and searching for Stella or, at the very least, Marco. He couldn't see either. Stepping inside, he could see that Marco had excelled himself. He spotted star-shaped balloons and a table with food that had the remains of a birthday cake, but still no sign of Stella. And when he heard a laugh, he recognised it immediately. The sound of it lifted his heart. Until he heard the deep rumbling of Marco Martelli's laugh joining hers, he raised his eyes from the table to see them both reappearing from the corridor that led to the bedrooms.

Shit!

Marco's laugh was so loud. When the door opened to the bedroom he had been working on just last week, Stella stumbled out. Marco followed close behind her, fastening his shirt as Stella pulled her high-heeled shoes back on. Marco smirked, his eyes transfixed on her rear. William glared at both of them. *Is this what he meant when he said, 'If you don't go there, someone else will'? Did he mean himself?*

When the happy couple saw his face, the laughter stopped. He knew he wasn't hiding his emotions very well, but Stella looked angrier than he felt, if that was possible.

“Hello, stranger. Better late than never.”

Shit, why can't I just be there for her? I want to be.

"Hey Stella, Happy Birthday. I was expecting you for dinner."

"Will, my man, you're missing all the fun." Marco's grin was wide even when Stella reached back and slapped his chest.

"Behave, Martelli. Would you like a piece of my cake?"

"It looks like I'm a bit too late for that."

"Oh, sorry, I didn't think … you didn't mention dinner, so when Marco asked me to look at a job, I didn't think it would be a problem."

"It's not a problem." He couldn't look at her anymore. Even Marco couldn't arrange this in the hour he had been late. When had Marco decided to do this? He swallowed.

"You look like you've been enjoying yourself." He took in the new hair and nails, and she was wearing a silky-looking dress with an intricate neckline. *Did she do all that for Marco? She does like him.* That had been obvious since the day she found out he lived next door. *Had these two planned tonight? When did she decide to get her hair cut?*

Marco's face held a broad smirk. *Is he playing with me? He knows I like her; hell, he's been teasing me about it enough. How do I save this? How do I get her back home to give her presents? She needs to know I didn't forget.*

Will looked around at the people filling the room. John Kingston waved at her from a group that was dancing. *Dancing? You can't dance! I can try.*

"If you didn't save me any cake, did you save me a dance?" He didn't wait for a reply. He pulled her hand and gently coaxed her to a spot with a little more space to move, and then he took her in his arms. One glance at Marco showed him smiling and shaking his head.

"So, how was your day? Your hair looks wonderful, by the way."

"It was a last-minute decision. My mum called at daft o'clock this morning. I guess she was trying to make up for missing last year. She reminded me to call Maribeth. Then, when I rang her, she wanted to take me out."

"Well, you look wonderful. I'm sorry I missed you this morning. I tried to get off early, to be back for your birthday."

"How did that go?"

"There were a couple of problems to deal with, but I've a present for you from Sarah. She had it sent to the office."

"She said when she rang."

"I hope you didn't think I forgot."

"Why would I think that?" She spun out of his arms, dancing just a tantalising distance away from him. He searched her face, but she wasn't making eye contact with him, so how could he tell what was happening in her head? Was he ever sure what was happening in that brain?

It was torture to dance so near but not close enough to touch her. He looked across at Marco, trying to assess the cause of the smirk he was wearing. Will knew the room they left was Marco's bedroom. Why would they be there during her birthday party if not to … As images of Marco with Stella filled his head, John Kingston emerged from a group near the table. He took Stella's hand and twirled her into his body. William's eyes closed as he felt a physical pull, watching her body spin away from him.

John was older than him and probably nearly twenty years older than Stella. Will's brain buzzed, searching for answers to a hundred different questions. *Where does he live? He's not playing tennis now. What does he do? Isn't he married? How serious is he?* He shook himself. *He's only dancing … but you were dancing, and you certainly wanted more.*

When John dipped his head to whisper into Stella's ear, he had to walk away. He didn't like dancing except with her. How could he dance watching her with someone else? He moved towards the open door, not sure whether to retreat to his own place. He hesitated at the doorway, looking out at the house he was trying so hard to turn into a home.

"I hope you aren't going to abandon her again, Will. I seriously thought you cared for her more than that."

Will spun around, for the first time, totally frustrated with Marco and his behaviour.

"Why? Why, when you can have any girl, would you want to take her? Why would you do that?"

"Take her? I was just entertaining her until you were ready." The smirk aimed at him hurt, and William's fists clenched.

"Ready?"

"Ready to see she has grown up, ready to be there for her. Ready to take that next step."

"I … I …"

"Look at her, Will. She is not just an attractive woman; she is bright, intelligent and has a heart as big as a house. If you don't make a move, someone else will. If I weren't a friend, I would have done it the day I met her. I can't be sure John would hold back the same. He has talked

about her nonstop since that night we played pool. He was the first one here when he knew it was her birthday, and you should see the tennis bracelet he bought her. Why wouldn't everyone love her?"

"I … but …"

"I know all that rubbish about your family and her family and your sister. It's crap, William, my man. You are the best guy for her because she thinks the same about you."

"She couldn't …"

"When you kissed, did she behave as if she wanted you to stop?"

"Well …"

"Oh, go home, Will. I'm sure someone will see she enjoys her birthday for once." Marco stormed off, leaving Will staring back at Stella, still dancing with John.

His hands clenched as he stared at her, unable to stop or walk away. Stella turned as she danced and saw him looking at her. She smiled as she held his gaze. He recognised the familiar, gentle smile—the one gracing her face after his kiss on the unfurnished cinema floor—the same smile he had seen when he woke after her nightmares that night.

Barely aware of what he was doing, he walked hesitantly towards her. Stella returned the stare, and the gap between them closed. He watched as she said something to John, who moved slowly away, squeezing her hand as he left her. Will took the last three steps much faster, and now she was standing alone, looking at him.

"I …"

"Take me home, Will." She took his hand, and together they walked back to the door leading out into the garden.

Chapter 32

Stepping out into the cool night, Stella stopped abruptly, and Will walked into her back.

"I should say goodbye and thank Marco."

"Maybe you should, but please don't." Will looked over his shoulder at their host. "He's big-headed enough. We can both thank him tomorrow. He looks happy already."

Stella followed his gaze over to Marco, who was grinning wildly and waving them off.

"OK. In that case, let's go."

As they left, William took her hand and held it close to his side, his thumb stroking her wrist.

"I'm sorry. I had plans. I was late … and the traffic…"

Stella struggled to listen; she felt bad for not waiting for him.

"I didn't realise it was a party … I went to look at the room …" Stella quickened her pace to keep up. "He did say he would do dinner … it was a surprise…it was nice, though." *Just stop talking. You aren't making it any better. It was nice to have someone make a fuss of my birthday … why should I feel so guilty about that?*

"Your presents are on the table."

"Really? And cake?"

"If you still want cake, I might just have a proper birthday cake." Will smiled down at her. "It's OK, Stella."

Despite rushing, with short legs and high heels, Stella struggled to keep up with Will's long strides. He was on a mission to get back. With a firm grip on her hand, he pulled her along. In the dark, neither of them saw the branch lying on the lawn until her foot caught in it. Stumbling forward, she clutched William's arm with her free hand. Will turned to catch her, but she still found herself sitting on the damp grass.

"Are you OK?"

"I can't keep up with you. It's those long legs."

"I'm sorry, let me help you up." He took her hands in his. "Oh, you're bleeding."

"It's nothing."

Looking up at Will, she smiled, wiping her hands together. Once she found her feet, he crouched down.

"Here, let me give you a ride."

"I said it's nothing."

"Come on, Stella."

"I'm a big girl now. I don't need a piggyback."

"Please, Stella. Come on." Stella reluctantly clung to his back, her arms around his neck, her legs clamped around his waist. Will's hands slipped under her thighs. He carried her into the house, past her bedroom, and then past his.

"Wait! Where are we going?"

"To sort that foot!"

In the kitchen, he spun around until Stella felt a little dizzy.

"Will! What the …"

"Just hang on!" Eventually, he sat her on the new island that dominated the room. Stella dropped her shoes as she squirmed on the cold marble, pulling down her dress.

"I shouldn't be up here," Stella clutched at her hem. "What if I get blood…"

"Sit. Still!" William rushed about opening cupboards, his hair flopping in his eyes. Stella shuffled to the edge of the island.

"What about the service kitchen?"

"Sit still!" He filled a bowl with water and emptied it. He refilled it, checking the temperature. Carrying it back, his face softened.

"Now, let me see your war wound." That made Stella smile. Would he always remind her of being at home?

He lifted her foot tenderly, but too fast for Stella, who was hanging on to the hem of her dress. Once the heat of his palm warmed the sole of her foot, she began to relax.

"It's fine."

Will tenderly cleaned the gash where her foot had hit the branch. Stella flinched as she felt the sting of the wet cotton wool. Will stepped away, his hand going straight to the back of his neck.

"Sorry, I didn't want to hurt you."

The words held a lot of meaning for Stella.

"I know that, Will, but no one can protect us from pain all the time. We get through it."

Their eyes locked. Will broke the contact first as he glanced down at her foot, but she couldn't take her eyes from his face.

"I think it's swelling. Is there any ice?"

"Yes … but I don't need …" Will charged off again, leaving her stranded on the counter. Frustrated, she shuffled to the edge, looking down to see where her shoes had landed.

"Star! Sit. Still."

"Will, just slow down. I think we can safely say I'm not about to bleed to death. Look, it's stopped bleeding."

Will walked back in, wrapping some ice in a tea towel.

"It's my fault. If I hadn't been in such a rush to get you back …" he blushed, keeping his eyes firmly fixed on her foot as he held the ice pack in place. Stella giggled.

"You might have been in a rush, but I don't think you were alone."

Will looked up, his eyes trained on her again, his smile shifted. Stella's heart fluttered as her own face matched his. He was still holding the ice to her foot, and she still hung on to that hem.

"You mean …"

"I wanted to see my presents." She tried to protest.

"Is that all?"

"Yes!" she laughed.

"I don't believe you." He leant forward and kissed her. Just a fleeting kiss. Too fleeting for Stella, who released the bottom of her dress and all sense of modesty as she reached for him.

Her hands cupped his face as she fell into a more extended kiss. Deeper than any they had tried before.

Will pulled away. He shook his head. "Star. Lock outside doors." His eyes darkened as he explained. "No interruptions tonight."

<<The house is secure.>>

"Is that a promise?"

"Well …"

"I can't keep getting this far, and then something happens. We don't talk about it. We just act like it didn't happen."

"Stella, this isn't easy for me."

"And?"

"Seeing you come out of that bedroom … well, it woke me up."

"Was that because it was Marco?"

"No." He pulled down her dress for her. "Possibly. I don't know."

"You realise I was just looking at his room. For a job, that's all."

"It was Marco's face. He knows how I feel about you, and he looked so smug. I …"

"Excuse me!"

"I think he was doing it to wind me up," he explained.

"I mean, what you said about Marco knows how you feel about me. See what I mean? We haven't talked about it. And yet you've discussed it with Marco!"

"Not by choice!" he snapped. Stella shook her head.

"Keep digging, Will." She snarled.

"I'm sorry. Can we start again?" His shoulders sagged.

"I'd like that." The soft smile was back.

Encouraged by the smile, Will leant forward to touch his lips to the crease at the corner of her mouth, slowly kissing across her lips, teasing and tempting her. Her hands gripped the edge of the island as her legs dangled between his.

This time, it was Stella who pulled away.

"I thought we were going to talk about…" Will's lips stopped her mid-sentence.

"Actions speak louder than words, they say. I thought I'd show you just how much you mean to me." With a smile, he returned to kissing her. Stella let go of the counter and took hold of his waist, ensuring he didn't move away again. Instead, she tipped her head to one side.

"Actions? So, I'm going to see some action?" Her hands clasped around his neck.

"Yep!" He said, lifting her. "Hold on tight."

"Where are we going?"

"You'll see." Will sat her down on the large conference table. A set of parcels waited for her, together with a birthday cake that had chocolate frosting and was decorated with different coloured chocolate chips. Such a simple cake, but very much like the ones she had as a child. Across the top, in white icing, it read, "Happy Birthday Star."

"Is this for me?"

"It is. Someone owed me a favour."

"Can I open my presents now?" Will didn't answer. Instead, he dipped his head and kissed her.

"I think I would rather open my present first." He played with the drawstring on her neckline. "I haven't seen this dress before."

"It's not really suitable for work," she scoffed, stroking the material downwards. Will smiled his reply as he pulled at the strings holding the neck of her dress closed. The dress fell open, revealing just the barest hint of a black lace bra. Stella shuddered as his fingers traced the outline of the lace as it swept over the fullness of her breast.

"Hmm, very nice. Are you wearing this for someone special?" *Of course I did.*

Her bravado had left her.

"Will … I …" Stella bit her lip. Will gently released her lip as his thumb stroked it. He kissed her delicately again before catching her bottom lip between his teeth. He let go and eased her pain with a swift sweep of his tongue. As her lips parted, his tongue darted into her mouth to dance with hers. Every thought left her brain. All she could think about was the heat building inside her as his lips teased her mouth.

Stella ran her fingers through his hair, holding his face still as she returned his kiss with her own, more heated kisses, searching for something more than the kisses they'd exchanged before. This time, she was desperate for there to be more to this connection.

Will slipped the straps of her dress off her shoulders as she sat on the table before him. The silky fabric pooled at her waist, allowing him to run his fingers over the black lace she wore underneath. Stella swallowed. *This is what you have been waiting for, isn't it? This is a man who will respect both you and your work. This is someone you've always trusted.*

Will pulled her inch by inch closer to him as he leant between her thighs. Stella sought the buttons on his shirt and began to undo them deliberately and slowly. When the toned body of this man she adored was gradually revealed, her fingertips explored the curves of his body. Her eyes were drawn to the defined muscles of his chest. *Swimming. It has a lot to answer for.*

Will's tiny kisses reached her jaw and trailed around to her ear. A small groan left him as he released her perfect breasts from her bra. Stella's head dropped back, opening up more access. This slow, teasing exploration of each other was becoming too much for her.

With Will's shirt resting on the floor, she pulled at the belt on his jeans. The stiffness of the leather meant it took more effort than she expected to release him. She batted away his hand when he reached

down to help her, which brought his smile back. She huffed as she managed to undo first the belt and then his jeans.

She slipped her hand inside the warmth to cup his taut buttocks. Will's lips found her mouth again, and as she pulled him closer, the intensity of his kisses grew. Stella returned them with equal heat. Their bodies matched, the chemistry clearly working between them. Stella wanted to squeeze her thighs together, but with Will standing between them, that wasn't possible. When he stepped back, she couldn't resist that urge any longer. Her lips missed his as soon as they left.

Another groan left her as he dropped to his knees. He pulled her closer to the edge of the table. He removed the black lace and then gently opened her legs.

"Thank you for trusting me," he whispered as he pulled the rest of her clothes free from her body. Stella lay back on the table, her hands now searching for the texture on its surface.

First his fingers and then his lips continued to explore her body. Her skin responded by becoming hypersensitive to his touch. She wanted to twist and jerk as Will eventually entered her with his fingers.

"Are you OK there, my little Star?"

"Hmmm."

"That's good. Now, let me see if I can find a birthday gift for you. Something to make you feel special on your birthday." Stella could hear the smile in his voice, although her eyes were firmly closed. The urge to close her thighs was growing again, and yet she resisted. When his lips found her clitoris, she lifted from the table, such was the intensity of her reaction to all this attention. It wasn't long before her whole being tensed and throbbed as he probed deeper. The euphoria that followed swiftly washed over her. Will kissed her inner thighs as he raised his head.

"Are you alright there?"

"Hmmm."

"Good. Come on." He helped her sit up. Lifting her again, he left the room.

"Where are you taking me?"

"I was thinking somewhere with a bed … and condoms … but I'm open to ideas."

"I can go with that. Your place or mine?"

"Very funny, but I think we will use mine."

"OK."

"It's closer!" He puffed, hitching her up a little.

"I could walk."

"Where is the fun in that?"

"Star, open the bedroom door." The door swung open in time for him to carry her into the room. "Star, lights three."

The room lit up with soft pink lights around the headboard and the floor edge. Soft music was playing so low that Stella could hardly hear it.

Will stumbled as he reached the bed. Stella fell from his arms, landing with a bounce on the deep mattress. His eyes widened at her almost naked body sprawled on his bed beneath him. "I'm so sorry."

Stella was too busy laughing to respond.

"Are you laughing at me?"

"It's all a bit staged. Do you do this often?"

"No. This is something new I've been working on."

"Who for?"

"You, of course. Now move over."

"Actually, can you go around the other side? I'd rather stay here." Will's eyes narrowed.

"Don't tell me you like to sleep on this side because …"

"No, I was just thinking about my foot. Then maybe I'm not staying."

"Is there a limit to how many times we can start again?"

"I think so, but we haven't got there yet."

Chapter 33

William had spent the last month trying to control his body's reactions to this grown-up version of the girl he knew. His expectations from the previous night, his plans for her birthday, and images of her at Marco's tonight built up inside him, pushing him to move forward with her. Whatever doubts he'd had before, had been overshadowed by the last 24 hours.

"Now, where were we?" Will knelt on the bed at her feet, crawling up her body until his lips hovered inches from hers.

"William Thoresby, is this your attempt to leave me wanting again? Kiss me and then make some excuse."

"No." He shook his head slowly. "No, I want this, Stella. I can't begin to tell you how much." He lifted a hand, wiping his thumb across her bottom lip. "But I won't be mad if you say no." He dipped his mouth and touched his lips to hers. "I need to be sure that you—"

"I'm not going to say no, Will. I want this."

"Thank God." His lips crashed into hers. Stella's head lifted towards him. Increasing the pressure of their kiss. Her eyes closed as the intensity of the kiss increased. William groaned, pulling back from her mouth, and he trailed his lips down her body.

He cradled her injured foot as he gently kissed her instep, moving up the inside of her ankle and then her calf. His kisses were soft and warm, both comforting and teasing in the same moment. Stella wriggled beneath him, unable to lie still. His attention travelled up her inner thigh, teasing inch by inch. He paused at the apex of her leg. Blowing playfully across her. Still sensitive, her hips twisted and lifted towards him once more. He stopped, looking down at her body, so alive to his touch. *She looks so perfect. Has she done this before? What if this is her first time?*

"Will, please."

"In good time, Star."

"Will!"

"Just relax, let me…"

"Will, I think I've waited weeks."

"Star." He reached over to the bedside table and pulled a foil package from the drawer. Stella took it from him with the confidence of a woman who knew what she wanted. It was Will's turn to close his eyes. He

opened them slowly to watch her nimble fingers open the packet. Gripping his length, she calmly rolled the condom onto him. With relief, he realised she had done this before, and he had no more doubt that she wanted this. Stella looked into his eyes as she massaged his thighs.

"So powerful."

Will moved forward as Stella eased back. She didn't break eye contact with him.

"Star. My Star," he murmured as he positioned himself over her. The blue eyes he knew so well looked up at him. Her want was clear, and he knew he couldn't wait much longer. Taking a deep breath, he tried to control what he did next. He stroked his hardness against her heat. He knew how wet she was from their earlier playing. His heightened senses could smell her desire. She had orgasmed once and was still sensitive but ready. He placed the tip of his erection inside her and pushed slowly and deliberately forward. Studying her face for a response.

As he filled her, he paused as more blood pulsed through him. He'd had enough sex in the past, yet somehow, this felt brand new. Will wanted to worship her, to bring her pleasure in any way he could. He fought his own body's desire to drive forward, claiming her as his own.

The image of her dancing with John taunted him. He wanted her for himself. He'd struggled with the idea of making love to her, but it didn't compare to the idea of someone else claiming her. He pulled out and pushed back harder and further. Stella groaned, her eyes now firmly closed. Her body was warm and soft beneath him. It took every ounce of his self-control not to rush this first time inside her.

"Yes." His eyes closed. "That feels …" He froze, holding himself above her, sweat beading on his forehead.

"God, don't stop, Will. Please. I need more."

The sound of her voice woke him; he pushed forward again, filling her. This time, as he pulled out, he didn't hesitate to push back in again, and again. He put every inch of his body and his soul into filling her, watching her face still.

Stroke after stroke, his pace quickening as she gripped his shoulders. He needed to bring her to a climax again. They'd both waited for this.

"Oh, Will." It wasn't the scream he'd heard so many people talk about, but it was music to his ears. It was followed by her hips lifting when her body tightened around him. The throbbing pulse of her gripping him pushed him over the edge as his own body flexed and

pulsed. Pumping out for longer than he thought possible. He collapsed over her as her body continued to pulse around him.

"I'm sorry." He rolled off her, and she turned to look at him.

"Sorry? Why on earth are you sorry?"

"Well, that wasn't very spectacular."

"Oh, Will, don't you think we've been putting this off for too long for that? I mean that first kiss."

"You've been wanting this ever since then?"

"Well, yes. What about you?"

"Since I banged my head on that wall after looking up your legs when you arrived two days early."

"I was NOT early!"

"I know." He kissed her. It was wonderful to have her here in his bed, knowing she'd be there when he woke up. It wasn't a dream anymore.

"I just need to deal with…" he waved his hand to the condom.

"Oh yes, of course."

Will hopped off the bed and walked to the bathroom. *Is that it? Are we in a relationship? Can I tell Marco to leave her alone now?* With the condom gone and himself washed, his thoughts turned to how long he had with her. His Star. *Will she still leave when this is done? What does this mean to her? Does she do this often? Shit! What will Sarah say?*

He took some tissues and a glass of water back to the bed.

"I'll just leave these here. How's your foot? Can I get you anything — a cup of tea? Some pain meds?"

"I'll settle for a cuddle."

"That I can do."

He lay back beside her, and she curled into him. Her head on his chest. *What do I say now?* Pulling her closer, he kissed the top of her hair and prayed this was the beginning and not the end.

Stella drifted off to sleep quickly, breathing softly. She'd had a busy day, they both had, and he still hadn't given her a present or cooked her a meal. *I guess there is always tomorrow.*

Chapter 34

Although Will woke several times during the night, Stella was always asleep when he checked. He wished he could sleep as well, but recently, all the worry about this project and how the money tied up in it was affecting Thoresby Technologies meant sleep eluded him most nights. At least with the big launch coming up, the wait might be over. If they could just secure the sale of one plot, it would be great; two would be even better.

He reached over for his phone and disconnected the wake-up sequence on the computer. If Stella could sleep, let her. He wanted to go for a swim to think all this through, but he didn't want her to wake up and find him gone. He did as much work as he could on his phone and then decided it was time to get up. Looking at Stella curled away from him; he toyed with ideas of how to wake her.

Playing it safe, he pulled on shorts and went to the kitchen to fetch her a drink.

"Morning, Beautiful."

Will placed a tray of tea and orange juice on the table by the window. Stella roused and propped herself up on her elbows.

"Do I smell toast?"

"I thought we could have this and then maybe try starting your birthday again."

"Another restart?"

"There are presents and cake."

"Cake for breakfast?"

"Why not?"

Will tried not to stare as Stella sat up in his bed for the first time since that first night. He hoped it was a sight he would get used to.

"What time is it?" She pulled at her new shorter hair.

"It's after seven."

"Oh. What happened to Star?"

"I cancelled the alarm. Tea?"

"Yes, please. I must use the loo first."

"Knock yourself out."

"My clothes are in the kitchen."

"Hu hu."

"So…"

Will looked at her askance. "You are shy? After last night?"

"Will!"

William sighed and held up his hands.

"OK. I'll close my eyes. You know where the T-shirts are."

"Are they closed?" With another sigh, he put his hands over his eyes.

"Yes."

When he heard her move, he dropped his hand from his eyes, sneaking a look at her retreating naked body—the body that he had slept with, his Star. *I could get used to that view.* When she returned wearing a large white T-shirt with his company logo on, he couldn't shake the smile. *My Star. MINE!*

"Happy Birthday," he said as he pulled her into a hug, pressing a soft kiss to her lips. "I feel like it's my birthday." Eventually, he moved away to pour the tea, and Stella sat back on the bed, slipping her legs under the sheet. He passed her the orange juice. Her eyes lit up as she took her first sip.

"This is amazing."

"This is California." He smiled. "Toast first or straight to cake?"

"Both! For some reason, I'm hungry this morning."

"Me too! I wonder why?" His grin was so wide he thought his face might crack. It really did feel like his birthday, too. Excitement bubbled up inside as he arranged everything on his bed around her.

Will watched transfixed as Stella bit into the toast, the crumbs falling down his T-shirt, which looked so good on her. He sat on the ottoman, watching her, and steadily spread Marmite on another slice of toast.

"I know, now come on, open these presents. I've tried rattling them, but I still don't know what's in them."

She sat back on the bed and squeezed the presents herself.

"What about the ones from you? Do you know what's in them?"

"I'll admit I had help, but yes, I do know what's in them."

Stella started with the parcel from her family. She opened everything annoyingly slowly. Amongst the cards, she found a bracelet from her grandmother, a clutch bag from India, and a pair of quirky earrings that Stella seemed to love. Her father sent a note saying he had deposited

some money in her account. Will couldn't wait for her to open his gifts, or perhaps he could; he felt so tense.

His sister, Sarah, had sent her a bottle of sun cream, a romance book, a sarong, and a bright red bikini. The card read:

For Working on Your Tan.

When the time came to hand over his present, his anxiety grew; he swallowed as he passed her a picnic basket. His voice cracked.

"I had help. I did the shopping, but Tina, my PA, baked the cake and arranged everything in the basket for me." Will held his breath. From her comments last night, he already knew he'd got the cake right.

"I thought your mother had made it. It looked so much like the ones Sarah used to get."

William tried to regulate his breathing. He thought he was pretty safe with the food treats that had inspired the picnic basket. Stella's delight at the snacks from home shone in her eyes, but he wasn't ready to relax yet. When she pulled out a plush toy in the shape of a dog, her puzzled look made him rush to explain.

"I wish I could've bought you a real puppy, maybe one day…"

"It's lovely, Will. Thank you." She stroked the dog's head.

"There is one last present in there." Stella pushed both hands into the tissue paper and drew out a small jewellery box. She didn't open it; she just looked into his face, waiting.

"Open it then."

Relief flowed through him as a wide smile spread across her face. She pulled out the delicate silver locket. Inside, he had placed a photo of the three of them as children—a copy of the one he kept in his wallet.

"Oh, Will, it's lovely. Thank you. I've had the nicest birthday in a long time."

"I'm glad you liked it."

"This cake is amazing."

"Oh, so the cake is the best bit."

"I didn't say that."

"So, what was the best bit?"

"I think you know."

"Are you going to tell me, so we are sure?" He teased.

Stella straightened the duvet as she blushed.

"Well …" Before she could explain, the computer announced a new arrival.

<<Grigori is at the gate.>>

"Star, let him in." Will pulled on some jeans, talking to Stella as he dressed.

"Don't think you got off that easily. I'll go meet Grigori. You take your time."

"I'll have a shower if that's OK?"

"Of course." He kissed her swiftly, moved towards the door, and stopped. "Are we telling the world yet?"

"Can we get used to it ourselves first?"

"Sure."

Will walked to the kitchen to put on the kettle, ready to talk through the day with Grigori. Panic hit when he saw Stella's dress on the floor near the table, along with high-heeled shoes. He crammed them into the filing cabinet in his office just as his site manager walked in. William couldn't look at him, afraid of what was written on his face. Damn, his whole body felt different.

Chapter 35

Stella looked at the debris of her birthday breakfast. She wanted to lie back down and luxuriate in the bed simply because it belonged to William Thoresby. Today was a workday and one of just a few left before the big day. The launch. She had every reason to get up and make this happen.

She might have moved to the next level with Will, but what did that really mean? *I love you, Star.* But did that mean he was in love with her? For now, she had to focus on finishing this job and juggling the finances.

She slipped silently down the corridor in just the borrowed T-shirt, her footsteps hastened by hearing Will talking to Grigori. She hadn't worked much yesterday, so she promised herself she would make up for that today. Her cut-off shorts would do nicely for that job with the newly acquired T-shirt. Her foot was a little tender, so she decided to go to the primary suite barefoot for now.

Grigori found her in there, tape measure in hand.

"Your hair looks nice. Did you enjoy your birthday? I hope Will found you."

"He did, and yes, I did enjoy my birthday, thank you." Convinced she was blushing, Stella turned away from him, using her tape to check the space for the shower.

"So, what are you planning in here?"

"I really want to make this room a sanctuary for him. I've some artwork lined up. In terms of design, I'd like to repeat that pattern we added to his pocket doors elsewhere in the room." She spun around to point to the central open area. "To be exact, I want it in at least two more places. I was thinking one would be a screen. This is a large area. I'd like to make the bed space a bit more intimate by adding an open screen here. The other will probably be in textiles, so that can come later.

Grigori was staring at the door. His face worried Stella. *What is the problem?* She rushed to fill the silence.

"So, the screen? Do you have an idea how we could cut that out? I could ask Jenny about a laser cutting group she mentioned."

"I think we can do it with the CNC machine. We have the cutting files from making the door. I'm not sure we have deep enough wood, though. How deep did you want it?"

"If it were ten centimetres, sorry, I mean four inches, it would be brilliant. But I just want it to break the eye line, really. Actually, I want to come and see what timber we've got because I've got another idea for the kitchen."

"OK. What else?"

"The bathroom. I'm guessing the suite has been ordered already."

"It's been delivered, and it cost a fortune," Grigori paused, "but you aren't going to like it."

Stella froze; her finances really wouldn't stretch to the sort of bathroom suite she would need for this space.

"If it's here and paid for, I'll have to work with it," she shrugged.

"If you say so. Here, let me show you." He pulled out his phone and scanned through the images on it. "Here you go." Stella took the phone. Her heart sank when she saw a heavy black suite with gold taps. The price tag made her want to cry. She could've done the entire room for that sort of price.

"I told you it's more Marco than Will." Grigori laughed.

"G, you are a genius. This would work great in that room for Marco." Stella's eyes lit up as her brain buzzed. "If we sell it to him, I'm guessing we can fund the whole suite here. Not only that, but it would inspire a whole theme of black and gold for Marco."

"Worth a try, I guess."

"I just need to frame it in the right way. Maybe on the right mood board, some nice Carrara marble with plenty of black in it, and gold fittings." Stella now had so many ideas for a room that Marco would love and just wasn't Will:

"If it helps, Vanessa had it delivered early because there is a long wait list for this design."

"I'll go throw some ideas together, then go talk to Marco if you can look at the screen, and then we can go from there. I'd better put some shoes on."

"If I were you, I would put a bit more than shoes on." Stella looked down at the cut-offs and bare legs.

"Maybe you are right."

The shoes she'd chosen caught on her foot, and she walked gingerly over to the next house.

At Marco’s, the debris of last night’s party littered the lounge.

“Morning Gabriella, is Marco about?”

“If my ears are still working, he’s in his bedroom. I can call him.” Gabriella stood up, but before she could move, Marco walked into the room.

“I thought I heard voices. Morning, beautiful girl. I hope you enjoyed the rest of your birthday after William dragged you home.”

“I did.” She looked at her hands, hoping he wouldn’t see her blush. It was futile. Marco missed nothing.

“Marco, I wanted to show you some ideas for your project. I was thinking about how powerful black and gold would look.” Stella pulled out her phone to show him the bathroom suite. “I found this, and it made me think of you and how we could use it as a jumping-off point for your entire suite.”

“I love it. Any chance you can get started on it soon?”

“Grigori and the team can do the work. I can’t be sure I’ll be here. I can’t assume Will wants me to stay. He wasn’t that happy when I arrived.”

“Really?” Marco shook his head. “I’m sure he feels differently now.”

Stella looked away.

“OK. Then I’ll pay now … a design fee and for the materials you need.”

“It would certainly be helpful to have the materials paid for now.”

“Yes. Let me do that. How much?”

“I know how much the bathroom suite is, but I’ll have to get back to you when I have the fabrics.”

“Let me just pay you something before I leave for Rome in the morning.” Marco’s hands were in his pockets as he rocked on his heels. “And Stella, thank you. You know, for looking after Will.”

An awkward silence sat between them. It felt strange.

“Marco, why did you do all that last night?”

“The party? Because it was your birthday, and you haven’t had a fuss made for a while.”

“How did you know that?”

“Will told me.”

“Did he tell you he had plans?”

"He was just going to cook you a steak and give you a stuffed toy. You're a woman, Stella. I thought you deserved more than that."

Stella suspected there was more to this than Marco was saying. It didn't matter what Marco's intentions were; the result was that she and Will finally took the next step. She stood on her tiptoes and kissed him softly on the cheek.

"Thank you, Marco, for looking after Will, too."

"Don't be saying things like that. It will be terrible for my reputation."

"It'll be our secret."

"Oh, I like secrets."

As Stella made her way back to give Grigori the good news and order a different bathroom suite for Will, she had to wonder just how many secrets Marco had.

Chapter 36

Waking up alone didn't feel anywhere near as wonderful as waking up curled into William. He'd returned home late, if he'd returned at all. She'd given up and settled down in the room that would become Sarah's.

With Grigori's team focusing on the kitchen, Stella worked alone in the main bedroom. The desire to make this room about Will had been building since she arrived. He worked so hard and came back so late, she wanted to create a place he would like to come home to, somewhere he would enjoy being.

Sleeping alone last night had left her confused about her feelings for him. She missed his warm body beside hers. The intensity of her emotions caused her to toss and turn all night. Still, she knew she wanted him to be happy. For Stella, building a home was a way to show love. It had been a long time since she'd felt like Hursts Bridge was truly home. It might still be the same house she had always lived in, but it certainly didn't feel like it anymore. Her father's new wives had made sure of that. Growing up, she couldn't wait to leave Yorkshire and move to London. Sadly, the big city hadn't lived up to her small-town girl's expectations.

Right, today is about this room. Focus. You need fabrics. Then you need paint. You know what paint colours you want. Prussian Blue and Chantilly Lace. She shook her head. *Yes, but I'm not buying them until I find the fabric. I might move a shade or two.* She stood up and stretched her legs. It was time for lunch, and maybe there was time to talk to India. She set off for the service kitchen, still mulling over her thoughts.

You can't really buy fabric until you have some money. Will said I could use that bank card. No, you know money is a problem for him. Stella shook her head again. *If I don't have to use that card, I won't.*

She started a list as she ate a sandwich and checked her phone. A message from Maribeth asking questions on behalf of two interested clients sounded positive. Stella answered them and asked if there was anything else she could do before the Agent's Open House.

At last, her bank app announced a payment from Marco.

Bless him. So now I can buy fabric. Talking to Susan and stroking the fabrics always makes me feel better. Am I unhappy? How can I be unhappy after...? I'm not sad I did it. It just doesn't make it any easier to decide what to do next. If anything, it's made it more complicated.

Her body flushed as she recalled the previous night and the birthday breakfast the next morning. *We haven't talked about the future. Who talks about the future the first time they have sex? Is that one of the differences between men and women? They have sex. Great Sex. He's wondering what there is to eat, and she is picking out towels.*

Stella took her list back to the room to walk herself through everything she would need. There was a space by the window that overlooked the garden. Grigori was making most of the furniture now, but perhaps a chair would be a good addition there. He didn't need any more storage. She pulled out her phone and searched for a seat to fill the space. A classic Eames lounge chair would be ideal, but would she be able to get one that fits her scheme, not to mention her budget? An advert for a second-hand lounge chair caught her eye. It didn't say original, and she very much doubted it was. The question was, would it solve her problem?

As Stella ran her hands over a pile of inky blue fabrics, Susan was looking at the chair on Stella's phone.

"Is it Eames?"

"No. Just looks like a copy to me. But that's good."

"Oh?" Susan didn't hide her surprise, and Stella laughed.

"I want to alter it, and I don't think I've the heart to do that to an original."

"I see." Susan handed back her phone.

"Do you know an upholsterer?"

"There's Elaine, who buys from me. I've some photos of her work." Susan rummaged through a stack of papers on the counter and handed Stella a small photo album.

"I like these. Do you think she will be available?"

"I could ring her."

"Great, thanks," Stella replied, her eyes firmly fixed on two different velvets she was comparing with her paint swatch. Stella took the bolts of fabric and the swatch over to the door to get more light on the colours. Susan called from the back.

"She's on her way over. I'll make some coffee." Stella smiled down at the fabrics, having made her choice.

"Thank you. That's very kind."

“Nah! Two customers working on projects together increases the chance of my materials being used.” Susan laughed as she came over to help Stella. When she had a nice pile of blues and creams, she sighed.

“Now I need black and gold. And hopefully, something patterned in both to pull this scheme together.”

Susan looked puzzled. “Is this for the same house?”

“No, this is for another client.” Stella didn’t mention Marco’s name.

“I didn’t think they could be the same person.”

“Obviously not!” said the tall woman, who had just entered the shop. *But they were meant for the same person. The black and gold is what Vanessa had chosen for sweet William.*

“That was quick. Stella, this is Elaine. I’ll fetch that coffee whilst you explain about the chair.”

Stella had no problem getting Elaine to understand the vision for the chair. Together, they picked out a Prussian blue velvet and some dark-washed heavy denim.

“I want it to be durable.” She explained.

“Obviously.”

“How long would it take you?”

“Are you in a rush?”

“This is a tight timeline, so the sooner, the better.”

“I’m working on something for my mum. She won’t mind waiting. If you can get the chair to me today, I can probably make the weekend.”

“I can work with that, but if you get it finished earlier …”

“Of course. I’ll let you know.”

Susan measured and packed the blue fabrics while Elaine swapped addresses with Stella as they all drank their coffee. With her future in the balance, she knew she couldn’t leave the work for Marco undone, especially as he’d paid her.

As she fingered other black and gold fabrics, she tentatively sounded out her companions.

“Would either of you be interested in doing the work with this black and gold? Cushions, headboard and the like?”

“I’d love to do it.” Elaine jumped in quickly, and Stella thought Susan had let her. This only made Stella like them both more.

“That’s great then, and I’ll take some swatches and make up a list of measurements for when you deliver the chair.”

"Those are pretty standard fabrics, other than that one you keep stroking. If I just pop that in the back room until you know…"

"I'll take what you have left." Stella thought hard. "I'll take it with me now. Hopefully, I'll have time to make something for that room before I go." Both women looked at her.

"Go where?"

Stella sank down on a stool in the corner, clutching the brocade fabric.

"I wish I knew."

"OK, new question. Why are you going?"

"I'm staying with Will."

"He's the blue project," Susan explained to Elaine. Who now nodded as if that explained everything.

"And when the project is done, I guess I'll have to go home."

"That's a shame," Susan sighed. "I love the choices you make. It inspires me. Is there any chance you'll stay?" *Wake up next to Will every morning? Have someone to hold me when the thunder comes. For the rest of my life? That would be wonderful, but that would have to come from him. I can't ask to stay.* Stella shook her head.

"So where is home?" Elaine asked innocently.

"That's just it, I don't know." Stella's fingers on the fabric stopped moving, and her eyes glazed over.

Susan and Elaine fussed around and helped her get everything packed and loaded without asking her any further questions. They told her they loved her choices and liked the pewter embellishments she showed them. They talked about the weather but didn't pry anymore.

Stella knew they were being kind, but it didn't help her one bit.

She drove over to pick up the second-hand chair and dropped it at Elaine's. At both places, they spoke about nothing in general, and Stella drifted through the conversations. *How can you not know where home is? And even if you don't know, you can't expect William just to move you in. Life doesn't go like that.*

As she kicked off her shoes and rubbed her sore foot. As scared as she felt, Stella made a promise to herself that she couldn't tell Will about not knowing where home was because she didn't want him to feel sorry for her and make decisions based on what he thought she should do.

Chapter 37

Checking her e-mail, she searched for a reply from India. Stella had asked her to use her skills on some of the landscape photographs from Hursts Bridge. She wanted monochrome blue tones to better suit William's space. When she found the file, she was delighted with the images India had sent her. She didn't hesitate to call her cousin.

"Hello?"

"Did you have a nice birthday in the end?" Stella considered her answer carefully.

"I did. Thanks for the images."

"Did you get them?"

"Yes, thank you. I think they're going to work great in the primary."

"So, you're going with blue then?"

"With cream and touches of pewter."

"Sounds like you have a plan. I guess you always do."

"It's going to be a whole lot better than the black and gold it was going to be."

"Black and gold can look good."

"Oh, it can, and I'm doing that for Marco."

"How is it going with the big guy?"

"I'm doing another room for him. His bedroom this time."

"That sounds intimate."

"Don't be getting any ideas, anyway, William, with his blonde hair and blue eyes, needs blue. Black is much too harsh for him."

"To wear?"

"He's too soft for something as brutal as black and gold."

"Anymore kisses?" Stella closed her eyes, and India backpedalled. "Forget I asked. I know how complicated life can get. When things were new with Charlie and me, other people's questions drove me crazy. I was so busy trying to work it out in my own head, but then I had Katie to talk to."

"Yes, well, it's not like I can talk to Sarah, is it?"

"Look, Stella, I'm not Sarah, and I'm not related to William. But I do know your family, I've met his. You can always talk to me. I'm good at keeping secrets."

"I wish this wasn't a secret, but thanks for the offer."

"I'd say don't work too hard, but I know I'd be wasting my breath. So, you take care. If I can help with anything, let me know."

"Thanks, I'm going to head for a shower. It's been a long day.

It was past midnight when Stella stepped out of the shower and wrapped herself in a large white towel. Unplugging her phone from the charger, she made her way over to the bed and slumped down. Being unsure where she stood with William, she'd buried herself in work, and now she could feel her body complaining. The sex, if that's what it was, had been incredible, but was it just sex, or was it a statement of something more? She still didn't understand what was happening with Vanessa. William insisted it was nothing, and yet Vanessa behaved as if William belonged to her.

Men, why was it always so complicated with men?

India said it had been complicated with Charlie, and yet she'd not met two people more suited to each other, and she couldn't begin to understand what had kept them apart in the first place.

Stella rubbed her hair with a small towel, undecided if now was as good a time as any to see how her last video had done. She'd spliced together some footage from Davey to show how Will's technology could integrate with design. As soon as her phone powered up, it came alive with notifications.

What on earth have I missed?

She spotted a series of messages from Davey.

Davey: Congratulations. Way to go.

Davey: Have you seen your Instagram?

Davey: Stella, I'm so proud of you. Thank you for tagging us.

Davey: Is there any chance I can pop over and do some setup videos?

Davey: I was thinking time-lapse. What do you think?

Stella: It's a crazy week. I'm sure we can fit something in.

Stella: Can I call you tomorrow?

Davey: Sure. Have a great night.

Wondering what all the fuss was about, she opened her profile. The number of views and comments on her last video hit her first. It was one thing for people to watch the video and then move on; it was another for them to stop and leave her a message.

The excitement bubbled in her veins, and she couldn't wait to share this with someone—not just anyone. Stella needed to share this with William. Clutching her towel, she set off running down the corridor, shouting his name.

William appeared at his bedroom door.

"Hey, steady on there, I'm here. Where's the fire?" Will held her wrists, and Stella gripped her towel.

"Will, look, they love it."

"Who? What do they love?"

"My latest video of all your magic. The numbers are amazing. Look at how many people have watched it."

"How many of those are going to buy this place?"

"I know it's not buyers, but it's agents and the press."

"The press?"

"Yes. I think we are going to need to extend the press event."

Will tightened the towel around her and smiled.

"Come in here and explain it to me." He ushered her into his room and passed her a hairdryer.

"You get dried, and I'll go get some champagne. Then you can explain it all to me."

Stella was so excited that when William arrived carrying two glasses and an open bottle, she was still struggling to juggle his hairdryer.

"I can't do the simplest thing. Is it this dryer? It's silly." She confessed. Will smiled as he handed her a glass of champagne.

"Here, you drink this and let me do your hair."

"Oh no, you don't have to do that."

"I want to." Will sat on the bed, with the dryer beside him. "Come here." He patted the space between his legs. Stella perched on the edge, and he pulled her firmly back between his thighs.

"That's better." He ran his fingers from the base of her scalp up into her hair. "This is so soft. It's always been like this, hasn't it?"

Stella nodded without speaking. She could feel the warmth of his body behind her. It felt too good, and she didn't want to break the spell. She took another gulp of her champagne.

"Hey, don't get drunk without me." He tugged gently at her hair. "Actually, don't get drunk at all."

Stella began to wriggle. The adrenaline from seeing her account explode like that was still coursing through her veins. The bubbles from the champagne only heightened her buzz. On his bedside table, notifications kept dinging on her phone.

She closed her eyes as Will worked on her hair, his fingers coaxing her to relax.

"That's it, sit still. That's a good girl." His arm swung around her waist and pulled her closer to him. She leant into his hard body. He was clearly aroused, which only made Stella squirm more between his legs.

The dryer was gone now, and William's fingers gently ran along the muscles up and down her neck. Stella's eyes closed as she leant into the feeling. William began to knead her shoulders, and Stella rolled her head as he moved over her skin.

She let out a soft moan when his lips trailed down her neck and across her shoulders. Her skin was alive under his touch. This morning, she had felt confused; now, she just wanted more. She stood up from the bed, leaving him bewildered. His hands stuck in mid-air, his eyes closed.

"Stella. I'm sorry. I should have asked."

"Will, we need to talk." He nodded his reply as her towel fell to the ground. "But not right now."

"OK." Will still looked lost.

"Right now, I need you to make love to me."

Without a word, William stood up from the bed, carefully placing both glasses on the side. He picked up the towel from the floor and folded it neatly on his ottoman.

Stella sat on the edge of the bed, and he approached her. She pulled at the waist of his jeans, manoeuvring him to stand between her legs, and without pause, she undid his jeans with much more ease than the first time.

Stella looked up to watch his face as she eased his erection into her hands. The silky softness over the steel-like core held her transfixed until

she let her lips explore him. William's hands went to the hair he had so lovingly dried earlier.

"Much as I'm enjoying this, I'm going to ask you to stop."

"No. I think you need to let go. We have all night, Will."

His grip tightened as she licked slowly now, up his length and let her tongue circle his crown. Stopping to taste the pre-cum that sat on the tip. With a smile, she took all she could into her mouth and stroked her hand around his sac. Pulling him closer with a second hand on his thigh, she could feel the muscles under her fingers contract.

"Stella. I'm going to …"

She didn't stop. She wanted him to have this release so they could relax and enjoy the next stage of their lovemaking. His rush came with a force that shocked her, and she pulled back.

She lay down on his bed, watching as Will gripped himself and left to clean up.

Stella felt exposed, lying naked on his bed. She shuffled her way up to the soft white pillow she knew would smell of him.

William walked back towards her, naked himself, and threw three condom packets on the pillow beside her.

"Three?"

"You said we had all night. I can get more." He smiled. This was the playful William she loved. "Now, where were we?" He reached over and passed her glass and took his.

"I was telling you about our viral video."

Will leant over her and took her empty glass away.

"I like how you said, 'our video', but I think you should give yourself more credit." His lips touched hers. The news and the alcohol had helped Stella's excitement levels, but the touch of his lips as his hand trailed up her arm, lit up her skin.

William Thoresby didn't just know how to light up furniture.

He pulled her under him, with short laps, he licked his way up her neck to her ear. He nuzzled in, whispering to her.

"You don't know what you do to me, do you? When you asked me to make love to you and then undo my jeans like that." The hum of his voice on her neck buzzed her flesh. "Now, tell me more about what you want me to do."

Stella didn't answer him. Instead, she slipped away from him and moved onto her hands and knees. William moved behind her and bent to nip at the soft roundness of her behind.

He took his time stroking her and exploring between her legs. Stella felt frustrated and looked over her shoulder to encourage him.

"Patience, little one. After all, we have all night."

"I'm starting to regret saying that now."

William reached for a condom and, without wasting any more time, put it on and leant back towards her.

"I hope you are ready for this." He teased her entrance with his crown and pushed gently forward. Easing himself into her slowly. He pulled back and thrust forward again. Working deeper inside her.

Stella pushed back. She needed more. One night without him had left her so hungry.

Together, they set up a rhythm that worked. Stella felt herself clenching around him as he seemed to grow. William growled in her ear as he pulled out.

"I need to see your face. Roll over."

She shuffled up the bed, watching his face and the perspiration on his forehead. She reached up to wipe her finger across his brow.

"You're making me work hard again." He grunted. She smiled softly as he moved to enter her once more. This time, their eyes locked as he pushed into her. His hands went under her hips, lifting her and changing the angle.

"Star, that's it. Fuck Star. Come for me. I want to feel it. Star now, let go."

As they came together in a wonderful climax, a jumble of arms and legs, the computer interrupted them.

<<I'm sorry, William, I don't know how to do that.>>

"I think we need a new wake word for the computer."

They rolled together on the sheets, laughing, their arms locked around each other.

"Please sleep here tonight?"

"I think I can be persuaded."

It was the beginning of a night of making love, sipping champagne and sleeping peacefully in each other's arms. When light filtered into his bedroom, Stella woke to Will sitting on the edge of the bed, ready for his swim. She forced her eyes to open and then look at his face rather than that delicate piece of skin just under his arm.

"Star, can you sleep in here again tonight?"

"Do you want me to?"

"I don't want to spend all day distracted by wondering if I can make love to you tonight."

"But we still aren't telling the world yet?"

"Is it wrong that I want to keep you to myself?"

"So, it's not because you don't want to tell Sarah?"

"I was hoping you would do that."

"Maybe we can do it together ... when we have got past this launch."

"But tonight?"

"I think I can do that."

William kissed her. "Good."

He framed her face and dropped his lips to hers. This kiss was something more—a feeling of being home. Will's arms had felt like home for a long time, but Stella was no longer wondering where this was going.

Chapter 38

On Friday afternoon, Grigori and his team were trying to install the appliances in the kitchen, and Stella attempted to stay out of the way. She needed to focus as she painstakingly added pewter outliner to the glass shades for the lights at the side of the bed. The sketch for the headboard lay across the table from her. Her eyes kept flicking to it. Every time her eyes landed on it, she had to fight the idea of Will making love to her in it.

Even when she'd finished, she became so utterly lost in her thoughts that she jumped when Will burst through the workroom door whilst she was scrubbing outliner off her hands in the huge sink. Her heart pounded faster at his sudden appearance from her daydreams.

Rushing up behind her, he threw his arms around her waist, lifting her into the air.

"God, you smell wonderful." He breathed into her neck.

Stella shrieked as her wet hands waved in the air.

"Will! Put me down."

"No, I'm going to hold on to you. I'm not letting you go."

"I didn't realise it was that late."

"It's not. I'm back early."

"Ha. And you think I'm going to stop working too?"

"Well …"

"We've a deadline, or did you forget?"

"Then maybe we can get something done together. I loved working with you in the cinema."

"The team have been busy in the kitchen all day. It's probably best that we stay out of their way. So that limits things a bit."

"Did I miss anything here today?"

"Not in here." Stella's eye ran around her room and landed on the parcel that had arrived an hour earlier. "Oh, that came from New York."

"Is it a surprise?" Will whispered in her ear, sending a shiver down her back.

"It's from my mum for my birthday. A painting. Do you want to see it?"

"Yes." Will glanced over to the brown paper package. "It's big."

"Now, can I dry my hands?"

"If I can have a kiss first."

Stella's wet hands were still up in the air as Will held her face, kissing her tenderly but firmly on the lips. Stella turned away with a smile and finished washing and then drying her hands.

Will picked up her fabric scissors and passed them to her. Stella looked at him, her brows pulled together.

"I thought a guy like you would understand about tools." She took them from him, hung them back up in place, and pulled out a box knife. She ran her hand over the top of the package. "Oh! She sent two!"

The knife slashed through the top layer of brown paper, exposing more packaging. William sat down, and Stella continued the unpacking. It didn't take her long to reveal two paintings in shades of bright orange. She stood them up against the wall and took a step back. Will touched her hand and laced his fingers with hers as she silently admired the artwork. When she still didn't speak or move her eyes, he gently pulled her to sit on his knee.

"Don't you like them?"

"Oh, I love them, and I know just where we are going to hang them."

She stood and picked up a tape and a level, then smiled at Will.

"If you want to work with me, can you carry these?"

Will didn't hesitate to pick up the paintings.

"Follow me," she said from the doorway.

"I'd follow you anywhere."

Will was very precise in hanging the paintings. It made her smile. He was always making her smile.

"I haven't done anything about dinner." She said over her shoulder.

"We still have steak; we can cook outside and avoid the kitchen."

"Could we swim first?" Stella's eyes sparkled. "I have a new bikini," she teased, "the red one."

"Huh, together?" He asked, and Stella nodded. Will's eyes glazed, then he shook his head. "You go swim. I'll set up dinner, and then I'll join you."

Chapter 39

Will had no problem imagining what Stella would look like in that red bikini. After all, he had been doing it all day. In theory, he was trying to find some money to cover the costs of statuary testing their latest product so they could release it. He knew that if his team said it was ready, it would pass all the necessary tests. He'd tried to concentrate, but thinking of her warm body next to his when he woke up that morning made any other cognitive thought impossible. He'd gone back to the house, telling himself he could work in his office there.

Relief flooded his system as soon as he found her still there, and he realised how much he loved her. He wanted to come home to her every day. *How can I ask her to give up her life to stay here with me?*

He needed to make tonight special, so they both had a great memory of their time together. He hoped it might encourage her to want to stay.

Outside, the air was cooler, so he lit the fire pit before moving the pool cover and checking the water's temperature. He was fussing in the outdoor kitchen when Stella slipped quietly into the pool. *His Pool! His Star, in his pool.* Just the idea caused his skin to tingle.

His eyes remained glued to the water as Stella's body, clad in the simple Santa red costume, glided towards the opposite end. The tension had left her face as she turned to swim back. William knew only too well the effect that swimming could have. It'd become a daily ritual for him. He lit the grill and replaced the cover, leaving it to heat.

When he joined her in the water, he noted how quickly her body responded to his presence. Will pulled up beside her as her fingers touched the end of the pool. She stood smiling up at him, shaking the water from her hair. Will reached out to wipe a few drops from her brow.

"I've missed you today." He said softly.

"Is that why you came home early?"

"It might be. Did you miss me?"

Stella's smile was wide, her head tilted back to look up at him.

"Why would I miss you?"

"Let me remind you." He kissed her as tenderly as he could. The passion was building up inside him, but he pulled away.

"Are you hungry yet?"

"Hmm." She nodded.

"You swim some more; I'll go organise dinner."

Usually, Will struggled with the urge to move the steak around on the grill. Tonight, it wasn't an issue. He seasoned the meat and laid it on the grill, then watched as Stella swam lengths in his pool beneath a Southern California sky. The sunset was spectacular, and Will had to ask himself if that was because she was there in his pool in that red bikini. Only when he smelt the steak browning did he remember to turn it over.

"These need a few more minutes to rest, if you want to get dressed."

Stella's blue eyes sparkled as she watched him from the pool. The hint of mischief he knew so well was there. *I think she lives to tease me.*

"There doesn't seem much point in getting dressed again."

Will pulled a robe out of a locker and held it open.

"Hang on, I'll take this wet costume off." Remembering how coy she had been that morning, Will closed his eyes and offered up the robe.

"You can stop pretending, Will. I know you peeked last time."

"Sorry," he said softly.

"Don't be, hell, we had just slept together. I guess it's me, or should I say it, because of our history." She held out her arms for him to slip on the robe. Will eased it onto her naked body, wrapping his arm around her and giving her a gentle squeeze. The robe was far too large for her delicate frame, and she tried to turn back the cuffs.

"This is going to make eating dinner a bit difficult." He muttered.

"The cuffs, you mean?"

Will laughed. "No, you being naked."

"Will, I've had to cope with you in those tiny things you swim in."

"I'm pretty sure I haven't sat at the table to eat in them."

"Like you are now."

They exchanged smiles, and Will carried two plates over to the table he'd prepared earlier. Standing back next to the grill, he asked.

"Now, what would you like to drink?"

"I guess this is my birthday meal. What did you have planned?"

"I picked out a nice red wine to go with the meat. But you can have whatever you want… well, as long as we have it."

"If you chose the wine before, let's have that."

Will produced two wine glasses and a bottle of Châteauneuf-du-Pape.

"How come you've no furniture but such well-matched glassware?"

"Well…"

"And Châteauneuf?"

"I couldn't decide between a wine I knew you'd know and something local. I had this in. I'm hoping you will stay longer to try the local wines. I've got some of Patrick's wine you can try another time."

"Patrick? The shy guy from Marco's?"

"Yes. He owns a vineyard with his sister. You'll love her, and their wine is amazing. I've been working on creating a better monitoring system for their fermentation vats."

"Will, have you realised yet that right now, you need to be calling in any favours you can?"

"Favours?"

"Like when we dress that wine cupboard, would Patrick be able to lend us some display bottles?"

"I don't think I could ask."

"It might help the winery to be seen in these photos. It couldn't hurt."

"I'm not sure."

"Do you have any of their wine around?"

"Yes, he gave me a case when I was working over there."

"Right, I'll get my phone; you go fetch some bottles." Will was confused but followed her into the house.

By the time Will returned, Stella was rearranging the table.

"I'm sure the steak will be going cold."

"This won't take long. Just open that wine."

"I already opened the other …" The look on her face stopped him from saying more. Instead, he opened the wine and poured two glasses. Stella then took what Will thought were more than enough photos.

"Can we eat now?"

"Sure."

She finally sat down at the table, and Will waited for her to cut and put the first piece into her mouth. She closed her eyes, tasting and enjoying the food. Finally, he could relax. He had fed her.

Stella crossed her legs as she tasted Patrick's wine. Her robe fell open, and Will could see the full length of her legs below the glass table. She opened her phone, looking through the images.

"This one will work." He watched her brightly coloured nails tapping across the screen.

Enjoying all the tastes of SoCal with the team from @ThoresbyTech and @WhitesWines. #watchthisspace #designerslife

The phone went into her pocket, letting them finish the meal in peace.

"How's the foot?"

"Tender, but I'll live. Don't worry, it didn't stop me working."

"Look, I appreciate all you are doing. Please take care of yourself."

"Says the man who leaves the house before I get up." Will sighed and looked away from those eyes that seemed to see right to his core. "And I'll stop when we get to the big day; I'd like to guess that you always work these long hours." When she squeezed his hand, he looked back to meet her gaze. "Promise me, when we sell, you'll look at your team's and your own workload."

"If we sell."

"WHEN we sell." She insisted. Her smile melted William.

"OK, when we sell – now, is there any cake left?"

"Yes. Don't think I missed you avoiding the point about workloads."

"I'll get the cake."

Stella swiped her finger to pick up the last crumb of cake. Will couldn't help but broaden his smile as she climbed onto his knee.

"Thank you for a wonderful birthday, Will." He leant forward to kiss her, and as their lips touched, his phone vibrated on his thigh.

"Get it."

"It can wait. I'm not sure I can."

His hand trailed between her legs. His excitement grew as his lips played with hers. Teasing and tormenting.

When the answerphone kicked in, he recognised Patrick's voice.

"Hey, Mr Thoresby Tech. Why didn't you tell me who your Star was? I'm glad to see you are enjoying yourself. Call me."

"How the…"

"I tagged him, well, the winery." Stella popped a kiss on his lips, then stood up. Bouncing on her toes.

"Call him!"

"Now?"

"He said to call. We need 240 bottles."

"I can't ask …"

"Look, give him a chance to say no … but don't be afraid to ask. We can build them into the photography. I was thinking that the wine cellar you designed is pretty special. We could look at doing a series of articles on the different fabulous units and gradually release them. We just need to find the right journalist … and photographer."

Will gripped her robe and pulled her closer, kissing her stomach.

"I was busy."

"I can wait. Now, ring the man."

With Stella now off his knee and pacing whilst looking through her phone, he pulled out his own and returned Patrick's call.

"Hey man, what's happening? Got that house finished yet?"

"We're getting closer. I'm just returning your call."

"You should be enjoying that wine. I hope it's just the two of you."

"Yes." His eyes travelled to Stella, her brain clearly working overtime as she strode around the pool, her robe blowing in the evening breeze.

"Well, thank her for the tag. The website blew up, and we were wondering why. My sister went wild when she saw Stella's post. So now I'm in trouble for not telling her Stella was at Marco's. When she found out she was designing for you, she went crazy."

"I presume that's a good thing?"

"Er, yes. Is she there much longer? Can I send another case?"

"Any chance of you sending some more bottles?"

"Sure, how many?"

Stella stood in front of him, jigging about. Her eyes danced across Will's face.

"Look, Stella was pretty excited herself. I'm in trouble for not telling her about the winery. Can I let her explain?"

"Hello, Stella."

"Hello, Patrick. I need 240 bottles to dress this new wine store Will designed. If we could have them for the launch event and some product photography, that would be ace. We could look at returning them or buying them if the plot sells." Having spewed it all out, Stella bit her lip.

"Sale or return?"

"Yes." William studied her face and took her hand.

"When's the big day?"

"Just over a week away." Will gave her hand a gentle squeeze.

"I could bring them myself on Thursday. Would that be OK?"

"That would be perfect."

"Can I ask who is doing your catering? Do I need to talk to Will?"

"I'm not sure, maybe Vanessa…"

"Oh, her, forget it. Hang on. My sister is talking in my ear. It's probably easier if you two speak to each other."

"Hi Stella, I'm a big fan."

"Thanks."

"Is it a press day?"

"Exclusive agents in the morning. We've invited the press for later."

"Could we elbow in – provide wine and glasses, etc?"

"Sounds wonderful, but I'd need to check."

"OK. Look, why don't you come out and see for yourself?"

"That's kind. I'll talk to Will and see what we can do."

William watched an excited Stella swapping contact details with Poppy. It made his heart sing that she was happy.

"OK, see you soon." She ended the call and threw her arms around his neck; kissing him hard, she declared, "I love you!"

At last. He lifted her as she swung her legs to wrap around his waist and carried her to his bed.

Chapter 40

On Sunday morning, Stella and Will had a leisurely breakfast and then went their separate ways to work for a few hours before lunch. Having the house to themselves always felt good, and Will hummed as he worked in his office. He was looking forward to taking Stella to the winery; it almost felt like a date. It was a romantic location, and he had plans for the return journey.

He knew that Poppy would love Stella. It sounded like she already knew her blog from the comments she made when he had called to make the plans for today. *Of course, everyone loves Stella, and why not?* But part of him was itching to see how the monitoring systems he had worked on for Patrick were performing, too.

The time was dragging, and he didn't feel like he was making any progress. His brain was far too distracted by thoughts of his little sister's best friend. As if to summon her, his sister's name appeared on his phone screen.

"Morning, sister, how are you?"

"I'm fine. The better question is, how are you? I've tried ringing Stella, but she isn't answering my calls."

"Well, we're working again today, so she might not have heard it, but that's par for the course. Just over a week left, the construction team are having a day off, but Stella and I are doing a couple of jobs this morning." Will knew that Stella had her phone glued to her.

Why is she avoiding Sarah? Probably for the same reason I don't really want to talk to her. I don't know how I'm going to tell any of my family about this, especially my sister.

"Are you going to make her work all day?"

Will smiled.

"No, we are going to visit a winery this afternoon. I admit it's partly for work, but I think she will enjoy the trip out. It's a fabulous drive."

"That sounds wonderful. She needs some downtime, Will. You promise you'll look after her."

"Of course, you don't have to ask."

"Sadly, I feel I need to remind you. And tell her to ring me."

It was just the excuse William needed to leave his desk and go looking for Stella. He found her washing the tiniest paintbrush he had ever seen. She never ceased to amaze him.

"It's going to take you a long time to paint a wall with that brush."

It was an awful joke; one his dad would be proud of. It didn't stop Stella from smiling at him.

"Hilarious, Will. It's a good job I haven't been painting walls. I mainly leave that to Paulo; he's pretty amazing. Did you see how quickly he sprayed the basement?" Will pulled her into his arms, kissing her nose.

"God, I love that we are alone, and I can do this whenever I want."

"It is rather nice, isn't it?"

"Sarah phoned. She's worried because you aren't answering her calls."

"Agh! I'm trying to get to the 'we can tell everyone stage' before I talk to her. She always asks awkward questions that I'm tiptoeing around."

"I know," he fingered the locket she wore. Another sign she was his.

"I'd better get showered. What time did you want to leave?"

"Poppy said two o'clock would be a good time. So, we can eat lunch here or on the way."

The approach to the winery was littered with orange poppies with smatterings of blues from the shrubs. Stella pressed her back into the butter-soft seat in William's swish red car.

"You always wanted a car like this, didn't you?"

"Yes. I guess I did." Having her at his side as he drove through this fabulous landscape made his heart dance. *How can I make this last? Would she ever stay here with me? Would this ever be enough to get her to leave her friends?*

"Does it make you happy?"

"On days like today, it does. Are you happy, Stella?"

"Yes." She smiled across at him. "Yes, today, I'm very happy."

They drove on, with Stella taking what seemed to Will to be hundreds of photos. She was happy, and that made him happy. He hadn't been able to stop smiling all day.

My face is aching, but I love it. Who knew life could feel like this?

"I knew they were called California poppies. I didn't realise they grew so wild."

It had been a few months since he'd been at the winery to help Patrick. It looked to have undergone a few changes. Red, white and blue bunting hung over a barn at the side. Over the door hung a huge red sign that read 'Poppy's Kitchen'. Will took her hand and led her over to the large barn door.

"That must be Poppy's new venture." Before he could think or react, Poppy bounded out into the courtyard, followed by Patrick. He looked down at their hands locked together. *Shit, Marco will know in half an hour.*

"Don't tell me Marco is right again?"

Will's eyes closed. Stella dropped his hand and rubbed her arm. He knew it was probably a waste of energy, but he had to try.

"Could you leave off spreading the news until we get past the big day? Please?"

"You mean, would I keep him in the dark for a whole week so I can gloat when he tells me? Now let me think," he teased. "I think I could do that. And I won't even ask why."

He moved his attention to Stella. He hugged her and kissed each cheek.

"Lovely to see you again, Stella. May I introduce my sister? This is Poppy." Poppy hugged Stella tighter than her brother, and together they rushed into the barn, leaving William and Patrick to follow behind.

"I was going to ask which wines you wanted me to bring over on Thursday, but I'm guessing those two will be sorting all that out."

"I'm pretty sure Star will be picking bottles for the aesthetic. Sorry, mate."

"It's a good job they all taste great, then, isn't it?"

In the barn, they found Poppy making coffee from a large Italian machine as Stella browsed the shelves of jars and packets. Patrick indicated a table covered with a red and white cloth, and they sat down to watch.

"Well, I take it things are going better with Stella, but what about the build? Do you think it will be ready?"

"In theory, yes, but with a build, anything can and usually does go wrong."

"After seeing what you've done here, I'm looking forward to what you've done with a wine fridge. Would it work in here?"

Will's eyes scanned the large barn. It still had a rustic feel, from the signage to the wine barrels stacked at one end.

"Possibly, or I could create something that suited your needs more."

"We've spent a fair amount of money already, or should I say Poppy has. She says that events make sense. They drive people to come out here on any particular day."

"She's right," Stella said as she slipped into a chair next to Will. "It's a great space. Love the signage, it goes with the country look". Stella nodded at the barrels in the corner.

Poppy placed a tray of coffee onto the table and took the final chair.

"It goes with the budget."

"The barrels couldn't be cheap, even if you are in the trade."

"They fell off a lorry, quite literally. They wouldn't hold wine anymore. Just don't look around the back. I'm glad you like it, though. I can't wait to hear what you think I can do to improve it." Both Poppy and Stella seemed to be lit up from inside, and Will couldn't help wondering what it would be like with her permanently in his life. Patrick was the one to get the conversation back on track.

"So, what can we bring you? Will seems to think the labels might be more important than the wine." He used a mock, offended voice, which made Stella blush. Will saved her.

"I love all your wine, so I can go with her picking for the looks."

"The thing can have three different temperature zones if that helps," Stella said, trying to talk about the wine rather than how good it looks. "I hope that means we can display more of your range."

"Don't tell Poppy that, or we will definitely need to buy one."

"You can see it properly on Thursday, but here's a photo." She passed her phone to Patrick, who passed it on to Poppy.

"Right, you and I could pick out some labels. We've eight varieties at the moment, but we change the label each year, so we could pick out two vintages in a couple of varieties."

"Whatever works for Stella. Are you sure you are OK with us buying after the event or returning them if we haven't sold?"

"I'm sure. If you don't sell, we can talk about buying that fridge." Patrick grinned.

“Judging by the number of comments on the video you posted, you’ll be selling plenty.” Poppy pulled out her phone. “You have 50 thousand views now and over a thousand comments. It's gone even higher today.”

“I haven’t looked.”

“I don’t suppose I can persuade you to do a post whilst you’re here. It might help our geotag.”

“Of course. Let’s go do something now, and you can show me what you were thinking about for refreshments.”

“Does that mean we could do the catering?” Poppy looked excited until she saw Stella’s face.

“Sorry, I won’t know until tomorrow. I’m presuming we already have something in place. We can find out in the morning; we may be able to cancel it or switch to something else. We can talk through the possibilities, though.” They wandered off talking as fast as ever, both seemed happy to have made a new friend.

“Another coffee?” Patrick offered.

“No thanks. How is the monitoring going?”

“Great, it's far more accurate than the commercial system we had, but I guess we’ll know better when we taste the wine. Do you want to look?”

Will stood up and followed Patrick to the barn containing the fermentation vats and other machinery he hadn’t worked out yet. His eyes were still focused on Stella as she talked animatedly with Poppy.

“You can take your eyes off her, she isn’t at Marco’s now.”

Will pulled his eyes away from Stella and looked at his companion and the stainless-steel towering above them.

“I’m sorry.”

“It’s new, I get it. It was pretty funny watching Marco play with you.”

“How did he even know she was here?”

“I don’t know how he does it, but I’m pretty sure all that information is how he makes money. He pretends to be the Playboy, so people don’t see him as a threat.”

“Except the husbands.”

“Well, yes.”

Patrick seemed excited to share how much easier he was finding the new systems that Will had created. As they walked back to meet the others, Patrick turned his head to look at Will.

“You could sell these, you know.”

Will gulped, looking out at the pristine rows of vines beyond the barn.

"Happy to keep helping you and working on what you think you need, but right now I need to focus."

"On the building project … or Stella?"

It was a huge sigh that Will let out as he looked back at Patrick.

"So, you were all having a laugh at my expense that night?"

"I don't know, John was pretty flattered she knew who he was. He isn't so well-known over here. And Marco, well, he is always interested in a pretty girl." Will scowled. Patrick laughed at him. "Don't worry while he thinks you've a chance; he won't risk your friendship."

"Are you sure? He sails pretty close to the wind so much of the time." As he said back at the table, his eyes were drawn to Stella, who walked towards them carrying a plate. "Time to change the subject."

"Will, taste these cheeses." Stella thrust the plate under his face, and he leant back. "We could have these, look how great these platters look, and they will pair well with the wine…"

"Stella, steady; as we said, I like the idea, but we need to check what is already in the pipeline."

"I know, but you need to taste this stuff. Even if we don't use it this time, you might want to think about it for other events. You must need stuff at the office, even."

"I don't usually get involved in that."

"I know you leave it to Vanessa, but…"

Poppy's face screwed up at that name.

"Say no more. I've tried talking to her about catering at Christmas. Is she just a snob?"

"Vanessa … she just wants to protect the brand." Stella frowned, and Will tried again. "What I'm trying to say is, although she can come over as protective, she is very good at her job."

"If you say so." Poppy didn't seem convinced, and Will didn't like the scowl on Stella's face. *Is she jealous? And Poppy? Does everyone have a problem with Vanessa*? It made him study Stella's face again before continuing.

"I really want to use you guys, it makes sense. It really does. Stella is the one who can see the ways we can use your products in our images. She's the visual one."

"Stop, Will," she blushed, and he finally made himself look away.

"Marco is right, it really is love, isn't it?" Poppy sighed. "Let's go pick some wine by the labels then."

Patrick's groan made Stella blush.

"I'm sorry, Patrick."

"It's good to be honest in business." Patrick offered them both a weak smile. "It's interesting, although we look at labels as a sales tool, I don't think we've ever considered how they would look lying in a fridge."

Poppy stood up, "Come on, Stella."

"Do you want me to come?" William's half-hearted offer made everyone else laugh.

"It's OK, spend some time with Patrick."

"Are you sure?"

"Yes." He watched her leave.

"You look like a couple. It feels like you belong together, but you did that night at Marco's. I guess that's why he's so sure about you two."

"We grew up together. That's what makes it so easy and so difficult at the same time."

"Don't they like her?"

"They adore her."

"Oh, I see, is this about you worrying about things going wrong before they even start. Damn, Marco is so good at this."

"Marco said that?"

"Come on, you know the guy. He loves watching people. It's like we are all some social experiment for his entertainment." Will froze. "I mean in the nicest possible way. He's always helping his friends. I've never seen him drink wine, but he has me deliver three cases every week, even when he's away."

"He does have a lot of people over. I'm sure it gets drunk."

"And he was right about you two. So why is it a secret?"

"I don't know about you, but I haven't really had a serious relationship. And this one is just so different."

"That's good, isn't it?"

"I mean the set-up. I know her so well, so we aren't getting to know each other. Our parents know each other. We're already living together. But I hadn't seen her in ten years, and this trip is the nearest thing we have had to a date since she arrived." Will stopped talking, but he could

see that Patrick was beginning to see the problem. “There is nothing normal about this relationship.”

“I see.”

“And we are both so focused on the launch.”

“Then what?”

Will took a deep breath, and before he could find the words to explain that he had no idea, Stella returned with Poppy.

“We’ve got wine to taste.”

“What’s in the bag?” A puzzled Will clutched the back of his neck, making Poppy laugh.

“I’ve packed up some snacks for the workers.”

“Does that mean you’re ready to leave?”

“I guess so.”

Will jangled his keys as they made their way to the car. Patrick carried a new case of wine. Stella and Poppy carried bags of cheese, crackers, biscuits, and fruit.

“Thanks, Poppy, this will keep the team going.”

“Patrick and I’ll be over on Thursday. I'm looking forward to seeing it all.”

Stella shook her hand as William closed the trunk of the car.

“I can't thank you guys enough. We’ll be in touch tomorrow.”

The hugs that followed showed Will that he had done the right thing in bringing Stella to meet them. Poppy's kitchen looked like an event space that they could use in the future. This had been such a great day, the two of them being together without hiding. Still working, but so relaxed. William wanted it to last forever. He knew it must end sometime, but not just yet.

As they set off toward home, the sun was slowly reaching the horizon over the ocean, and Will took a right turn.

“Tonight, I want to sleep in my room, I mean, Sarah’s room, you know what I mean.” Will felt that like a physical slap.

“If that’s what you want.” They drove a little further to enjoy the fabulous colours of the sunset, and Stella took image after image. She turned her camera to Will and snapped a few photos of him, too.

“We don’t need to have sex; we could just cuddle … or sleep if that's what you want.”

"Pardon?"

"I get that you might want to keep your own room and all that, I get that … and I understand you might not want sex every night, but…"

"Will, let me stop you there. I'd like us both to move into Sarah's so I can start working on the room you're currently in before the launch. The main bedroom is still a work in progress, but Sarah's room is finished."

"Oh!" He blushed.

"Oh indeed."

"Yes, that makes sense. I'm sure you are enjoying it, but I will be so happy when this is all over."

"Do you think the team will notice?"

"From the comments I've been picking up all week, I'm not sure we are fooling anyone." He sighed. "It will all be over soon." Stella's face twisted away as he spoke. When she bit her lip, he reached over and squeezed her hand. Stella resumed taking photos.

"Thanks for this, the winery. It was a great idea. You were right; I do like them. Their marketing team has started sharing our posts, which is helping my posts reach a wider audience. I do like a good Win-Win."

"I can't say I understand it, but if it works, I will be very grateful."

"Is this a different road? Aren't we going home?" *Home? She called it home.* If only she meant what he wanted her to mean.

"I thought we would go back the scenic route. You haven't seen much of the coast."

"Thank you."

They drove through incredible landscapes under a multi-coloured sky. Stella looked relaxed at his side, and he wanted to feel the same. There was something comforting about knowing he would be sleeping with her again tonight, but he couldn't help but fear what happened next. The idea of her leaving was more than he could face.

Eventually, William turned into a car park set amongst an area of dunes. Stella looked at him, her questions in her eyes.

"I wasn't ready to go back just yet. I wanted to enjoy our day together a little bit longer before the rest of the world invades us."

"I love a walk at the coast. The air is so … inspiring, is that the word?"

"It's not my area, but there are people who'll tell you all about the coastal air here. They say these amazing sunsets are not just the water vapour over the ocean, but the smog particles from downtown L.A."

They'd reached the beach and Stella slipped off her shoes. William took them from her and held her hand.

This would be a good opportunity to talk about our future.

He squeezed her hand and smiled at her.

Nope, I'm not going to spoil this perfect day.

They didn't speak until they came to a rocky outcrop.

"I hate to say this, but I guess it's time to go back."

"One last selfie, Will. I don't want to forget today."

Will stood behind her, his arms locked over her shoulders, and they both smiled into the lens, with the magical sunset behind them. Stella tapped at her screen and looked up at him.

"I've sent you a copy."

"Thank you." Will kissed her nose and took her hand to walk back to the car.

Chapter 41

Waking up in Sarah's room, Will knew he needed to change things, but how did he tell Stella? Rolling over, he wrapped his arm across her waist, pulling her closer.

"Star, are you awake?"

"Good morning."

"I was just thinking …"

"Yes?"

"Should we put some of the old linen on this bed until the launch? I mean, keep this nice?"

"That is probably a brilliant idea. I can get this laundered and pressed." She kissed his cheek.

"Great." Will didn't hide his relief. And Stella raised on one elbow.

"Is this too much colour for you?"

"I didn't want to say that."

"Will, this is your home; you should speak up."

Isn't it your home too?

"I only want you to be happy."

And sleeping in a bed, you keep calling my sister's, is not helping.

"I am happy. Didn't I tell you that yesterday?"

"I had a great time. Can I take you to the ocean again? Get you out of here for a while. Somewhere we can hold hands and just be."

"It would be lovely, Will. Right now, though, I need to pee." She left Will alone in the colourful bed that hurt his eyes. He got up and padded over to her open laptop.

The mood boards on her screen confused him. It looked rather like an English country cottage.

"Is this for someone back in the U.K.?" He called out.

Stella dashed over, closing the laptop. "Don't look at that rubbish."

"It didn't look like rubbish. Where is it for?"

Stella blushed. "Nowhere. It's not real life; it's just a dream."

Will smiled, "I hope you'll show it to me one day."

He patted her leg. "When you trust me enough. But Stella, we all have dreams. I'll show you mine if you show me yours."

“That’s not funny, Will.”

“I know.” Will kissed her forehead and left to start his day.

Once he’d settled at his desk, he needed to call Tina with a list of jobs.

“Right, boss, so you want me to cancel the catering for next week. And you need the cleaning crew on Wednesday and Sunday.”

“Yes, get them to come at two o’clock both days. They shouldn’t need to stay too long on Sunday. But if they can clean thoroughly on Wednesday before the new furniture comes in.”

“Fine, I’ll get on to that straight away.”

It was time for lunch when the computer announced a new arrival.

<<Welcome, Vanessa. William is in his office.>>

William cringed as he heard her walking towards his office. *How many times do I have to tell her she can’t just turn up?*

“Sorry for calling in, but I actually felt I should check in about this catering. How can you cancel it?”

“Will it cost me to cancel it?”

“We will forfeit the deposit, but how are you going to get someone as good on such short notice? William, you know I only pick the best.”

“I do realise that, Vanessa, and I appreciate that, but hopefully, you now realise that the budget is tight on this project.”

“I warn you; this is actually a false economy. We need to impress these people. Who do you think can do better than the top company? They do all the dealer open days.”

“So perhaps it’s good that we are bringing in White’s winery then.”

“White’s Winery?” Her eyebrow rose. Will nodded.

“That’s actually an excellent choice, but if you are bringing someone like that in, where are you getting the staff?”

“The winery will provide them. Stella has it all arranged.”

“That damn girl! Why do you put so much faith in her? She is going to cause you enormous problems, William, you mark my words.”

Chapter 42

Stella stroked the kitchen island that Grigori and William had created.

"Glad you like it. I'm hoping my team will finish in here today. I'm guessing you want to be in here dressing the room."

"What?"

"The kitchen, you can have it tomorrow. Not long left to get it looking like you designed it."

Panic hit the pit of her stomach. This room really wasn't her style. She'd simply made the best of what had already been ordered and delivered.

"I haven't looked at what's already here. I'd better check it out."

"Sorry to disappoint you, but Vanessa did nothing about that."

"You mean there is nothing? No fancy food storage that costs the earth? No hideous vase for flowers? No Italian fruit bowls?"

"Nothing at all. I don't think our friend does kitchens 'actually'." Grigori used air quotes for actually, and Stella collapsed into giggles.

"Don't make me laugh. But she does say, actually, so many times, I find myself saying it back to her."

"Don't worry, she doesn't notice. Well, she hasn't when I do it."

"I guess that tells me what I'm doing today, then."

It was a major setback for Stella and a lesson not to assume anything about Vanessa. She hadn't factored in the time or the budget to decorate the kitchen. Needing to calm down and think, she made a coffee and took herself outside. Pulling her legs up, she looked out at the wide blue sky from the chair. She'd enjoyed the sunset last night.

The evening had been blissful, with the two of them cuddled up close in front of the fire, talking about the project and reminiscing about the past. Stella couldn't help noticing they didn't talk about their future. That little fact still bounced around rent-free in her brain.

For the first time in her life, Stella didn't know what came next. Well, that is since the day she walked in on Jackson and his new assistant. Those five minutes changed so much of her life. Most of all, it rocked her confidence in her own judgment.

The time with Will had been so lovely, and she tried to put her finger on why. Was it just being outdoors? Was it because they knew each other

so well? Or was it because it was Will? Each kiss seemed more intense. Her lips tingled, remembering how he'd kissed her awake that morning.

Stella checked her bank account. *Damn, that's not really enough to do this massive room justice. I really don't want to use that credit card Will gave me. I so want this to be a professional job. There has to be another way—time to get creative, Stella.*

The artisans she'd been buying from might lend her a few pieces; certainly, Eric seemed keen to showcase more of his work. Marco was away; she could maybe borrow some tableware from him. Who else could she ask? In the end, she composed a brief message and sent it to ten of her contacts to see if they could help. And then she rang Maribeth.

"Good morning, Stella. How are you?"

"I'm good, but I could use help. I'd totally missed that I needed to dress the kitchen before the launch and, well, the budget … In short, I'm looking for any ideas where I can borrow, hire, or buy inexpensively."

"It is one of the most important rooms, Stella."

"I do know that, but I took over this job from someone else, and I thought the props would be organised."

"Well, I can probably help. The agency has a box of empty food packaging that we keep. You'd be amazed at what we find in clients' fridges. So, we store some nice pasta tins, you know the sort of things I mean, for when we must do a showing in a house someone is living in."

"Thank you. I've sent messages out to the artisans I've been working with. I'm sure they will help with the artistic side of it all. I have some money; I just don't want to end up spending my airfare home."

"You won't need that for a while, though, will you?"

"Who knows?"

"I understand. I always wanted to have my fare home. How about I pop around tomorrow with what I have, and maybe I can ask a few questions I have for clients?"

"That would be great. See you tomorrow."

Next, Stella called Poppy at the winery.

"It seems I don't just have to fill the wine fridge; I need to decorate the whole kitchen. Could you bring some pickles and things tomorrow?"

"I don't see why not. What do you need?"

"Can I send you a few photos?"

"Brilliant. Do that, and I'll see you tomorrow."

As she ended the call, she found a reply to her text.

Jenny: Come to my house. We can drink coffee, draw up a plan, and raid my mother's garage. It will be fun.
Stella: I'll be there in half an hour.

Already feeling better, Stella drove over to Jenny's. Her mum had been just as great as Jenny herself. They offered her lots of advice, and having other people to talk to really helped to dispel the butterflies that had hit her stomach when Grigori had dropped the bombshell.

Jenny had mentioned a set of pretty shops she could visit on her way back. A little bit of retail therapy was good, and it gave her a chance to buy something for dinner.

Seeing William's slick car parked next to Grigori's truck filled her heart, and she felt at home. She left most things in the jeep and carried the fresh food into the kitchen.

<<Welcome, Stella.>>

"Star, where is William?"

<<William is in his office.>>

He must've heard the announcement because he appeared to help her bring in the food.

"This looks interesting."

"I'm sorry, this is window dressing. Just an instant dinner tonight."

"That's fine. I don't expect you to feed me."

"But I'd like to cook a proper meal for you."

"Ah, there will be time for that one day. Another few days and we can relax." *Is he talking about a future?*

"Until then, I guess we'll do what we need to do to get the job done." She pushed the hair from her face as she unwrapped their dinner.

"Star, don't do too much, though. This is important, but Grigori says we are on top of things, and I'm sure we could buy a few cushions."

Stella shut the oven door firmly and adjusted the temperature.

"Come with me!" She strode through the door and down the corridor towards the bedroom.

"Oh! I like this, very commanding Stella."

"It's not what you think, so get your mind out of the gutter." She swung open the door to Sarah's room.

"Look at this space." She lifted the cushions off the bed and threw them down the corridor. "I know there are pillows and fabrics on the surface; now look past that." Will didn't say a word. He looked slowly around the room.

"Yes, I could have bought the cushions in here and maybe even the bedding. If I'd bought them off the shelf, we'd have had standard pillows. They wouldn't mix and coordinate like these, which is why I take the time to make them bespoke. It's more than that, Will, take out the cushions, can't you see what else has been added?" Stella crossed her arms and stared at Will.

"Right. You're right. You are always right. Now dinner. Could I get you some wine?" Stella thumped his arm.

"You're trying to get me drunk."

"No. But being relaxed would be good. I'm sorry if I upset you. I didn't want to do that." William sat down on the bed and took her hand. "Come here." He pulled her down onto his knee. "Star, the next few days, I mean, up until this launch. If things get tense, just know that I love you, whatever happens."

He loves me? Really? Stella bent her head to kiss him. The day had been a challenge, but her panic from that morning was under control.

"That chicken bake will take half an hour."

"A whole thirty minutes. And we're alone. Whatever will we do?"

"Are you sure we're alone?"

"Star, lock down the house."

<<The house is now locked down. Shall I set an alarm?>>

"Star, do not set the alarm." William's arms went around Stella's waist.

"Star, close the blinds."

Chapter 43

As she raised the blinds, still sitting in bed, Stella watched Will already out in the pool. He's early this morning. *I guess that means there is more going on in his brain than he lets on.*

Stretching out her arms above her head, she recognised the familiar ache of waking up after a night in bed with Will. They were growing to know each other's bodies more each day, and yet there always seemed to be more to discover.

This project will soon be over, and we can both enjoy some relaxed time. Will that be together? It won't be easy telling my parents, but I hope he is telling his family. How do we begin to explain this to Sarah? I've never kept any secrets from her before.

Stella sprang out of bed, inspired to complete her lists.

She enjoyed the morning, finally unpacking furniture. If the grin on his face was anything to go by, William appeared to be enjoying it, too.

"Thank you for doing this."

"It's my pleasure." His smile broadened. "Grigori and Paulo are busy; I'm just happy to be doing something useful that didn't involve a lot of thought from me."

Stella dropped the section of the sofa she'd been holding. Will dropped his end and stepped back.

"You're supposed to be helping me decide where to put things!"

He laughed softly and pulled her into his arms. "You keep asking me what I think and then answering your own questions."

"But I want you to feel like this is your home." She sighed as she looked up into his face. He hugged her closer.

"Having you here is what's making it feel like home."

"Really?"

"Yes, you cook British food and buy the Hobnobs."

Stella thumped his chest as he tried to hold her closer.

"I'm not eleven anymore, William. You can stop teasing me."

"I'm not sure I could ever do that, even if I wanted to."

Stella pulled out his arms and picked up her end of the sofa.

Despite being tired, seeing everything finally come together brought her renewed energy. All her many lists were getting ticked off one by one.

"Is this the coffee table?"

"Yes, it is."

"Hallelujah, now I've somewhere to put my nuts."

"Oh, William, all this work, and you just want a place to leave the snacks. If you would only …"

Stella didn't get to finish the sentence as her phone called yet again. It had been non-stop for the last two days.

"Sorry, it's the winery. I'd better take this."

"That's OK. I've something I want to check in my office."

"Morning, Poppy."

"Hi Stella, can I just ask what was wrong?"

"Wrong?"

"I think you need to have a word with your assistant."

"My assistant?" Stella thought her head would explode. *What now?*

"Yes, if you didn't want us to bring things this afternoon, it was a bit late. Whilst I understand you might have decided to go a more upmarket route, it wasn't very nice to be told that."

"I'm lost. You're going to have to say that again, but only after I tell you I don't have an assistant, and we are looking forward to seeing you."

"Oh!"

"Look, did she give a name?"

"No," Stella heard the hesitation in Poppy's voice. "She said she was Ms Barrington Jones' executive assistant and needed to cancel because you wanted something, and I quote, 'more upmarket.'

"What can I say? Will and I discussed this plenty, even before Sunday. Will wants to support a business that employs him. It could lead to other things together. We both want press coverage; this should work for both companies."

"Patrick is so excited because after the two posts you've already made, we've seen a huge surge on the website, and sales are up, too, which is great news at this time of year."

"I'll try to work out what happened. I'll see you when you get here."

Will had wandered off when her phone rang, and she had to find him to put the coffee table in place. *Much as I'm fairly sure who did this, now is not the time to tell Will. Anyway, how do I prove it?*

"Can you help me remove the packaging from this?"

Will nodded, his smile broad. "I can't wait to have this."

"Because we can have snacks and drinks so much easier now?"

"Am I that easy to read?"

"I've known you for ages. At least it's not Jelly Worms anymore."

"Only because I can't find them."

They ate lunch outside with the rest of the team. Having stopped, Stella struggled to go back. Much more appealing to stay out there with the spring sunshine warming her cheeks, so different from the way the icy winds had nipped her face when she arrived in New York just a few weeks ago. The arrival of the winery folks helped her to get on her feet again.

<<Welcome, Patrick. Stella is in the kitchen.>>

"Sweetie, can you make the drinks? I'll go meet them."

"Don't you need me to lift the boxes?" Will flexed his biceps, smiling. "You've been using me for my body all day."

Stella couldn't help the smile that crept across her face. Things were finally falling into place, with the build and with Will.

"Patrick is here now, though." She smirked.

"So, you don't need me now, then?" Stella laughed at his mock pout.

"I think I'll always need you." She said softly as she turned away, not sure if she wanted him to hear her confession.

Poppy's head spun around as she tried to take in the space.

"Wow, you've done so much already."

"I've not really started on the kitchen yet. I didn't choose these units; they were already delivered when I arrived."

"It's unusual what you have done over there, though, the way those doors are configured." Poppy stroked the island. "I just love this. The wood is so sensual."

"Well, I didn't have to use the exact layout they were originally intended to be in."

"A little bit of creativity goes a long way." Poppy sighed.

The words made Stella's chest swell. Every day felt like an emotional roller coaster; some days, she'd been overjoyed with the results, and

other times, Vanessa's voice of doom rang in her ears. *You're a silly little girl who could ruin everything for William.* Even the cruel things Jackson Wilde had said as he entertained his next assistant. And her mother's warnings.

"Are you OK, Stella?" Stella snapped back out of her dream state.

"Me? Oh yes, just a bit distracted … a lot on my brain today."

"I'm not surprised. Now, where do you want these?"

"Let's start in the service kitchen, then just bring out here what we need." Poppy put the box she'd been carrying down on the stainless-steel surface and started to open it.

"WAIT!" Stella's hand stopped her from doing more. "Hang on. I'll get a tripod, and we can film an unboxing." Poppy watched transfixed as Stella worked.

"I've told Patrick we need to do that sort of thing; he didn't get it. But since that poolside post of yours, he can see the impact it can have."

"It's always good to have a plan, take plenty of photos and videos, then use the best you can."

"If we do an unboxing post today, the fridge tomorrow, enjoying some wine with dinner on Sunday and then there's the Open Day buzz. Of course, we will film the first three of them today."

"You make it look so easy, Stella."

"It's down to the fact I do it every day, so I get quicker. I think the other thing is not getting too precious. If you take enough photos, you don't worry about the ones that don't quite work."

"Can I help you put the wine in the fridge?"

"You are welcome to do the whole job if you want."

"Will that help?"

"God, yes."

They found Patrick drooling over the wine fridge with Will.

"What do you think, brother?"

"I like the idea for your events at the barn. Although I don't know about something guests could just open."

"Stella has been bending my ear about making things more child-friendly, so we discussed putting some sort of lock on it."

"Child-friendly? That's quick." Patrick teased, making William blush. Stella simply batted at his arm.

"It's not for us, silly. It's for potential investors. I thought if we could get them to see this as a home suitable for a family and not just the Playboy set …"

"Do you always talk about Marco like that? Does he know?"

"Well… I didn't mean …" Stella babbled. *He's teasing me like Will earlier.* Patrick threw his arm around her shoulder.

"Relax, Stella. Perhaps I spend too much time around my little sister, I don't know when to stop." *Little sister, little sister? Does Will still see me as his little sister? Is that why he teases me?*

"Patrick, stop. You go too far. Stella, will you show me around the rest of this place before we go?"

"I'd love that." Poppy took her hand and encouraged her down the hallway off the kitchen. Once they were out of earshot, she stopped to apologise.

"I'm sorry about Patrick. If it helps, it probably means he trusts you."

"That's OK."

Poppy narrowed her eyes and looked hard at Stella. Stella sighed and began to explain.

"I tend to be a bit sensitive about those two words, 'little sister'."

"OK?"

"It's how Will saw me before I arrived here — another little sister."

"Ouch. But clearly, he's got over that now. I mean, the way he looks at you. It makes me melt."

"Yes, I thought so too. Then, this morning, he was tormenting me like that. And me being an idiot reminded him that I was a grown-up now." Stella hung her head. "I'm always doing it."

"How has it been since you came to the barn?"

"Good, I think. It's so strange, really. I've never been out with anyone I know as well as I do Will. And we are living together… It just seems to have shifted things."

"I'm guessing this launch thing isn't helping with the tension stakes."

"It isn't like any other relationship I've had before."

"You not only live together, but you are also working together, and there are so many people around you. Are you still trying to hide it?"

"We are, I know it's madness, but I don't think either of us wants to be the one to tell everyone back in Hursts Bridge."

"So, after the launch, you said, then what?"

Stella looked at the floor. She liked Poppy, but what could she say?

"I'm sorry, Stella, it's none of my business. How about you show me some of the bedrooms?"

"Thanks for caring, though, Poppy. It's not like I have many friends here. And I certainly can't phone my best friend to download about it."

Stella showed Poppy the first guest room. "I've kept this one fairly neutral as far as colour is concerned."

"So, you piled on the different textures."

"That's the idea." Stella desperately wanted to ask, *'do you like it?'* Polly's eyes searched the room. It felt like forever before she spoke. As the seconds stretched out, Stella's chest tightened. *She doesn't like it.* Eventually, Poppy spun to face Stella.

"Stella, it's fabulous; it's all tonal and textural and … well, I love it. Show me more." The next bedroom was the one she'd designed for Sarah, the one she was now sleeping in with Will. His need for straight lines meant the bed was made very neatly every day. There would be nothing out of line unless you opened the cupboards or drawers that Stella was using.

The colours were fabulous. Stella knew in her heart that Sarah was going to love it … but it was probably best she didn't tell her she had been sleeping in that bed with her brother.

"So, this is the first room I did for Will. When I saw these fabrics, I knew they would speak to Sarah." When Poppy's eyebrows rose, she quickly explained. "Sarah is Will's sister … and my best friend."

"OMG, this is so like three romance books rolled into one. I was thinking it was about the rich boss falling for someone who works for him." Stella didn't answer. Instead, she focused on watching the landscapers working around the edge of the deck. She regretted she hadn't had time to work on the plans for the outside—just one more regret.

"I'm doing it again. I met you once, and now I'm digging through your love life." Poppy shook her head. "I guess because I've followed you online for so long, I feel like I know you. Hey, can I take some photos for my socials?"

"As long as you don't post them before Tuesday."

"Of course. Thanks for that. Can I tag you in them?" Stella just smiled. Poppy was new to social media, but she seemed to be learning fast. The next room was for a small child. Stella's heart clenched when

her eyes fell on the cot. She looked at her watch; she needed to finish unpacking furniture.

"I don't mean to be rude, but I need to get back to bossing William around. You're welcome to look some more if you like. There are two more bedrooms down here you can check out."

"Thanks, Stella, I don't want to hold you up. I wanted to help, not distract you."

"Meet me back in the kitchen." Stella strode purposefully towards where she had left Will talking to Patrick. Muttering to herself about how he could be totally focused on his own work and yet so easily distracted when doing anything else. *You know that's who he is. And you still love him.*

She was a little taken aback to find Will was busy unpacking some of the larger pieces, with Patrick's help.

"There she is. Now, you tell us where to put these things, and Patrick here can do your share of the lifting."

Stella didn't answer. Her brain had finally frozen.

"Unless you want to lift, and I'll decide where everything is going." Will teased her with a boyish grin.

"Let me help, Stella. My sister has already distracted you enough."

With a certain amount of unease, Stella guided them in arranging the seating around the fireplace and the spot where the TV emerged from the floor. As she stood back to admire the look, Poppy returned to the room.

"Stella, the artwork is amazing. Where did you find it all?"

"Mostly locally. Some came from my mother in New York."

"I've lived here all my life, and it all looks new to me."

"She's being modest. Stella has done a lot of the art herself. Then, most of the work she's commissioned, she has had some input in. The glass guy, what's his name, is amazed by her ideas."

"He's called Eric. I believe his grandfather came over from Sweden in the sixties, and he inherited all his equipment and know-how."

"But how do you find so many?"

"On social media, I've a friend I already knew online who lives nearby, Jenny. She has been fabulous."

"Talking of help, what can we do before we get out of your hair?"

Together, the four managed to get most of the great room furniture in place. Polly seemed a champion at chopping cushions, and the friendly banter lifted Stella's mood, especially as the jobs on her mental list were being ticked off at an amazing rate.

Poppy also did a brilliant job filling the wine fridge while Stella supervised the men in unpacking and arranging the new dining table and chairs.

"What will you do with the table? Leave it like this or set it?"

"I haven't decided yet. I'll definitely put some flowers on it, and if I want tableware, I can borrow it from next door."

By the time she returned with one of the boxes, Patrick and Poppy had already left, leaving a note and a brown bag containing a quiche and salad for their evening meal. Will had disappeared, nowhere to be seen.

She opened the bottle of wine left next to the paper bag and poured a drink as she considered what William would want. She let out a long breath as she felt the tiredness creep across her back and shoulders.

"That was a big sigh. Are you OK?" Will tenderly rubbed the nape of her neck, kissing behind her ear.

"Just tired. Glass of wine?"

"Sure, what's in the bag Patrick left?"

"Quiche and salad. I guess that's dinner sorted."

"I wanted to take you out," Will said quietly.

Stella smiled softly. "We could go outside. Does that count?"

"It's a start. You take the wine and get sat down; I'll find some plates."

Chapter 44

A nervous Stella woke early and was looking through the parcels that had arrived from Eric and the other artisans. She separated out the ones that would be useful somewhere other than the kitchen and labelled them with the rooms she wanted them moved to.

<<Welcome, Grigori. Stella is in the kitchen.>>

Grigori walked in carrying a cumbersome parcel wrapped neatly in brown paper.

"Do I want to know what this is?"

Stella giggled. "Can't you tell?"

"It looks like someone parcelled up a giraffe. This thing is taller than I am."

"Why don't you open it?" Stella watched Grigori over the top of her teacup as he pulled out his pocketknife to cut the string. He carefully removed the brown paper to reveal a plush toy that was indeed a six-foot-tall giraffe. As he removed more paper, he found between its legs an identical toy, this time just a foot tall.

"I'm guessing this isn't for the boss's office."

"No, it's not," she laughed.

"I'd better take this for you. It's taller than you."

"Thanks."

"I'll do that now, while you finish breakfast, and then we can discuss what you need help with today."

Stella downed the rest of her tea and dismissed the idea of another cup. There was a lot to do today. She was fetching the things she'd picked up from Jenny when the woman herself arrived.

Stella waved as Jenny retrieved a box from the back of her car.

"I've potted some herbs; I've put them in the pots we weren't sure about. What do you think?" Stella asked, needing to be reassured.

"Actually, they look quite good now with the plants in them. It's a huge difference, isn't it?"

"We need this place fresh and clean, but not bare."

"Stella, it's a case of balance. You seem calmer today; how do you feel?"

"I guess I'm like the proverbial swan. It might look smooth above the waterline, but everything below is paddling like mad."

They had finished the cleaning and were enjoying a break with coffee when Maribeth arrived with the things she promised. Stella and Jenny helped her add it to everything else they had lined up.

From a black jute shopping bag, Maribeth produced three bottles of champagne.

"These are to wish you luck for Monday."

"More champagne. William's business manager insists he keeps some in to celebrate every little win."

"It's a good theory. One of the business gurus suggests it."

"And there I was thinking she had an original thought!" Stella's bitter tone shocked both of her companions. Maribeth was the one to speak, though.

"My dear, that sounded like you have an issue with this woman. I'm going to guess it's the one who sent out all the invitations." Stella didn't respond. Maribeth was a potential client, a good one at that. Maribeth didn't seem to worry about it.

"It didn't go unnoticed how selective the invite list was. The way she fawned over the men that day, too." Stella went red and tried to busy herself with unwrapping a fabulous fruit bowl from Eric. She desperately wanted to share the things she suspected Vanessa of, but now was not the time. Maribeth seemed to get the message and changed the subject.

"Another couple of questions have come up. I hope you can answer them. Then, hopefully, on Monday, I'll be ready to make a bid on behalf of one of them."

"Of course. I'm not sure why it bothers me, but something makes me want you to be the one who buys them all." Stella sighed.

"OK, so, the computer system. Is it voice or touchpad activated?"

"The computer system is something that's evolving all the time. Currently, it supports both voice and touchpad operation. Star, turn on the fire." Maribeth spun around as the fire in the lounge area sprang into life. "Star, close the blinds." As the computer followed instruction after instruction, the potential client in her aunt looked impressed.

"You can create sequences, too. For example, when he gets up in the morning, William sets his alarm to play music, followed by his shower. Five minutes later, it will start the coffee machine, and when he picks up his drink, he gets the Morning News. All the showers are digital, which

means each person can set their personal preference, temperature, and rate, even how long the shower lasts." Maribeth looked impressed.

"William could tell you more, but I know he has a lockdown routine and a nighttime routine. The extensive integrated technology is what makes this build so special."

"I realised that, but Stella, please don't underestimate your input. This lighting system may be technologically wonderful, but it also looks great. I think the pair of you make a winning combination." Stella blushed again; it was becoming a habit.

"Let me show you the primary suite. That should be a good example of how we can create something bespoke… within limits, of course."

"Stanford and I've been looking at plots. Will we be able to select the plot we want?"

"We can only sell each unit once. When a plot is sold…"

"That's why I need to be confident in making our bids on launch day. You know what they say about location."

Through the kitchen window, she spotted a small van pulling up, and Elaine got out.

"Great, that's the last piece for the primary." Finally, Stella was getting excited. When Grigori called her phone, she was quick to tell him what to do.

"It's for the primary. Can you bring it in?" Grigori carried the chair covered with a blanket as Elaine brought in the ottoman. Relieved to have this final item to complete the room she'd poured so much love into, Stella bounced down the corridor, followed by both Jenny and Maribeth.

"Do you think this is better than the bedroom we saw before?" Maribeth asked, and Stella laughed.

"They are each perfect for the person they were designed for. This is the primary, so it has more components."

"I do hope it isn't too big. I hate a bed in the middle of a huge space."

"I like it a bit more intimate, too." Stella opened the decorative pocket doors and led them all into the room. It was clear where the chair belonged, so Grigori positioned it, and Elaine carefully placed the ottoman next to it. She held both covering sheets in her hand as she looked at Stella.

"I hope you like it." She whisked away the covers to a series of oohs and aahs from her audience. The dark, inky stain on the wooden frame

perfectly complemented the fabrics. It was the crown of the room. Stella's heart sped up in anticipation of showing it to Will.

“Elaine, it's just what I asked for. I don't suppose you’ve another example of your work for Monday?”

“I've got something I could finish and bring over on Sunday night if it'll help.” Whilst Elaine showed Stella some pictures on her phone, Jenny and Maribeth took in the room.

“Oh, Stella, it’s wonderful,” Jenny exclaimed. “I love that screen. Wait a minute, does it match the door? Where did you get doors and screens to match?”

“That comes with working with such a talented team.” Stella grinned at Grigori. “Between us, we can make quite bespoke items that coordinate. And now I'm building up my contacts with other artisans like Elaine here. I’m confident we could do just about anything.” Stella swallowed; she needed to sound positive in front of Maribeth.

They all went back into the kitchen to finish there. Maribeth picked up a cloth and helped wipe down the surfaces as Stella unpacked the props she’d brought.

“I have to say, you look a whole lot better than you did the last time I saw you. Is it because you can see the end, or did something else happen? Anyone would think you were in love.”

“I’d noticed that, but I didn’t know how to ask. Are things easier with Will now?”

Stella didn’t answer either question; she pushed on with the job in hand.

“What do you think we need in the fridge?”

Elaine and Jenny both seemed to have a good eye, and Stella was grateful to have the help. Eventually, they all stood back to look at the finished room.

<<Welcome, William. Stella and guests are in the kitchen.>>

The three women all waited for him to see their efforts. Stella's stomach tumbled over and over. It felt like it took much longer than normal for William to find them. Stella was desperate for his approval, not just in the kitchen but in his room too.

When he eventually arrived in the room, he froze. Stella watched as he looked from Elaine to Jenny and finally to Maribeth. His eyes flittered around the room they’d all been decorating. Stella knew he’d be finding this hard. Her hands itched to hold him and tell him it was all OK. But

they were still keeping this to themselves. The room around her buzzed with voices telling him what they liked or loved the most about the kitchen, the great room, and the primary bedroom. All the time, Stella stared in silence like William. Jenny broke the mood.

“Look at the time. It was nice to meet you, but I need to go. I'll see you on Sunday.

“I'll walk out with you. See you on Sunday with that chaise, Stella.”

“No, that's fine. I'll see you both on Sunday. Thanks for all your help today.” Stella tried to smile. Maribeth hung back.

“William, can I ask a question?” Stella had tuned out, but she watched as William led Maribeth to his office.

Left alone, she scanned the great room, looking for what she still needed to do in there. It was the many minor things that made her head spin. She pulled out her phone to make another list. She was still doing that when Maribeth and William returned. Stella walked Maribeth out.

“I’m so grateful for everything you’ve done, and not just today.”

“Don't mention it, I've quite enjoyed myself. After all, we're family. And thank you too, I've talked to William about Stafford and I being the marketing agents for this and the other projects he's working on going forward.”

“What did he say?”

“I think he's interested. I pointed out that the young lady might be suitable for his tech business, but he will need professional help in the longer term. One thing my husband and I know is the property business.”

“I think he needs to focus on supplying the tech rather than the whole project.”

“What does he think?”

“I don't know, we haven't talked about our future… oh, I mean, after the launch, it's so close.”

“William is a lovely guy. Has your mother met him yet?” Stella smiled. Maribeth didn't miss much.

“She knows the family. They were friends back in Hursts Bridge.” *But how would she feel if I moved here for him?*

“I see.” She held Stella’s arm. “We will be here on Monday. Don't be afraid to ring me if I can help.”

“Thank you. It’s been wonderful having you here today.”

When Stella returned to the kitchen, Will was plating up sandwiches.

"I know it's hardly Friday dinner, but…"

"You didn't want to make a mess, I get it. I've got work to do later, so a sandwich is fine. What is it?"

"Ham with cheese and salad. Wine?"

"Is there any more of that orange juice? And cake?"

Grigori popped in.

"I'm letting the team go tonight, but they are all going to be here over the weekend."

"I guess they can have Monday off," William mumbled.

"I'm sending them over to work next door on Monday."

"Oh!" Will scratched the back of his head.

"The lads don't mind, they are working, and they are earning."

"See you tomorrow. The tech team will be here too."

"Goodnight, boss," Grigori nodded to Stella. "Star, I mean Stella."

And they were alone. Without any discussion, they took the sandwiches into Will's office. Stella took one bite and groaned as mayonnaise spilt down the side of her mouth. William laughed and wiped it away with his thumb. He leant over and kissed her softly on the cheek.

"Have I told you I love you?"

"Yes." She grinned and wriggled in her chair. "I hope you still feel the same when you see your room."

"It's finished?"

"Yes, that's why Elaine was here. She's been making the final piece."

"When can I see it?"

"When you've eaten your sandwich."

Will took a hungry bite and chewed dramatically.

"And when I've finished mine, so no need to rush." The next couple of bites saw them grinning but not talking. Their eyes fixed on each other.

<<Welcome, Vanessa. William is in the office.>>

"Now what?" Stella wiped her mouth and put the sandwich back on the plate. She closed her eyes to centre herself as she heard the click, click of Vanessa's heels coming towards them. Her white, blonde hair in a tight and long ponytail from the crown of her head swished as she swept into the office. Stella looked down at Will's T-shirt, feeling

underdressed when she saw the tight black dress that clung to Vanessa's curves.

"Won't that spoil your dinner? It is still seven o'clock for Friday night dinner, isn't it? You didn't say it had changed."

Will stood and met Vanessa at the door. He took her elbow and led her away. Stella could just hear his voice over the clicking of her heels as they moved away, but she couldn't hear what was said. Doubt and insecurity reared their head again for Stella. Conversations she wasn't part of.

What is the problem? Is she always going to keep turning up in our lives? Is he still sleeping with her? Am I just a fool again? Is that why he isn't talking about a future?

Chapter 45

"I thought I made it clear you weren't to come over without it being arranged." His voice rose higher than he liked.

"Not even for Friday dinner?"

Will shook his head. He tried to moderate his voice. "Not at all." *How does she not get it?*

"Well, I'm here now."

"I'm afraid there's no dinner tonight, the kitchen's finished, so we are not using it until after Monday."

"Good idea. I'll get us a table. I take it we'll only need the two places?" Vanessa pulled out her phone as she spoke. Will's temper rose.

"No! We're working. That's why we're in the office."

"I did wonder." She smirked.

"I'll walk you out."

The tension was palpable as he sat in silence with Stella, finishing his meal. The haste from early now gone. *Vanessa's arrival has upset Star again. How do I convince her that she has nothing to worry about?*

Eventually, he stood up and took Stella's plate from her.

"Now do I see this room?" Stella stood up and jiggled her shoulders. He watched her close her eyes and then look back at him. *I'm sorry, Star.*

"Let's do this."

It felt strange walking down this corridor in his own home, so much had changed in the past week.

"Is it only a week since I've been down here?"

"I hope you like it." He watched her swallow. "Can you close your eyes?" She took his hand. "Are you ready?" William nodded his reply, the lump in his throat so large that he couldn't speak.

Stella gently stroked his palm as she led him to stand in front of the door. Her soft hands, warm in his, eased his concern.

"OK, open them." The pocket doors that he had helped to fit now looked so different. He stretched out his fingers to feel the raised textured finish. It appeared to be made of pewter, but when his fingers stroked the smooth curves, he realised it had been constructed from wood.

"Stella, that's… well, it's so dramatic." She took hold of his hands again as she spoke.

"Star, open the master door." William gently squeezed her hand as his heartbeat quickened. He wanted to like this space so much. He hadn't liked the black bathroom on the plan, yet he had every faith that Stella would've done something extraordinary with it.

He liked the place he slept in for now. The main bedroom was too big and grand for his taste. *Maybe I can stay in my old room.*

He gave her hand one last squeeze and walked in. She let go of him and encouraged him forward. He loved it in the first moment, and not just because she had created it for him. The simple blues and creams were soothing and uplifting. A screen featuring the same design as the pocket doors created an intimate space for a bed with a padded headboard, its sections upholstered in a range of blue fabrics. His fingers trailed the textures. The widest panel had an interesting pattern on it.

"Is it a map?" His brows raised.

"Yes, it's Hursts Bridge. I had it printed." Will couldn't speak. He wanted to thank her, but he had no idea where to start. This was beyond anything Vanessa had shown him, and, more than that, he loved it. But the blue and cream map fabric was a hint of how much she had put into this for him.

"You hate it!"

"No, no. I love it. I just keep seeing more. Stella, it's amazing. I loved it the minute I walked in, but I keep seeing something else." He studied the artwork on the sidewall. "Is that Jack's landing?"

"Yes." William's fingers caressed the curves of the screen, looking at the artwork through it.

"How did you do this?"

"Teamwork. I did have help."

"I'm sure you did, but I'm guessing Grigori didn't pick out the artwork." He walked over to the chair, his fingers trailing over the bentwood frame. "This chair… I've always liked them… is it?"

"No, sorry, it's not an original. But if it were, I wouldn't have wanted to stain the wood."

William sat in the chair, stroking the fabric. As he lifted his feet onto the ottoman, he sighed.

"It's wonderful. I can't thank you enough. I presume we should wait until after the launch before we sleep in here."

“Yes.” Stella's voice was soft, and her eyes were focused on something outside. Will didn't know what she was thinking, he could only hope that she was looking forward to occupying that big bed with him as much as he was with her. He tried to break the mood.

“So, your place tonight?”

“Sure, now you said there was cake, perhaps we could have a drink to celebrate. Then let's go over the list so we can work out who's doing what tomorrow. There's so much work left, and we need to prioritise and make sure we aren’t undoing work.” She suddenly turned to Will. “If there are a lot of people here, how are we going to feed them?”

“Oh, don't worry, I had an assistant order some sandwiches to bring in. He's going to pick them up on the way here; it's all arranged.” Stella looked at him, obviously wanting to say something more, but she didn't speak. William waited patiently, giving her the time she needed.

“Will, is Vanessa coming?” She was quick to continue, “It's not a problem, I just like to know.” Stella examined her toes. “When she simply arrives out of the blue, like today, it throws me.” Stella lifted her eyes to his face. “Did you know she was coming this evening?”

William shook his head and took her hand.

“Let's get through this launch. She shouldn't need to be here after that. I'm not expecting her tomorrow. If she thinks it's going to be hard work, she'll stay away. She must be here on Sunday to prepare for the next day.”

“OK.”

“I hate that she upsets you.” Will threw his arm across her shoulder. “Star, I need you here, and I think we need her for this launch. After speaking with Maribeth, I believe that by Monday, we can hand over some of this to them. I'm certainly going to talk to them about it.” He pulled her to him. “Do you want to rest tonight?”

“I'd rather get a bit more done. Why don't we dress the bathrooms?”

Will smirked, “Well, I guess if we only need to use one bedroom and one bathroom, it will save on work.” Stella battered his arm.

“Is that just an excuse? I also want to decorate in here a little more. Maybe we could bring some things out of the room you've been using.”

“Come on, I'm not sure I can stay in here much longer without throwing you on this bed. What have you done in the other bedrooms?”

"You can see them as we finish the bathrooms." Stella produced two piles of towels, one the softest of white, the other a wonderful deep blue. She left the blue ones outside the room that Will had been using.

"This is going to be for a teenage boy."

"Are you trying to say something?"

"It just seemed the easiest thing to upgrade yours to. We don't need to hide all your gaming stuff then." Will followed her as she carried the white towels into the last room. Will froze in the doorway.

"I thought I would do this for the family market. Maribeth seemed to think it was a good idea. She said, People often just make the extra rooms look like hotel rooms, and people can visualise that without any help." Stella stroked the tall giraffe. Watching her face as she smoothed its neck warmed the space in his chest.

William stood by the crib, gripping the edge tight. He reached down to finger the embroidered quilt.

"What would we call her?" He picked up the soft velvet teddy and stroked its head.

"Who?"

"Our little girl."

Chapter 46

Stella woke with an uneasy feeling. She reached out to Will, but his side of the bed felt cold. *He must have been gone a while. I hope he isn't working. He needs to rest, too.*

She pulled on the borrowed T-shirt. It was her comfort blanket now, and she padded out of the room to find him. A gentle blue light spilt out of the primary, and she cautiously opened the pocket doors. She discovered Will sat in the chair, his eyes closed and his feet on the ottoman.

"Am I forgiven for using it before the big day?" he asked without opening his eyes.

"Of course, if it were mine, I wouldn't move out of it for a week." She walked over to stand next to him, and he took her hand.

"You are so clever; how do you know all this about me?" He waved at the room. "Anyone who has seen my previous homes would think I wanted black and white."

"Just because you did that doesn't mean it's what you want."

"That's very profound. Come here." He tugged her to sit on his knee. Stroking her leg, he searched her face. "Now, why are you out of bed?"

"I woke up, and you were gone. I hoped you weren't working."

"Ha, I was, it'll be manic here tomorrow. I'm very much used to my own space. I work better like that."

So, what does that mean for us? Is that why he hasn't mentioned the future? Do I get in his way? She looked out the window at the lights of the city below them. It all seemed so far away. She swallowed.

"So why are you here, in this chair?"

"I finished what I was doing, and I didn't want to disturb you."

"Disturb me?"

"If I got back in that bed with you, I wouldn't be able to leave you alone." He kissed her hand and entwined their fingers. "You are just too tempting." *I guess I don't have much time with him. After this is over, he will return to working in that office full-time.*

She turned to kiss him. It was a slow kiss meant to tease him enough to forget his worries.

"What if I want to be disturbed?"

Will returned the kiss, leaving no doubt that he wanted her body even if there wasn’t room for her in his life. She led him back to her bed, and they made love for the third time that night. It was much slower and gentler than the other times. His languid movements saddened her. She tried to remember every touch, kiss, and every thrust. She couldn’t see a time when she wouldn’t miss him not being in her bed.

When the sun poked its face above the horizon, Stella stretched, aware of Will’s arm resting heavily across her stomach. As she moved, a hand pulled her closer, back into the man behind her. Will’s chin rested on her shoulder, stubble from his day-old beard cut into the delicate skin.

“Ouch,” she muttered.

“Oh, I'm sorry. I forgot.”

He kissed away the pain on her skin, leaving her wanting more. She reached her hand back to pull his body closer to her own.

“Good morning, Beautiful, and how are you?” His fingers traced her collarbone and touched the locket.

“I’m good, and how are you too? Feeling what is nudging into me, I think you are quite well yourself.”

“You could say that. You could say that waking up with you always puts me in a good mood.” He pulled her closer to him. “You might even say just seeing you always puts me in a good mood.”

“Always?”

“Since the moment you arrived.” He affirmed. Her hand touched his erection.

“This sort of good mood?”

“Huhu.” The urgency of his presence behind her was enough to wake Stella’s desire as well as her brain.

“It’s a busy day today. We've got to get the jobs finished.”

“I really want to get that games room completed, Will. Do you think we can do it?”

“I don’t see why not, if we work together. I have an idea for adjusting the electronics to improve the game table. It came to me when I woke up.”

“So why are you still here and not out there sorting it out?”

“Because you're next to me. Your warm body is just too tempting. I couldn't find the energy to pull away.”

"But if I get up?"

"Why would you want to? Surely you want to stay as well. Why would either of us want to get out of this warm bed?"

"Well, you're usually out of bed ready for a swim. I really don't know what's got into you."

Will's hand came up to her breast, stroking her nipple.

"Well, this is what got into me, feeling you, knowing you would be here, how could I leave this?"

"Did you lock down the house last night?"

"No, and Grigori will be here soon."

"Yes, come on time to get up."

Chapter 47

Saturday was a day full of people hustling and bustling around. When his phone showed an incoming call from his father, he stood back from the activity buzzing around his house. His office was still his sanctuary.

"Hello, Dad."

"Just want to check in with you and see how it's going."

"Really?" Will sighed. "Why call today, Dad?"

"Sarah's here, and she mentioned she's moving. I didn't know you were selling your flat. Is everything OK?"

"It's a cash flow thing. It's only temporary." *God, I hope it is.*

"She also mentioned Stella; I thought she was only staying a week or so after whatever it was that happened in London?"

"Stella's helping with the project. I'm not exactly good at this sort of design."

"I guess she gets that from her mother. Just be careful there, son; she might be like her mother in other ways."

"I'm sorry, what?"

"I know how soft you are. She left her flat in London before Christmas. God knows where she'll go next. You know what her mother did. The way she left…"

"Look, Dad, I need to go. I have the team here."

"On the weekend?"

"Yes." William swallowed. "We've a deadline."

"Goodbye, son. Like I said, be careful."

What did that all mean? Stella is not her mother, or is she? And what the hell happened to make her run? Will cleared his desk, and as he closed the drawer. *I have to talk to her, I want to understand what she is running from. Maybe it can wait until after the launch.*

He didn't have time to worry for long. It was a busy day for him and his team, finishing off projects.

After a long day of working in different parts of the house, Will walked into Stella's workroom and, with no pleasantries, barked out.

"Right, get changed."

"I beg your pardon!" Her face told him he needed to soften his tone.

"You've worked on that long enough. You can stop now. Get changed. I'm taking you out."

"William Thoresby, are you really trying to tell me what to do?"

"Yes, sorry. Let me try again." He offered her a soft smile. "Stella, this is the third day in a row you have worked solidly. I think we will both enjoy a change of scene. I would love to take you out for something to eat. I'm happy to wait while you change out of your work clothes."

"Oh, Will, I'm tired."

"Nothing fancy, Star, but there's a brilliant Chinese restaurant. I'm sure you'll love it."

"Is it posh? Do I need to get dressed up?"

"No, I'm going in my jeans."

Stella examined his smart jeans and a white shirt.

"You're going dressed like that?"

"Yes?"

"OK. Just wanted to know." Stella turned the work in her hand and ran it through the sewing machine for one last seam.

"I'll be ten minutes."

Will laughed. "Stella, I'm hungry. Please don't be long."

Stella hurried through the process of getting ready as an excited buzz filled her. *Taking me out for a meal - is this a date?* There had been a lot more than a kiss now, and part of Stella wanted this to be more. She hadn't stopped worrying about what Sarah would say or think, but when she was with Will, there was no doubt in her mind that she wanted more.

Back in the soft leather seats of William's red sports car, Stella felt the connection building. Music played quietly over the gentle hum of the engine. The seat hugged her as William drove them to a small town a couple of miles from his house. Stella settled down into her seat, looking out at the bright neon lights that lit up the darkness outside the window. It might be a cold spring night, but she felt snug and safe with Will.

The Chinese restaurant stood proudly at the end of the street. Red lanterns lit the front and sides of a traditional building. The place seemed huge compared with any sort of restaurant she had seen back home.

Maybe she was excited, or perhaps she had forgotten which country she was in, but she looked the wrong way as she started to cross the road. A large black SUV flew past in front of her. William grabbed her hand and pulled her by his side. He held her all the way to the door, where he stopped to open it before ushering her through.

A small man in a black suit greeted William as if he were a long-lost son. He led them to a table surprisingly close to the kitchen door. Will helped her remove her coat and pulled out a chair.

"Do you think my mum would be happy?"

"With the car, with the coat, and the chair bit, sure. Although I don't know if she'd appreciate the choice of venue."

William passed her a menu and asked what she would like to begin with.

"Oh, there are so many lovely things I can't make up my mind."

"That's good. I'm glad you think so. Can I suggest I pick things we can share?" When Stella excitedly nodded her agreement, Will passed the menu to the server.

"I think four to start." The server nodded and walked away.

"I take it you come here often."

"Eating out is quite the norm around here. And you know me, I like things kept simple. Once I find somewhere I like, it's easier just to keep going back to the same place."

Their server returned with glasses and a bottle of wine. Before Stella had taken her first long drink, two more servers arrived with full plates and set them on a lazy Susan in the middle of the table. Small bowls were placed in front of Will and Stella.

And so began the most wonderful Chinese banquet Stella had ever enjoyed. Will did little more than nod and smile at the servers, and yet, more wonderful, fragrant food kept arriving at the table for them to share.

"I'm sorry I can't eat another mouthful."

"Then we should go home. I'll just organise paying the bill." Will handed over a card, and the server disappeared. He returned and spoke quietly in Will's ear. Although she couldn't hear the words, Stella could tell that his card had been declined. She swiftly produced her own card to pay the bill. Will was perplexed and hadn't noticed that she'd settled the bill. He was busy tapping on his phone to try to find out what had happened with this account.

"Come on, Will, we can sort this out later." Stella took his hand and led him back to his shiny red car.

"But…

"Don't worry about it, Will. I've paid."

"But…"

"Come on, Will."

"I just don't understand it, Stella. I'm so sorry. I'll pay you back."

Stella laughed.

"The first time you take me out, William Thoresby, and you can't pay the bill."

"But Stella, something is wrong."

"Stop worrying, William, it's the sort of thing that happens every day. I don't know how banks get away with it, but it happens. Don't worry, it'll get sorted out." She pushed against his shoulder. "Now, are you going to let me drive this car?"

"I would, Stella, you know I would, but you're not insured." Stella opened her mouth to complain, then laughed.

"Anything you say, William." And she climbed back into the softest car seats in the world.

That night, they slept in Stella's room. It was becoming a habit.

Chapter 48

Will could not sleep. He didn't understand why the restaurant declined his card. The account he had given to Stella to use to buy anything she needed was now empty. At three in the morning, he slipped out of the bed Stella had created for his sister and made his way in the darkness to his office.

As he studied the latest purchases, all of them in the last four days. They were all furniture stores, and he thought the names might be designers. Turmoil filled his whole body. His hands shook as he rechecked the transactions.

Has she just been pretending to make things? Are these just last-minute panic buys? God! Star, do you know anything about budgets?

He stayed in his office all day. William couldn't bear to watch her. He could hear the cheerful voices of his team working away in the rest of the house. Every now and then, Stella's voice would rise above them, every time it did, it made him stop. He simply didn't understand all the emotions he was feeling right now. His father's voice rattled around in his head. *Be Careful. She ran away. She could be like her mother.*

After tomorrow, there was no reason for her to stay. She still had some work to do for Marco. Maybe he should talk to him about money. Just because Marco had more cash than him, it didn't mean he would be happy to lose some. *Perhaps that is why she is so interested in working for him? She can see that the Italian clearly has far more money than me.*

He tried to block these thoughts from his mind and focus on the latest project for his technology company. They had been perfecting a new computer screen mounting system. If he could return his attention to that, they might get it to market as soon as he had some capital back to pay for the statutory testing.

He sent a series of curt messages to the group chat.

Busy in my office. Only disturb me if necessary.

Food will be available from eleven.

The cleaning crew arrives at 2, so you should be out by then.

He had disabled the computer door entry with so many people coming and going. He was shocked but not surprised when Vanessa walked into his office. She was the only one who had disturbed him.

"William, why are you in here?"

"I'm working on the paperwork for that new screen mounting."

"Do you have any idea what's going on out there?"

"It all seemed to be getting there yesterday; the cleaners will be here soon."

"Look, just say the word, and I can have a team here to sort this out tonight. You can't seriously think that is OK. I mean the primary suite … it's blue. A very dark blue at that. It would take a few coats, but I'm sure my team could have it sorted by the morning."

Will swallowed. Whatever had happened with this money, he felt sure Stella was on the right track. If they sold two plots, they would be solvent again. He knew he had to stand by her and hope the financial issue could be resolved after the launch.

"No. Leave it."

"I don't understand you, William Thoresby. You've been a different man since that girl arrived." Vanessa stared at him, and he returned her stare until a text bounced in.

Marco: How many rooms do you need?
Will: Just me and Stella, so two.

I'm not ready to tell him. What the hell will I do there? I'll go to work.

Will: I need to go to the office. I might be late. Look after her.
Marco: Always

How am I going to tell Marco? How am I going to tell anyone?

Stella was busy, but not too busy to realise Will was avoiding her. *Has he always been this moody, and I just conveniently blocked it out?* Grigori had suggested it was typical Will behaviour when his head was

in work mode, and he didn't seem at all worried. Stella, though, felt convinced it was something to do with her.

She was nursing a coffee and trying to stay focused on getting everything done before the two o'clock deadline. Try as she might, she couldn't stop thinking, *What happens after this?* She had the primary suite to finish at Marco's, and Maribeth had hinted she might have more work to discuss with her.

Stella had seen Vanessa slip out of Will's office. She had no idea how long she had been in there or why he was seeing her when he claimed he was busy. *"Have I done it again? Now that this project is finished, is he back with her?"* She mindlessly flicked through her phone, looking for flights. A text message bounced in, making her jump.

John K: Is that house up for sale?

Stella: Which?

John K: The one you are living in?

Stella: At the right price, I guess. It all goes on the market tomorrow.

John K: Any chance I can come and look at it today?

John K: For my parents. They want something, and Marco says it's very British.

Stella: It's a bit crazy here, and I still need to go out and buy lemons and oranges and flowers, probably if I can find any on a Sunday, that is.

John K: If I deliver lemons, oranges and flowers, could I look around whilst I was there?

Stella: I don't know.

Stella looked at her long to-do list. *How would John know what flowers to buy? I can always go myself whilst the cleaners are in.*

Stella: Do you know anything about buying flowers?

John K: I know a florist, and I mean really know :)

Stella: OK, can you make it about 2:30?

John K: Sure.

With that sorted, Stella got back to the last few jobs with renewed energy. That energy was buoyed up even more when Patrick arrived with Poppy to set up the refreshments.

"Stella, it looks amazing." Patrick seemed to see it all for the first time, despite being there just a few days before.

"Was it her?" Poppy hissed.

"Sorry?"

"Your executive assistant, was it that woman. What did Will say?" Stella's eyes flew to the office door.

"I haven't told him. He has enough to worry about. Anyway, how would I prove it?"

"She is …"

"Look, we probably need her tomorrow. She's careful about who knows what. She particularly protects Will from having to worry about the details."

Grigori came in with a second box of wine glasses.

"Don't tell me she has been up to her old tricks again?"

"Let's just get through this, and we can all talk to Will."

Patrick looked over Poppy's shoulder.

"If you need me to say anything…"

"Not today, please."

The team had left when Will came out of his office for more coffee. Stella was talking to the cleaning crew and explaining what was needed when John Kingston arrived with two large arrangements of flowers and some fruit.

"I wasn't expecting you?"

"I'm just bringing these for Stella," he said, holding up the bag of fruit. "Is she around?"

Will didn't need to answer because Stella swooped in and kissed John on the cheek.

"John, they are fabulous. Thank you."

"I'm hoping it was worth my while."

"Come this way." And she took him down the corridor towards the bedrooms.

"I didn't know what to say." John hissed.

"I think it's best we don't say anything at the moment. Everyone is tense enough about tomorrow."

"Is that what is wrong with William?"

"I hope so. To be honest, he hasn't spoken to me all day. Here, this is one bedroom. There are five down here like this. Plus, two more down the primary suite hallway."

"Mum and Dad have six grandchildren. I'm pretty sure they won't all be here, but Mum lives in hope. Thank you for doing this. I've been so stressed trying to find the right place for them. They find it all so different from what they are used to in Surrey.

What John saw impressed him, and they wandered back towards the freshly finished kitchen.

"This is a nice size."

"I think so."

"Would you mind if I took a few photos?"

"As long as they are only for your parents, it should be fine."

"Do you think William would sell this one? Marco said he might need an immediate sale."

"I couldn't say, you would need to speak to Will, probably on Tuesday."

"If I could get a few photos of the bedroom, I should have thought of it before."

"Sure, we can do that."

John took numerous photos of all the bedrooms, and Stella explained the areas that could be easily changed. As they left the bedroom Stella had designed for Sarah, John hugged her.

"Thank you, Stella, that's exactly what I needed."

"You're very welcome."

As she pulled away from the hug, she saw a scowling Will disappearing around the corner. *Surely, he doesn't think anything about that.*

Chapter 49

Stella had slept fitfully at Marco's last night, but as far as she knew, William hadn't turned up. She tried not to think about where he'd slept, but that didn't stop her from imagining him laughing about her with Vanessa. *Where else could he be?*

Stella examined her fingers. Every scratch, every mark, every pinprick had come down to this. The success and reward for all that effort would be known by the end of the day. She looked around for Will. She'd hardly seen him since he'd disappeared from her bed in the middle of the night. They'd been so close; now she missed his constant need to touch or kiss her. All those stolen moments, then nothing.

When the first agent arrived, Stella's stomach tumbled before it rumbled. It had been a long time since breakfast, where she'd only managed a black coffee and a yoghurt. *It's today. All this work is the big test. This is it.*

Poppy and her team had set up in the service kitchen. Vanessa had swooped on the first agent to arrive and began by showing him the technology around the television. Poppy's red goodie bags stood ready to collect at the side of a neat pile of twelve named packs, explaining that the plots would go on the open market on Friday.

Maribeth arrived dressed to impress and in a cloud of Dior. The twinkle in her eye was a sign of her excitement. She hurried over to hug Stella, kissing her on both cheeks.

"Can we look at the children's bedrooms and the outside?" Pulling Stella out of the room, she whispered, "I might need you to talk to one of my clients." Safely inside the cutest room Stella had ever produced, Maribeth started again.

"First, I need to say you look great, as does the house. Where's Will?"

"Still in his office, I think."

"Definitely want to buy one. I want to pick the plot for that today."

"Sure."

"Now, the client I'd like you to help me with is a new mum. She's seen a blog you did on technology for little ones. When she came to me last year, she talked about this post on how important it was. It was only yesterday that I realised you wrote it. She is so excited."

"I've been working on an update for that post based on Thoresby Technology. I've learned so much whilst I've been here." Stella opened the door to the little girl's bathroom. Maribeth stood soaking in the soft colours and fabrics. Stella had added the paintings from her mum and the two differently sized giraffes. The smallest one had a ribbon around its neck with the name Martha on it.

Maribeth studied the paintings. She turned to Stella, smiling.

"Are these Judy's work?"

"Yes, I love them in here."

"Let me get my client on FaceTime. I'll show her the room and then pass her over to you." Maribeth stood to one side and lifted her phone.

"Morning, Freya."

"Where have you been? It feels like forever…"

"I had to get here first. Look, I've brought Stella down to the bedrooms so we can talk. Just look …" Maribeth scanned the room with her phone.

"Oh, that's fabulous … I haven't seen giraffes like that before."

"They are bespoke. You could have elephants, crocodiles, whatever…" Maribeth handed the phone to Stella.

"I couldn't believe it when Mrs Stanford told me that you had designed the children's rooms."

"She's designed it all," Maribeth called out in the background.

"The point is you can have exactly what you want," Stella said.

"Is there a nanny's room?"

"In this current design, you've got five rooms on this wing … You can configure them how you like. These are just a few ideas for showcasing our partners. Let me show you the technology we've used here. The shower and the bath filler are both digital. That means you can set a precise temperature for the shower or the bathwater. You can set the depths of the bathwater. So, every shower and every bath are just right for your little one at the touch of a button or a word to the computer." Stella paused to show the client the room. "This computer can be the ultimate baby monitor. So, nanny, or you can check on the baby. It's also flexible; it can grow with them. We can add locks on cupboards and windows for when they start moving."

"Bespoke?"

"Yes, within our structure, there is capacity to make most things bespoke. Watch … Star play lullaby mode." The computer played soft music accompanied by simple dancing lights.

"And you will help me, Stella?"

"I will."

"Go ahead, Maribeth, buy it… As we discussed."

"I think we'd better go and find Will."

Stella opened the door to Will's office. He didn't look pleased to see her. When Maribeth followed her in, his face changed. That moment Vanessa called her name, so she left them talking plots and money. She knew Maribeth wanted to finalise her role as the agent by Monday.

Vanessa stood talking to a tall man she didn't recall from the preview.

"Stella, this is Vincent Lancaster. He has some questions about the artwork. As you've changed so much since you came on board, I think you are best suited to help him."

"I'll do my best." Stella offered them both a smile.

"From what I've seen already, the primary suite might be a good place to hold this conversation." The man's deep voice was full of authority.

"This way then." Stella smiled. "Did I miss you at the preview?"

"I sent my number two."

"I see. Could I offer you a drink, something to eat?"

"Maybe later. I'll get straight to the point. I didn't come myself, as the invitation suggested it would be like another box with the same art by LaRoche. I sent my guy because I was intrigued about the technology."

"But you're here today, yourself?"

"The photos of the preview made me look online. Could you help me understand how everything ties together? How available is all this?"

"You certainly can buy Thoresby Technology for any building, home, or office. This home was built for Mr Thoresby, so it has the latest ideas. These may be made available on the open market if pricing allows. You'd need to talk to Will. I thought you wanted to talk about the art."

"I do. Is that available elsewhere?"

"We engage with a range of local artisans who make the individual pieces to work with Thoresby Technology. You could commission work from them, but not our designs."

"So, this screen, for example …"

"Designed and made by the team. Unique to this development."

"And this artwork?"

"The image is personal to the owner, I'm sure you're not asking me as the artist, details of my process."

"You personally produced the art in here?" Stella spun around the room, taking in all the individual pieces she had created for William.

"Yes, Mr Lancaster, I did. Each piece of artwork and furniture was individually designed for Mr Thoresby." Stella's heart clamped as she thought of all the love she poured into this room for a man who was struggling to look at her. She'd caught him whispering to Vanessa once too often in the last two days. Had she really been that stupid again?

"Can you show me some more. I saw a child's room."

"Of course, this way. The team has used Thoresby Technology to create a safe environment for young ones. We think it will help young families buy with confidence." She pushed open the door.

"You haven't skimped on artwork in here, though." He stopped in front of the colourful painting her mum had sent.

"These remind me of Judy Finch. But these are new, and she hasn't sold work in over twenty years."

"Twenty-three years. When she had me."

"You mean they are Judy Finch? Are they for sale?"

"Not at the moment."

"There are ten plots available, is that correct?" Maybe it was the anger she was feeling towards William, but Mr Lancaster and his tone were seriously making it hard for her to stay polite.

"We did have ten plots. We've sold two this morning. Two more are in talks. And a fifth has inquiries." Stella crossed her fingers with that last statement, but she felt Marco was still keen. "I do not doubt that when we go to the open market on Friday, they will sell quickly."

"The open market? Will you have an agent in place by then?"

"As I said, you would need to talk to William Thoresby, but I believe that's in place, too. I could be wrong. It's a shame you missed the preview, Mr Lancaster. Other companies have turned up today ready to secure the plots they want for their clients."

"I'd better not waste any more time."

The agents were lingering, chatting to each other, and enjoying the wine. Poppy and Stella began clearing the food and glasses to prepare for the next event. William stayed doggedly in his office. Stella watched as Vanessa made up a plate for his lunch. *Let her... I hope they'll be very*

happy together. Every time Vanessa spoke, it felt like a dig. Vanessa waltzed out of William's office and was now flirting with Mr Lancaster. Poppy came over with some lunch for Stella.

"I don't know how you work with her, she's busy flirting with that man, whilst bragging about how hard it is being engaged to someone you work with." Stella's heart stopped beating just for that fleeting second. The lump sitting in her chest was slow and painful. *Did she mean Will? Poppy obviously didn't think so. I have. I've done it again.*

The atmosphere was very different after lunch. Davey and Hidir arrived early, which helped to lift Stella's mood. The look on Vanessa's face still unnerved her. People wanted to interview William and her. Poppy and Patrick were busy making contacts and booked some visits to the winery. The red bags for the press were larger, and Stella had provided a thumb drive with exclusive images for the afternoon group.

She could see that Vanessa was getting bored because no one was talking to her. Davey winked at Stella as he and Hidir videoed an interview with her.

"I'm going to send you a copy of this," Davey whispered to Stella.

"Why?"

"I'm also sending you a copy of the emails she sent me this week."

"Emails?" Davey took her into another room to explain the situation.

"Yes, emails, saying it had been moved to Tuesday. She had one guy still coming. Hidir messaged everyone else to make sure they came." Stella was a little stunned but not surprised.

"It's becoming a bit of a pattern with her. I'm not sure I can keep going with her around. She tried this with the winery, too. Thankfully, they thought to check." Vanessa was hovering outside the room as they left.

"Love the winery idea, Stella," Hidir said softly.

"Oh, that was William's idea," Stella said loud enough to ensure Vanessa would hear.

Chapter 50

The success of the day put a skip into Stella's step as she went to the kitchen for a snack. It had been a long day, and even she was aware she hadn't eaten or drunk nearly enough. At last, Will's comments about looking after herself were starting to sink in.

Finally seeing the results of her work, Stella could see a future for herself here in Los Angeles. Opening the fridge, she saw the champagne. Yes, she'd had a successful day, but without him to share it with, she had no desire to celebrate. Instead, she took a glass of water and an apple over to the window to look at the newly furnished deck. It was next to Will's pool and her favourite place. With her eyes locked on the storm rolling across the other side of the valley, she wasn't looking at the apple and knocked it onto the floor. It rolled behind the heavy fabric dressing the portman doors.

Stella followed, lifting the fabric in search of the fruit. She froze as angry voices entered the room.

"Will, you're being so blind. Surely you know, actually, to check references when you employ someone."

"But it's Star!" Stella froze. They clearly didn't know she was there, and now didn't seem like a good time to tell them.

"You still don't even know how she lost her job." Stella gripped her glass. She was sure they would hear her swallow. It was so loud.

"She doesn't want to talk about it, and I didn't want to push her."

"You're an idiot!"

"So, you keep saying."

"Well, I've done some checking. This morning, I spoke to a Mr Jackson Wilde." Stella's appetite had left her. She stood clutching her glass, the apple forgotten on the floor. "At first, he refused to say anything, but when I pushed, he said he should have kept a better eye on her spending. She was buying lunches and gifts for everyone, including champagne. Have you been checking her use of your card?"

"If she had done something wrong like that, I'm sure Sarah would have told me."

"What has your sister told you?"

"Nothing."

"If she has been sacked for misappropriation of money, would Sarah actually know?"

"You seem sure, V."

"Why would Mr Wilde lie?"

Stella listened, waiting for Will to defend her. Will had always defended her. She didn't hear the words she was waiting for. This time, she had to watch Will walk off with his arm around Vanessa's shoulder as they disappeared into the primary suite. The space she had put her heart and soul into for him.

How do you sleep after that? I believed him when he said he wasn't sleeping with Vanessa. Are all men compulsive liars or just the men she worked for?

The dark silence of her room did nothing to comfort her. Her body felt like lead, and she hadn't even started to get ready for bed. She lay curled on her side, looking out at his pool, with Spike firmly clutched to her chin. *Who can I even talk to about this?*

Hey Sarah, I slept with your brother, he thinks I'm stealing from him, and yes, he's sleeping with someone you are going to love.

Hey India, I did it again, I slept with my boss, and exactly like Jackson, he is sleeping with his assistant.

Hey Zach, I should have come with you because I've worked myself into the ground yet again for a guy, I believed cared for me, and yep, he is sleeping with someone else, just like my last boss.

Hey Mum, guess what just happened again?

When her phone announced a notification, she hoped it was someone awake she could talk to.

> Stella,
> The bank account is now completely empty.
> Please make sure I have a complete copy of the accounts, including receipts, if available.
> Will.

Stella didn't hear William's caramel voice when she read the email. No, she heard the leering voice of her old boss. Heat hit her face.

I haven't spent any of his bloody money. How could he think I'd …
Of course, if he listens to Vanessa and her new friend Jackson…

Stella jumped up from the bed and, with trembling hands, put her laptop on the desk. She had good records, but the last few days had been so busy that she still had a few last things to update on the spreadsheet. As silent tears slid down her cheeks, her fingers stabbed at the keyboard. She wasn't sure who she was most angry with. Logic said Jackson or Vanessa, but Will's behaviour hurt more, and yet she was probably the most furious with herself for believing Will loved her and wasn't simply keeping her working above and beyond, as her last boss had.

She wrote the email, attached the invoice and receipts file, and saved it to her drafts. She couldn't be here when he got this. She wouldn't slap William's face like she did Jackson. She knew she couldn't watch Will with Vanessa or anyone else he took into that room. *If I'm leaving, I might as well go now.*

She ordered an Uber, and that gave her thirty minutes. She packed her laptop first and then just the clothes she came with. This was the time to travel light; she didn't even bother to clear the bathroom.

She swapped today's smart dress for jeans. With a heavy heart and her trainers in her hand, she made her way through the house. In the hall, her eyes fell on the canvas scene of Jack's Landing, which brought fresh tears to her eyes. *Surely, I can't have any more tears. When I get home, I'm giving up crying forever.*

Still walking as softly as she could, she realised the front door won't work, and she didn't want the lift to make a noise. She swallowed her sobs, walking barefoot would be wasted if she woke the house up with her crying. *What am I thinking, if they are christening that master on those soft sheets he asked for, they won't hear me in the basement.*

Her lift would be here soon. She worried Will would be alerted when the gate opened, even if she used her fob, so she waited inside the gate until her Uber arrived.

In the back of the car, she finally let go of the emotions she had been holding onto so tightly. The sobs were over now, but silent tears flowed endlessly down her cheeks.

Her flight wouldn't leave until six a.m. In thirteen hours, she would be home. She desperately needed to be in the air and on her way. She sat at the same table that she had waited for William at nine weeks earlier. *Why hadn't I seen that as a sign? Why didn't I just go when I saw him dismiss my call that first day?*

Stella sipped hot tea and nibbled at a raspberry and white chocolate muffin. They were her favourite, but today it gave her no joy. She didn't

know if all the tears had ruined her taste buds or if the airport had rubbish muffins. What did it matter?

She mused over what to do with all the material Davey had forwarded to her. Who did she share it with? Would Will believe her? Watching the video where Vanessa claimed ownership of the project and yet still managed to disrespect Stella's input left her baffled. Davey had assured her that they wouldn't be using the footage, so could she even share it with anyone?

When her flight time approached, she headed to the bathroom and washed her face, determined to find some dignity. Squaring her shoulders in front of the mirror, she scolded herself once more.

Stella wasn't a nervous flyer, but today her stomach was filled with a strange foreboding, like the worst hadn't even happened yet. Queuing to board, she pulled out her phone. It was time to press send on that email to Will. Before she put her phone back in her pocket, a text bounced in.

SARAH: How did it go?
STELLA: Sold three.
SARAH: I wasn't expecting a reply so quickly.
STELLA: At the airport. 6:05 flight. See you soon.
SARAH: What happened?
STELLA: Just boarding. Phone is going off.

Stella had the length of her flight to decide what to tell Sarah. That wasn't going to be an easy decision.

Chapter 51

Will had settled Vanessa in the primary suite, then left to sleep in his old room. He had fallen in love with the room Stella had created for him, just like he had fallen in love with Star. Knowing she had drained his bank account to do it had taken the edge off it. He couldn't enjoy it. To him, it was a visual reminder of how she had betrayed him.

He had one hope, that in the morning, when she got his email, she would be able to explain everything. He turned over and started to replay all their conversations. He thought, based on everything she said, that she was spending a lot less than Vanessa. *I presume I have to pay her fees, though, whereas I was already paying V. I've no idea how much she charges. Why didn't I ask? She has worked a lot of hours.*

He woke to his phone ringing. It came as a shock that he had actually fallen asleep. He fumbled with his phone, and eventually he saw Sarah's face on the screen. The call dropped out, and he lay back, trying to get his bearings. Almost immediately, Sarah called again. By the time he pushed on his glasses and answered, his sister was beside herself.

"What have you done now?"

"Sorry? I'm not sure I've done anything."

"I don't believe that. And if you don't even realise it, well..."

Will pushed the hair off his face and sat up on the bed.

"I've got a question for you, sister. Why on earth didn't you tell me Stella had been sacked because of money irregularities?"

"What?"

"My assistant spoke to someone called Jackson Wilde. He explained why she was sacked."

"And you believed it?"

"Well, why would he lie?"

"I said I wouldn't tell anyone, so if you repeat this, I really am going to kill you. But when Stella RESIGNED, she handed in her notice by slapping his face." She stopped for the briefest moment. "I might add the guy had no trousers on at the time, and they weren't alone. If you'd like a reference for Jackson Bloody Wilde, ask India, or any of her friends. They'll tell you what a snake he is. So, maybe he'd lie rather than admit the truth. Of course, that is, if it was Jackson Wilde and not some story from that assistant of yours."

Well, that is something I hadn't considered.

Grrr. The fact remains that the account is empty.

"Look, it's six thirty here. I'm going to get to the bottom of this as soon as Grigori gets here, and Stella is up. I've asked for her receipts…"

"You asked her?"

"I sent an email last night.

"You mean after weeks of work, you emailed her on the day she sold three plots for you? You email her after the hours she has put in this for receipts? Seriously, Will!"

"Stop it! Sorry, you're scaring me." Will rubbed the back of his head. "I'm going to sort it this morning. Grigori will be here by eight, and then I can talk to Stella, too."

"I think you might be out of luck there, my brother."

"If Stella's done nothing wrong, then this can be quickly sorted."

"Can you get to your emails as we talk?"

"Hang on, I was asleep when you rang, and I'm not in my own room."

"Whose bedroom are you in, for God's sake? What have you done?"

"Relax. Just a spare one."

"Do I even want to know why?"

"Vanessa's in mine, and to be honest, I felt so betrayed by Stella last night, I couldn't face seeing all her work in there. Hang on, I'll go to my office."

"Betrayed! Jesus Will." She muttered.

Whilst he walked, he kept talking to Sarah. "What made you ring in the first place, Sarah? Have you been in touch with Stella?"

"I just sent her a text to ask how the big day went. She said you'd sold three plots. She said she couldn't go into detail because she was about to board a plane and that she would see me very soon."

"Sorry, what was that last sentence? It sounded like you said she was getting on a plane."

"That is because I said she was getting on a plane." He quit the call.

Will made his way to her room and threw open the door.

No Stella.

He was still confused as he found some clothes still hanging in the wardrobe, and her bathroom was the usual mess of bottles; he couldn't understand the need for them. And yet some things were gone. Her case, all her many bags, and her laptop. He slumped down onto the empty,

unmade bed. She had, after all that, fled. Had she really abandoned him? His dad had warned him.

He dropped his head on her pillow, still full of her scent. And under the pillow was still Spike, the knitted puppy with the pink nose. It broke his heart again to think of that lost little girl. He hadn't been very old, but he knew what pain she must have felt that day. Giving up Spike seemed the thing to do. He certainly didn't want her to give him back.

He closed his eyes.

>>Welcome, Grigori.<<

"Star, start the coffee."

>>Coffee is ready in the kitchen.<<

It took a great deal of effort for Will to leave her room, closing the door carefully. He didn't want anyone else in there. He found Grigori in the service kitchen looking for mugs.

"I thought I'd better use the old ones. What are we doing about the kitchen? Do you want to keep it dressed and ready?" Will looked blank. Grigori pulled out a third mug. "Is Stella joining us?"

"No."

"No to the kitchen or Stella?"

"No to Stella, I don't know about the kitchen." Grigori poured two coffees and took the milk from the fridge. Will didn't want to tell him she'd left. If he did, that would make it all so much more real. He was pretty sure his project manager wouldn't be pleased with the news. The two men sipped their coffee in silence.

"So yesterday we had a stream of deliveries that I assume arrived courtesy of your business manager."

"Vanessa?"

"Who else? She was just waiting to sweep in and save your day yet again. You do know she didn't cancel the catering, and I had to send them away?"

"Vanessa?"

"I don't know why you sound so shocked. I see her car is still outside, so I presume she is still here, and we can go through how much of this we can send back. I can't see Marco buying all this."

"I guess so." Will was still struggling to understand everything he'd been told.

"I really think you need to talk to her. We can't be having all this hassle with every house we build."

"No, you're right. It's not as if I haven't tried telling her to focus on the office and the direct product market. The good news is I have three buyers for you to start work on, so you will be able to start on them as soon as the paperwork has cleared."

"We've enough work next door to keep us busy for a couple of weeks, and I'd like to give the team some time off after how hard they've worked over the last couple of weeks."

"Good idea."

"I'd better go find Stella then and ask her about this bedroom at Marco's." *Shit, so much for keeping to myself for a while.*

"She's not here."

"When will she be back?"

"I don't know." *Damn,* "Look, I need to be honest; she's flown back to the U.K. I only found out when I spoke to my sister this morning."

"I knew things were bad on Sunday. I didn't realise it was that bad."

"Sunday?"

"You ignored her, and she was struggling. I thought she must be tired, carrying all that in her head, alone sort of."

"Alone?"

"Well, she was the one everyone was asking questions. You were hiding in your office, and she was doing it all alone."

"I wasn't hiding. I was working."

"I'm sure you were. It still left her having to do it all out here. And now she isn't here, but Vanessa is. I'm telling you now, boss, I can't work with that vampire again.

William felt sick.

I'm such an idiot. Maybe it's just as well she left, if I can't support her.

Chapter 52

Will couldn't make sense of what he was looking at. All the invoices and receipts from Stella had no relation to the purchases on his now empty bank account. He felt physically sick as he checked off each of her receipts. They all made sense. What didn't make sense were all the purchases on his account. He wanted to speak to Stella so much, but her phone was turned off; he could only assume she was still on the plane.

He knew Grigori wanted to talk to him about returning the pile of deliveries he'd intercepted on Monday, whilst they'd been busy with the launch. He was hoping that those deliveries would match the amounts spent recently. When he couldn't stand looking at the numbers any longer, he took himself outside. Unable to sit down, he paced around the pool.

He sat, staring at the water. In his mind, he could see her swimming in that damn red bikini. The vision vanished the moment Vanessa walked out of the door towards him; he felt his fists clench.

Everyone had warned him about her, so why hadn't he listened?

"OMG, I've the worst headache from sleeping in that room. All that blue. It should come with a warning."

"I don't suppose the headache has anything to do with the wine you were drinking?"

"You could be right, William. I did warn you about serving an inferior product." William choked on his coffee.

"Which brings me to what I tried to tell you last night. I won't stay here working for someone who won't take my advice. I can't believe what you let happen yesterday. It was pretty much a disaster. If I hadn't been here to smooth over the cracks, I don't know what would have happened." William hadn't shared with Vanessa about the sales he had confirmed yesterday.

"Do you think you made any sales yesterday?"

"Well, I might have managed several if it hadn't been for that little girl you brought in to play with her paints. The people want to buy art from someone they've heard of."

"I see. And did you say you were leaving?"

"My new boyfriend, I should say fiancé, doesn't want me upset when my advice is ignored, so I'm going to be his new executive assistant."

William thought he should feel relieved, but he still felt heavy. It was too late; his Star had gone. He swallowed the hurt.

"In which case, hand over your keys, your phone, and your laptop, and I will ensure that you get every penny you are owed."

"Well … it's nice to know all my hard work has been appreciated." The sarcasm was strong as Vanessa snarled at William.

"I hope you know I did appreciate your work, Vanessa. But that didn't give you the right to do some of the things that you have done recently."

Don't start a discussion about it; you can't win. Just get her out of here.

William wondered if he should escort her off the premises; her behaviour had become so extreme. He was relieved when Grigori came around the corner.

"G, Vanessa is leaving. I wonder if you could help her carry her things to the car?" Grigori nodded.

"Vanessa, if you have your phone, etc., here, please leave them. It will save you a trip to the office." He knew full well she had them with her yesterday. Grigori smiled at him.

"I can do that, boss. The people from the winery are here to collect their things. I thought you'd want to know."

"Thank you."

William walked slowly to the service kitchen, where Patrick was packing boxes. Poppy walked in, carrying a huge basket of flowers.

"I wanted to thank Stella. She's been so generous. We've made so many contacts with the press. And I've booked three events for the bar just this morning. Where is she?" William looked at his watch.

"I guess she'll be somewhere over the Atlantic."

"Already?"

William sank into a chair. Patrick and Poppy sat down with him.

"Are you OK?"

"No, I've been so stupid. Someone told me things about her that were hard to believe. I don't think I really ever believed it, but I was so shocked, so upset, that I asked her to explain." He sighed. "I guess she thought I did believe it, and she left."

"But you've cleared it up now?"

"I tried, but I haven't managed to speak to her yet."

"Did she tell you that Vanessa tried to cancel us, pretending she was Stella's assistant?"

"No." Will shook his head.

"She tried to cancel the press, too, Davey told me."

"And Stella knew?" Poppy nodded. "I don't get why she'd protect Vanessa."

"I think it was more a case of her protecting you." Poppy offered.

"She's gone, Boss, but why was she in your room?"

"I didn't sleep with her if that's what you are suggesting."

"I'm sorry if I got the wrong impression. I hope no one else did."

"God! You mean Stella might have thought, but I told her I wasn't. I haven't ..."

<<Welcome, Marco. William is in the great room.>>

Will dropped his head into his hands.

"Please! Please not now."

Marco wasn't alone. John Kingston followed him into the room. Will remembered the sight of him leaving Stella's bedroom on Sunday. *Is that something else I've been stupid about?*

"What do you want, Kingston?" Will snapped out, pulling himself up to his full height.

"Didn't Stella tell you?"

"Tell me what?" His patience had gone.

"I want to buy this house; well, my parents do. I explained it all to her when she showed me the place on Sunday." Will's stare must have unsettled him because he tried to explain more.

"Stella did say not to mention she'd shown me around on Sunday. I'm sorry if that is a problem."

"You came on Sunday to look around? And not to see Stella?"

"Yes."

"But you arrived with flowers?"

"That was the price. That doesn't sound good. She said she was too busy to show me around and that she still had to buy flowers and lemons. So, I persuaded her that I could save her time if she could show me around the house. I needed to speak to my parents, and I knew we couldn't come on Monday because it was your big day..."

"So, you brought the flowers for the launch?"

"And oranges and lemons. Look, is there a problem?"

"No."

"Where is Stella? I still have a couple of questions for her."

William's head dropped again, and Poppy stood with her arm around his shoulders. It was Patrick who explained.

"Stella's gone. She took an early flight back to the U.K."

The group sat down with Will, each of them quiet except, of course, Marco. He didn't hide his feelings.

"I knew you could be an idiot sometimes, Will, but I thought you had a breakthrough as far as Stella was concerned. Hell, I was taking bets on the name of your firstborn. I felt sure Stella would want to call him Marco, but Patrick here thought you would want something more English." *Martha, I want to call her Martha.*

"Shut up, Marco," Poppy interrupted. "This isn't the time. Look, Will, what did she say? Couldn't you stop her?"

"She didn't say anything. That's the whole point. I woke up to my sister screaming down the phone at me. Her room is empty. Well, not empty, but she's gone, and so has her laptop and stuff."

"If she was upset because she thought you didn't believe her, she might not have wanted to pack everything." Poppy sighed. John shook his head.

"She might be upset about other things," Grigori muttered.

"Look, I saw your face when I left on Sunday, and you clearly thought the flowers were a romantic gesture. If I've caused all this, I'm sorry."

"No. It's about money. Someone has emptied an account, and I stupidly thought it could be her because it was all art stuff. I'm sorry, Marco, but it looked like she could have been ripping us both off."

"Now I know you must be ill. I would have gladly paid her double for the work she did for me. She's undercharging."

"But she sold you my bathroom suite."

"Did you want it?"

"Well, no, I prefer the one I have."

"I liked it, so I bought it. I paid the list price for it, but I didn't have to wait weeks for delivery. I think she funded your room for what she sold it for."

Grigori walked over carrying a tray of coffee.

"That's right, boss. I did the figures with her. The bathroom had been delivered, and she didn't like it for you. She thought that it would suit

Marco much better, so she worked out a design that would allow her to do your whole suite for the cost of it. Marco's happy, and you got the blue room." Grigori handed the coffee around the group.

"Why do you think she's been working for me? To buy materials for you. Why do you think she spends hours at the sewing machine?" Marco paused to take a drink.

"Because it helps her to think and stay calm."

"That might be, but it also saves you money whilst making you something totally unique." Marco didn't stop. "Can't you see how she got the screen and the door pattern on so many things? Because it's her design, granted G does some of the work and the Paulo guy is a genius, but they'll both tell you they can't put it together without her. Grigori, tell him how she understands materials and construction, will you?"

"So that's why I need her?"

"No, you idiot. You need her because she is the other half of you. I like you, Will. I always have, but when she's around, it's different."

"That's what V said."

"Fuck V. It isn't a bad thing. How did you feel when she was here? That last week when you were sleeping with her? Don't look like that. Of course, I knew, we all knew; you were both so alive. The big question you've to ask yourself in life is, how do you want to feel? Not good enough, like you did with V, always trying to improve you? Or happy as yourself with Stella?" Will said nothing, but Marco couldn't stop.

"Come on, Will. How do you want to feel?" Will looked at his face, realisation slowly dawning. "Now what are you going to do to feel the way you want to feel?"

Chapter 53

Stella wasn't looking forward to the tube ride back to Putney. She wanted to crawl into her bed and hide there. And yes, Sarah was in her flat. *Everyone is probably laughing at me. How could I be so naïve?*

Despite it being over twenty hours since she left Will's house in L.A., she still did not know what she was going to do. She'd finally decided L.A. and working and living with Will would fulfil her ideas for a next step. She just hadn't found a way to talk to William about it.

Marco had been encouraging, and Maribeth had suggested there would be plenty of work. *That was when I believed that Will cared for me. I got that wrong yet again.*

Stella needed to apologise to Sarah, but she wasn't ready to do it today. No, she'd just get a train up north. When she opened her phone to check trains for Leeds and Hursts Bridge, she was greeted by a photo of them together on the beach at sunset. With a sigh, her thumb stroked over the screen.

She was still debating a destination as she came out of baggage claim and bumped straight into Sarah Thoresby.

Sarah grabbed her by the shoulders and hugged her.

"Stella, I'm so sorry. I should learn to stop messing in people's lives."

"How… I mean, I didn't ask…"

"You said you were getting on a plane; even I could work out which flight and where you would be. When Will didn't know you'd left, I knew it must be bad. You look terrible."

"I've had a long couple of days and a long flight …"

"I'm sorry. What sort of friend am I? The sort who asks you to help my helpless brother only for him to behave like the idiot he is."

"Sarah, look …" Stella didn't have the words to explain to Sarah the pain she felt or how much she was already missing Will. She'd been missing him since Sunday morning. She'd now processed what Jackson had said, and it explained why he'd always insisted on her being the one to sort the payments when they were out. It explained his threatening emails. *Was it his insurance policy with the women he employed?* It wasn't hard to work out Will's empty bank account, his bad mood, and his email to her were all connected.

"Stop, let's get you back to the flat. We can sort all this out."

"I thought I would go home… to Hursts Bridge, that is."

"If you wanted to be there, you'd have gone there and not New York."

"I'm not going to kick you out of my flat, Sarah. You're my best friend." A single tear fell as Sarah stopped to hug her again.

"Let's just get to the flat." Sarah took her bag and ushered her into a taxi. They sat together in the back of the cab. Stella couldn't find the words to say anymore to Sarah. The roads were clear so early in the day. The streetlights lit the wet pavements as Stella fought the urge to close her eyes. Sarah gripped her hand as they pulled up outside the wine shop near Putney Bridge. Although it had only been three months since Stella was here, it felt like a lifetime.

Sarah paid the driver and took charge of the bags, and Stella followed her into the building and the first-floor flat. Both girls were quiet and trying not to disturb the peace of this early London morning.

"I'll go home as soon as it's a proper time."

"Don't be silly. You need to rest first. Go and get into bed, have a shower first if you want one."

"Won't that wake up Dan and Tasha?"

"They'll be happy to see you. I'll move out quickly, I'm sorry …"

"No. Stay Sarah. I need to go home for a while."

"You aren't thinking this through. You need to speak to him." Stella stared at her friend. *I'm not sure I can. What good would it do?*

Stella felt too exhausted to argue with Sarah anymore. She went to bed, knowing she would be gone as soon as she could. *I'd better phone first. I can't see that going down well at* … She checked her phone to see it was just after 2 a.m., and she'd had a dozen missed calls from William. *Maybe Sarah is right. I'll have to talk to him. I can let him say what he has to say, and then I don't have to do anything more.*

Stella fell asleep quickly, although her body had forgotten how noisy the road outside her window was. By six a.m., she was up and dressed. Sarah was still asleep, so Stella slipped out quietly without going in to get any breakfast, not even coffee.

She took her bags to a café around the corner and ordered breakfast until it was late enough to call home. Sarah was correct in that life with her dad wasn't really a brilliant idea, but she couldn't upset her grandma.

She found a train that left at nine and would arrive in Doncaster before eleven. In the end, afraid to speak to her dad, she sent a text.

Stella: Catching the train up this morning.
Can you pick me up from Doncaster at eleven?

She wasn't expecting a quick reply, but one bounced in immediately.

Dad: I can drive down there and pick you up.

Shit, he knows, but what does he know and how?

Stella: The train will be fine.
Dad: Someone will be there. I'll let you know who.

Sarah: You didn't need to leave like that.
Stella: I'm sorry.
Sarah: You need to talk to Will. He knows he's been stupid.

On the tube, making her way to King's Cross, she could hear more messages bouncing in, but she didn't want to look during the early morning crush. In the café, she'd worked out that the second train was cheaper, meaning she could afford a first-class ticket. She would still get to the same station, and she was in no rush to get there, now that she realised they knew. It wasn't just her bag weighing her down. She felt ridiculously heavy and so relieved to sit down as the train pulled away.

When the refreshments were served, she accepted a coffee but refused anything to eat. The coffee in the paper cup was wet, but it didn't even smell like coffee, let alone taste like the drink she'd enjoyed so often from Will's magic coffee machine. She would miss great coffee. *But will you miss him? I missed him as soon as he stopped talking to me.*

Stella spent the journey reading all William's emails and text messages and thumbing through photos. She wasn't ready to listen to the voice messages, so she tried to create reasoned responses. In the end, she sent one simple reply.

Stella: I'm sorry. Please give me some space.

The moment she saw the bright scarlet coat on her grandma, Stella knew she'd made the right decision to come north. Her granddad took her bag as she was enveloped in a hug from her grandma.

"It's good to have you back."

Chapter 54

Walking away from Stella's house, all Will wanted to do was turn back and bang on the door until she listened. But she'd be upstairs, and it would be her laid-back dad coming to the door. William couldn't imagine Stella's father chasing after a woman who was 'playing hard to get'. He could remember his smart comments on a beach in France as a teenager, before Star's mother left.

He sank onto the grass at the end of the drive. He'd run out of ideas and needed to think. He'd apologised. He'd explained, and she'd accepted his apology and then closed the door. She was hurting; he could see that. It was why he so wanted to hold her.

Why had he let her down like that? He knew Stella; how could he think she would steal from him? He didn't believe that at all; he simply thought she'd got carried away with the shopping. Lord knows Vanessa had spent more than enough before Stella arrived. He couldn't believe he'd fallen for all of Vanessa's lies. He had done that, though, so now he had the job of putting as much of that right as he could.

He'd foolishly believed Stella would listen to him. She had listened. Well, she didn't speak; she waited until he'd finished, said a polite, sad thank you, and closed the door. Sitting on the grass wasn't the answer. So, what did he do now?

A text buzzed in on his phone.

Sarah: Did she listen?

Will: She listened.

Sarah: And?

Will: And nothing. She said thank you and shut the door.

Sarah: SHIT.

Will: What do I do now? She looked so ... I've never seen her without that bounce.

Sarah: Falling in love can do that. So, are you just going to give in?

Will picked up the phone and called his sister.

"I wish I could just walk away. But I can't. I need her to know … to understand how sorry I am, how much I want her, no, need her in my life."

"Come home, Will. We can talk about this."

When he walked through the door, his sister hugged him so hard.

"Thanks."

"I'm sorry. That was for me. I want to hug Stella to tell her I'm sorry, as I can't, I'm hugging you."

"Why can't you hug her?"

"She's avoiding me. You see, in Stella's head, she's let me down."

"And you think it's your fault?"

"Of course it is. I underestimated how hurt she was, and then I begged her to go to L.A. because I was worried about you."

"But you weren't to know all this would happen."

"I didn't know you would upset everything by accusing her of stealing, no. But like everyone else, I realised you would end up together. Of all the people in the world, you are the last person I thought would hurt her. I never expected it from you. She was a mess in London. Everyone could see it. I naively thought you could help each other. Heaven knows you needed to get away from Vanessa."

"I was so stupid."

"The question is why, Will. Why did you get involved with her? Vanessa, I mean."

"She's a great business manager. She was what I needed when I hired her. The problem started when the edges got blurred. It started with advice about what to wear to meetings. I listened, and she just kept doing more. Where I should be seen, things like that. I felt I needed her support at the social events. And then she started to behave as if they were dates. I started to put on the brakes, but she didn't take any notice. I should have known when she met Marco, they'd hated each other."

"He's asked Stella to decorate your old flat in London."

Will stared at his sister, trying to understand what she'd just said.

"Marco … has been in touch with Stella?"

"He didn't tell you?"

"No. And he's the one who bought the flat. Actually, that makes sense. It even makes sense that he would contact her to make sure she

was OK and offer her work. That's Marco. From what I understand from Grigori, the projects she did for Marco funded a lot of the work for me."

"You've paid her now?"

"Yes."

"You've sold five plots now."

"Sarah, I don't think you understand. Stella sold those plots herself. The people she knew and spoke to, those she showed around. They all bought plots. And through that, I now have a marketing agency I can work with, a relation of her stepfather. They've brought in more clients. We could have all the plots sold if I could bring her back."

"How many did Vanessa sell?"

"None, but she found herself a new boyfriend and resigned."

"You didn't sack her?"

"Didn't need to. It was a relief, really."

"But did you tell Stella that she left with her new boyfriend?"

"Yes."

"God! Sometimes you are so stupid, William Thoresby."

"What?"

"Don't worry, Stella, she left me for someone else, not me. I've sacked her for what she did to you. It sounds like she left, so now I've come for you, eventually."

Will swallowed, his eyes blank. His sister kept going.

"And I need you to help me sell the rest of the units! God Will, really!"

"I've explained I needed to sign contracts on those properties."

"And these friends of Stella wouldn't wait? I'm sorry, Will, I love that girl, and I'm broken that she is so hurt because of something I asked her to do."

"I love her too, and it's seeing her so hurt that's killing me."

Chapter 55

Stella stared at the empty screen. Nothing. She had absolutely nothing in her head. Nothing, she wanted to share with the world. She was resisting thinking about William. The rain rattling her window was loud, but it didn't drown out the noise from downstairs. Stella shivered with a feeling of déjà vu. The storm was nothing like the weather in SoCal. She'd told William she'd outgrown her fear of storms. It was a lie. Living with William, she'd felt so much safer, and the anxiety was less. There! Just thinking about rain, and she was thinking about him! The lead in the bottom of her stomach weighed heavier than ever.

She could hear Gemma screaming at her dad. She wasn't sure, but she had to believe it had something to do with her. Gemma had certainly been short with them both since she arrived back in Hursts Bridge. The shouting stopped when the front door slammed.

Who had left this time? What happens if my dad leaves me now?

Unable to stop herself, she looked out of the window to check which car was driving away. Seeing her dad's car still sitting in its usual place in front of the garage was a brief relief. It was one thing to be grateful for. It didn't stop her from feeling sick. *Should I talk to him? What would I say?*

The rain didn't let up. Beating down, the petals from the magnolia her mother loved so much lay sodden on the ground. The garden would look very different in the morning. What would her life look like? Had Gemma left for good or just for the night? Would she need to find somewhere else to live? Did she even care anymore?

Stella closed her laptop and drifted past the window and her bookshelf, finally lying back in her bed. Her fingers went to her locket. *How can you forget him if you insist on wearing his locket?* She tried to lift her head, but it felt too heavy. Her whole body felt heavy. She rolled her head to look out of the window again. Even when sheet lightning lit the sky, it didn't shed light on her life. All it managed to do was help her miss William Thoresby more. She wanted to be back on the floor of the cinema with him. Laughing and sharing chocolate. She wanted to be safe. And in Will's arms, she felt safe.

She closed her heavy eyes, attempting to blot out the darkness and remember the sunsets by Will's pool. Instead, she was filled with the

same haunted feeling she felt when he shut down and pulled away from her. *Was that why I'd turned him away yesterday? Am I trying to avoid facing that feeling of loss again?*

A vision of William walking away filled her head as a quiet knock came on the bedroom door. Her eyes flew open to see her dad's head appear.

"Hey, sweetheart, can I come in?"

"Sure."

In response, he pushed open the door with his foot and carried in a sandwich on a plate and a mug.

"I thought you might be hungry."

"Thanks, Dad. Is everything OK? Did I hear Gemma leave?"

"Ha, yes, don't worry, she's gone to her sister's for a week. It will give us some time together." Stella tried to smile, but she couldn't imagine spending much time with him. What she really needed right now was her mum.

Richard Barrington Jones stood back from his daughter's bed and pulled the house phone from his back pocket. "I nearly forgot, your mum phoned to speak to you." He blushed as he pushed the handset toward her. Stella hadn't heard the phone ring; she knew it was her father who had made the call.

"Hello Mum."

"Hello darling, I just thought I'd see how you were doing?"

"What did Dad say?"

"I forgot you're grown up. I miss the days when we could tell you what we thought you wanted to hear. Your dad says you've been in your room, and you've been avoiding them."

"I have to admit I haven't been down to meals. I don't know how to talk about this or if I even want to. And now I think I've ruined another of my father's marriages."

"I think you're going to have to explain that. Which of your dad's marriages have you ruined, as you call it?"

"All of them, of course."

"Gemma has just gone away for a few days. She can see you need time with your dad. She's not all that terrible. I'm pretty sure your dad didn't need any help with the other two."

“And what about you? Was having a child, being a mum, part of what you were escaping from?”

“Stella, I loved your father, but living with him, being a mother in that environment, sucked everything out of me. At the time, I was still very young, and I blamed everything on you and him. On reflection, I think the problem was what I thought I needed to do as a mother.”

Stella rolled over. Her stomach clenched again.

“Maybe I was trying to be the mother that I wanted to have when I was growing up, and when I couldn't be that perfect mother, I didn't know how to be something second class, and I missed me. I missed the artist. I missed even the bad days in the studio.

“Look, I'm not saying all this to make you feel guilty. I'm saying all this, so you understand that I didn't have it all figured out. I may have made some mistakes. You've grown up into a wonderful woman, and I couldn't be prouder of you. I don't regret leaving your dad because Mike, well, Mike's so much more. He has a way of supporting me without suffocating me. He’s able to encourage my soul to flow.”

An image of Will helping her hang the paintings filled Stella’s brain; it made her swallow. *I thought that was Will. Was I so wrong about him?*

“I did love Richard, but we were both far too young to start a family. Not much changed for him. He went to work and continued to work the same long hours. I was very lonely in that house.

“Whatever you do in life. Stella, whatever you decide to do next, please be yourself. Find something that makes your heart sing, a place, a person, a job, a passion, or a purpose. You need a reason to get up every morning with a song in your heart, that's all I want for you. It's all your dad wants for you. We just want you to be happy and healthy.”

Chapter 56

"You're her dad. You must want to help me."

"Listen, Will, my boy, don't push it. Come on, let's go get a drink."

"But this is important. How do I make her understand? It kills me that she is hurting so much. I can't just leave it at that."

Richard Barrington Jones ordered two pints of beer and passed one to William.

"Why, Will? Why can't you just let her go?"

"If she's happy …" William looked at Stella's dad. "Is she happy?"

"No," Richard sighed. "I can't say she's happy, and she won't talk about it. What is so terrible she can't tell me?"

"My sister claims what happened in London caused her more damage than anyone suspected. So, when I was stupid, even our normally strong Stella broke." Will offered, taking a first sip of his beer.

"If Stella wants to live in the U.S., she'd be in New York with her mother. She'd be with all the fancy designers alongside all the weird ones." The men exchanged glances, and Richard shrugged.

"Don't ask me, it's something my wife said. Gemma can't understand why Stella would want to live in Hursts Bridge … when she has the flat in London and her mum's place in New York." He shook his head. "I don't think she's happy having another woman in the house."

"She's probably here because New York isn't far enough away from me!" muttered William.

"So why Hursts Bridge? So close to your parents, William, tell me that. What did she hate about California so much?"

"Being close to me?"

"Did you do something?" Richard stared straight at William. "Didn't you want her there? Did she paint those damn flowers everywhere?" William looked down into his beer.

"Only for Marco," he muttered, his eyes trained on the bubbles at the top of his glass. Richard's eyebrow raised. "My neighbour, Marco, is my neighbour." He tried to explain. Richard laughed.

"She can be pushy when she gets a paintbrush in her hand."

"She worked so hard."

"I know. I don't know where she gets that from. My dad, maybe? But ..." Richard sighed heavily. "My last wife suggested Stella was trying to prove her worth to me and her mother. She got the impression Stella felt neither of us cared for her. So maybe the damage was done a long time ago. You can't take all the blame. That being said, I don't think we would have stayed together so long if not for her. But her mum struggled with being away from the States. We met and got married there. Stella was born there. And then I had to drag her here, to Hursts Bridge of all places. It would never have been big enough for Judy." Richard took a drink from his pint and looked off into the distance.

"My dad suggested we try London, which is why they bought the place in Putney, but it needed work. She left the following week." It was William's turn to stare.

"Why didn't she take Stella?"

"New fella, I think?"

"But she took the dog?"

"I know, God! I missed that dog."

William groaned. "Mr Barrington Jones, what can I do?"

"Are you looking for suggestions from me? I'm not sure I'm the right person to give relationship advice. Look, I called your dad ... your mum's coming."

William's mum gripped his hand on the table. "It's going to be OK."

"Don't tell me I'll be fine without her because ..."

"Did I say that?"

"No," William shook his head. "But ..."

"William, I presume from the way you have been stomping around and from what your sister says, you love Stella."

"Sarah?"

"Well, I made her explain why she looked like she wanted to jump off a cliff. I thought that guy in London had dumped her or something."

"Guy? Sarah has a guy?"

"Stop getting off topic. Your sister is upset because she thinks all this," she waved her hand around the table, "is all her fault."

"I guess Stella is holding back because of Sarah and you guys," he waved at the company.

"Us? How are we part of the problem?"

"You guys being friends."

"Friends is a bit of a stretch … I guess we were close at one point, but we hardly see this man and his many wives these days." Richard's face dropped, but William didn't give up.

"But if we split up … Dad said …"

"Are you splitting up already?" Richard didn't hide his anger. "Look, just go back to Southern California. There must be some pretty girls over there."

"Stella is not a pretty girl!" William banged on the table. "Well, obviously she is, but she's more than that, a lot more."

"But you're thinking about splitting up?"

"No!"

"But you're worried about how we'd feel?"

"No!" He sighed, "But Stella is." He said quietly. "I think … she won't talk to me."

"Did she leave California because she doesn't care about you?"

William shook his head, and Richard scoffed.

"She's acting as though someone ripped her heart out, again, that's what Gemma said."

"I can't believe I have done this to her. Why won't she listen?"

"She must care, or why would she be upset because you did something stupid. Has it occurred to you to tell her how we all feel? More importantly, how do you feel?"

"She doesn't listen. I don't think she believes me."

"Then show her!" Will had no doubt his mother was feeling frustrated at his shitty communication skills.

"How?"

"You're the clever one."

Chapter 57

Stella was desperate for something to do, preferably something that would make a post for her blog. The weather was rubbish, and that didn't help her mood or the problem. Since her return from California she'd struggled to keep posting. Her bedroom wasn't exactly small, but there was only so much she could do there. She'd done a few projects locally, she suspected, because her grandma had been dropping giant hints to everyone she knew. She didn't want to see Sarah, well, she did, but … It was a relief when India called to say she would be back in Hursts Bridge for a few days if she wanted to have lunch.

She chose to walk into town and to The Bridge Inn in an attempt to extend the lunch date. The lush green landscape and traditional buildings were a vast contrast to her time in L.A. Her steps were slow as she tried to soak up the atmosphere of being home, but her heart couldn't stop feeling lost without William being close. As she crossed the old bridge, her steps quickened when she spotted India parking her car by the green.

Kissing her cousin on the cheek, she sighed.

"I haven't been here for years."

"Nor me," laughed India.

"I don't suppose it's changed." She tried to smile as she pushed open the heavy door.

Indeed, The Bridge Inn was much as she remembered it.

"I think that old man was sitting in that same corner the last time I came in."

"Mr Binch? Most likely. He's always sat there."

They took a table in the dining area and ordered soup and a sandwich. When the server left with their order, the small talk was over.

"So, L.A.?"

"What about it?" Stella's fingers smoothed over her locket.

"I wondered how you felt about it all, now that you're home."

"It was lovely. So much warmer than Yorkshire." Stella tried to laugh.

"So, you had a good time. The project went well?"

"Doing a whole house, for a client who didn't want to butt in every other day, yes, I loved it. Challenging work because of the time scale,

not to mention working in yards instead of metres. But yes, I enjoyed it. He even had nice neighbours."

"You didn't want to stay?"

"How could I? What was I supposed to say? I know you think I've stolen all your money, and you keep sleeping with that witch, but would you mind if I stayed in my best friend's bedroom? Sarah won't be bothered."

"You offered her your flat."

"She hadn't slept with my brother."

"I see. Why did you? Or do I mean how did you fudging force him?"

"I didn't, but he was managing to resist. If I hadn't pushed, I don't think he would have gone that far."

"He resisted? So, he was thinking about it? He didn't start anything?"

"Well, I guess … he kissed … Well, I mean, yes, there was something there. I'm not that crazy. I wouldn't have pushed if I hadn't thought, well, you know."

"What has Sarah said?"

"She claims she doesn't care. I've hardly seen her, though. I can't look at her. She looks so sad."

"And do you know why she is sad?"

"Well, because of what I did?"

"Because you slept with him, or that you won't speak to him?"

"Well, because …" Stella's hand went to the locket again.

"I think you're making a lot of assumptions." India's face softened. "Why don't you have a heart-to-heart with her?"

"It's not a conversation you want to have with your best friend. I slept with your brother. It was fabulous, and I can't stop thinking about him. I think I love him. Walking away was the hardest thing I've ever done."

"You love him?"

"I do, but is that enough?"

"Have you thought about talking to him?"

"I can't do that!" Stella looked out of the window.

"What happened when he came to the house?"

"I think he was trying to apologise," she shook her head. "But in doing that, he was blaming her and blaming me for not telling him about Jackson Wilde."

"Ouch!"

"Ouch, indeed." At that point, the food arrived, and the subject was changed.

"OK. Positivity time. What are you thinking about next?"

"I'm glad you asked. I guess I need to decide on a location before I can look at clients." Between bites of her sandwich, Stella shared her Hursts Bridge or London debate.

"And then I thought, what about Leeds?"

"If you really want to do that, we've a spare room. You'd have to share a bathroom with Zach."

"Ah, maybe that is not a good idea."

"There's a problem with Zacho?"

"Not a problem as such, but he's been texting … a lot. Just friendly … but living with him?"

"Zach is a lovely guy, I mean, I know a few girls who would kill to get his attention."

"He does seem nice, and I can't say I haven't enjoyed the banter," Stella smirked, then looked out of the glass doors to the river. Her smile had disappeared, and a heavy sadness hung over her whole body again.

"I guess that tells me you are still thinking about William."

Stella didn't look back from staring at the river. What could she say?

"Well, Leeds is a good place. You could probably use my office space for work. You know me and Tilly." They both took another bite of their sandwich, thinking as they chewed.

"Have you thought of anywhere else?"

"No, nothing really seems to stick."

"Well, think about it and maybe come over for a week or so."

"I don't suppose you'd let me do up a room or two so I could blog?"

"I'd have to speak to Charlie. He keeps saying I can do whatever I like, but it's his house."

"I know each of my dad's wives wanted to change something. They actually changed a lot."

"It's not terrible, it's nice, but it's a bit beige. But talking about your blog, I've been wondering what I can do while I'm here. Charlie's going to be in Sri Lanka for another week, so how about I take some promo photos for you and maybe film some B-roll? It would be stuff I could use on my social media, too. Win - Win."

Stella’s hand went to her face, and she nodded, pushing the hair off her forehead.

“I'd better do something with my hair. I haven't been making much of an effort since I got back.”

“You do that. It will also give your mood a boost. So, shall we have a pamper session this afternoon?”

India had left to drive back to her mum’s house. As she drove away, Stella switched her phone on.

Zach: Is the sun shining there yet?
Stella: Not yet.

She was about to switch her phone off again when another text bounced in, this time from William. He’d sent her something every day. She thought she might have to block him, if only to make the pain stop, but she just couldn’t do it to him.

Will: I miss you, Star.

A silent tear fell down Stella's cheek as she typed I miss you too, and then she pressed delete and pushed her phone firmly into her pocket.

Chapter 58

Stella spent yet another night tossing and turning, going over and over what India had said. The only positive thing she had to take forward was the idea of going back to Leeds with India for a week or so. It made a lot of sense while Charlie was still away, and Zach was still in Australia.

Unable to sleep, Stella was more than ready by the time India arrived with her camera case.

"Let's take a few of you flicking through colour charts. What else would you be looking at?" Stella picked up her paint charts and searched on her desk for something else. But her brain was full of cotton wool. She couldn't think positively at all. When she looked at the things on her desk, it took her straight back to working for William. India took stills and some video close-ups of Stella's hands. Stella may have been distracted, but she noticed India was constantly checking her watch.

"Do you need to get off?"

India blushed. "No, I struggle to work out the time difference with Sri Lanka. Let's try a few more, looking over your shoulder, then I thought we could take a walk along the river. You know, start at the bridge, walk up to Jack's Landing, and then back. I could do various angles; it would give you another look." Stella felt the unease in India's voice, but she went along with the suggestion.

As they were putting on their coats, India's phone rang.

"That will be him. I'll just get this." She stepped out, leaving Stella to stare at the mirror. *No wonder India's been focusing on my hands and looking over my shoulder. Even I can see the dark circles now.*

The sun was still quite hazy as it hung over the water. The rain over the last week had the river running up fast and high. Stella was walking along on her own with India behind her, letting her walk further and further ahead. She'd become lost in her own thoughts again. She'd never spent so much time in her head as since that first kiss.

As the wooden rail of the landing came into sight, Stella saw a balloon tied to the handrail. It was a silver star helium balloon with a tag hanging from it. She turned to look at India, who shrugged.

"I don't know, but it works. Walk up and see what the tag says, and I'll keep filming. I can always edit it out." For some strange reason, the star shape made Stella's heart thump that little bit faster, and she walked

quickly towards the balloon, aware that behind her, India was filming each step. She looked back at India. *Is she smiling? Is this something India has set up to try to cheer me up? Do I look that miserable?*

The tag hanging from the balloon simply held a QR code. Stella didn't hesitate to take out her phone and scan the code. Excitement was building inside her, although she had no understanding of what was happening or why. A breeze tugged at the balloon, and Stella had to grip the tag to scan the code.

The loading sign spun on her screen, and she panicked about what she might have done. Her screen finally filled with a room full of people, all waving at her. It took a moment to realise the people filling her screen were her family and Sarah with the rest of William's family. They were waving and shouting. Eventually, she worked out what they were saying.

"Behind you!" "Behind you!" "Behind you!" It was just like a pantomime. Finally, the message sank in, and she turned to look behind her. She rocked back on her heels as William stood in front of her.

Her body ached with the need to touch him, but she was frozen trying to assimilate everything that had just happened. *He's here. What does that mean?*

William could see the shock in her eyes. Despite the make-up, she looked tired and drawn. It broke his heart that he had caused any of it. She came to him broken by another man, and he'd tempted her back to life, then shut her out. He'd hid in his office, hurt by what he'd imagined she'd done to him, completely missing who she was. He couldn't see that she was as much committed to him as he was to her.

William had to stop holding his breath.

"I'm sorry I haven't been able to put into words how I feel about you." He said, taking both her hands in his. She hung on to her phone. William slipped it out of her hand and passed it to India along with his own phone. He turned to look at Stella again. Holding both her hands as firmly as he could without hurting her. He desperately wanted to keep her focused on what he had to say. *At least she can't slam the door in my face here.*

"As I was saying, I didn't have the words to explain what I felt. What I feel now, and Stella, I'm sorry if you thought you weren't the most important thing for me." Stella looked away towards the fast-moving

water in the river. "It's something so deep inside here. I can only hope you feel the same." He sighed; Stella didn't speak.

"I thought you felt it too, that connection. Do you?"

"I know what you mean about not having the words, if that helps." It was a start, and it made William smile. When he glimpsed the locket he'd bought, his smile widened. *They were good signs, weren't they?*

"What do you feel in here?" His hand sat on her stomach. Stella's eyes filled up.

"Will, I'm scared," she whispered.

"Me too!" he laughed. "I've never been more scared."

"What scares you most?"

"How much it will hurt." He confessed.

"It hurts now," she scoffed.

"I know. Stella, do you trust me?" He held his breath as he waited for her response.

"I trust you. Don't you trust me?"

"I do."

"Really? Then why did you believe I would spend …"

William sighed and shook his head.

"I don't know why I doubted you, maybe because the money had disappeared too. Will you ever be able to forgive me?"

"I accepted your apology, didn't I?"

"Stella, I need you."

"I know. Maribeth's been in touch about the nursery, and Marco says he has finally persuaded you to sell him a plot."

"So, you do talk to some people?"

"They were emails!"

"We're getting off the point." Will sighed. "When I said I needed you, I didn't mean for work."

"Your house is finished?"

"That's another thing I want to talk about, but not today." He shook his head.

"Stella, I love you. I probably always have. But in that short time we had together, Stella, I know you felt it too. It was everything I couldn't put into words. Marco said you were the other half of me. I guess that's the closest I can get, in words, I mean. You complete me. It sounds

soppy, but I do want you back in my life. Please, Stella, can we find a way to be together?"

"Why are they here?" She nodded to the two phones India was holding. One screen filled with their families in the U.K., and his screen filled with Marco and the gang in California.

"They are here so that you can't use them as an excuse."

"I wasn't … I mean, I do want to be with you." A cheer went up from Stella's phone. "But how?"

"I'm pretty sure we can work that out. That's if you want to."

"I want to." Another cheer went up. William let go of her hands and cupped her face. His thumb stroked her bottom lip, and then he kissed her, softly at first and then with more passion when Stella started to respond.

"Do we need the audience now?" she smiled. Will smiled at her looking around, but India had walked away, her camera hanging in her hand. The plan had worked so far. Now he was on his own.

"I do know I don't want to live somewhere that doesn't have you, Stella." He pulled her into his arms, and her face settled on his chest.

"I thought my life was here, Will." His heart sank; he had to keep trying.

"If it is, we can live here and visit L.A., or we can live in L.A. and visit here. Or anywhere."

"No." She shook her head. "This, being here with you, when you hold me, I'm home. My home will be where you are. I can work from anywhere."

"You are the only one who makes me feel like I'm home," he said with a smile and then shook his head. "Look, I still have five more plots to sell, and I know I'd like your input on that. So how about we go back and finish that job?" He studied her eyes. "It'll give us time to decide what we do next and where. Could you give it a year, Stella? What do you say?" Stella didn't reply; she turned away. Watching as she gripped the rail, looking at the balloon as it danced in the breeze, he had to keep trying.

"Do you still want a dog? And children?"

"I've spent a lot of time looking at puppies online," she blushed.

"A puppy? Is that what you want?"

"I've had too much time to think." Stella paused, turning to look into his eyes. "Maybe I felt I wanted a dog because I didn't have a person to cuddle. But if I had you?"

"Me?"

"You are pretty good at the cuddling."

Her face lit up with the smile he loved her for. It was so soft, and yet it melted his core. He was still struggling to know whether she would agree to live with him.

"How is the house?" She asked, her face more serious again.

"I sold it … to John's parents. I didn't want to live in it without you."

"But Will…"

"I know you put so much into it. I kept most of the artwork and my chair. But if you come back, we can do it together this time. Let's build a home together from the ground up."

"Together?" Will nodded. "In L.A.?" He nodded again.

He reached out to touch her locket. His finger stroked the hair from the side of her face.

"Yes. I want to marry you, Star, and I know that's a big ask." He took her hands again. "So, for now, let's go back and finish what we started."

"Yes. I would love to do that, Will. What do we do first?"

"First, we need to go and tell everyone the news."

"Together?"

"Together."

Epilogue

Stella felt the edge of the bed dip despite how gently he'd tried to sit next to her. It was William, fresh from the pool. When his hand slid slowly down her back, she allowed her lashes to flick up to take in his smooth body sitting at her side. His hair wet and falling forward. The temptation to pull at the towel around his waist brought a smile that lit up her face.

"Are you OK, Star?"

"Hmm, I'm fine. I'm simply enjoying a little longer in bed today."

"It's just you used to watch me swim when you first got here, and now you sleep through it."

"I'm trying to be strong and save that pleasure for Friday mornings only." A smile snuck out of the side of her face. She fought to straighten it. "You weren't supposed to notice that."

"I couldn't help but check out your window."

"Well, a gentleman wouldn't mention it. Anyway, I'm out of the habit, with you swimming in your old pool. What's it like? The new pool, I mean."

"I love it. The Kingstons were kind to let me use the pool at the old house, but this... Well, it feels like we've finally finished what we started. It's the same design as the last place, only in a different spot." He wiped the hair from her forehead. "I'm glad to be able to swim straight outside our window again; it's the one thing I missed about that house."

Stella's eyes widened.

"Is that really all you missed?" She started to sit up, pulling the sheet with her.

"I know it's the place we had all our firsts in. But I'm glad we've had this fresh start. It's taken a while, but I like to think this house is better because we built it together instead of making do with what was already bought."

"I know what you mean."

He stroked her face again.

"I was getting worried you weren't feeling ... I mean, I wondered if you were feeling sick again."

Stella frowned, but the care written all over his face softened her.

"I just feel shattered."

"Do you want to cancel today?"

"God, no! It's taken me a month to fit this in with Hidir. He's only in California this week. It's exactly a year since he was here for the launch day."

"Is it really 12 months since that day?"

"Don't you have that date etched in your brain? I know I do. I don't think I'll ever forget it."

"If it's all the same with you, I'd rather not remember it."

"It wasn't all bad, the relief of getting the job finished and the way people reacted. We sold plots and saved … well, everything. Then, seeing you walk her into that room. The one I'd poured so much of my soul into for you. I couldn't breathe. Then your email about the money."

William's face twisted as he looked away.

"I know, I'm so sorry I listened to her, but you know I didn't sleep with her that night."

Stella swung her legs out of the bed and headed for the bathroom. Over her shoulder, she smiled.

"Oh, I know that now. And you should realise, I wouldn't be here now if you had."

Hidir looked stunningly attractive in his dark suit as they sat on the terrace by William's beloved pool, enjoying the afternoon light.

"Thank you both for agreeing to show us around the final building on this development. I love the way you've created this space outside. It really is an extension of the home."

"This is California. What can I say? William likes to swim, and I like the view." Stella smiled as she looked at Will. He hated the cameras, but as it was Davey, he wasn't feeling so nervous as he had last year.

"Would it be fair to say you have saved the best until last?"

"I think we can say we continue to learn and find new solutions with every property we work on. With this one, the bonus being, we knew the

client really well." They all smiled, and William could feel his shoulders relax.

"Stella has been storing up ideas for a while now. This was her first chance to work on something for herself. For us both."

Stella grinned, and Hidir's face lit up.

"Our followers were so excited we were coming back to meet you again; they sent us some questions. Are you OK to answer them?" Stella nodded, and Hidir pulled out five sheets of yellow paper and laid them on his knee.

"So, first question for you, Stella. Claire from Bewdley wants to know how you match your paint colours to your fabrics so well."

"That's an easy one, Claire. I use a scope. It scans the colour and matches it to the component colours, which are then combined to make the closest paint match possible."

"It's been 12 months since we were last here. Roly from Peterborough would like to know how Thoresby Technology has developed in that time."

"We've several new products already on the retail market that have come from working on this house together, and many of those link to products we were already producing, so we've made it easier to create consistent programmes. It means more and more you can create a house that works for you and your family." Stella's warm hand squeezed his arm as she clarified what he was trying to say.

"Making things personally tailored to you is a big motivation for all the team at Thoresby Technology. We like our tech, but we want it to work for us and to fit into our lifestyle."

"I notice that there is an increasing number of items on your website shopping categories that are designed for the nursery. Is there any significance in that?"

William swallowed hard. It was his turn to help her.

"Before we ever worked together on a project. Stella had been researching and reporting on ways of creating a safe environment to raise children in." She took over again.

"That is to say, I was looking at what paints were safe. What sort of edges you want on furniture. The physical things. Working with William, I learned how much technology can contribute to a safe home." She looked at him, and his heart stilled.

"So, it's not for personal reasons?" Will looked from Hidir back to Stella as her face reddened. She looked away. He spoke to take the focus from her. Clearing his throat, he forced a laugh.

"Oh, that's where you were going, and there we were getting all designy and geeky. Sorry to disappoint you, but we've no plans to add to our family in the immediate future."

"I'm sure a lot of fans out there would be interested to see that sort of outcome." Neither of them spoke in reply.

Hidir shuffled the yellow paper on his knee.

Why didn't I just cancel when Star was sick this morning? He wanted to take her away from all these questions. Silence hung in the air for the first time. Hidir looked at his pages for what felt like an hour to William. He swallowed hard and held Stella's hand. At last, Hidir spoke again.

"Now that this project is finally finished, Aurora from Cumbria is asking what comes next for this dynamic duo."

"James and Alison Kingston, who bought our first house, have asked us to work on a project to build six holiday cabins."

Stella seemed to have recovered, and she took over.

"It's hard to describe, really. Cabins make them sound a bit basic, but they are large luxury cabins, personally tailored to six families, all on the same plot of land. It's on the edge of the golf course that their group is developing in Scotland."

Hidir smiled. "I've never been to Scotland. Have you?"

"I haven't, but Stella has an aunt who lives in Hawick. This new development is located close to the Scottish border region. So, she's aware of the area and all its attractions. She tells me we're going to be working with a lot of wool and tweeds."

"I can see that's going to be inspiring for you. Stella."

"Oh yes, I've got mood board upon mood board inspired by the landscape, the heathers, and those beautiful traditional woven blankets that you find in the Tweed mills around Hawick. To be honest, it was a mood board I've been working on for a long time. It's going to be wonderful working back in the U.K. and being closer to family for a time. But that's not the only project we're working on."

"Yes, I notice that your social media posts are from all over the U.S. and Europe at the moment. Any plans to move outside that territory?"

"Well, Canada is definitely on the list for the next six months, but I think I might be working with similar fabrics and colours to those I'll be

using in Scotland. That should be interesting, and I'm working on an apartment in London for Marco."

"Marco Martelli? "

"Yes, he's our neighbour here in California and possibly the biggest fan of our work. He always seems to have a job lined up for us."

"Well, this time last year, we filmed some of your work for Mr Martelli. So, we'll put a link to that video in the comments, and you can check out what these two got up to when they were working for him last year."

"Now we're going to take a tour of the house you're living in. Is this going to be your permanent home?"

William smiled. The sun was shining down on them.

"I'm relieved to say we are looking to keep it for now, although we will be looking for something possibly smaller in the U.K., too."

"Is there a location in the U.K. you're focusing on?"

"Yes, we're going to be looking around Hursts Bridge, probably not in the town itself. It's so small. But we both have families living close to Hursts Bridge, so that is our jumping-off point."

William reached for her hands and stroked his fingers over her knuckles.

"We both rather like the river, so something with a view of that water would be ideal, but I'm sure we'll know it when we see it."

"I think what William means is. I will know it when I see it. I'm flying over next week and leaving William here to get a new project to market. It's a really clever piece of equipment that works with hydraulics and thermocouples."

"So, Will, you're letting Stella pick out a house for you."

"I can't think of anyone else I would trust to do that, but Stella has a way of knowing what I want or need even before I know myself."

"And would we be welcome to come and see you in this new place in the U.K.?"

"Davey and you would be welcome at our home at any time, as long as you leave those cameras behind. The house in Yorkshire will be very much a retreat. It's not likely to be large, but you would still be very welcome. I don't see it as a project that we will be filming and promoting. I think one of the ways in which you can survive a life on social media is to have something that is yours and that you keep for you and your family."

“That's excellent advice. I think I would agree with that. Do you have any other advice for people wanting to make a success of their business using social media?”

“The easiest thing to do is to be yourself and find the audience that likes who you are, because whoever you are, whatever you try to be, someone won't like it. That's hard, and you need to find a way to live with it. But if you keep something of yourself, something that you're not necessarily sharing with the whole world, that helps your mental health.”

“Well, thank you, William and Stella. It's been lovely to meet you again and spend time with you. Again, thank you for providing us with such valuable insight into the work you do. I think I can safely say our viewers like your style. The one comment that is consistent across everything we've done for you is how well your work complements each other. It's hard to see in a piece like this, a light fitting where William ends and Stella starts. It’s the perfect marriage of technology and design.”

“Well, I'll take that as a compliment. I can't speak for Stella, but I like working with such a clever person, who gives me so much inspiration.”

“William is a ‘let's do it’ sort of person. He never says, ‘I don't think that'll work,’ even though he sometimes thinks that. He likes to find a way to make it work.”

“That sounds like a great place to finish this interview.”

Back in the kitchen, Davey was winding up cables and packing the black bags with all the equipment. William had taken Hidir to his office to show him some plans for the Scotland project.

Stella stared out of the window, slowly sipping water and trying to hold on to her breakfast. She was relieved that this morning was over and that for the rest of the day, it would just be her and Will.

“It’ll be OK, Stella. I’ll edit it out.”

“Sorry, what?”

“That question about kids.”

The blood throbbed in her temples, and she tried to rub away the confusion in her brain. Why was everyone suddenly talking about babies? *Is it tattooed on my face?*

"What? I don't understand..."

She felt a pair of strong arms slip around her waist. She relaxed onto Will's chest as his lips caressed her neck. His voice rumbled in her ear.

"I think that would be a good idea. Thank you." Will squeezed her shoulder, but Stella's brain still wouldn't let her speak.

"We are here to do a job, but we still think of you as a friend. If you don't want to share, I get it."

Hidir stepped forward. "I'm sorry I asked."

"It's just that it's early and a lot can happen. We haven't spoken to anyone yet. I wasn't lying when I said we had no plans."

Davey and Hidir busied themselves with the packing. Stella wanted the ground to open up. Will continued to hold her.

"This might not be planned, but if there is going to be a baby, then you can bet we will not only be ready for it, but we will also be so pleased to welcome it into the world."

Stella finally smiled. Will hadn't said much since she voiced her fears to him, and she knew he was right. This baby, if it were coming, was going to be so loved.

"Don't worry, I'll send you the edited tape before we publish."

Finally alone, they'd settled down to eat by the pool. Stella had nodded off. As she started to wake, she could feel Will's strong fingers stroking her hair, and he whispered into the back of her head.

"I don't care what happens in the next couple of days, I'm going to love you and our babies for the rest of my life."

"Thank you."

"Hey, I thought you were asleep."

"Does it change what you said?"

"No, come here. Let me see your face." Stella sat up, and Will pulled her closer. "I'm not sure why we are in this position; it wasn't what we planned, but I'm happy. I'm happy this has all worked out."

"My birthday."

"I'm sorry?"

"How this happened, I think it could have been my birthday. Another anniversary."

"Oh really... Star, are you happy? It's just you seem down, that's all."

"I feel exhausted. I've been pushing this week to have things ready for filming today. I don't know if it's that or the baby, if it is a baby."

"Why don't you go and see a doctor?"

"Let me rest. If I don't feel better now that this is over, I'll make an appointment."

"Can I get you a drink?"

"A cup of tea would be nice."

Stella sat on the terrace as the sun slowly dropped in the sky. A year ago, she had fled the States, sad to leave the house she had created for him. Upset that he had believed the woman who worked for him. He'd asked for a year, but the project had been a dream, and now she had no doubt that she had made the right decision to come here to build a home with him. She knew they would survive this pregnancy hiccup, whatever the outcome, because William made it home.

When the man himself appeared carrying a tray with tea for them both and biscuits, the smile on his face mirrored hers.

"What's that smile for?"

"The biscuits or the tea, I'm still trying to decide. It could be just because of you, William Thoresby. You make me happy, very happy."

A Note from the Author.

I loved writing Stella and Will's story. They are fabulous people, and they are both so creative. I sincerely hope they are able to build a business that showcases their talents. Personally, I've enjoyed the creative issues and solutions they faced.

I have so many more stories to write, and some hints to some of them may be found in this book, as well as characters who will appear in the next series. I promise you that my stories will be filled with strong women who have problems to solve and brave men who will join them on their journey. Most of all, I promise you many, many happy ever afters.

As I send you this book, I would like to express my gratitude to those who have helped me. The ones who have encouraged me, the ones who have written alongside me at silly times of the day, and the ones who have helped me lick the story into shape. I have listed them here in alphabetical order. Ben, Christine, Elaine, Giorgia, Katie, Lesley, Lynn, Joanne, Linda, and Martin.

Also in this book, I would like to thank three readers who provided me with names for Hidir's interview. Claire, Nicola, and Aurora,

Please come and find me on social media. Cheer me on as I write more.

Please check out my other stories.

BEE

Find Belinda online at www.booksbybelinda.com.
Facebook @BelindaEdwardsAuthor
Instagram @booksbybelinda
Twitter @BooksByBelinda

Printed in Dunstable, United Kingdom

68545601R10170